THE FIRST FIVE YEARS
OF THE
COMMUNIST INTERNATIONAL

Leon Trotsky

The First Five Years
of the
Communist
International

In Two Volumes
VOLUME TWO

NEW PARK PUBLICATIONS

First published in 1924 as
Pyat Let Kominterna
by State Publishing House, Moscow

Translated from the Russian by

JOHN G. WRIGHT

First English Edition: 1953
This Edition: 1974

Foreword Copyright © 1974
New Park Publications, Ltd.

Published by
NEW PARK PUBLICATIONS LTD.,
186a Clapham High Street,
London SW4 7UG

Set up, Printed and Bound
by Trade Union Labour

Distributed in the United States by:

Labor Publications Inc.,
135 West 14 Street, New York,
New York 10011

ISBN 0 902030 52 3

Printed in Great Britain by
PLOUGH PRESS LTD. (T.U.)
r/o 180 Clapham High Street, London, SW4 7UG

CONTENTS

II. THE FOURTH WORLD CONGRESS

III. AFTER THE FOURTH WORLD CONGRESS

FOREWORD

THE SPEECHES and documents by Leon Trotsky which are contained in this second volume of the 'First Five Years of the Communist International' date from the period when it was at the height of its authority as the general staff of the revolutionary movement. Lenin and Trotsky himself, more than any other leaders, embodied that authority and left their mark on the proceedings and resolutions of the International. These volumes contain the reports and speeches made by Trotsky in connection with its work and the theses which he wrote. It shows not only his mastery of the main currents of political and economic events as they unfolded after the First World War but also of the details of the inner life of the Communist Parties in Europe with which he was particularly concerned.

Unlike Stalin and his epigones, Trotsky had unbounded confidence in the revolutionary capacities of the international working class given the right leadership. At the same time, he was completely aware of the continued strength and vitality of the bourgeoisie, once it had survived the immediate post-war crisis, and the carefully thought out counter-revolutionary strategy which it was putting into effect. Hence the most urgent task before the International was to build and strengthen the young Communist Parties, to cleanse them of reformist and centrist elements and to deal patiently with their problems and their mistakes. In the period covered by the second volume these questions were posed most sharply in the case of the French party, which had been founded as the result of a split in the Socialist Party—an old reformist party—at its Tours Congress in December, 1920. Trotsky followed closely the situation which subsequently resulted from the continued presence in the party of leaders who assumed that they would be able to continue with their previous methods. A number of the most important contributions in this volume are concerned with the struggle to transform the French

Communist Party into a party of a new type, a Bolshevik party. It was a task, in fact, which was never to be completed before the party itself was overtaken by the virus of Stalinism.

This volume deals with the period after the Third Congress of the Communist International which had taken place in Moscow in June, 1921. At this Congress an important turn took place in the tactical line of the Communist Parties. As Trotsky put it in his preface to the two volumes in 1924: 'the parties take into account that they have yet to win the masses, and that an assault must be preceded by a more or less protracted period of preparatory work. There opens up the zone of the united front, that is, the tactic of fusing the masses on the basis of transitional demands.'

In France, the major victor country on the continent, the revolutionary possibilities may have seemed less immediate than in defeated Germany, plunged into a deep social crisis which on three occasions—1919, 1921 and 1923—seemed to open the way for the working class to take power. Trotsky regarded the situation in France as in many ways decisive. The most powerful country in Europe, it was also inherently weak and unstable. Moreover, the Socialist Party, after the Tours split, held a position in no way comparable with that of the Social Democratic Party in Germany. It was rejected by those workers who took a syndicalist position as well as by those who followed the lead of the young Communist Party.

As Trotsky saw it: 'The French Communist Party has every opportunity of gaining the complete and individual leadership of the labour movement before the decisive events occur. But to do so French Communism must divest itself once and for all of the ancient husk of political conventionalities and equivocations, more rigid in France than anywhere else.'

He thus carried on an implacable struggle against those leaders who still continued with the political methods inherited from the Second International. They were steeped in a parliamentary environment and rubbed shoulders with middle class politicians in the lodges of the Free Masons and the meetings of the League for the Rights of Man. They resisted centralism and disciplined organization and took up a centrist position on major political questions which prevented the party from giving a clear lead to the working class. It also prevented it from winning over those militant workers whose suspicion of opportunist politicians left them under syndicalist influence.

Trotsky's efforts to shape the French Communist Party into a disciplined, revolutionary party with its roots in the working class and enjoying its confidence deserve close study today by all those concerned in the building of revolutionary parties in the advanced countries. They bring out the irreconcilable differences between Marxist method and those of the opportunists and centrists in the party. The tendencies which Trotsky had to take up arms against were deeply rooted in the French movement and were not easily to be removed.

Precisely the same tendencies and methods repeatedly re-appeared to hold back the communist movement in France. Stalinism reflected and made its compromises with them. Trotsky continued his struggle against them after his exile from the Soviet Union in the course of building up the forces for the Fourth International. They were carried over into the Trotskyist movement itself and found their ultimate expression in the Organization Communiste Internationaliste which finally broke with the Fourth International when it moved to an openly centrist position in 1971.

In Germany and Italy, as well as France, there were at this time numerically strong Communist Parties although a majority of the working class still followed the reformists of the Second International. These parties had come into existence too late to take advantage of the post-war revolutionary opportunities which by 1921 appeared to have faded away. The prime task of these parties in the new situation was to find a road to the masses and prepare for the next opportunity. There were those inside the communist movement who refused to accept the evidence for such a tactical shift and urged the policy of 'continuous offensive'. The futility and danger of launching an offensive when the working class was not prepared had been demonstrated in the March action in Germany in 1921.

The question of the united front occupied an important part in all Trotsky's discussion and polemics with Communist leaders from other countries. Important lessons for today are to be drawn from Trotsky's analysis in this book of concrete cases in the different countries. Resistance came from ultra-lefts, who saw in it only unity with the reformists, and opportunists from whom the communists had so recently broken.

In fact, as Trotsky explained many times, the united front was a programme for action by the working class, not for passive co-operation with those leaders who were the agents of the bourgeoisie inside the labour movement. Are we to seek agreement with them, he asked?—'Yes, in all those cases where the masses that follow them are ready to engage in joint struggle together with the masses that follow us and when they, the reformists, are to a lesser or greater degree compelled to become an instrument in this struggle'.

The united front meant that the Communists should take the lead in putting forward proposals for joint action in defence of the living standards and basic rights of the working class. This provided the basis for breaking the workers in the reformist organizations from their leadership in the course of the struggle. At the same time, the Communist Party had to retain its unconditional independence and its right to criticize all participants in a joint action. It had to continue the process of strengthening its own ranks by education and training and by struggle against centrist or sectarian tendencies.

United front action aimed to show the political character of every class conflict, so that it prepared the way for a struggle for power and educated the masses to that understanding. Many of those who opposed the united front with talk about a compromise on principles were actually resisting the turn to new forms of mass work in the trade unions and elsewhere which it required. Work for the united front meant a break with political passivity, old forms of activity and mere propagandism. It called on the Communists to become leaders in mass struggles and challenge the reformists for the leadership of the working class.

In arguing for the united front Trotsky was not, of course, putting forward a line of his own. It had been hammered out within the leadership of the International itself against the opposition of Zinoviev and others. It was the basis for the work of the sections from the time of the Third Congress. The Stalinists later abandoned it and adopted, after 1928, the suicidal policy of the so-called 'third period' in which the Communist Parties described the Social Democrats as 'social fascists' and refused to enter into any type of joint struggle against the rising menace of fascism. Consistent with his analysis of the early 1920s and the programme of the Communist International at that time, Trotsky put forward the demand for the United Front in the 1930s as the only way in which the working class could bar the way to Hitler. The Stalinists repeated the threadbare arguments of the ultra-lefts and put forward the fatuous cry of 'the united front from below'. But if the Social Democratic workers were prepared to go against their own leaders what was to prevent them coming directly over to the Communist Party? This would not happen until their faith in those leaders had been shaken and destroyed; and that meant placing demands on them, through a call for united action, and testing them out in the course of struggle. The 'united front from below' was thus no more than a phrase which could not win the Social Democratic workers nor shake the power of the reformist bureaucracy.

On all the questions of the hour Trotsky's approach was profoundly internationalist. Deeply as he was concerned with the success of the workers' state in Russia there was no question of the parties of the International being subordinated to its needs. On the contrary the question was to feed into those parties, still young and inexperienced, all the lessons of the history of the Bolshevik Party, the October revolution and the struggles of the Soviet state to overcome its domestic and foreign enemies. Trotsky spoke with all the authority of a participant whose prestige was second only to that of Lenin, but he counted on patient explanation and discussion to persuade even those who resisted the decisions of the International. What a difference between these speeches and the colourless reports and peremptory directives of the Stalin period!

Despite his enormous responsibilities in the Soviet government Trotsky obviously found time to follow closely the economic and political developments in the capitalist world as well as to pay close attention to the internal life of the major European Communist parties. Moreover, Trotsky prepared his speeches and reports with a sure grasp of the

Marxist method which makes them enduring contributions to theory and not a dry record of historical events.

Trotsky at all times opposed a mechanical interpretation of Marxism of the kind which found more than an echo inside the International itself. His method comes out particularly clearly in connection with the trends in capitalist development, especially in the article entitled 'Flood-tide'. Here Trotsky analyses the dialectical interconnections between the ups-and-downs in the economy—what is called the conjuncture—and the possibilities for revolutionary action by the working class. He points out that the political effects of an economic crisis 'are determined by the entire political situation and by those events which precede and accompany the crisis, especially the battles, successes or failures of the working class itself prior to the crisis. Under one set of circumstances the crisis may give a mighty impulse to the revolutionary activity of the working masses; under a different set of circumstances it may completely paralyse the offensive of the proletariat and, should the crisis endure too long and the workers suffer too many losses, it might weaken extremely not only the offensive but also the defensive potential of the working class'.

In the same way, a period of stabilization of uncertain duration of the kind which capitalism had entered did not mean that there were no longer any possibilities for revolutionary action. On this point Trotsky came into collision with the advocates of the 'continuous offensive' who denied the possibility of an end to the post-war crisis and a period of temporary stabilization. Trotsky explains how the rythmn of capitalist development itself produced such a stabilization at the same time as he points out its fragile basis. Neither slump nor revival in the conjuncture leads mechanically to the conditions for the victory of the working class. A decisive part would be played in any case by the revolutionary party itself. It was the ability of the party to grow, to educate the working class and establish roots in it which was the barrier to a relapse into barbarism brought about by capitalism in its death agony and the only guarantee of a victory for socialism. Just as the defeat of the post-war revolutionary wave had resulted from the failure to build in time the parties which could lead the working class to victory, so the class would not come forward again until it had been convinced by experience of 'the correctness, firmness and stability of communist leadership'. Throughout his life, and above all in his struggle to build the Fourth International, Trotsky emphasized the crucial importance of revolutionary leadership. It finds expression in all his contributions to the work of the first four Congresses of the Communist International which passed into the heritage of the Trotskyist movement.

Trotsky was well aware, and expressed more clearly than any other leader of the International at this time, that the failure of the revolution to spread opened up immense dangers for the workers' state in Russia and the working class internationally. There was, therefore, a close dialectical relationship between the building of the Communist International and its sections and the defence of the gains of the October Revolution. This is expressed in this volume in the analysis of the economic situation of the Soviet state which resulted because of its isolation in the enforced retreat of the New Economic Policy and the lessons to be drawn from the socialist conquests of the October Revolution.

Already from the five years' history of the Russian Revolution it was possible for Trotsky to draw important conclusions about the tasks of socialist construction not only in backward Russia but also in the advanced countries of capitalism. But it was also possible to draw lessons about the strategy of revolutionary struggle. The lessons of the Russian Revolution had not been lost on the European bourgeoisie, immensely more powerful and self-confident than its debile Russian counterpart. This was shown, for example, in the resort to fascism which had already taken place in Italy. At the same time the Soviet Union provided a base for the organization and mobilization of the international proletariat through the building of Communist Parties, not to devise means of peacefully co-existing with capitalism but of preparing to take power as soon as the next revolutionary opportunity presented itself.

There was at this time, i.e. down to the Fourth Congress, no open dissent from this position in the International or from the leadership of the Russian party. But the isolation of the revolution in backward and still predominantly peasant Russia, the ebb of the struggle in the capitalist countries, had prepared the conditions for the growth of a bureaucracy in the party and state, sceptical of the prospects of the working class taking power in other countries, which was shortly to adopt a self-centred, nationalist policy and impose it on the international Communist Movement.

The emergence from the shadows after Lenin's death in 1924 of the figure of Joseph Stalin, holding the administrative post of general secretary and playing no part in the early history of the Communist International, was followed by the enunciation of the theory of 'socialism in one country' and a complete break with what the International had hitherto stood for.

The consolidation of Stalin's power, first in alliance with Zinoviev and Kamenev, was assisted by the defeat in Germany in 1923 which further exposed the isolation of the Soviet state. Within a few years, despite the struggle waged by the Left Opposition for the continuity of Marxism in the International, the theory of 'socialism in one country' had become mandatory for the sections of the International. They ceased to stand by the programmatic documents of the first four Congresses, which were consigned as far as possible to historical oblivion. The Communist Parties became subservient instruments of the Soviet bureaucracy. Their leaders went periodically to Moscow not to discuss tactics and strategy and to thrash out differences on a fraternal basis but to receive their instructions and pay their respects to the all-wise Stalin. By the 1930s the leaders of these parties were hand-picked sycophants with no will of their own.

It is well to be reminded of what the Communist International had been founded to do and how it set about doing it in its first five years when it was still the international of Lenin and Trotsky. We can return with enormous profit today to study its experiences and apply its lessons to the building of the revolutionary party and the Fourth International which Trotsky founded in 1938 to continue its work.

PREFACE TO THE 1974 ENGLISH EDITION

Five Years of the Comintern, as it was originally called, was published by the State Publishing House in Moscow in 1924 bringing together the majority of Comintern reports and documents for which Trotsky was responsible, and a number of other articles of his closely relating to the activity of the Communist International and its sections.

The English edition which was translated and edited by John G. Wright appeared in two stages: Volume I, covering the period up to the end of the Third World Congress in 1921, was published by Pioneer Publishers of New York in October 1945 and republished in a new edition by New Park Publications in 1973. Volume II, which is devoted to material dating from 1922 together with several articles of 1923 dealing with questions emerging from the discussion at the Fourth World Congress, was first published by New Park Publications, London, in July 1953.

This new English edition of Volume II is a reprint of the 1953 edition; the titles of a number of items have been re-translated from the Russian by R. Chappell.

From the Third to the Fourth World Congress

AIRES DE TOUS PAYS UNISS

Picture: The main hall of the Tours Convention, December 1920, where the split between the social-democrats and the group which became the French Communist Party took place.

A School of
Revolutionary Strategy

Speech at a General Party Membership Meeting
of the Moscow Organization.   July 1921.

COMRADES, THE internal causation and lawfulness of historical development was formulated for the first time by Marxist theory. The
theory of Marxism, as Marx himself wrote in the introduction to his
work *Critique of Political Economy*, established approximately the
following proposition with regard to revolution: No social system
departs from the arena until it has developed the productive forces to
the maximum degree attainable under the given system; and no new
social system appears on the scene unless the economic premises
necessary for it have already been prepared by the old social system.
This truth, which is basic for revolutionary policy, unquestionably
retains all its meaning as a guide for us to this very moment.   But
more than once has Marxism been understood mechanically, uni-
laterally and therefore erroneously. Wrong conclusions may likewise
be drawn from the foregoing proposition.

Marx says that a social system must leave the scene once the
productive forces — technology, man's power over nature — can no
longer develop within its framework. From the standpoint of Marxism,
historical society, as such, is an organization of collective man—man
in the aggregate—for the purpose of increasing man's power over
nature. Of course this goal is not posed extrinsically by human beings,
but in the course of their development they struggle for it, adapting
themselves to the objective conditions of their environment and
constantly increasing their power over nature's elemental forces.

The proposition that conditions for a revolution—for a deep-going social revolution and not simply for superficial, though sanguinary, political overturns—conditions for a social revolution which replaces one economic system by another, are created only when the old social order no longer leaves room for the development of productive forces—this proposition does not at all mean that the old social order unfailingly collapses as soon as it becomes reactionary in the economic sense, that is, as soon as it begins to retard the development of the technological power of man. Not at all. For while the productive forces constitute the basic driving force of historical development, the latter nevertheless occurs not separate and apart from human beings, but through them. The productive forces—the means whereby social man dominates nature—take shape, it is true, independently of the will of any single individual and are only slightly dependent upon the common will of human beings alive to-day, because technology represents the accumulated capital inherited by us from the past, which impels us forward, and which under certain conditions also holds us back. But when the productive forces, when technology become too restricted within an old framework, say that of slavery, or feudal or bourgeois society, and when a change of social forms become necessary for the further growth of mankind's power, then this is not accomplished automatically, like the sun rises and sets, but must be accomplished through human beings, through the struggle of human beings welded into classes. To replace a social class, governing an old society that has turned reactionary, must come a new social class which possesses the program for a new social order meeting the needs for the development of productive forces, and which is prepared to realize this program in life. But it by no means always happens when a given social system has outlived itself, i.e., has turned reactionary, that a new class appears, conscious enough, organized enough and powerful enough to cast down life's old masters and pave the way for new social relations. No, this does not at all always happen.

On the contrary, more than once, it has happened in history that an old society exhausted itself, for example, the ancient slave society of Rome—and preceding it there were the ancient Asian civilizations whose foundation of slavery opened up no room for the development of productive forces. But within this outlived society there existed no new class strong enough to overthrow the slaveholders and institute a new, a feudal, system, because the feudal system was, compared to slavery, a step forward.

In its turn, within the feudal system there was not always to be found in the hour of need a new class, the bourgeoisie, to overthrow the feudalists and to open the road for historical development. It has more than once happened in history that a given society, a given nation, or people, or a tribe, or several tribes and nations, living under similar historical conditions, have run up against the impossibility of developing any further on a given economic foundation—slavery or feudalism—but inasmuch as no new class existed among them capable of leading them out to the main highway, they simply fell apart. The given civilization, the given state, the given society disintegrated. Mankind has thus not always moved upwards from below in a steady, rising curve. No, there have been prolonged periods of stagnation and there have been regressions into barbarism. Societies rose upwards, attained certain levels, but were unable to maintain themselves upon these heights. Mankind does not remain standing in one place, owing to class and national struggles its equilibrium is unstable; a society that is unable to move forward, falls back, and if no class exists to lift it higher, this society begins to fall apart, opening the road to barbarism.

For a clear conception of this extremely complex problem, the general abstract considerations I have just developed do not suffice, Comrades. Young Comrades with little experience in such questions should apply themselves to a study of historical works in order to master the factual material pertaining to the history of different countries and peoples, particularly and especially their economic history. Only then is it possible to attain a more concrete and clearer conception of the inner mechanics of society. This mechanics must be clearly understood in order to apply Marxism correctly to tactics, i.e., to the class struggle in practice.

Questions of Revolutionary Tactics

Some comrades have a far too simplified approach to the victory of the proletariat. There obtains to-day not alone in Europe but on a world scale a situation which permits us, from the standpoint of Marxism, to say with complete assurance that the bourgeois system has completely drained itself. The world productive forces cannot develop further within the framework of bourgeois society. On the contrary, what we have witnessed during the last decade is the falling apart, the disintegration of the economic foundations of capitalist society coupled with the use of machines for the destruction of accumulated wealth. We are now living in conditions of the most appalling and unprecedented crisis in world history, not simply a periodic "normal crisis" unavoidable in the process of the development of productive forces under capitalism, but a crisis which signifies that the productive forces of bourgeois society are falling apart and decomposing. There still may be ups and downs, but, in general, as I told the comrades in this very hall a month and a half ago, the curve of capitalist economic development swings through all the fluctuations, not upwards but downwards. But does this mean that the doom of the bourgeoisie is automatically and mechanically predetermined? No. The bourgeoisie is a living class which has risen on specific economic, productive foundations. This class is not a passive product of economic development, but a living, dynamic, active historical force. This class has outlived itself, i.e., has become the most fearsome brake upon historical development. But this must not at all be taken to mean that this class is prone to historical suicide, that it is ready to say, "Since the scientific theory of historical development finds me reactionary, therefore I leave the scene." Of course, there cannot even be talk of this. On the other hand, the recognition by the Communist Party of the fact that the bourgeois class is condemned and subject to elimination, is likewise far from sufficient to assure the victory of the proletariat. No, the bourgeoisie must still be defeated and overthrown!

If the further development of productive forces was conceivable within the framework of bourgeois society, then revolution would generally be impossible. But since the further development of the productive forces within the framework of bourgeois society is inconceivable, the basic premise for the revolution is given. But revolution in and of itself signifies a living class struggle. The bourgeoisie, even though it finds itself in a complete contradiction with the demands of historical progress, nevertheless still remains the most powerful class. More than that, it may be said that politically the bourgeoisie attains its greatest powers, its greatest concentration of forces and resources, of political and military means of deception, of coercion, and provocation, i.e., the flowering of its class strategy, at the moment when it is most immediately threatened by social ruin. The war and its terrible consequences—and the war sprang precisely from the fact that the productive forces had no room to develop further within the framework of bourgeois society—the war and its consequences, I say, have confronted the bourgeoisie with the terrible threat of destruction. This has rendered its instinct of class self-preservation sensitive in the extreme. The greater the danger, all the more does the class, like the individual, exert its vital forces in the struggle for self-preservation. Let us not forget also that the bourgeoisie finds itself face to face with mortal danger, after having accumulated colossal political experience. The bourgeoisie has created and destroyed all sorts of regimes. Its development occurred under pure absolutism, under constitutional monarchy, under parliamentary monarchy, under a democratic republic, under a Bonapartist dictatorship, under a state bound up with the Catholic Church, under a state bound up with the Reformation, under a state separated from the Church, under a state persecuting the Church, etc., etc. All this varied and rich experience which has entered into the blood and marrow of bourgeois ruling circles has now been mobilized by them in order to maintain themselves in power at any cost. And they act the more resourcefully, cunningly, ruthlessly, all the more clearly their leaders take cognizance of the threatening danger.

From a superficial standpoint there appears to be some sort of contradiction here: We have brought the bourgeoisie for judgment before the court of Marxism, i.e., the court of scientific knowledge of the historical process, and found it obsolete, and yet at the same time the bourgeoisie discloses a colossal vitality. In reality there is no contradiction here at all. This is what Marxism calls the dialectic. The gist of the matter lies in this, that the different aspects of the historical process—economics, politics, the state, the growth of the working class—do not develop simultaneously along parallel lines. The working class does not grow parallel, point for point, with the growth of the productive forces, while the bourgeoisie does not decay nor wither away parallel with the growth and strengthening of the proletariat. No, history proceeds in a different way. Productive forces develop by leaps, now whirling forwards, now dropping back. The bourgeoisie, in its turn, developed through a series of shocks and impulses. So, too, has the working class. In a period when the productive forces of capitalism have run up against a blank wall and can go no further we see the bourgeoisie gathering in its own hands the army, the police, science, schools, church, parliament, the press, the White Guard gangs; tightening the reins and mentally saying to the proletariat, " Yes, my position is dangerous. I see an abyss yawning under my feet. But we'll wait and see who plunges first into this abyss. Perhaps before I perish, even if such is to be my fate, I'll succeed in casting you, the working class, into the abyss." What would this signify? This would signify the collapse of European civilization as a whole. If the bourgeoisie, which is doomed historically, were to find sufficient strength, energy and power to defeat the working class in the impending terrible combat, it would signify that Europe is condemned to economic and cultural decomposition, as happened in the past to many countries, nations and civilizations. In other words, history has brought matters to such a pass that the proletarian revolution has become unconditionally necessary for the salvation of Europe and the whole world. History has provided the basic premise for the success of this revolution—in the sense that society cannot any longer develop its productive forces on bourgeois foundations. But history does not at all assume upon itself—in place of the working class, in place of the politicians of the working class, in place of the Communists—the solution of this entire task. No, History seems to say to the proletarian vanguard (let us imagine for a moment that history is a figure looming above us), History says to the working class, "You must know that unless you cast down the bourgeoisie, you will perish beneath the ruins of civilization. Try, solve this task!" Such is the state of affairs to-day.

We see that in Europe, after the war, the working class is trying semi-spontaneously, semi-consciously to solve the task set before it by history. And the practical conclusion which all the thinking elements of the working class in Europe and the whole world had to draw after the three years following the termination of the world war, reads as follows: Overthrowing the bourgeoisie, even though it has been condemned by history, is neither so simple nor so easy as it might have seemed.

Europe and the whole world are passing through a period which is, on the one side, an epoch of the disintegration of the productive forces of bourgeois society, and, on the other side, an epoch of the highest flowering of the counter-revolutionary strategy of the bourgeoisie. We must understand this clearly and precisely. Counter-revolutionary strategy, i.e., the art of waging a combined struggle against the proletariat by every method from saccharine, professorial-clerical preachments to machine-gunning of strikers, has never attained such heights as it does to-day.

Lansing[1], the former U.S. Secretary of State, in his book on the Versailles Peace remarks that Lloyd George is ignorant of geography, economics, etc. We readily incline to believe him. But for us it is absolutely incontestable that this same Lloyd George has stored in his head all the usages of duping and coercing the toilers, from the most cunning and subtle tricks to the bloodiest; he has assimilated the entire experience provided by English history on this score, and has developed and perfected all this in the experience of the last three stormy years. Lloyd George is in his own way a superb strategist of the bourgeoisie, threatened with historical ruin. And we must say, nowise minimizing thereby either the present or all the less so the future of the English Communist Party which is still very young—we must say that the English proletariat possesses no such strategists as yet.

In France the President of the Republic, Millerand, formerly a member of a working class party, and Briand, the head of the government, who once used to propagate the idea of "General Strike" among the workers—both of them have used the French bourgeoisie's entire rich political experience plus the experience which they themselves had gained in the camp of the proletariat—used it in the service of the cause of the bourgeoisie, as its skilled counter-revolutionary strategists. In Italy, in Germany, we see how carefully the bourgeoisie promotes from its ranks individuals and groups that concentrate the entire experience of the bourgeoisie's class struggle for its own development, enrichment, consolidation and self-preservation.

The School of Revolutionary Strategy

The task of the working class—in Europe and throughout the world—consists in counterposing to the thoroughly thought-out counter-revolutionary strategy of the bourgeoisie its own revolutionary strategy, likewise thought out to the end. For this it is first of all necessary to understand that it will not be possible to overthrow the bourgeoisie automatically, mechanically, merely because it is condemned by history. On the highly complex field of political struggle we find, on the one side, the bourgeoisie with its forces and resources and, on the opposing side, the working class with its various layers, moods, levels of development, with its Communist Party struggling against other parties and organizations for influence over the working masses. In this struggle the Communist Party, which is actually moving steadily to the head of the European working class, has to maneuver, now attacking, now retreating, always consolidating its influence, conquering new positions until the favorable moment arrives for the overthrow of the bourgeoisie. Let me repeat, this is a complex strategical task and the last World Congress posed this task in its full scope. From this standpoint, one may say that the Third Congress of the Communist International was the highest school of revolutionary strategy.

The First Congress convened after the war at a time when Communism was just being born as a European movement and when there was a certain justification for reckoning and hoping that the semi-spontaneous onset of the working class might overthrow the bourgeoisie before the latter succeeded in finding a new orientation and new postwar points of support. Such moods and expectations were by and large justified by the objective situation at the time. The bourgeoisie was terribly frightened by the consequence of its own war policy which, in its turn, had been imposed upon the bourgeoisie by the objective conditions. I dealt with this in my report on the world situation and will not repeat it here. In any case, it is unquestionable that in the era of the First Congress (1919) many of us reckoned—some more, others less—that the spontaneous onset of the workers and in part of the peasant masses would overthrow the bourgeoisie in the near future. And, as a matter of fact, this onset was truly colossal. The number of casualties was very large. But the bourgeoisie was able to withstand this initial onset and precisely for this reason regained its class self-confidence.

The Second Congress in 1920 convened at the breaking point. It could already be sensed that by the onset alone the bourgeoisie would not be overthrown in a few weeks or in one, two or three months; that needed was a more serious organizational and political preparation. But at the same time the situation remained very acute. You will recall, the Red Army was then advancing on Warsaw and it was possible to calculate that because of the revolutionary situation in Germany, Italy and other countries, the military impulse—without, of course, any independent significance of its own but as an auxiliary force introduced into the struggle of the European forces—might bring down the landslide of revolution, then temporarily at a dead point. This did not happen. We were beaten back.

After the Second Congress of the Communist International it became increasingly clear that the working class was in need of a more complex revolutionary strategy. We see the working masses, after acquiring a serious postwar experience, themselves moving in this direction, and as a primary result of this the Communist parties everywhere experience growth. During the initial period millions of workers in Germany threw themselves into frontal assaults upon the old order, almost without paying attention to the Spartacus League. What did this mean? After the war, it seemed to the working masses that now was the time to make demands, to press forward, to deal a blow—and there would be a change in many things, if not in everything. That is why millions of workers deemed it unnecessary to expend their energy on building the Communist Party. Meanwhile, last year saw the Communist parties in Germany and France—two of the most important countries on the European continent—transformed from circle-groups into organizations embracing workers by the hundreds of thousands. In Germany there are about 400,000; in France, between 120,000 and 130,000, which is a very high figure under the French conditions. This shows how deeply the working masses during this period became imbued with the realization that it is impossible to win without a special organization where the working class is able to weigh its experience and draw conclusions from it—in a word, a centralized party leadership. Herein is the great conquest of the period just elapsed—the creation of mass Communist parties, among which should be listed the Czechoslovak Party, numbering 350,000 members. (After fusing with the German Communist Organization of Czechoslovakia this Party will number about 400,000 among a population of 12 million.)

It would, however, be a mistake to expect of these young and just risen Communist parties that they immediately master the art of revolutionary strategy. No! Last year's tactical experience testifies all too clearly to the contrary. And the Third Congress came to grips with this question.

The last World Congress, taken in its most general aspects, had two tasks before it. One was and remains: To cleanse the working class, including our own Communist ranks, of elements *who do not want to struggle,* who fear struggle and who use this or that theory in order to cover up their aversion from struggle and their inner inclination to conciliate with bourgeois society. The purge of the labor movement as a whole, and all the more so of the Communist ranks, of reformist, centrist, semi-centrist elements and moods is twofold in character: Where conscious centrists, case-hardened conciliators or semi-conciliators are concerned—they must be forthwith driven out of the ranks of the Communist Party and the labor movement; where it is a question of vague semi-centrist moods, such elements must be given firm guidance, subjected to influence and drawn into the revolutionary struggle. This is the first task of the Communist International

—to purge the party of the working class of all elements who do not want to struggle and who thereby paralyze the struggle of the proletariat. But there is a second and no less important task: *To learn the art of struggle*, an art which by no means falls from the skies like manna for the working class or its Communist Party. The art of tactics and strategy, the art of revolutionary struggle can be mastered only through experience, through criticism and self-criticism. At the Third World Congress we told the young Communists: " Comrades, we desire not only heroic struggle, we desire first of all *victory*. During the last few years, we have seen no few heroic struggles in Europe, especially in Germany. We have seen in Italy large-scale revolutionary struggles, a civil war with its unavoidable sacrifices. Of course, every struggle does not lead to victory. Defeats are inescapable. But these defeats must not come through the fault of our party. Yet we have seen many manifestations and methods of struggle which do not and cannot lead to victory, for they are dictated time and time again by revolutionary impatience and not by political sagacity."

This was the axis of the ideological struggle that took place at the Third World Congress. I must, Comrades, make a reservation here to the effect that this struggle was not at all embittered or " factional " in character. On the contrary, the atmosphere at the Congress was deeply comradely, serious and businesslike; and the ideological struggle was of a rigidly principled character and there was at the same time a businesslike interchange of opinions.

The Congress was a big revolutionary-political Soviet of the working class. And there, at this Soviet, we, the representatives of various countries, on the basis of experience in these countries, on the one hand, verified, once again reaffirmed in practice and rendered more precise our theses concerning the need of purging the working class of all elements who do not want to struggle and who are incapable of struggle; and, on the other hand, we for the first time posed bluntly and in its full scope the following issue: The revolutionary struggle for power has its own laws, its own usages, its own tactics, its own strategy. Those who do not master this art will never taste victory.

Centrist Tendencies in Italian Socialism

The tasks of struggle with centrist or semi-centrist elements were delineated most clearly in the case of the Italian Socialist Party. You are acquainted with the history of this question. The Italian Socialist Party passed through an important internal struggle and a split even prior to the imperialist war. This cleansed the party of the worst chauvinists. Besides, Italy entered the war nine months later than other countries. This made it easier for the Italian party to conduct its anti-war policy. The party did not fall into patriotism but preserved a critical attitude toward the war and toward the government. This impelled it to participate in the anti-militarist Zimmerwald Conference², although its internationalism was rather formless. Later the vanguard of the Italian working class pushed the leading party circles still farther to the left and the party found itself inside the Third International—along with Turati who contends in his speeches and articles that the Third International is nothing except a diplomatic tool in the hands of the Soviet power, which, under the guise of internationalism, is waging a struggle for the " national " interests of the Russian people. Isn't it monstrous to hear such pronouncements on the lips—with your indulgence—of a " comrade " in the Third International? The abnormality of the Italian Socialist Party's adhering in its old form to the Communist International was most glaringly revealed during the large-scale mass action of last September. One must say that in the course of this movement this party *betrayed* the working class.

If one were to ask how and why did this party retreat and capitulate in the autumn of last year, during the mass strike, during the seizure of factories, plants, estates, etc., by the workers? If one were to ask what was the dominant element in this betrayal? Was it malignant reformism, or indecision, political light-mindedness or something else? To such questions it would be difficult to give an exact answer. The Italian Socialist Party came, after the war, under the influence of the Communist International, which enabled its Left Wing to express itself more vociferously than the Right Wing. This fully corresponded to the moods of the masses. But the organizational apparatus remained for the most part in the hands of the center and the Right Wing. The party carried on agitation in favor of the dictatorship of the proleariat, in favor of the Soviet power, in favor of the hammer and sickle, in favor of Soviet Russia, etc. The Italian working class *en masse* took all this seriously and entered the road of open revolutionary struggle. In September of last year matters reached the point of seizure of factories, plants, mines, large estates, etc. But precisely at the moment when the party should have drawn all the political, organizational and practical conclusions from its own agitation, it became scared of the responsibility and shied away, leaving the rear of the proletariat unprotected. The working masses were left exposed to the blows of fascist gangs. The working class thought and hoped that the party which had summoned it to struggle would consolidate the success of its assault. And this success could have been sealed, such hope was fully justified, inasmuch as the bourgeois power was at that time demoralized and paralyzed, unable to depend either on the army or on the police apparatus. It was only natural, I repeat, for the working class to think that the party standing at its head would lead to its conclusion the struggle that had commenced. But at the most critical moment the party, on the contrary, beat a retreat, beheading the working class and rendering it powerless. It then became definitely and absolutely clear that politicians of this sort had no place in the ranks of the Third International. The ECCI acted perfectly correctly in recognizing, after the split which presently occurred in the Italian Party, that only the Left Communist Wing constituted a section of the Communist International. Therewith the party of Serrati, i.e., the leading section of the old Italian Socialist Party, found itself outside the Third International. Unfortunately—it might have been owing to exceptionally unfavorable conditions, or perhaps also owing to mistakes on our part—unfortunately, the Communist Party of Italy when it was formed drew into its ranks less than 50,000 members, while Serrati's party kept about 100,000, among them 14,000 transparent reformists, constituting an organized faction. (They held their own conference at Reggio-Emilia.) Naturally, 100,000 workers, belonging to a Socialist party, are under no circumstances our adversaries. If we have been unable up to now to draw them completely into our ranks, then we are not entirely blameless here. The correctness of this thought is evidenced by the fact that the Socialist Party of Italy, which had been expelled from the Third International, sent three of its representatives to our Congress. What does this mean? The ruling circles of the party had, by their policy, placed themselves outside the International, but the working masses compel them again and again to knock on the doors of the International.

The worker-Socialists have thereby shown that their mood is revolutionary and that they want to be with us. But they sent people who have by their conduct revealed that they failed to assimilate the ideas and methods of Communism. By this the Italian workers belonging to Serrati's party showed that while being in their majority revolutionary in their moods, they had not yet attained the necessary political clarity.

There came to our Congress the aged Lazzari. Personally, he is very likeable, unquestionably an honest man, an old fighter, an irreproachable individual, but in no case a Communist. He is completely under the sway of democratic, humanitarian and pacifist views. He argued at the Congress: " You exaggerate Turati's importance. You generally incline to exaggerate the importance of our reformists. You demand of us that we expel them. But how can we expel them when they submit to party discipline? If they provided us—said Lazzari—with a *fact* of openly opposing the party, if they joined the government against our decision, if they voted for the military budget against our instructions, then we could expel them. But not otherwise."

We called his attention to Turati's articles which are directed wholly against the ABC of revolutionary socialism. Lazzari objected that these articles did not constitute *facts,* that they have freedom of opinion in the Italian party, and so on. To this we again answered him : " By your leave, if to expel Turati you need an accomplished ' fact,' i.e., his accepting a portfolio from Giolitti then it is unquestionable that Turati who is a *clever* politician will never take this step. For Turati is not at all a shoddy careerist whose sole concern is to obtain a portfolio. Turati is a case-hardened conciliator, an irreconcilable enemy of the revolution, but in his own way, an ideological politician. He wants to save at any cost the bourgeois-democratic ' civilization ' and therefore to defeat the revolutionary tendency in the working class. When Giolitti offers him a portfolio—and this probably happened more than once in secluded places—Turati makes approximately the following reply: ' My acceptance of the portfolio would constitute the very ' fact ' referred to by Lazzari. The moment I accept the portfolio I would be caught up on this ' fact ' and driven out of the party. But the moment I am driven out of the party, I won't be of much use to you, either, my dear godfather Giolitti. For you need me only so long as I am connected with a large workers' party. It follows therefore that after I am expelled from the party you would boot me out of the Ministry."

That is approximately how Turati reasons, and he is correct; he is much more far-sighted than the idealistic and pacifistic Lazzari.

" You overestimate Turati's group," said Lazzari. " It is a small group. As the French say, a negligible quantity."

To this we replied, "And do you know that while you take the floor at the Moscow International with the demand that you be admitted into our ranks, Giolitti is calling Turati on the phone and asking: 'Are you aware, dear friend, that Lazzari has gone to Moscow and that he might make there in the name of your party some dangerous commitments to the Russian Bolsheviks?' Do you know what Turati answers to this? In all likelihood he says, 'Don't worry, my bosom friend Giolitti, our Lazzari is a *quantité négligeable,* a negligible quantity.'" And he is infinitely more correct than Lazzari.

Such was the dialogue between us and the vacillating representatives of a considerable section of the Italian workers. It was finally decided to put an ultimatum to the Italian Socialists: They must convene within three months a party conference, expel at this conference all the reformists whose roll-call was taken by themselves at their Reggio-Emilia Conference, and unite with the Communists on the basis of the decisions of the Third Congress. What the immediate practical results of this decision will be, it is impossible to say exactly. Will all the followers of Serrati come over to us? I doubt it. But this is hardly desirable. Among them there are some we have no use for at all. But the step taken by the Congress was correct. Its aim is to win over the workers to us, by effecting a split in the ranks of the vacillating leaders.

Italian Communism—Its Difficulties, Its Tasks

Among the delegates of the Italian Communist Party and also among the representatives of the youth there were to be found, however, some very incensed critics of this step. The Italian Communists, most of whom deviated to the left, critized the Congress most sharply for having "opened the doors" to the Serrati-ites, opportunists and centrists. This expression—"you opened the doors of the Communist International"—was repeated scores of times. We pointed out to them, "Comrades, you have as yet about 50,000 workers while the Serrati-ites have about 100,000. After all, it is impermissible to rest contented with such a result." They disputed the figures a little, pointing out that there had been mass departures from the Socialist Party, which is quite possible. But their chief argument ran as follows: "The Socialist Party as a whole, and not its leaders alone, is reformist, opportunist." We asked, "How and why, then, did they send Lazzari, Maffi and Riboldi to Moscow?" The young Italian Communists gave me an answer that was quite vague, "You see, the whole point is that the Italian working class *as a whole* is gravitating toward Moscow and is pushing the opportunists in this direction." This is an obviously forced explanation. If the situation were such that the Italian working class as a whole was surging toward Moscow, it had a widely opened door to get to Moscow, namely: the Italian Communist Party, adhering to the International. Why then did the Italian working class choose such a round-about way to Moscow, keep pushing Serrati's party instead of simply joining the Communist Party of Italy? It is quite obvious that all these objections of the Left Communists were spurious, arising from an insufficient understanding of the basic task —the need of winning over the vanguard of the working class and first of all, those workers, by no means the worst types, who remained in the ranks of the Socialist Party of Italy. It was precisely these workers who brought Lazzari to Moscow. The mistake of the " Lefts " stems from a special kind of revolutionary impatience which causes one to lose sight of the most important preparatory and preliminary tasks and which invariably brings the greatest harm to the interests of our cause. It seems to some " Lefts " that since the immediate task is to overthrow the bourgeoisie, therefore is it really worthwhile pausing along the road in order to engage in negotiations with the Serrati-ites, open the doors for workers who follow Serrati, etc., etc.? And yet that is the chief task today. And it is not at all a simple task. Needed here are negotiations as well as struggle as well as exhortations; involved here are new unifications and in all likelihood new splits. But some impatient comrades wanted simply to turn their backs upon this problem and consequently also upon the worker-Socialists. Let those who are in favor of the Third International come right into our Communist Party. On the surface this seems to be the simplest solution of the problem but in reality it skirts the question, for the latter precisely consists in knowing *how*, and *through what methods* to attract the worker-Socialist into the Communist Party.

This task cannot be solved automatically by "shutting the doors" of the International. After all, the Italian workers know that the Socialist Party, too, belonged to the Third International. Its leaders made revolutionary speeches, summoned to struggle, called for the Soviet power and precipitated the September strike, the seizure of factories and plants. Then they capitulated, failing to join the battle when the workers were engaged in fighting. Today the vanguard of the Italian proletariat is mentally digesting this fact. The workers see that a Communist minority has separated from the Socialist Party and has addressed itself to them with the same or virtually the same speeches which they heard yesterday from Serrati's party. The workers say to themselves, " We must wait, we must see what this means, we must examine. . . . " In other words they are demanding perhaps not very articulately or consciously but in the nature of things very persistently that the new, Communist Party prove itself *in action,* that the leaders demonstrate in practice that they are made of different stuff from the leaders of the old party and that they are inseparably bound up with the masses in their struggle, no matter how harsh may be the conditions of this struggle. It is necessary by word and deed, by deed and word to conquer the confidence of tens of thousands worker-Socialists who still remain at the crossroads but who would like to be in our ranks. If we were simply to turn our backs on them, allegedly in the name of immediately overthrowing the bourgeoisie, then we could cause no little harm thereby to the revolution. And meanwhile, precisely in Italy the conditions are very favorable for the triumph of the proletarian revolution in the rather near future.

Let us imagine for a moment—this is only by way of example— that the Italian Communists, say, in May of this year were to summon the Italian working class to a new general strike and an insurrection. Suppose they said: "Since the Socialist Party, whose ranks we have left, proved itself bankrupt in September, it therefore follows that we, Communists, must now erase this blot at any cost and lead the working class immediately into the decisive battle." From a superficial standpoint, this might actually seem to be the duty of the Communists. But that is really not the case at all. According to elementary revolutionary strategy, such a summons would be a piece of insanity and a crime, in the given conditions, because the working class which had, under the leadership of the Socialist Party, cruelly burnt its fingers in September, would not believe it possible to successfully repeat this experience in May under the leadership of the Communist Party with which it had not yet had the opportunity to become really acquainted. The Socialist Party was guilty in the main of " calling " for a revolution without first drawing all the necessary conclusions, that is, it really made no preparations for the revolution, failed to explain to the advanced workers the questions bound up with the conquest of power, failed to purge its ranks of those who did not want the conquest of power, failed to select and train reliable cadres of fighters, failed to create assault groups capable of handling weapons and capable of seizing weapons at the necessary moment. . . . In brief, the *Socialist Party called for the revolution but did not prepare for it.* If the Italian Communists were now simply to call for revolution they would be repeating the mistake of the Socialists—only under far more difficult conditions. The task of our sister party in Italy is to *prepare* for the revolution. That is to say, first of all conquer the majority of the working class and organize its vanguard in a proper way. Anyone who curbed the impatient section of the Italian Communists and said to them: Before calling for the uprising you must first win over the worker-Socialists, cleanse the trade unions, elect Communists there in place of opportunists to responsible posts, conquer the masses—he who said this might superficially appear to be dragging the Communists back but in reality he would thereby be pointing out the real road to the victory of the revolution.

The Fears and Suspicions of the Extreme " Left "

All of the foregoing, Comrades, is ABC from the standpoint of serious revolutionary experience. But there were some " Left " elements in the Congress who saw in this tactic a shift " to the right." And some young revolutionary comrades, lacking in experience, but brimful of energy and readiness to struggle and self-sacrifice, literally felt their hair stand up on their heads when they heard the first critical and admonitory speeches of the Russian comrades. Among these young revolutionists there were some, who, I am told, kissed the Soviet soil upon crossing the frontier. And although we still work our soil far too poorly to make it worthy of such kisses, we nevertheless appreciate the revolutionary enthusiasm of our young foreign friends. They think it a shame and a disgrace that they have been so laggard and haven't as yet accomplished their revolution. They came with these feelings into the hall of the Nikolayevsk Palace— and what happened? Russian Communists took the floor there and not only failed to demand an immediate summons to insurrection but, on the contrary, issued all sorts of warnings against adventures and insisted upon attracting the worker-Socialists, upon conquering the majority of the toilers on the basis of careful preparation.

Certain extreme Lefts even decided that not everything was above-board here. Semi-hostile elements like delegates from the so-called Communist Workers' Party of Germany (this group has a consultative vote in the International) began reasoning to the effect that up to recently the Russian Soviet power did actually entertain hopes of a revolution in Europe and did shape its policies accordingly, but that later its patience became exhausted and it began concluding trade agreements and developed through its People's Commissariat of Foreign Trade a large-scale world commerce. Commerce, on the other hand, is a serious business requiring tranquil and peaceful relations. It has long been known that revolutionary convulsions are harmful to commerce, and from the standpoint of Comrade Krassin's' Commissariat we are, you see, interested in postponing and retarding the revolution as long as possible. (*General laughter*.) Comrades, I am very sorry that your friendly laughter cannot be transmitted by radio to certain extremely Leftist comrades in Germany and Italy. The hypothesis concerning the opposition of our Commissariat of Foreign Trade to revolutionary disturbances is rendered all the more curious by the fact that as recently as March of this year when tragic battles broke out in Germany, with which I shall presently deal—battles which terminated in a cruel defeat of a section of the German working class—the German bourgeois and Social-Democratic news-papers, and in their wake the press throughout the world began howling that the March uprising had been provoked by orders from Moscow; that the Soviet power, in difficult straits at that time (peasant mutinies, Kronstadt, etc.), had issued, to save itself, you see, an order to stage uprisings regardless of the situation in every given country. It is impossible to invent anything sillier than this! But no sooner had the Comrade Delegates from Rome, Berlin and Paris arrived in Moscow, than a new theory arise, but this time at the opposite and extreme left pole—according to this theory, we not only fail to " order " uprisings to be staged immediately and independently of the objective situation, but, on the contrary, we are infatuated with our beautiful trade turn-over and are interested in postponing the revolution. Which of these two diametrically opposed stupidities is sillier, it is not easy to decide. If we were to blame for the March mistakes—insofar as it is possible to speak here of blame—then it was only in the sense that the International as a whole, including our own party, has up to now failed to carry on enough educational work in the sphere of revolutionary tactics, and for this reason failed to eliminate the possibility of such mistaken actions and methods. But to dream of completely eliminating mistakes would be the height of innocence.

The March Events in Germany

In a certain sense the question of the March events occupied at the Congress the central place. And this was not accidental. Among all the Communist parties, our German Party is one of the most powerful and best prepared theoretically. And as regards the order of revolution—if it is permissible to express oneself in this manner —Germany stands in any case in the front rank.

As a defeated country, Germany's internal conditions are the most favorable for revolution. The numerical strength and the economic role of the German proletariat are entirely adequate to assure victory to this revolution. It is only natural for the methods of struggle applied by the German Communist Party to assume an international significance. Beginning with 1918, major events in the revolutionary struggle have transpired on Germany's soil, and the positive and negative aspects can be analyzed here from living experience.

What was the content of the March events? The proletarians of Central Germany, the workers in the mining regions, represented in recent times, even during the war, one of the most retarded sections of the German working class. In their majority they followed not the Social Democrats but the patriotic, bourgeois and clerical cliques, remained devoted to the Emperor, and so on and so forth. Their living and working conditions were exceptionally harsh. In relation to the workers of Berlin they occupied the same place, as say, did the backward Ural provinces in our country in relation to the Petersburg workers. During a revolutionary epoch it happens not infrequently that a most oppressed and backward section of the working class, awakened for the first time by the thunder of events, swings into the struggle with the greatest energy and evinces a readiness to fight under any and all conditions, far from always taking into consideration the circumstances and the chances of victory, that is, the requirements of revolutionary strategy. For example, at a time when the workers of Berlin or Saxony had become, after the experience of 1919-1920, far more cautious—which has its minuses and its pluses too—the workers of Central Germany continued to engage in stormy actions, strikes and demonstrations, carting out their foremen on wheelbarrows, holding meetings during working hours, and so on. Naturally, this is incompatible with the sacred tasks of Ebert's Republic. It is hardly surprising that this conservative-police Republic, in the person of its police agent, the Social Democrat Hoersing, should have decided to do a little " purging " there, i.e., drive out the most revolutionary elements, arrest several Communists, etc.

Precisely during this period (the middle of March), the Central Committee of the German Communist Party arrived firmly at the idea that there was need of conducting a more actively revolutionary policy. The German Party, you will recall, had been created a short while before by the merger of the old Spartacus League and the majority of the Independent Party and thereby became confronted in practice with the question of mass actions. The idea that it was necessary to pass over to a more active policy was absolutely correct. But how did this express itself in practice? When the Social-Democratic policeman Hoersing issued his order, demanding of the workers what Kerensky's government had more than once vainly demanded in our country, namely: that no meetings be held during working hours, that factory property be treated as a sacred trust, etc.—at this moment the Central Committee of the Communist Party issued a call for a general strike in order to aid the workers of Central Germany. A general strike is not something to which the working class responds easily, at the party's very first call—especially if the workers have recently suffered a number of defeats, and, all the less so in a country where alongside the Communist Party there exist two mass Social-Democratic parties and where the trade union apparatus is opposed to us. Yet, if we examine the issues of *Rote Fahne,* central publication of the Communist Party, throughout this period, day by day, we will see that the call for the general strike came completely unprepared. During the period of revolution there were not a few blood-lettings in Germany and the police offensive against Central Germany could not in and of itself have immediately raised the entire working class to its feet. Every serious mass action must obviously be preceded by large-scale energetic agitation, centering around action slogans, all hitting on one and the same point. Such agitation can lead to more decisive calls for action only if it reveals, after probing, that the masses have already been touched to the quick and are ready to march forward on the path of revolutionary action. This is the ABC of revolutionary strategy, but precisely this ABC was completely

violated during the March events. Before the police battalions had
even succeeded in reaching the factories and mines of Central Germany, a general strike did actually break out there. I already said
that in Central Germany there existed the readiness to engage in
immediate struggle, and the call of the Central Committee met with an
immediate response. But an entirely different situation prevailed in
the rest of the country. There was nothing either in the international
or the domestic situation of Germany to justify such a sudden transition to activity. The masses simply failed to understand the summons.

Nevertheless, certain very influential theoreticians of the German
Communist Party instead of acknowledging that this summons was
a mistake, proceeded to explain it away by propounding a theory that
in a revolutionary epoch we are obliged to conduct exclusively an
aggressive policy, that is, the policy of revolutionary offensive. The
March action is thus served up to the masses in the guise of an
offensive. You can now evaluate the situation as a whole.   The
offensive was in reality launched by the Social-Democratic policeman
Hoersing. This should have been utilized in order to unite all the
workers for defense, for self-protection, even if, to begin with,
a very modest resistance. Had the soil proved favorable, had the
agitation met with a favorable response, it would then have been
possible to pass over to the general strike. If the events continue
to unfold further, if the masses rise, if the ties among the workers
grow stronger, if their temper lifts, while indecision and demoraliza-
tion seize the camp of the foe—then comes the time for issuing the
slogan to pass over to the offensive. But should the soil prove unfavorable, should the conditions and the moods of the masses fail to
correspond with the more resolute slogans, then it is necessary to sound
a retreat, and to fall back to previously prepared positions in as orderly
a manner as possible. Therewith we have gained this, that we proved
our ability to probe the working masses, we strengthened their internal
ties and, what is most important, we have raised the party's authority
for giving wise leadership under all circumstances.

But what does the leading body of the German Party do? It gives the
appearance of pouncing upon the very first pretext; and even before
this pretext has become known to workers or assimilated by them, the
Central Committee hurls the slogan of the general strike. And before
the party had a chance to rally the workers of Berlin, Dresden and
Munich to the aid of the workers of Central Germany—and this could

perhaps have been accomplished in the space of a few days, provided there was no leaping over the events, and the masses were led forward systematically and firmly—before the party succeeded in accomplishing this work, it is proclaimed that our action is an offensive. This was already tantamount to ruining everything and paralyzing the movement in advance. It is quite self-evident that at this stage the offensive came exclusively from the enemy side. It was necessary to utilize the moral element of *defense,* it was necessary to summon the proletariat of the whole country to hasten to the aid of the workers of Central Germany. In the initial stages this support might have assumed varied forms, until the party found itself in a position to issue a generalized slogan of action. The task of agitation consisted in raising the masses to their feet, focusing their attention upon the events in Central Germany, smashing politically the resistance of the Labor bureaucracy and thus assuring a genuinely *general* character of the strike action as a possible base for the further development of the revolutionary struggle. But what happened instead? The revolutionary and dynamic minority of the proletariat found itself counterposed in action to the majority of the proletariat, before this majority had a chance to grasp the meaning of events. When the party ran up against the passivity and dilatoriness of the working class, the impatient Communist elements sought here and there to drive the majority of the workers into the streets, no longer by means of agitation, but by mechanical measures. If the majority of workers favor a strike, they can of course always compel the minority by forcibly shutting down the factories and thus achieving the general strike in action. This has happened more than once, it will happen in the future and only simpletons can raise objections to it. But when the crushing majority of the working class has no clear conception of the movement, or is unsympathetic to it, or does not believe it can succeed, but a minority rushes ahead and seeks to drive workers to strike by mechanical measures, then such an impatient minority can, in the person of the party, come into a hostile clash with the working class and break its own neck.*

* Paul Levi, former Chairman of the Central Committee of the German Communist Party, has come forward with a criticism of the Party's tactic during the March events. But his criticism is so absolutely and impermissibly disorganizing in character as to injure and not benefit the cause. The internal struggle led to the expulsion of Levi from the Party and this expulsion was approved by the Congress of the International.—L.T.

The Strategy of the German Counter-Revolution and the Leftist Adventuristic Elements

Let us review from this point of view the entire history of the German revolution. In November 1918, the monarchy fell and the proletarian revolution was placed on the order of the day. In January 1919, there occurred the sanguinary revolutionary battles of the proletarian vanguard against the regime of bourgeois democracy; these battles recurred in March 1919. The bourgeoisie quickly oriented itself and elaborated its own strategy: it proceeded to crush the proletariat, section by section. Therewith the best leaders of the working class perished—Rosa Luxemburg and Karl Liebknecht. In March 1920, after the Kapp-Luettwitz attempt at a counter-revolutionary overturn had been swept away by the General Strike, there was a new partial uprising, the armed struggle of the workers in the Ruhr coal basin. The movement terminated in a new defeat and countless fresh victims. Finally, in March 1921, there came a new civil war —once again partial in character—and a new defeat.

When in January and March 1919, the German workers engaged in a partial uprising, suffered defeat and lost their best leaders, we said, recalling our own experience, that these were the " July Days " of the German Communist Party. All of you remember the July Days in Petersburg in the year 1917. Petersburg at that time out-distanced the rest of the country, and rushed ahead by itself; it did not have sufficient support in the provinces, while in Kerensky's army there still remained backward regiments that could be employed to crush the movement. But in Petersburg itself the crushing majority of the proletariat was already with us. The July Days in Petersburg became the premise for October. It is true that we, too, did some foolish things during July. But we did not elevate them into a system. The January and March battles of 1919 were viewed by us as the German " July." But in Germany what came next was not " October " but March 1920—a new defeat, let alone other and smaller partial defeats and the systematic massacre of the best local leaders of the German working class. I say, when we observed the March movement of 1920 and later the March movement of 1921, we could not help but say: No, there are too many " July Days " in Germany, what we want is—October.

Yes, it is necessary to prepare the German October, the victory of the German working class. And it is here that the questions of revolu-

tionary strategy rise before us in their full scope. It is perfectly clear
and obvious that the German bourgeoisie, i.e., its leading clique, has
completely unfolded its counter-revolutionary strategy: It provokes
separate sections of the working class into action; it isolates them in
each province; it lies in ambush with rifles cocked and always aims
at the head, at the best representatives of the working class.   In the
streets or in the police cells, in an open battle or during alleged
attempts to escape, at the hands of courts martial or in the clutches of
an illegal gang, there perish by ones and twos, by the score, by the
hundred and by the thousand those Communists in whom the best
experience of the proletariat is embodied.   This strategy is rigidly
calculated, cold-bloodedly executed, and it encompasses the entire
experience of the ruling class.

And under these conditions, at a time when the German working
class as a whole instinctively senses that one cannot cope with such
an enemy with bare hands, that needed here is not merely enthusiasm
but cool calculation, lucid appraisal, serious preparation, and while
the working class expects this from its party, it is instead informed
from above that: It is our duty to pursue only the strategy of the
offensive, i.e., attack under all conditions because, you see, we have
entered the epoch of revolution.   This is approximately the same thing
as an army commander's saying: " Since we are at war, it is therefore our duty to assume the offensive everywhere and at all times."
Such a commander would be unfailingly smashed even with a preponderance of forces on his side.   But that is not all, there are to be
found " theoreticians," like the German Communist Maslow, who in
connection with the March events talk themselves into something
really egregious.   Maslow says: " Our opponents indict our March
action for something which we consider to be to our credit, namely:
that the party upon entering the struggle did not ask itself whether
the working class would follow it or not."   This is a verbatim quotation!

From the standpoint of subjective revolutionism or of Left-S.R.'ism,
this is superb, but from the standpoint of Marxism this is—monstrous!

Adventuristic Tendencies

" Revolutionary duty demands that we launch an offensive against
the Germans," proclaimed the Left S.R.'s in July 1918.   We'll be
crushed?   But it is our duty to march forward.   Do the working
masses object?   Very well.   In that case, it is possible to throw a

bomb at Mirbach[5] so as to compel the Russian workers to engage in a struggle in which they must unfailingly perish. Moods of this sort are very strong within the so-called Communist Workers Party of Germany (KAPD). This is a small group of *Proletarian Left S.R.'ism.* Our native Left S.R.'s have—more accurately they had—their deepest roots among the intellectuals and peasants. But apart from this social distinction, the political methods remain identical. This is an hysterical revolutionism capable of applying at any moment the most extreme means and methods without taking either the masses or the general situation into account. It is impatience in place of cool calculation. It is intoxication with revolutionary phrases. All this wholly characterizes " The Communist Workers Party of Germany." At the Congress one of the speakers, talking in the name of this party, said approximately the following: " What can you expect? The working class of Germany is permeated through and through (he even said *verseucht,* diseased) with philistinism, with middle-class ideology, petty-bourgeois spirit. What then can you do about it? Without economic sabotage, you will not get them out into the streets. . . ."

And when asked what he meant by this, he explained that no sooner did the workers begin living a little better than they become contented and do not want a revolution. If, however, the mechanical operation of production is interrupted, if factories, plants and railroads, etc., are blown up, this acts to worsen the condition of the working class and consequently renders it more capable of revolution. Bear in mind that this is spoken by a representative of a " workers " party. This is indeed absolute skepticism!

It thus turns out—if we draw the corresponding conclusions for the village—that the advanced peasants of Germany ought to set villages on fire, let loose the red cocks throughout the country and in this way revolutionize the rural population. Here one cannot help but recall that during the very first period of the revolutionary movement in Russia, in the Sixties, when the revolutionary intellectuals were completely powerless to express themselves in action, when they were squeezed in by their circle existence and continuously ran up against the passivity of the peasant masses—precisely at that time, certain groups (the so-called Nechayevites[6]), came to the conclusion that fires and arson constituted the real revolutionary factor of Russia's political development.

It is perfectly obvious that this sort of sabotage directed essentially against the majority of the working class is an anti-revolutionary measure which brings the working class into a hostile clash with a "workers" party, whose numbers are hard to estimate. But in any case, this "workers" party counts no more than 30,000-40,000, while the United Communist Party has, as you all know, about 400,000 members.

The Congress raised the question of the KAPD quite bluntly, presenting this organization with the demand that it hold a convention within the next three months and either merge with the unified Communist Party or definitely take its place outside the Communist International. From many indications the KAPD in the person of its present anarcho-adventuristic leadership will not submit to the decision of the International, and thus finding itself outside our ranks will probably try to form a "Fourth International" together with some other "extreme left" elements. A few notes on the same little pipe were blown at the Congress by our own Kollontai. It is no secret that our party remains for the time being, the core of the Communist International. Meanwhile Comrade Kollontai painted the situation in our party in such colours as to make it appear that, give or take a month, the working masses, with Comrade Kollontai at the head, will have to make a "third revolution" in order to establish a "genuine" Soviet system. But why only a third revolution and not a fourth? After all, the third revolution in the name of a "genuine" Soviet system occurred last February in Kronstadt. There are extreme leftists in Holland, too. Perhaps in other countries as well. I do not know whether all of them have been accounted for. But in any case their number is not excessive and a "Fourth International," should it arise, runs the least danger of becoming very large numerically. Naturally, it would be sad to lose even a small group, because there undoubtedly are good worker militants in its ranks. But if this sectarian split is ordained to occur then we shall have in the next period not only the Two-and-a-Half International on our right but also International Number Four on our left—where subjectivity, hysteria, adventurism and revolutionary phrase-mongering will find expression in a completely finished form. We will thus obtain a "left" scarecrow of which we shall make use in order to teach strategy to the working class. Everything, as you see, has two sides: positive and negative.

Leftist Blunders and the Russian Experience

But within the United Communist Party, too, there were anti-

Marxist tendencies which revealed themselves quite crassly in March and afterwards. I have already cited the astonishing article of Maslow'. But Maslow is not alone. In Vienna there is published a magazine *Kommunismus*, an organ of the Communist International in the German language. In the July issue of this magazine, an article devoted to the situation in the International states approximately the following:

" The principal characteristic of the present period of the revolution lies in this, that we are now compelled to conduct even partial battles, including economic ones, i.e., strikes, with the instrumentalities of the final battle, i.e., with arms in hand."

Here, Comrades, is strategy turned topsy-turvy! At a time when the bourgeoisie is provoking us into *partial* sanguinary battles, some of our strategists want to elevate battles of this sort into a guiding rule. Isn't this monstrous! The objective situation in Europe is profoundly revolutionary. The working class senses it and throughout the postwar period it rushed impetuously into the struggle against the bourgeoisie. But it gained victory nowhere except in Russia. The working class then began to understand that it faces a difficult task and started to build the apparatus for victory—the Communist Party. Along this path it has marched with seven-league boots during the last year. We now have genuine mass Communist parties in Germany, France, Czechoslovakia, Yugoslavia, Bulgaria. . . . The growth has been enormous! What is the next task? It is for these parties to conquer as quickly as possible the majority of industrial workers and the decisive section of rural workers and even of the poor peasantry, just as we had conquered them before October—otherwise there would have been no October. Certain unhappy strategists say instead that since the epoch today is revolutionary, therefore we are duty-bound, at every opportunity, to wage the struggle, even a partial one, with the methods of armed insurrection. The bourgeoisie couldn't ask for anything better! At a time when the Communist Party is growing at a splendid rate, and its wings are becoming extended more and more over the entire working class, it is the aim of the bourgeoisie to provoke the most impatient and combative section of the workers to plunge prematurely into battle —without the support of the basic mass of the workers—in order, by defeating the working class piecemeal, to undermine the proletariat's faith in its own ability to conquer the bourgeoisie. Under these conditions, the theory of always taking the offensive and waging partial battles with the methods of armed uprising is so much grist to the mill of the counter-revolution.   That is why the Russian Party, supported by all the maturer elements at the Third Congress, firmly told the Comrades of the Left Wing: You are superb revolutionists and you will fight and die for the cause of Communism, but that is not enough for us.   We must not only fight, but conquer!   And for this it is necessary to master more fully the art of revolutionary strategy.

In my considered opinion, Comrades, one of the most important reasons why there is an underestimation of the difficulties of the revolutionary struggle and revolutionary victory in Europe, is to be found in the actual course of the proletarian revolution in Russia and partly also in Hungary.   We had in Russia a bourgeoisie, belated historically and weak politically, a bourgeoisie greatly dependent upon European capital and with weak political roots in Russian soil. On the other hand, we had a revolutionary party with a great tradition and heritage of underground struggle, trained and tempered in combat, consciously utilizing the entire past experience of revolutionary struggles in Europe and throughout the world.   The position of the Russian peasantry *vis-a-vis* the bourgeoisie and *vis-a-vis* the proletariat, the character and mood of the Russian army after the military debacle of Czarism—all this made the October revolution unavoidable and greatly facilitated the victory of the revolution.   (Although this did not at all eliminate future difficulties but, on the contrary, prepared them on a colossal scale.)   Because of the relative ease with which the October revolution was accomplished, the victory of the Russian proletariat did not present itself commensurately to the leading circles of European workers as a politico-strategic task, and this aspect of it was not adequately assimilated by them.

The next experience in the conquest of power by the proletariat occurred on a smaller scale but nearer Europe—in Hungary.   The circumstances there unfolded in such a way that the Communists gained power almost without any revolutionary struggle.   Thereby the questions of revolutionary strategy in the epoch of the *struggle for power* were naturally reduced to a minimum.

From the experience of Russia and Hungary not alone the working masses but also the Communist parties of other countries acquired first of all the knowledge that the victory of the proletariat was inevitable and then they directly passed over to acquiring knowledge concerning the difficulties which flow from the victory of the working class. As touches the *strategy of revolutionary struggle for the conquest of power*, it presented itself to them as something exceedingly simple, as something that could almost be taken for granted. It is not at all accidental that certain prominent Hungarian Comrades, who have rendered big services to the International, reveal a tendency to simplify in the extreme the tactical questions facing the proletariat in a revolutionary epoch; and to replace tactics with a slogan of waging an offensive.

The Third World Congress said to the Communists of all countries: The course of the Russian revolution is a very important historical *example* but it is by no means the political *rule*. And furthermore: Only a *traitor* could deny the need of a revolutionary offensive; but only a simpleton would reduce all of revolutionary strategy to an offensive.

The Positive and Negative Sides of the French Communist Party

Over the policy of the French Communist Party we had a less stormy discussion, at any rate during the sessions of the Congress itself, than took place over the German policy. But during sessions of the ECCI there once occurred a rather heated dispute among us over questions of the French labor movement. The French Communist Party was formed without the external and internal paroxysms that gripped the German Party. In consequence there still remain within the French Party unquestionably strong centrist moods and old methods of parliamentary-Socialism. In its recent past the French proletariat has experienced no revolutionary struggle—a struggle that would have revived its old revolutionary traditions. The French bourgeoisie emerged victorious from the war, and was thus enabled until recently to throw, at pillaged Germany's expense, isolated sops to privileged sections of the French working class. Revolutionary class struggle in France is just beginning to take shape. Prior to the first serious battles the French Communist Party gained the possibility of utilizing and assimilating the revolutionary experience of Russia and Germany. Suffice it to recall that in Germany the civil war was already blazing when the Communists still comprised only a handful of Spartacists; but in France, on the contrary, there has been no open postwar revolutionary struggle, and in the meantime the Communist Party of France already embraces in its ranks 120,000 workers. If we take into consideration that there are in France revolutionary syndicalists who "do not recognize" parties although they do support the struggle for the dictatorship of the proletariat; if we take into consideration that the organization in France was never as strong as in Germany, then it becomes apparent that these 120,000 organized Communists carry not less but probably more weight in France than do 400,000 members in Germany. This is shown most clearly by the fact that in Germany there are to be found to the Right of these 400,000, the parties of Independents and of Social Democrats who possess jointly many more members and sympathizers than do the Communists, while in France to the Right of the Communists there is only the insignificant split-off group of the followers of Longuet and Renaudel. In the trade union movement of France the relationship of forces is on the whole likewise undoubtedly more favorable for the Left Wing. But on the other hand, the general relationship of class forces in Germany is undoubtedly more favorable for the victory of the revolution. In other words, in France the bourgeoisie still continues to depend mainly upon its own apparatus—the army, the police, etc.; in Germany the bourgeoisie depends primarily upon the Social Democracy and the trade union bureaucracy. The French Communist Party has every opportunity of gaining the complete and indivisible leadership of the labor movement before the decisive events occur. But to do so, French Communism must divest itself once and for all of the ancient husk of political conventionalities and equivocations, more rigid in France than anywhere else. The French Party stands in need of a more resolute approach toward events; its agitation must be more energetic and irreconcilable in its character and in its very tone; it must take a severer attitude to any and all manifestations of democratic parliamentarian ideology, intellectual egotism and careerism. During the discussion of the French Party's policy by the ECCI, it was brought out that the party had committed such and such mistakes; that the Communist deputies in parliament not infrequently engaged in excessive" discussions" with their bourgeois enemies instead of appealing to the masses over the heads of these enemies; that the party papers must speak a great deal more in a simpler and sharper revolutionary language so that the most oppressed and down-trodden French workers would here feel a response to their sufferings, their demands and their aspirations. In the course of this discussion a young French Comrade took the floor and in an impassioned speech, which met with the approbation of a part of the assembly, shifted the criticism of the party's policy to a totally different plane. This representative of the youth said:

" When the French government entertained designs, early this year, to seize the Ruhr province from the Germans, and announced the mobilization of 19-year-olds, the party did not summon the draftees to resist, and thereby revealed its utter bankruptcy."

We wanted to know what sort of resistance he had in mind.

" The party did not summon the 19-year-olds to refuse to submit to the mobilization order."

We asked what he meant by this " refusal to submit." Did it mean not to appear voluntarily until a gendarme or a policeman came to the flat? Or did it mean actively resisting a gendarme or a policeman, arms in hand?

This young Comrade, who made a very good impression upon all of us, immediately exclaimed: " Of course, we must go through to the very end, we must resist arms in hands . . . ."

This answer revealed how hazy and confused still are the conceptions of revolutionary tactics in the minds of some elements. We then engaged in a discussion with our young opponent: Among you in France under the tricolor of the imperialist army there are today, as the French say, several " classes," that is, draft ages. Your government deems it is necessary to call up one more " class," the 19-year-olds. This " class " (or draft-age) numbers in the country, let us say, 200,000 youths, among whom there are, let us suppose, from 3,000 to 5,000 Communists. They are dispersed, unorganized; some are in the villages, others in cities. Let us grant for a moment that the party does actually summon them to resist, arms in hand. I don't know how many agents of the bourgeoisie will be killed in the process, but it is a certainty that all the Communists will be plucked out of the class of 19-year-olds and exterminated. Why don't you summon those draft-ages who are already in the army to stage an insurrection? After all, they possess arms and are assembled in the army's ranks. You don't do it because you evidently understand that the army will not fire against the counter-revolution until the working class in its majority demonstrates in action its readiness to struggle for power, in other words, until the proletarian revolution begins. How then can you demand that the revolution be made not by the working class as a whole but by the " class " of 19-year-olds? If the Communist

Party—let us also grant this for a moment—were to issue such an order it would be the best possible gift for Millerand, for Briand, for Barthou, and all other candidates for the role of hangmen of the proletarian revolution. Because it is perfectly self-evident that once the most daring section of the youth is destroyed, the more backward section of the working class would be terror-stricken, the party would find itself isolated and its influence would be impaired for months, if not for years. Through such methods, that is, through an impatient application of the most drastic forms of revolutionary struggle, at a time when conditions have not yet matured for a decisive collision, one can obtain only negative results, and even bring about a revolutionary abortion instead of a mighty revolutionary birth.

We have a classic example of a completely unprepared call for mass action in the attempted general strike of May 1920. As you all know, the idea of this strike was treacherously " supported " by the syndicalists and the reformists. Their aim was not to allow the movement to slip out of their hands and thereby make it all the easier for them to wreck it at the first opportunity. They succeeded completely. But in behaving so treacherously, these people remained true to themselves. One couldn't expect anything else from them. Yet the opposing side, the revolutionary syndicalists and the Communists, failed completely to prepare the movement. The initiative came from the railway unions which had been won over for the first time by the Left-Wingers, with Monmousseau at the head. Before the Left-Wingers had succeeded in any way consolidating and securing the most important positions, before they had even properly surveyed the situation, they hastened to summon the masses to a decisive action under slogans that were muddled and ambiguous, and with the treacherous " support " from the Right. In every respect this was an unprepared attack. The results are well known: Only a small minority took part in the action; the conciliators blocked any furfher extension of the strike; the counter-revolution took full advantage of the manifest weakness of the Lefts and was enabled to extraordinarily strengthen its own positions.

Light-minded improvisations of this sort are impermissible in the movement. The situation must be appraised far more seriously; the movement must be prepared and coordinated persistently, energetically, in all spheres, in order later, when the signal is given, to lead it firmly and resolutely. But for this, it is necessary to have a Communist Party which unifies the experience of the proletariat in all its fields of struggle. Naturally, the mere presence of a party does not eliminate mistakes. But the absence of a party, as the directing vanguard, makes mistakes unavoidable, converting the struggle as a whole into a series of improvisations, experiments and adventures.

Communism and Syndicalism in France

The relationship between the Communist Party and the working class in France is, as I stated, more favorable than in Germany. But the party's political influence over the working class, which has greatly increased thanks to the radicalization of the party, still remains in an inadequate form in France, expecially with respect to the organizational side. This is to be seen most clearly in the question of the trade unions.

In France the syndicates (trade unions) are to a lesser extent multimillioned organizations than they are in Germany or the Anglo-American countries. But in France, too, the numerical strength of the trade unions has greatly increased in recent years. The relationship between the party and the class assumes, first of all, the form of the party's relations to the trade unions. This alone, this simple formulation of the question already shows how incorrect and how anti-revolutionary and how dangerous is the so-called theory of neutrality, the theory of complete " independence " of the trade unions from the party, and so on. If trade unions are, by their tendency, the organization of the working class as a whole, then how can this working class remain neutral toward the party or " independent " from it? After all, this would signify the neutrality of the class, that is, its complete indifference toward the revolution itself? Yet, on this basic question, to this day, there is still lacking necessary clarity in the French labor movement and, above all, this clarity is lacking within the party itself.

The theory that there is a complete and unconditional division of labor between the party and the trade unions and that they must practice mutual and absolute non-intervention is precisely a product of French political development. It is the most extreme expression of it. This theory is based on unadulterated opportunism. So long as the labor bureaucracy, organized in the trade unions, concludes wage agreements, while the Socialist Party defends reforms in parliament, the division of labor and mutual non-intervention remain more or less possible. But no sooner are the real proletarian masses drawn into the struggle and no sooner does the movement assume a genuinely revolutionary character, than the principle of non-intervention degenerates into reactionary scholasticism. The working class can gain victory only if there stands at its head an organization which represents its living historical experience, and is capable of generalizing theoretically and directing the entire struggle in practice. On account of the very meaning of its historic task, the party can include only the most conscious and active minority of the working class. The trade unions, on the other hand, seek to embrace the working class as a whole. Those who recognize that the proletariat urgently needs the ideological and political leadership of its vanguard, united in the Communist Party, thereby recognize that the party must become the leading force inside the trade unions as well, that is, inside the mass working class organizations. Yet there are comrades in the French Party who haven't assimilated this elementary truth and who, like Verdier, for example, wage an irreconcilable struggle to keep the trade unions "inviolate" from the influence of the party. Clearly these Comrades have joined the party only through a misunderstanding, because a Communist who denies the tasks and duties of the Communist Party in relation to the trade unions is no Communist at all.

Naturally this does not mean that the trade unions become subject to the party organizationally, or from the outside. The trade unions are organizationally independent. Within the trade unions the party wields the influence it gains by its activity, by its ideological intervention, by its authority. But to say this is to say that the party must strive in every way to increase its influence over the trade unions; it must deal with all the questions arising in the trade union movement; it must give clear answers to them and carry out its views through the Communists functioning in the trade unions, without in the least violating the organizational autonomy of the unions.

You all know that the so-called revolutionary syndicalist tendency used to wield considerable influence over the trade unions in France. Revolutionary syndicalism, despite its denial of the party, was essentially nothing but an anti-parliamentary party of the working class. The syndicalist party always waged an energetic struggle for its influence over the trade unions; and never recognized the neutrality or independence of the trade unions in relation to the theory and practice of the syndicalist party. If we leave aside the theoretical mistakes and excesses of French syndicalism and consider its revolutionary essence, then it is unquestionable that this essence found its full development precisely in Communism.

The core of revolutionary syndicalism in France was constituted by the group around the newspaper *La Vie Ouvrière* (*Workers Life*). I came in close contact with this group during the war. At the center of this group stood Monatte and Rosmer. Adhering to it from the Right were Merrheim and Dumoulin. Both of them later became renegades. Rosmer made the natural transition from revolutionary syndicalism to Communism. Up to now Monatte holds an ambiguous position, but after the Third World Congress and the Red Trade Union Congress, Monatte took a step which fills me with serious misgivings. Together with Monmousseau[3], secretary of the Railway Workers' Union, Monatte has published a protest against the Comintern resolution on the trade union movement and refused to join the Red Trade Union International. It must be said that the very text of this protest by Monatte and Monmousseau provides the best possible argument against their middle-of-the-road position. Monatte announces that he has left the Amsterdam Trade Union International because of its close ties with the Second International. Absolutely correct. But the fact that the overwhelming majority of trade unions are affiliated either with the Second or with the Third Internationals is the best possible proof that neutral or a-political trade unions do not exist and generally cannot exist, all the less so in a revolutionary epoch. Whoever breaks with Amsterdam and refuses to join Moscow runs the risk of creating a Two-and-a-Half Trade Union International.

I firmly expect that this unfortunate misunderstanding will be cleared up and that Monatte will take his rightful place inside the French Communist Party and the Third International where he belongs by virtue of his entire past.

Perfectly understandable and correct is the discreet and lenient attitude of the French CP toward the revolutionary syndicalists, in an attempt to draw them closer. But completely incomprehensible is the indulgence shown by the party in its toleration of the obstruction of Comintern's policy by its own members, such as Verdier. Monatte represents the tradition of revolutionary syndicalism; all that Verdier represents is muddle-headedness.

But above the questions of personalities and groups there stands the question of the party's guiding influence over the trade unions. Without in the least infringing upon their autonomy, which is wholly determined by the day-to-day needs of practical work, the party must nevertheless put an end to all disputes and vacillations in this important field and demonstrate in action to the French working class that it possesses at long last a revolutionary party, capable of giving leadership in all spheres of the class struggle. In this connection the decisions of the Third Congress, despite the temporary confusion and conflicts that may be evoked in the next few months, will exercise a great and most highly beneficial influence over the entire future course of the French labor movement. Only on the basis of these resolutions will a correct inter-relationship between the party and the working class be established, and failing this, there is not and there cannot be a victorious proletarian revolution.

Not a Right Turn But a Serious Preparation for the Conquest of Power

I will not deal with the Communist parties of other countries because my report is by no means intended to include the characterization of all the organizations adhering to the Communist International. It is my purpose simply to present to you, Comrades, the basic lines of its policy as unfolded and fixed by the last World Congress. For this reason I have characterized those parties which provided the maximum material for elaborating the tactical line of the International for the period ahead.

Needless to say, the Congress did not propose to " suspend " the struggle against centrists and semi-centrists, as some Leftist Comrades groundlessly feared. The entire struggle of the Communist International against the capitalist regime runs up against, in the first instance, its reformist, conciliationist entrenchments. These are the first positions that must be captured. On the other hand, it is impossible to wage a struggle against the Second and Two-and-a-Half Internationals without purging our own Communist ranks of centrist tendencies and moods. No one disputes this.*

---

* From the speeches of Comrade Kurt Geyer on the Third Congress which I have received, I note that this representative of the opposition not only tumbles into centrism, but is cognizant of it himself. His starting point is that the Third World Congress has fixed a new historical perspective and has therewith rendered tactics less dependent upon expectations of revolution in the next period. From this Geyer concludes that the tactical differences between the Third International and the centrists are becoming—mitigated. This conclusion is absolutely fantastic! The Third International is a combat organization which keeps marching toward its revolutionary goal, no matter

But this struggle against the Right, an integral part of our basic struggle against bourgeois society, can be conducted successfully by us only provided we are able to overcome within a minimum time those leftist blunders which arise from inexperience and impatience; and which betimes assume the shape of dangerous adventures. In this respect the Third World Congress accomplished a great work of education which turned it, as I said, into the highest school, the university of revolutionary strategy.

Apropos of our resolutions, Martov[9], Bauer and other arm-chair strategists of the little citizens have started talking about the decomposition of Communism, the foundering of the Third International, and so on. From the standpoint of theory this chatter merits only contempt. Communism is not and never was a dogmatic, time-setting program of the revolution. Communism is the living, dynamic, growing and maneuvering army of the proletariat which in the course of its activity takes into consideration the changing conditions of struggle, inspects its own weapons, gives the blade a new edge, if it has become blunted, and subordinates all its activities to the need of preparing the revolutionary abolition of the bourgeois order.

That we took up the tactical questions so carefully, so painstakingly and so concretely at the Third Congress represents by itself a tremendous step forward. It attests that the Third International has emerged from the phase of ideological and organizational self-deter

what changes in circumstances occur. The Two-and-a-Half International does not want a revolution and is built by a corresponding selection of leaders and semi-leaders, of groupings and tendencies, of ideas and methods.

At the moment when Geyer certifies that the differences between the Communists and the Independents are becoming softer, the Independents, with far greater justification, certify the softening of differences between themselves and the Social Democrats. If this were drawn to its logical conclusion, we would get the revived program of the old Social Democracy, as it used to be prior to August 1914, with all the consequences flowing therefrom. While we reject the dogmatic scheduling of the revolution for the weeks or months immediately ahead—which in practice gives rise to " putschist " tendencies—in our struggle against " putschism " we remain true to our fundamental task, that of building a revolutionary, dynamic and irreconcilable Communist Party which stands opposed to all reformist and centrist groupings within the proletariat. Kurt Geyer dogmatically relegates the revolution to the dim future and hence draws conclusions to the effect that there is a rapprochement with the centrists. There is every reason to fear that such a "perspective" will lead Geyer and his co-thinkers much further astray than they themselves suppose today.—L.T.

mination and has come, as a living, guiding mass organization, face to face with the questions of direct revolutionary action.

If among the younger and less experienced comrades in this hall, anyone were to draw a pessimistic conclusion from my report to the effect that the International is in an unfavorable position and that it is hard to defeat the bourgeoisie because of the prevalence of so many mistaken views and methods among the Communist parties, then this would be a completely false conclusion. In the epoch of abrupt changes in world politics, in the epoch of profound social shocks and convulsions, in brief, in the revolutionary epoch in which we live, the training of revolutionary parties takes place at an extraordinary speed, especially if there is a mutual exchange of experience, reciprocal control and a common centralized leadership—all of which is expressed in and by our International. Let us not forget that the strongest Communist parties of Europe are—literally! —only a few months old. In our epoch a month is equivalent to a year, and some months are equivalent to as much as a decade.

Although at the Congress I was a member of the so-called " right wing " and took part in criticizing the pseudo-revolutionary leftism— which, as I tried to show you, is extremely dangerous to a genuine growth of the proletarian revolution—I left the Congress in a far more optimistic mood than I came to it. My impressions, derived from an exchange of opinions with delegations from our sister parties of Europe and throughout the world, might be summed up as follows: During the last year the Communist International has taken a giant stride forward both ideologically and organizationally.

The Congress did not and could not issue a signal for a general offensive. It formulated the task of the Communist parties as the task of *preparing* an offensive; and in the first instance, as the task of winning over ideologically the majority of the toilers of city and countryside. This does not at all mean that the revolution has been " postponed " for an indefinite number of years. Nothing of the sort. We speed up the revolution and, what is more important, we assure its victory through a deep-going, all-sided and careful preparation of the revolution.

Naturally, it is impossible in any sense whatever to reduce the revolutionary policy of the working class and the military work of the Red Army to a common denominator. I am fully aware of this.

And it is especially "risky" for me even to attempt comparisons in this field, because of the almost traditional danger of being suspected of a "militaristic" bent of mind. The German Cunows and the Russian Martovs have already long ago proclaimed that I am seeking to replace working class politics and economics by "commands" transmitted through a military "machine." Nevertheless, having secured my rear by these prefatory remarks, I shall chance making a certain military comparison which seems to me not unfruitful for the purpose of clarifying both the revolutionary policy of the proletariat and the functioning of the Red Army.

Whenever it became necessary for us on any one of our many fronts to prepare for decisive operations, we would begin by sending there fresh regiments, Communists assigned by the party, supplies of munitions and so on. Without adequate material means there naturally could not even be talk of launching a decisive struggle against Kolchak, Denikin, Wrangel and the rest.

And so, the material conditions for decisive actions are more or less at hand. Upon arriving at the front we learn that the High Command of the front has fixed the date of a general offensive, say, for May 5, which is, let us suppose, three days hence. In the sessions of the Revolutionary Military Council, at the front, in the staff, in the Political Department, we proceed to discuss the conditions under which the decisive battles will take place. We learn that on our side there is a certain preponderance of bayonets, swords and artillery while the enemy has considerable superiority in aviation; but on the whole, the material superiority is on our side. Our soldiers are more or less adequately clothed and booted; the communications are secure. In this respect the situation is therefore quite favorable.

"And how was your agitation conducted prior to the offensive? How long did you carry it on? In what ways and under what slogans? How many Communists were detailed to the divisions to lead the agitation? Let us take a look at proclamations, circulars, articles in your army newspapers, your placards and your cartoons. Does every soldier in your army at your front know who Wrangel is? Does he know with whom Wrangel is tied up? Who is backing Wrangel and from whom his artillery and planes come?"

The answers we get are not definite enough. Agitation had, of course, been carried on; explanations concerning Wrangel had, of course, been made. But some regiments had arrived only a day or two days ago, from the center or from the other fronts and precise information is still lacking concerning their political moods and their morale.

" In what manner were several thousand Communists mobilized by the party assigned to divisions and regiments? Were the character and composition of each particular section taken into account in assigning the Communist elements? Were the Communists themselves sufficiently prepared in advance? Was it made clear to each group to just what section it had been assigned and what the peculiarities of this section were? Or what the special conditions of political work there were? Finally, has each company been assured of the presence of a Communist cell which is itself ready to fight to the bitter end and which is capable of leading the others forward?"

We learn that this work had been carried out only in rough outlines, without paying the necesary attention to the concrete conditions and special requirements of political agitation in the army as a whole, and in each regiment in particular. The agitation was not of a concentrated and intense character, meeting the actual needs of the direct preparation for battle. This was likewise apparent from the newspaper articles and the appeals to the troops.

" Finally, what measures have been taken to check the commanding staff and the commissar personnel? Many commissars had been killed in previous battles and accidental replacements for them had at first been made. Have the necessary replacements of commissar personnel been made? How do matters stand in relation to the commanders? Do they enjoy sufficient confidence? Have authoritative and energetic commissars been attached to those commanders who have as yet been little tested? And lastly, are there perhaps among the commanders, recruited from among former Czarist officers, those whose families are either abroad or in territories occupied by Wrangel?"

It would be quite in the nature of things for such commanders to try to be captured, and this could have fatal consequences for the outcome of separate operations. Has the commanding staff been checked from this standpoint? Has the commanding staff been replenished? Has it been strengthened? No? In that case, sound retreat!

It is necessary to cancel the offensive.

So far as the material aspects are concerned, the moment is propitious, the superiority of forces is on our side, the enemy has not succeeded in completing his concentration. This is beyond dispute. But preparations in the sphere of morale are of no less importance than material preparations. Yet this morale preparation has been carried out superficially and carelessly. Under these conditions it is preferable even to surrender part of the territory to the enemy, to retreat twenty or thirty versts, to gain time, to postpone the offensive for two or three weeks in order to carry the preparatory political and organizational campaign through to the end. If that is done, success is assured.

Those among you, Comrades, who have worked in the Red Army, and there are many in this hall, know that this illustration is no invention of mine. We made more than one strategic retreat solely because the army had been inadequately prepared in moral and political respects for decisive battles. Yet the army is a coercive organization. Once orders are issued, everyone is obliged to go into battle. Those who resist are subject to harsh military penalties. Failing this, there is no army and there can't be one. But in the revolutionary army the chief motor force is political consciousness, revolutionary enthusiasm, the undertaking on the part of the army's majority of the military task it faces and a readiness to solve this task.

How much more does this apply to the decisive revolutionary battles of the working class? There cannot even be talk here of coercing workers into revolution. There is no apparatus of repression here. Success can rest only upon the readiness of the majority of the toilers to take a direct or indirect part in the struggle and help bring it to a happy conclusion.* In its character the Third Congress was this: It was as if the Communist International in the person of its leading representatives had arrived at the front of the world labor movement, preparing to engage in the decisive battle for power. And the Congress asked:

" Comrade Communists of Germany, Italy, France and elsewhere! Have you won the majority of the working class? What have you done to make every worker understand what is at stake in the struggle?

---

* One jokesmith at the Congress " refuted " me by raising an objection to the effect that it is impermissible to command the working class, as one would an army. That's just it. And the burden of my whole argument was that even the Red Army could not be commanded in the same manner as certain politicians have tried to command the working class.—L.T.

Have you explained this in clear, simple and precise language to the toiling masses, including the most backward ones?   What did you do to verify whether these backward layers understood you?   Show us your newspapers, pamphlets, proclamations.   No, Comrades, this is still not enough.   This is still not the language which attests to genuine ties with millions of toilers. . . .

" What measures did you take to correctly apportion Communist forces among the trade unions?   Have you reliable cells in all the important organizations of the working class?   What did you do to check the ' commanding personnel ' in the trade unions?   What did you do to effectively cleanse the workers' organizations of all dubious, unreliable and, all the more so, obviously treacherous leaders?   Have you organized a far-reaching intelligence network in the enemy's camp?   No, Comrades, your preparations are inadequate, and in some respects you haven't even posed properly the task of preparation. . . ."

Does this mean that the decisive struggle is postponed for decades or even for a number of years?   Nothing of the sort!   In the case of a military offensive, the necessary preparations can sometimes be completed in the space of two or three weeks, and even less.   Disjointed divisions, shaky in their moods and with unstable commanding and commissar staffs, can be, through a correspondingly intense preparatory work, transformed in ten to fifteen days into a mighty army, firmly welded by unity of consciousness and will.   It is far more difficult to unite the proletarian millions for the decisive struggle. But our entire epoch facilitates this work in the extreme, provided we do not swerve aside to the right or stumble to the left.   It would not be wise to speculate how long this preparatory work will take, whether only a few months or a year or two, or even more.   This depends upon many circumstances.   But it is unquestionable that in the present situation our preparatory work is one of the most important conditions for bringing closer the revolution and its victorious consummation.

To all its parties the Communist International says: *To the masses*! Embrace them more extensively and more intensively!   Forge an impervious bond between them and yourselves.   Assign Communists to the most responsibile and dangerous posts in all the strata of the working class.   Let them conquer the confidence of the masses!   Let the masses together with them drive out of their ranks the opportunist leaders, leaders who vacillate, leaders who are careerists!   Employ every minute for revolutionary preparation. The epoch is working in our favor. Have no fear that the revolution will slip out of your hands. Organize and consolidate—and you will thereby speed the hour which will become the hour of the truly decisive offensive and the party will not only issue the command " Forward March! " but will actually lead the offensive to its victorious conclusion!

2

From the ECCI to the Central Committee of the French Communist Party (June 25, 1921)

Dear Comrades,

We find it necessary to draw certain conclusions from the decisions of the last Congress in applying them to the Communist parties of various countries.

1.   It is urgently necessary to establish more regular and frequent connections between you and the Executive Committee of the Communist International.   It is necessary to assign certain comrades to transmit to us all the Communist literature published by you in France.   It is indispensable for us to receive periodic reports about the life of the party and about the French labor movement as a whole. Finally, it is necessary to supply our magazine, *The Communist International* with articles illuminating the current problems of French Communism.

The basic directives for the French Communist Party in the tactical field are contained in a corresponding World Congress resolution. Here we merely wish to express our views primarily with respect to the party's parliamentary policy with greater clarity and frankness than is possible in theses intended for publication.   Naturally parliamentary activity is not decisive in character, but it is nevertheless of enormous *symptomatic significance*.   It enables one to appraise the degree of precision and clarity of a party's revolutionary line, its capacity for resisting bourgeois influences and its ability to speak to the proletarian masses over the head of the parliamentary majority.

In France, revolutionary precision in parliamentary tactics is more urgently required than anywhere else because the anarchistically inclined elements among the working class judge the party first of all by its parliamentary activity. The prejudices of those who deny the need and usefulness of the party can be surmounted only by converting the parliamentary fraction into an instrument for a genuinely revolutionary working class policy. This does not, unfortunately, obtain in your country as yet.

Thus, the parliamentary policy of our fraction during the recent tension in Franco-German relations was absolutely inadequate. The speech of Comrade Cachin could have been interpreted to the effect that the French Communist Party is backing the Anglo-French alliance as the mainstay of European peace as against the adventuristic policy of Briand. Yet it is perfectly obvious that in exposing the adventurism of the ruling clique there is no need whatever of suppressing the fact that the Anglo-French alliance is not a factor of peace but, on the contrary, a factor of pillage, robbery and new wars. A break between Britain and France would simply bring forth another combination for the self-same purpose. After Briand made his reassuring declarations, the Communist faction introduced a resolution limiting itself to a demand that draftees of the class of 1919 be released. In the given conditions this meant that the fraction took its stand on the ground of governmental policy, approving its dilatory course and demanding only that a purely practical conclusion be drawn from the general premises. No greater tactical blunder in principle could have been committed by the party under these conditions. The duty of the fraction was to expose in its resolution the new phase of the Anglo-French brigandage and to point out that the dilatory character of Briand's policy is only a prelude to new sanguinary depredations. In such a context the demand to release the 1919 draftees would have appeared in an entirely different light.

2. On a number of other questions the fraction disclosed its identity either too sketchily or failed to do so altogether; and in the eyes of the outside public it became dissolved in the " extreme left." With respect to parliamentary maneuvering, adapting oneself to an audience and achieving superficial oratorical effects, the superiority will invariably be on the side of the Dissidents, because they are a party *par excellence* of lawyers and deputies. All the more important, therefore, is it for us to pose questions flatly, to counterpose ourselves on

every suitable occasion to the followers of Longuet, exposing them openly and directly from the parliamentary tribune and formulating sharp, precise slogans which are comprehensible to the broadest layers of the labor movement.

Concurrently we must see to it, that the parliamentary reports in *l'Humanité* supplement, illuminate and render more precise the speeches of our deputies. It would do no harm but, on the contrary, would prove only beneficial if *l'Humanité* were, in specific cases, to point out directly a mistake in this or that speech by a Communist deputy. The bourgeois press will pounce upon this with malicious glee but the working mass will see that our deputies are not divinites, that they are subject to the party's control. This would have only an educational value.

The present parliamentary reports of *l'Humanité* are completely permeated with the spirit of parliamentary lobbies and therefore are positively inaccessible to the working masses.

3. The sharp declarations of Comrades Monatte[10] and Monmousseau against the Moscow Congress resolution on the interrelations between the party and the trade unions arise by and large from the fact that the French syndicalists have never heard an open criticism of their views from the French Communists. A tacit agreement reigns by virtue of which all questions of the trade union movement seem to have become something in the nature of an ideological monopoly of revolutionary syndicalism. As if by way of compensation, the syndicalists on their part have absolutely refrained from concerning themselves with the passivity of the party and especially its parliamentary activity. Such a mechanical cleavage can prove fatal to the revolutionary movement of France. The working class represents a unity. The proletarian revolution becomes the more possible all the more this unity manifests itself in all fields of the proletariat's class struggle. We must, before the eyes of the working mass, demand of the syndicalists that they openly express their views on the party's policy, and the negative aspect of the party. We must force them to explain why they refuse to join the Communist Party at a time when the Communist Party makes it obligatory for all its members to join the trade unions. We must listen with utmost attention to the criticism of syndicalists, because, as the entire past shows, they express by and large the moods and views of rather large revolutionary sections of the proletariat. At the same time, however, it is necessary

to criticize openly the narrowness of the revolutionary syndicalist position.

Constant references to the Charter of Amiens, refusals to join the Red Trade Union International, appeals for a new Trade Union Congress for the purpose of setting up a " broader " International—all this represents a repetition of the tactics employed by the Longuetists who likewise began by solidarizing with Moscow, then set themselves the task of " reconstructing " the past, refused to join the International, proposed to create a " broader " International and ended up by creating the tiny Two-and-a-Half International.   If Monatte and Monmousseau were to persist stubbornly on their present position, the end-result would undoubtedly be the formation of a tiny Two-and-a-Half Trade Union International, midway between Amsterdam and Moscow. All these dangers must be openly pointed out today. It is necessary to explain—through the spoken and written word—to broad working masses the meaning of the resolutions on trade union work adopted by the Moscow Congresses. It is possible and obligatory to permit in the columns of the party press a discussion on the question of the interrelationship between the party and the trade unions. It is especially important to draw the revolutionary syndicalists into this discussion. But it is in no case permissible to leave the masses without leadership. The viewpoint of the Communist International must be counterposed without fail from one issue to the next to the declarations, articles and resolutions of revolutionary syndicalists insofar as these resolutions diverge from the decisions of the International.

4. The basic task is the conquest of the working masses. The advanced section of the working mass is concentrated in the trade unions. For this reason the trade unions must become in the immediate period ahead the most important arena for a co-ordinated and organized activity of the party.

A close check must be kept on the Communists in the trade unions, they must be kept in touch with one another and brought under the control and guidance of the closest party organization. The Central Committee must give constant leadership to local party organizations on questions of trade union tactics.

In view of this it appears expedient to create a special and permanent functioning Commission attached to the Central Committee and devoting itself to questions of the trade union movement. This

Commission might be composed of several members of the Central Committee, intimately acquainted with trade union questions plus several worker-Communists who work primarily or exclusively in the trade unions. All questions of the trade union movement must come before this Commission. Especially important questions, or those over which differences arise inside the Commission must be referred to the Central Committee. This Commission shall organize in Paris a number of gatherings and conferences of those Communists who work in the trade unions for the purpose of clarifying the internal life of the trade unions, the ideological groupings there, the ways and means of conducting agitation, organization, and so on. To such conferences it would be desirable to invite the revolutionary syndicalists, giving them a consultative vote to enable them to gain an understanding in practice that the Communist Party is an organization of the proletarian vanguard, setting itself the task of conquering the leadership in all spheres of proletarian life and struggle.

We must at all costs educate and imbue the Communists, working in the trade unions, with the conviction that within the trade unions, too, they remain party members and carry out its basic directives. Communists who stubbornly persist in a blunder that in their trade union work they are independent of the party are subject, as a general rule, to expulsion from the party.

5. It is necessary right now to select worker-Communists who are capable of holding responsible posts in the trade unions when the latter have been partially or completely won over. These designated comrades must devote their main efforts to training themselves practically for trade union work.

6. In line with the resolutions of the last World Congress it is necessary to introduce serious and deep-going changes in the party's organizational apparatus and its methods of functioning.

We proceed on the assumption that this reorganization should begin with the Central Committee itself, devoting the interval up to the coming Party Convention to prepare carefully for this reorganization.

The Central Committee must: (a) be brought as closely as possible to the rank and file; (b) be composed of comrades who devote their efforts chiefly to party work.

Roughly speaking, not less than one-third of the members of the Central Committee should be professional party workers, kept on the party payroll and completely at the party's disposal. Next to them it is necessary to place in the Central Committee those who work primarily as functionaries in the trade unions. In view of the exceptional importance of the trade union question the aim should be to constitute approximately one-third of the Central Committee from among these workers. Under such conditions there would not be in the Central Committee more than one-third from among those comrades who devote the greater part of their time to parliamentary activity or to private work. It is our firm conviction that only a Central Committee composed in this way and with a large proportion of workers can assure this central party body genuine leadership of the movement. It is necessary right now to proceed to a selection of qualified comrades and a designation of the necessary candidates because in the absence of such careful preparatory work the Convention will not produce the necessary results in this connection.

7.   Under the existing set-up of federations the party is deprived of direct leadership. The Central Committee cannot direct, in all its concrete aspects, local work from Paris. There do not exist local committees, as elected and permanently functioning bodies. It is perfectly obvious that without permanent functioning local committees, the party is rendered incapable of action. The personnel of each local committee, too, must contain a number of comrades all of whose energies are at the party's disposal.

Unquestionably, in the person of party secretaries and treasurers we have inherited from the old party a considerable number of individuals who became Communists only because the majority of the party members came out in favor of the Third International. These old-type functionaries all too frequently prove incapable of grasping the character and the tasks of the new epoch and of the new work. Indispensable is a new selection from among the workers, including the ranks of the Communist Youth.

In each committee there must be comrades capable of sacrificing their personal interests for the sake of party work and equipped to set an example in this respect to others. In the cause of spreading literature, conducting agitation, propaganda, etc., it is necessary for party members to display the selflessness and energy that are required for the preparation of decisive battles facing us in the more or less immediate future.

8.   The party's internal life must be mirrored far more distinctly, effectively and efficiently in the columns of *l'Humanité*. It is necessary

to openly criticize the shortcomings of local work, to severely castigate those party members who, under the cover of the Communist banner, show the greatest opportunism in local work and are ready to engage in any horse trade with the powers that be. Only the vigilant strictness of the party toward its parliamentary deputies, municipal councilors, and others can assure it the confidence and respect of the working class.

9. An end must be put once and for all to a situation which makes it possible for party members, out of personal material consideration or because of their political views, to publish newspapers and periodicals over which the party has no control and which are, time after time, hostile to the party. Consciously or semi-consciously, covering themselves up by their proximity to Communism, publishers, editors and journalists of this type, use their connections with Communism as a cover in order to exploit the authority of the party and the revolutionary enthusiasm of the working masses for the benefit of their own private enterprise, in order later on at the most critical moment of the struggle to turn all the influence they wield against the Communist Party. In this field, considerations of political expediency dictate to the party a firm and resolute line of conduct.

10. The considerable success of *La Vague*[11], one of these obviously pernicious publications, is evidence, by the way, of how strong is the urge among broad circles of workers, soldiers and peasants to find in a newspaper or periodical some reflection of their own lives, their own experiences, thoughts, etc. We must at all costs bring the party press, including *l'Humanité*, closer to the life of the toiling masses. It is necessary to establish a far-flung network of correspondents in factories, shops, neighborhoods, etc. The reports of these correspondents should be condensed, cut, supplemented with a commentary. But it is indispensable for the working masses to find themselves mirrored in their own newspaper.

11. Complete mutual understanding and the establishment of close ties between the new ECCI and the Central Committee of the French Communist Party we consider to be a most important condition for the success of future work. For this reason we insist on requesting that Comrade Frossard, as Secretary of the party and Comrade Cachin, as chairman of the parliamentarian fraction, come to Moscow as soon as possible—together, or if this proves too difficult, separately —in order to discuss a number of questions most intimately connected

with the forthcoming Convention of the French Communist Party.

Having freely expressed our views on the tasks of the French Communist Party, we do not for a moment doubt that you, on your part, will take our criticism only as an expression of what it really is, namely: our profound and sincere attempt to render every possible assistance to the French Communist Party, one of the most important sections of the Communist International.

Please accept our fraternal greetings, and our wishes for your success.

                    Executive Committee of the Communist International.
June 25, 1921.

From the ECCI to the Marseilles Convention of the French Communist Party

3

Dear Comrades, the Communist International sends fraternal greetings to its French section assembled in this convention[12].

A year has elapsed since the Tours Convention where you took the necessary steps to liquidate the " socialism " of the war epoch and to free yourselves from the embraces of reformism by joining the Comintern. Those comrades who parted company with you, and whose defection was perhaps regretted by many in the beginning, have likewise put an end to all ambiguity. They had vowed that despite their leaving the party they would remain revolutionists, steadfast friends and defenders of the Russian Revolution. But their hostility to Communist principles, which drove them out of the ranks of the unified party, did not fail quickly to convert them into out-and-out counter-revolutionists mouthing the slanders which the capitalist press heaps upon the Russian Revolution. They have become the defenders of the counter-revolutionary Social Democrats who are among the bitterest enemies of the workers' and peasants' revolution. The party of the Dissidents is falling more and more under the influence and political leadership of Renaudel, Grumbach[13] and Blum, that is, of those who betrayed the French working class and international socialism during the war, those who have not renounced by an iota the policy of collaborating with the bourgeoisie and those who constrain their French Party to function as a connecting link between the Vienna International and the Their-Majesty's-Ministers' Second International.

The Tours Convention, the resulting split and energetic purge were the necessary and ineluctable products of working-class reaction to and anger against war-socialism and reformism which betrayed the class interests of the workers. But Tours, because it gave birth to the Communist Party, marked at the same time the point of departure for a new epoch in the history of the French revolutionary movement.

A year has elapsed since the Tours Convention. Among the French revolutionists there is no longer to be found anyone who regrets the split that occurred and the purge that followed. It is necessary, however, not only to survey the road traversed by the enemies of Communism but also to review what the Communist Party has accomplished during its first year's activity. The Comintern hails with joy the results of your efforts directed toward regrouping and reorganizing your federations into a large party numbering 130,000 members, with a widely circulated and flourishing press. Only the Communist Party and its press is capable of organizing resistance against imperialism and reaction, whose strongest citadel in the world is manned by the French bourgeoisie. Last year the party succeeded in effectively increasing its influence over the mass of the French proletariat and small peasantry.

Rejoicing over the achieved results, we nevertheless do not shut our eyes to those weaknesses and shortcomings which became manifest during this first year. Unlike the Second International, the Comintern does not rest content with offering congratulations and greetings to its sections. Being guided solely by the interests of the world revolution, it has the duty to fraternally point out to them their respective weaknesses and to try, in the process of intimate joint and harmonious collaboration, to eliminate these weaknesses. As regards the French Party, the Comintern has always taken into consideration the specific peculiarities of its evolution and of the milieu in which it is compelled to struggle. In appraising the work accomplished during this first year, we are likewise not unmindful of the condition in which the party found itself following the split at Tours; we are aware that a party subjected to such deviations as the French Party was during the war cannot suddenly turn Communist — by virtue of a resolution adopted by a convention. The vote at Tours was evidence of the party's will to become Communist. This first year was bound to signalize uninterrupted efforts and unremitting work directed toward investing the party with a Communist character. The party's efforts were enormous, but they were still inadequate. It is our desire to uncover together with you the reasons for this weakness; we are convinced that the Marseilles Convention sincerely wishes to pursue the work begun so energetically at Tours, and that your Convention will pay the closest attention to the directives of the International in order to strengthen the party's Communist character and policy.

The party has suffered from a weak leadership. The Central Committee immersed itself in a whole number of current administrative duties and failed to give firm political leadership to the party, failed to give day-to-day direction to the party's thought and diversified activities, failed to create a collective consciousness. The party has suffered from a lack of policy; it has lacked an agrarian policy, a trade union policy, an electoral policy. Fearful lest the federations accuse the Central Committee of dictatorial practices if it undertook to solve these questions itself, the Central Committee tabled the review and decision on all these questions until the Marseilles Convention. Yet as every revolutionist clearly understands, the Central Committee of the Communist Party is an elected body, elected by the convention and invested with confidence, and therefore vested with the broadest powers to direct the party's policy in accordance with the line of the theses and resolutions adopted by the national and international Congresses. Beginning with the Marseilles Convention, the Central Committee must steer a much firmer course and become a genuine leading political body, controlling and inspiring the press, guiding the parliamentary work, taking definite positions, day by day, on all the political questions, domestic and foreign. We consider it expedient to effect the transfer of all minor administrative duties to an administrative secretariat, and to select from among the Central Committee a bureau composed of at least five members whose main duty is to give continuous leadership to the thought and activity of the party.

Parallel with the installation of a firmer leadership it is necessary to promote the spirit of firmer discipline in the party. Communists must feel themselves to be, first and foremost, party members and to act as such in their entire social and private life.

The question of the party's trade union policy is undoubtedly the most important and touchy question on the agenda of the Marseilles Convention. The party has been unable to solve it during the first year of its existence. A Communist Party that seeks to become the vanguard and creator of the social revolution cannot ignore the trade union question. There is not a single labor question that falls outside the party's purview. And so the party must sketch out its line of conduct on questions pertaining to the trade unions. It must loudly proclaim to the working class its right and its duty to concern itself with these questions. It must demand of its members that they remain Communists inside the trade unions as well as in the party. A Communist Party cannot tolerate the fact that its members support the policy of Jouhaux and of the Amsterdam International. It must tell those who agree with Jouhaux that their place is in the party of Renaudel, Albert Thomas and Longuet. Similarly the party must wage an energetic struggle against the ideas of anarchists and ordinary trade unionists who deny the role of the party in the revolution. It must say in clear and precise language that the aim of both the party and the Comintern is not to subordinate the trade unions to the party but to get all party members to participate in the work and struggle of the trade union minority. Keeping itself constantly informed about the development of the trade union movement in France, the party must seek ways and means of establishing the closest collaboration with those syndicalists who have subjected their revolutionary ideas to a profound review on the basis of what has happened in history in recent years. While discussing fraternally all revolutionary problems with them, the party must try to make them render more precise their current conceptions and help them overcome the obsolete vestiges of anarcho-syndicalist thought. We do not doubt that the party, by showing itself to be a genuine, revolutionary Communist Party, will attract not only the sympathy and confidence of broad proletarian masses in France, but also those syndico-Communist comrades who still have an attitude of mistrust toward it. The party will win them over by its resolute policy, entirely alien to opportunism. The draft theses on the trade union question elaborated by the Central Committee signify only the first step toward clarity on this fundamental issue. Those who maintain that the economic struggle is of no concern to the party are either complete ignoramuses or individuals seeking to make a mockery of Communism. The party must draw into its ranks all the best elements of the working class; and as touches the ideological aspect, it must become the inspirer of all forms of proletarian struggle, including of course the economic struggle as well. The trade union as such is not subordinate to the party as such. In this sense the trade unions remain independent. But the Communists who work in the trade unions must invariably function as disciplined Communists.

Owing to a whole number of circumstances, many valuable revolu-

tionary elements who deem themselves syndicalists still remain outside
the ranks of the Communist Party of France.   Sooner or later we must
reach an agreement with them and unite in the ranks of a single Communist Party.   But we cannot and ought not foster syndicalist prejudices on questions relating to the party and to political actions.

During the French delegation's stay in Moscow on the occasion of
the Third World Congress, the ECCI called the attention of the delegates to the need of placing the unofficial party press under the control
of the Central Committee.   The ECCI had primarily in mind the
newspaper *La Vague* published by Brizon[14], and *Journal du Peuple*
by Fabre[15].   Both Brizon and Fabre were advocating a policy incompatible with the policy of the party and the Communist International.
The Second World Congress adopted the principled position that no
party member could use the freedom of the press as a flimsy pretext
for publishing periodicals not subject to the party's absolute political
control.   With the unanimous agreement of the French delegation in
Moscow, the ECCI adopted in this connection a resolution which
was transmitted to the Central Committee of the French Communist
Party.   But up to this day the ECCI has not received an official
reply on this question from the party's Central Committee.   The
ECCI requests the Marseilles Convention to give, in the name of
the party, a reply on this question, which we consider to be one of
the most rudimentary questions of Communist discipline, subject to
enforcement by the party's Central Committee.

Any delay in solving this problem would be all the more unfortunate in view of the fact that since the adoption of this (ECCI)
resolution, an opportunist tendency has crystallized around *Journal
du Peuple*, a tendency which bemoans the split that occurred at
Tours, and which to this day sheds tears over the departure of the
Dissidents and of Serrati, and which even advocates open collaboration with bourgeois parties in the form of a " left bloc."   It is hardly
surprising that those comrades who support a policy hostile to Communist principles should feel hurt by our resolution, and should try
to unload responsibility upon the French representatives in the ECCI.
We trust the Party Convention assembled at Marseilles will express
unambiguously its disapproval of such a policy and will call upon
this group of comrades to abide by Communist discipline.

We deem it necessary for the French Party to make an effort toward
establishing more intimate and stable ties with workers in factories

and shops. All too frequently the party press conveys the spirit of contending cliques and of dilettantism rather than genuinely revolutionary and proletarian spirit. Moreover, in the Central Committee there are far too few factory workers. In our opinion the worker-elements must be given greater representation in the election of the Central Committee.

We also wish to point out that somehow the French Party seems to have always remained on the side lines, apart from the life of the International. We trust that in the future more intimate ties and more frequent communications will enable the French Party to participate more actively and fruitfully in the life of the Comintern as a whole. We consider that all French questions are the concern of the entire International; just so do we trust that the French proletariat will consider as its own all questions pertaining to the proletariat of Germany, Russia, America and elsewhere; and that in the course of discussing these questions the French proletariat will take an active part in the work and struggle of all the sections of the International. All these vital questions, most of which should have been, in our opinion, already decided by the Central Committee in the course of last year, will come up for discussion at the Marseilles Convention.

It is our hope that the work of your Convention will, inspired by the single overpowering desire for and fervent hope in the victory of the social revolution, provide a new and great impulse to your party, placing it on a solid ideological foundation and outlining a clear tactic for it. Following the initial year of stabilization and organization, the Marseilles Convention must mark a new major stage and become the starting point for intense and fruitful work of large-scale Communist education and propaganda of our ideas among the working class and the peasantry; work directed toward a bold penetration of the capitalist army and particularly the army of occupation which may perhaps be destined to play the part of a connecting link between the German proletarian revolution and the French proletariat, which is ready to support and follow this revolution. The Marseilles Convention must become the starting point for internal work directed toward the creation of a firm party leadership and the establishment of discipline, cheerfully and voluntarily accepted by all, as well as of external work directed toward attracting broad masses to our ideals. The current year is likewise destined to be a year of fierce struggle against the reformism of Amsterdam, London, Vienna, Geneva[16]; a struggle against every variety of blocs with the bourgeoisie, whether it be a national bloc or a "left bloc"; a struggle designed to weaken and overthrow the most brazen and the most criminal of imperialist powers. At your convention you must forge the weapons and instruments for the battles and labors that await you. The Comintern trusts that Marseilles will become an even more famous date than Tours in the history of your party. With liveliest interest the Comintern follows your work, convinced that the French Party will fulfil its duty in the cause of working-class emancipation.

> Long Live the French Communist Party!
> Long Live the Communist International!
> Long Live the World Revolution!

> *Executive Committee of the Communist International.*

4

Speech on Comrade Zinoviev's Report: 'The Tactics of the Communist International' at the Eleventh Party Conference[17]

Comrades, According to today's newspapers, official recognition has virtually been extended to us after four years of the existence of our State. A conference will take place in the spring in which we, the Soviet Republic, will participate. This is unquestionably a fact of utmost importance. Nevertheless I believe that the entire European situation and the state of the world labor movement (and this bears directly upon the subject of Comrade Zinoviev's report) are such as to lead us to conclude that the path to our recognition will be far from smooth and easy.

The existing political situation, which exerts its influence both upon the working class as well as upon the different governments, and the economic situation in Europe and throughout the world, is complex in the extreme. On the one side, we have a profound economic crisis which is just beginning to pass away; on the other side, we have an influx of political self-confidence among the bourgeoisie and its respective governments.

On the one side, there still obtain the greatest economic difficulties, commercial and industrial life remains in the grip of an unprecedented crisis; but on the other side, there are the positions already conquered by the reorganized state apparatus and the resulting confidence among the bourgeoisies that they have already surmounted their most critical moments. If the bourgeoisie of England and the bourgeoisie of France are, in the person of their ruling circles, considering now the question of our recognition from the standpoint of a trade balance, from the standpoint of commercial

and industrial advantages, then the explanation for this is to be
found in the above-mentioned two causes. The bourgeoisie is in a
difficult economic position. It is looking for a way out that would
exclude Russia from the world economic circuit, but it feels so self-
confident politically as to deem it feasible to maneuver with so
weighty a body as Soviet Russia. This is the basic condition, determined by the entire postwar situation in Europe and the whole world.
The economic crisis is now expending itself. Both in Europe and
throughout the world there are unmistakably clear and weighty
symptoms of economic revival. And this is of utmost importance
for understanding the situation as a whole and the perspectives immediately ahead.

Those comrades who attended the last World Congress and followed the ideological struggle are aware that these questions came
up for discussion at the World Congress, especially at the Commission sessions. These questions were discussed from the standpoint
of the destinies of the labor movement in the period ahead. There
was a rather indefinite grouping whose contention it was that the
commercial and industrial crisis—and it was extremely acute—
through which we were passing on the eve of the last Congress constituted the final crisis of capitalist society, and that this final crisis
of capitalist society would inexorably worsen right up to the establishment of the dictatorship of the proletariat. This conception of
the revolution is completely non-Marxist, non-scientific, mechanistic.
There are some who reason as follows: Since we are living in a
revolutionary epoch, and since the crisis must unfailingly worsen
until the complete victory of the proletariat, it therefore follows that
our party must attack on the international arena, and the heavy
proletarian reserves, lashed by this worsening crisis, will sooner or
later come to our party's support in the final proletarian assault.
At the World Congress our delegation fought against this line of
reasoning, pointing out that such conceptions were neither correct nor
scientific.

There is no equilibrium between Europe and America. Europe
remains dismembered, the devastation of Central and Eastern Europe
is still unrepaired, and the blockade of Russia still persists in
essence. The tensions in international affairs, the lack of confidence,
the depreciated currencies, the huge indebtedness and the financial
chaos—these are the facts and factors bequeathed by the war. And

the elemental forces of capitalism seek to surmount all this. Can this be done? Or is it impossible?

Abstractly speaking, one could say that if these elemental forces were allowed to keep on operating while the proletariat remained passive and while the Communist Party continued to be an organization committing one blunder after another, then this would give rise to a situation in which the blind interplay of the economic forces would, availing themselves of the passivity of the working class and the mistakes of the Communist Party, restore in the long run some sort of new capitalist equilibrium upon the bones of millions upon millions of European proletarians, and through the devastation of a whole number of countries. In two or three decades a new capitalist equilibrium would be established, but this would at the same time mean the extinction of entire generations, the decline of Europe's culture, and so forth. This is a purely abstract approach, which leaves out of consideration the most important and fundamental factors, namely, the working class, under the leadership and guidance of the Communist Party.

We proceed from the postulate that side by side with economics, which provides the basis for the conscious maneuvering of a bourgeois state, there exists another factor which likewise rests upon this economic life, which takes the latter into account, appraising all its breaking-points and zigzags; and which also takes into account the maneuvering of the bourgeois state and translates all this into the language of revolutionary tactics. The postulate of an automatic offensive movement, which some comrades tried to promote in the conviction that the current commercial-industrial crisis must needs continue until the complete victory of the proletariat, runs completely counter to the economic theory of Marx. In the era of capitalist ascent as well as the epoch of capitalist stagnation as well as in the epoch of capitalist decay and economic disintegration, the crises occur through cycles: first comes a boom, then a depression, followed by another boom and another depression, with intermediate stages in between. Furthermore, as historical observations for the last 150 years attest, these cycles span on the average an interval of nine years. These oscillations have a profound internal lawfulness of their own and one can state with confidence that unless a victorious revolution takes place in 1920-21 in Europe, then in the course of 1920 or 1921 or 1922, the current acute crisis must ineluctably give way first to symptoms and signs and then to more obvious manifestations of a commercial-industrial boom. To a query concerning the character of this boom, its scope and depth, we might in answer employ an analogy with the breathing of a human organism: A man keeps drawing breath until he dies, but a youth, an adult and a dying man each breathe in a different way and the body's health may be judged by the breathing. But nonetheless a human being keeps breathing until death. Similarly with capitalism. The oscillation of these waves, these ups and downs are inevitable so long as capitalism is not snuffed out by the victorious proletariat. But it is possible to judge from the oscillating waves of boom and crisis whether capitalism is ascending, stagnating or declining. Today we can say positively that the crisis, which erupted in the spring of 1920, attained the peak of its acuteness in May 1921, after lasting, with various fluctuations, on the average some 15 to 16, or from 17 to 18 months, has succeeded in accomplishing the work of every crisis, that is, it got rid of surplus commodities and surplus productive forces, and has thereby provided capitalism with some supplementary room for growth. There are the beginnings of a revival, expressed by this, that prices are beginning to climb, while unemployment has started to drop. Those who are interested in pursuing this question further should read Pavlovsky's article[18] in the last issue of the *Communist International*. There is also the series of articles by Smith[19] in *Economicheskaya Zhizn*, not to mention the articles in special economic periodicals. Today it is superfluous to debate whether or not the crisis is continuing to deepen.

If we are to appraise the mounting wave now observable in the labor movement, then we are obliged to acknowledge that it is bound up most intimately with the incipient commercial-industrial revival. This commercial and industrial revival and its depth will of course depend on the condition of capitalism as a whole. After the commercial and industrial crisis has surmounted and leveled the first line of trenches—the monstrous prices—the paralyzed and wracked productive forces shall have gained to one degree or another the possibility of moving forward (we are now witnessing this). Tomorrow, or the day after, next year or two years from now (it is hard to guess dates), the productive forces will run up against the devastation of Eastern Europe, against the frightful condition of Western

Europe, against the very same currency systems which are a long way from recovery.

The boom will not be as colossal as the prosperity to which we became accustomed prior to 1914. In all likelihood this prosperity will be quite anemic, zig-zagging not only upward, but downward, too. This is beyond dispute. But nevertheless this boom marks a new phase, a new period in the evolution of economic life and of the labor movement's policy on the basis of the boom. Whence comes this boom? Let me briefly give you its chronology.

In 1914 a crisis was about to erupt. The imperialist war came instead. It intersected the curve of economic development and there ensued a frenzied war prosperity based on pillaging, burning, destroying material forces and resources, based on piling up debts, on disorganizing the economy, on aggravating the shortage of housing and of capital construction, disorganizing all the foundations, issuing huge currency emissions, and so on. The war came to an end. It was the year 1918. Demobilization. This was the most critical moment. The workers and peasants left the army in order to come home to their broken troughs. War contracts were canceled. The crisis deepened. Had the Communist Party been half as strong in this period as it is today in Germany or France, the proletariat could have taken power into its own hands. In 1919 (we can say this with complete assurance) there was no such Communist Party. The governments profited by its absence and, fearful of demobilization, continued their wartime economic policy throughout 1919. Emissions of paper currency were continued, old war contracts were extended or replaced by new ones solely for the purpose of averting the crisis. And the whole of 1919 passed under the sign of billions upon billions in huge subsidies granted by the bourgeois state, at the expense, of course, of the selfsame popular masses. This was a sort of moratorium—preservation through artificial and fictitious means. Capitalism granted political concessions and introduced the 8-hour day. A spontaneous wave of offensives by the workers unrolled without the leadership of the Communist Party, virtually non-existent at the time.

The time for settling accounts came in 1919: the crisis erupted. The bourgeoisie and its states reckoned with the crisis but it was beyond their powers to alter the laws of capitalist mechanics. The first revolutionary movements suffered failure owing to lack of experience and the absence of the Communist Party. This was followed by the outbreak of an internal struggle, splits and disillusionment among those broad working-class circles, who had book-learning and a much simpler conception of the state of affairs in 1918. The bourgeoisie attacked, wage scales were slashed—these were the symptoms of the hour. The lack of confidence was universal, strikes were smashed, the army of unemployed became enormous.

In these conditions the crisis was bound to engender reformist illusions on one pole and anarchist illusions on the other. The Communist Party began therewith to feel itself isolated from the masses for a while. And to the extent that the Communist Party missed the critical moment of the liquidation of the war; to the extent that the bourgeoisie was able to survive this critical period; to the extent that the crisis later scourged the masses who had already suffered their first political disillusionment, to that extent only the loosening of the tentacles of this crisis could provide a new and serious impetus to the revolutionary energy of the working masses. And this is what is happening now.

This crisis was, naturally, not one-tenth big enough to enable the bourgeoisie to solve a hundredth part of its contradictions or its difficulties; but this crisis is already powerful enough to enable the working class once again to feel that it is the bearer of production, that everything hinges upon it, that the bourgeoisie and capitalism are becoming more and more dependent upon it.

And what is most important is that this time the working class already possesses a guide in the Communist Party, which is experienced in struggle, in mistakes—and the experience of mistakes is the most valuable of all experiences—and experienced in successes gained by us by utilizing the lessons of the mistakes. Such is the situation facing us at the present time.

We can say with complete assurance that the phase of internal differentiation among the working masses which became acute early in 1920 and grew sharply defined toward the end of 1920—differentiation amid dispersion, the phase of isolation for the Communists, of their being converted into a pronounced minority which occasionally pretended to act as if it were the majority (we saw examples of it in Germany)—this phase, as a whole and in part, lies behind us. And this is the absolutely correct basis for the tactics which were proposed by the Communist International and which Comrade Zinoviev defended here.

It is hard to say, Comrades, how long this economic revival will last, or what forms it may assume. Most likely the form will be anemic. These ups and downs will resemble paroxysms, and for this reason they guarantee revolutionary impulses. Given the leadership of a Communist Party, one can say positively that the mounting wave of the revolutionary movement, this flood-tide, will raise up all the groupings inside the working class, i.e., it will lift to the top the opportunists, the centrists and the Communists alike. The requirements of this flood-tide impel and oblige us to seek practical agreements. But at the same time, precisely because it lifts up everybody, this flood-tide is beginning to stir the working masses into action and will submit all the groupings to test in action.

Everything that has previously been the subject of theoretical polemics, of discussions among minority political parties now become a test of methods by the majority. We will ride the crest of this upswing to the very end, while others drown in this flood-tide. And precisely all these circumstances completely determine the international situation.

The bourgeoisie is very self-confident, the economic difficulties are very great; the industrial boom likewise opens up prospects for the bourgeoisie, its top circles will of course skim the golden cream from this boom (the apparatus is in their hands). Backed by the experience of the International, of its leading parties and elements, we are probing into and formulating the symptoms of this boom but the bourgeoisie is not at all able to appraise its full historical meaning. The bourgeoisie's self-confidence is very great. And so, at this turning point, the bourgeoisie convenes its Washington Conference[20] and begins talking about inviting us to a new conference next spring. The self-confidence of the bourgeoisie, the famine in our country, our devilishly difficult economic situation—all these are indications that the bourgeoisie imagines that its negotiations with us will be far easier and simpler than they will actually prove.

America is the most far-sighted. It has concluded an agreement with Japan. Permission to Japan to plunder us is synchronized beautifully with philanthropic activities in our famine-stricken areas. The first is a perfect supplement to the second. A major maneuver is being executed there—in the Far East.

There are other maneuvers in the West, much closer home. The preparations of a Karelian drillground for future Karelian events are on a far larger scale than is commonly believed among us. Along our Western frontiers there are armed bands (at the Soviet Congress I will have a map showing the disposition of these bands) and there has been an increased concentration of Polish troops. All this means that there is, on the one hand, a wing of the European bourgeoisie—the Polish which, among other things, is closest to us and which wants to fight us at any cost. On the other hand, among the bourgeoisie there are some, perhaps even among the highest circles, who entertain a somewhat simplified conception of what is involved in recognizing us and coming to an agreement with us. They think somewhat along the following lines; " Well, we shall call in Krassin or Chicherin[21]. We shall add a little to the (proposed loan of) \$20,000,000; and then suggest to the Comintern that the thing to do is to carry out an internal purge. Let them give us some political guarantees. We shall properly clip the claws of this devil Communism, and then there will be smooth sailing."

There is little doubt that Lloyd George and a number of others have some such picture in mind. If negotiations over our recognition ever get started, there will be quite a number of zigzags akin to paroxysms and spasms. Both Lloyd George and Briand and many others will in the course of such negotiations require means of bringing pressure upon us. They have Poland, they have Rumania, they have Finland. The situation is very grave. And the historical perspective—internationally and for Russia alike—is that of a rising curve, but it will not be an evenly rising curve, but rather one with many ups and downs and the next break may occur precisely by next spring.

Suppose, however, that the negotiations are started; in that case we are, of course, bound to do everything possible to reach an agreement. I underscore this, on the one side, as a member of the Communist Party and also as the man who is most directly connected with certain aspects of this danger. But the unquestionable fact remains that the closer we come, on the international arena, to obtaining recognition, to being accredited by the bourgeois world, all the closer draws the moment when the bourgeois world will seek to gain our submissiveness in negotiations by supplementary blows and kicks and by direct military actions. From this standpoint the moves in the Far East and our nearby Western borders are profoundly symptomatic. For this reason I think that while we take stock of this entire international situation and wholeheartedly support the resolution of the Communist International which is absolutely correct and corresponds to the entire situation, we ought at the same time to say:

While the European and the world proletariat will, by resting upon the incipient economic revival, straighten out the united front of the revolutionary working masses, and will facilitate a gradual shift of the masses to our side, we must at the same time bear in mind and call the attention of the world proletariat to the fact that it is necessary to straighten out our own front too, in the full sense of the term. If this were to happen, and if by spring the revolutionary events were to assume a stormy character (this is of course hard to guess, but it is by no means excluded), then precisely this revolutionary upsurge coming at a time when the bourgeoisie is engaged in decisive negotiations with us could alter the situation drastically. Coming at such a moment in the midst of a political maneuver, these very first revolutionary developments might cancel out the plans for Soviet recognition and could impel our enemies to launch an open struggle against us through the medium of those who serve as the military agents of France and of all the other capitalist countries, that is, through the medium of our closest neighbors. That is why the Red Army must be in perfect order for that moment. (*Applause*.)

5

Summary Speech at the Eleventh Party Conference[22]

Comrades, the discussion on this question has assumed a somewhat academic character[23], in the worst sense of the word. It did not even enter my mind when I took the floor on Comrade Zinoviev's report that there would be any dispute over it. I found valuable material on this question in the last issue of the *Communist International* in Pavlovsky's article, which was published without any commentaries. And I think that the facts I cited are positively beyond dispute. This graph which I have sketched out roughly for the sake of illustration, this graph . . . [*Ryazanov*[24] *interjecting*: You can't get very far with each and every graph.]

I believe, Comrade Ryazanov, that you and I will get far enough with this one. . . . I say that although from 1920 up to May or June 1921, the curve of industrial development kept dropping, there then followed a movement which I called convulsive and spasmodic and which marks a certain upswing. The curve then drops again, starts climbing again and it may once drop again. But this line (pointing at the graph) sharply diverges from this line. Here we observe a decline in the course of twelve, thirteen or fourteen months. How does this decline express itself? Today there are, for example, a thousand workers, the next day are 999 or 998 or 997, and this decline continues systematically for 15 months. The 996th worker says to himself: "Tomorrow will come my turn." Since there has been a decline, a certain number of workers have been laid off in the factory. A mood of complete uncertainty prevails among the workers. The capitalist is not dependent upon them, while they are completely at his mercy. This depressed mood did prevail among broad circles of workers. Now let us instead suppose that one more worker has been added to the factory; There are now 1,001 workers, then there are 1,002 workers, and so on. From the statistical standpoint this is an

insignificant increase. From the standpoint of how the workers feel
it is of enormous importance. They originally number 1,000. Then
there are 1,001 of them, and then 1,002, and so on. This means
the factory is booming, and the worker begins feeling some solid
ground under his feet. Of importance is thus the very fact that a
change in the conjuncture has occurred in the autumn of this year,
because of the harvest, or because the strikes ended, or for any other
reason you care to mention. If I had no statistics at my disposal,
if I were confined in a solitary cell, but political and economic reports
nevertheless reached me to the effect that the mood of the workers was
such and such, the news was such and such, and then that there had
been some increase in the number of workers, I would deduce that
some things did change ; that some sort of economic shift had taken
place. Right now it is possible to dispute what will happen to this
curve in the future. Certain fluctuations are observable here. These
fluctuations prove that capitalist development either remains stagnant
or is declining. My reference was solely to the fact that this is an
uneven or downward line, that in it there are fluctuations, and that
to fail to take them into account means to disregard those living
impulses amid which the working class lives and fights.

Let me repeat, if I had no statistics at my disposal, I could even
in that case have told what has happened. But statistics are available.
I refer you to Pavlovsky's article. Major changes have occurred in
the textile industry. Nine-tenths of the spindles are or were in
operation during August and September. In the spring only half
of them were in operation. This is tremendous change. In America
the blast furnaces, the coal industry, the metallurgical industry underwent most important changes in August and September. We are now
living through a political reflection of these changes. Involved here
is an impulse which may bring down the landslide of the labor movement. Will there be another crisis? I will give my answer after the
impulse comes. Another crisis may not exert a demoralizing influence
because the need of fusing ranks has made itself felt, because the
need of unifying the political energy of the working class has made
itself felt. Within certain limits the working class acquires an independent significance. It is impermissible not to take these impulses
into account. Some comrades argue that this means the establishment of an equilibrium. What sort of equilibrium? If the present
boom were ten times greater than is indicated at present, it would
not reduce by a hundredth part those obstacles which bar the road

to prosperity. Sokolnikov is not logical ; he says that capitalism will
not reach an equilibrium. I explained the conditions under which an
equilibrium could be reached. If a million Europeans were to die
from cold and hunger, if Germany were converted into a colony, if
the Soviet power were to fall in Russia and the latter also converted
into a colony, if Europe were to become a vassal state of America
and Japan, then a new capitalist equilibrium would be restored. This
would require, say, 50 years of incessant struggle, in the course of
which we would be hammered, choked, mangled and finally strangled
to death. Then a new capitalist equilibrium would arise. This is the
perspective I painted.

A revival is now in progress. Prior to the war to which I made
reference, this revival has to run up against new trenches. The first
line of these trenches is constituted by the fantastically high prices.
Within two or three months this revival will run up against new barricades—the violent disruption of equilibrium between Europe and
America, the dismemberment of Europe, the devastation and isolation
of Central and Eastern Europe, the state of siege, and so on. When
capitalism, after attaining a certain semi-fictitious prosperity and after
giving an impetus to the labor movement, runs head on against the
barricades erected by the war, it turns toward the Soviet Union ; it
will turn ten times at the very first sign of deterioration. And in
November there was an unquestionable lag of some sort, which Varga
has cautiously characterized. This is a warning. In December there
will be a new upward swing. The feverish decline which lasted for
15 months since May of last year, or even since April or March and
up to June of this year, this feverish decline which came as a reaction
to the entire war will not recur. . . .

Will the boom be gradual and systematic? No. Will there be a
general upswing, punctuated by leaps? Quite possibly, but in no case
will it be a rapid one. How long will it endure? It is impossible to
foretell. But the change alone, the fact that from the cataracts we
have passed over to the narrows, where the waters of economic
development still swirl from side to side but there are no longer cataracts and the waters do not fall, this already constitutes a change,
a colossal change. I was told that there is no lack of poverty, misery,
unemployment and so on (I will not deal with unemployment in
England). These comments of Comrade Sokolnikov evoked the following train of thought in my mind: Suppose I had said that in
Moscow under Comrade Kamenev[25] the streets this year are cleaner

than they were in 1918, and then suppose somebody else were to get up and say that Trotsky claimed that Moscow is a picture of perfect luxury and then proceeded to adduce all the statistics pertaining to Moscow's filth and muck. My statement that the streets are cleaner than in 1918 would nevertheless remain a fact and it would be unfair to a Soviet municipality to disregard it.

Another fact is adduced, namely, that the currencies are whirling in a mad dance, the financial structure is disorganized and this, naturally, provides a basis for the revolution. But this development has its own zigzags, its own changes. Sokolnikov says that the conclusion from my speech is such as to lead to speculations on war. If it were my view that all indications point to the establishment of harmony and of equilibrium, then war would be sheer suicide. What means one chooses for doing away with oneself is a matter of indifference. Sokolnikov has labeled this as my logic. If capitalism is establishing equilibrium and I say that the entire policy should be directed toward war, then it simply means that I wish to cut my own throat with a razor, that I prefer to end matters in a bloody way. This is the philosophy of Comrade Sokolnikov.

But I said nothing of the sort. I pointed out that the trend toward extending us recognition is a significant fact in and by itself. It is not yet of historical significance, but it is of some symptomatic importance. If we gain recognition then it will have a historic significance, but there is only talk about it as yet and no one knows what the conditions for recognition are. When negotiations begin I will vote to send Sokolnikov to the conference; he is an excellent diplomat. When it comes to selecting a delegation to negotiate our recognition I would cast my vote for including in this delegation Comrade Sokolnikov who is in an anti-war mood and peaceably inclined, but at the same time I would warn that in a week or two Comrade Sokolnikov might inform us that Lloyd George and Briand are demanding nothing more nor less than that we banish the Comintern from Russia. [*Radek interjecting*: " To Riga."]

To Riga or to Revel—that's unimportant. That's the first minor demand. Secondly, that we yield the oil-bearing regions in the Caucasus and the industry in Petrograd to an English cartel—another trifle. England intrenched in Petrograd, and as mistress of the Caucasus, too. In the third place, that we dismantle the Red Army in view of universal disarmament proclaimed at Washington. Three minor demands, and therewith we might be told—in so many words, or by hints supplemented by deeds along our western frontiers—that if we find these conditions for agreement unacceptable, why then the French troops are ready to move into action, there is an excellent drill-ground in Karelia, a blow against Petrograd is being prepared from the north. . . .

Hence I draw the conclusion that while conducting these negotiations and utilizing to the utmost the supremely difficult position of capitalism, we ought to be on guard. Because the final phase of negotiations will be the most acute—when in order to make us more accommodating the threat of military intervention may be employed. And if this fails to have its effects, they may then employ intervention itself. Comrade Sokolnikov says that " my whole perspective is calculated for war, to wit, an offensive war." You have hit the bull's eye with your " to wit." In the party I am in complete agreement with the Central Committee in whose opinion it is the height of folly to make a slogan today out of the idea of offensive war. At the Congress of the Soviets, at each gathering of Red Army men, and at an authoritative party conference I have repeatedly declared that our policy is the policy of fighting for peace. But the fight for peace implies under the present conditions a strong Red Army. The approach of negotiations for recognition does not weaken this necessity but renders it all the more imperative. And the revival of the revolutionary movement in Europe, which places the bourgeoisie in an even more acute position, aggravates the possibility of the war danger.

Comrades, we have no political differences of any sort here. An attempt was made to transform into an ideal economic doctrine the propositions and arguments of an economic character which I had adduced. This attempt was made by Comrade Sokolnikov.

None among us talks about any kind of equilibrium. On the contrary, if anything may be charged against me it is this, that in the spring of this year, when the crisis was still very profound and unquestionable, I took a rather long-term view of the revolutionary perspectives. I maintained that there were no grounds for expecting an early revolutionary development. But today, on the contrary, I am wholly convinced that a turning-point has come, and especially that an impulse has resulted precisely from the economic revival. The cessation of the crisis and the incipient economic revival in the most important industrial countries will bring us politically closer to the possibility of a revolutionary mass movement. Should the deterioration continue in the future along the same course as in the last year and a half—which I consider improbable, impossible and economically un-founded—in that case, in my opinion revolutionary development would be retarded. Should developments proceed, as they are now doing, that would suit us perfectly. The bourgeoisie stands to gain economically a hundred times less than we shall gain politically. This is the gist of the matter.

To come back to Zinoviev's theses, I consider that they should be approved wholeheartedly and unanimously. This action of approval will become known to the entire Communist movement in Europe. There may be doubts among some elements here and there, along with prejudices, spurious, irrational objections, and so on. Having weighed them it is necessary to overcome them by our unanimous adoption of the theses. The conference will thus aid the genuine Communist elements in the world working class movement to shift their policy to an absolutely correct track.

6

Flood-Tide

THE ECONOMIC CONJUNCTURE AND THE WORLD LABOR MOVEMENT

The capitalist world enters a period of industrial upswing. Booms alternate with depressions — an organic law of capitalist society. The current boom in no way indicates the establishment of equilibrium in the class structure. A crisis frequently helps the growth of anarchist and reformist moods among the workers. The boom will help fuse the working masses.

I

Symptoms of a new revolutionary flood-tide are becoming apparent in the European labor movement. It is impossible to foretell whether it will bring with it the gigantic, all-engulfing waves. But there is no question that the curve of revolutionary development is obviously swinging upward.

The most critical period in the life of European capitalism came in the first post-war year (1919). The highest manifestations of revolutionary struggle in Italy (September days of 1920), occurred at a time when the acutest moments of the political crisis in Germany, England, France seemed to be already surmounted. This year's March events in Germany were a belated echo of a revolutionary epoch that had passed, and not the beginning of a new one. Early in 1920, capitalism and its state, having consolidated their first positions, already passed over to the offensive. The movement of the working masses assumed a defensive character. The Communist parties became convinced that they were in the minority, and at certain times they seemed to be

74

isolated from the overwhelming majority of the working class. Hence the so-called " crisis " in the Third International. At the present time, as I have stated, a turning-point is clearly indicated. The revolutionary offensive of the working masses is mounting. The perspectives of struggle are becoming more and more extensive.

This succession of stages is the product of complex causes of different orders; but at bottom it stems from the sharp zigzags in the economic conjuncture which mirror the capitalist development of the post-war era.

The most dangerous hours for the European bourgeoisie came during the period of demobilization, with the return of the deceived soldiers to their homes and with their reallocation in the bee-hives of production. The first post-war months engendered great difficulties which helped aggravate the revolutionary struggle. But the ruling bourgeois cliques corrected themselves in time and carried through a large-scale financial and governmental policy designed to mitigate the crisis of demobilization. The state budget continued to retain the monstrous proportions of the war epoch; many enterprises were artificially kept in operation; many contracts were prolonged to avert unemployment; apartments were rented at prices prohibiting the repair of buildings; the government subsidized out of its budget the import of bread and meat. In other words, the national debt piled up, the currency was debased, the foundations of economy were undermined —all for the political purpose of prolonging the fictitious commercial-industrial prosperity of the war years. This gave the leading industrial circles the opportunity to renovate the technical equipment of the biggest enterprises and reconvert them to peacetime production.

But this fictitious boom very quickly ran up against universal impoverishment. The consumer-goods industry was the first to come to a standstill because of the extremely reduced capacity of the market, and it threw up the first barricades of over-production which later obstructed the expansion of heavy industry. The crisis assumed unprecedented proportions and unparalleled forms. Starting in early spring across the Atlantic, the crisis spread to Europe by the middle of 1920, and reached its lowest depths in May 1921, the year now drawing to its close.

Thus by the time the open and unmistakable post-war commercial-industrial crisis set in (after a year of fictitious prosperity), the first elemental assault of the working class upon bourgeois society was already in its final stages. The bourgeoisie was able to hold out by dodging and veering, by making concessions, and in part by offering military resistance. This first proletarian assault was chaotic—without any definite political goals and ideas, without any plan, without any leading apparatus. The course and outcome of this initial assault demonstrated to the workers that changing their lot and reconstructing bourgeois society was a far more complicated business than they might have thought during the first manifestations of the post-war protest. Relatively homogeneous with respect to the inchoateness of their revolutionary mood, the working masses thereupon began quickly to lose their homogeneity — an internal differentiation set in among them. The most dynamic section of the working class, and the one least bound by past traditions, after learning through experience the need of ideological clarity and organizational fusion, cohered in the Communist Party. After the failures, the more conservative or less conscious elements temporarily recoiled from revolutionary aims and methods. The labor bureaucracy profited by this division in order to restore its positions.

The commercial-industrial crisis of 1920 broke out in the spring and summer, as has been said, at a time when the foregoing political and psychological reaction had already set in inside the working class. The crisis unquestionably increased the dissatisfaction among considerable working-class groups, provoking here and there stormy manifestations of dissatisfaction. But after the failure of the 1919 offensive, and with the resulting differentiation that took place, the economic crisis could not by itself any longer restore the necessary unity to the movement, nor cause it to assume the character of a new and more resolute revolutionary assault. This circumstance reinforces our conviction that the effects of a crisis upon the course of the labor movement are not all so unilateral in character as some simplifiers imagine. The political effects of a crisis (not only the extent of its influence but also its direction) are determined by the entire existing political situation and by those events which precede and accompany the crisis, especially the battles, successes or failures of the working class itself prior to the crisis. Under one set of conditions the crisis may give a mighty impulse to the revolutionary activity of the working masses ; under a different set of circumstances it may completely paralyze the offensive of the proletariat and, should the crisis endure too long and the workers suffer too many losses, it might weaken extremely not only the offensive but also the defensive potential of the working class.

Today, in retrospect, in order to illustrate this thought, one might formulate the following proposition: Had the economic crisis with its manifestations of mass unemployment and insecurity followed directly upon the termination of the war, the revolutionary crisis of bourgeois society would have been far sharper and deeper in character. Precisely in order to avert this, the bourgeois states took the edge off the revolutionary crisis by means of a speculative financial prosperity, that is, by postponing the unavoidable commercial-industrial crisis for twelve to eighteen months, at the cost of further disorganizing their respective financial and economic apparatuses. By reason of this, the crisis became still deeper and sharper: in point of time, however, it no longer coincided with the turbulent wave of demobilization, but came instead at the moment when the latter had already receded—at a moment when one camp was drawing up the balance sheet and re-educating itself while the other camp was going through disillusionment and the resulting splits. The revolutionary energy of the working class turned inward and found its clearest expression in the strenuous efforts to build the Communist Party. The latter immediately expanded into the biggest single force in Germany and in France. With the passing of the immediate danger, capitalism, having artificially created a speculative boom in the course of 1919, took advantage of the incipient crisis in order to dislodge the workers from those positions (the 8-hour day, wage increases) which the capitalists had previously surrendered to them as measures of self-preservation. Fighting rear-guard battles, the workers retreated. The ideas of conquering power, of establishing Soviet Republics, of carrying through the socialist revolution, naturally grew dim in their minds at a time when they found themselves compelled to fight, not always successfully, to keep down the rate at which their wages were being slashed.

Wherever the economic crisis did not assume the shape of over-production and acute unemployment, but retained instead the profounder form (as in Germany) of the country's being auctioned off and the living standard of the toilers being degraded, there the energy of the working class, directed toward raising wages to compensate for the declining purchasing power of the mark, resembled the efforts of a man chasing his own shadow. As in other countries, German capitalism went over to the offensive; the working masses, while resisting, retreated in disorder.

It was precisely in such a general situation that this year's March events occurred in Germany. Their gist comes down to this, that the young Communist Party, taking fright at the obvious revolutionary

ebb of the labor movement, made a desperate bid to exploit the action
of one of the dynamically inclined detachments of the proletariat for
the purpose of " electrifying " the working class and of doing everything possible to bring matters to a head, to precipitate the decisive
battle.

The Third World Congress of the Comintern convened under the
fresh impressions of the March events in Germany. After a careful
analysis the Congress fully assayed the danger inherent in the lack of
correspondence between the tactic of the " offensive," the tactic of
revolutionary " electrification," etc.—and those far more profound
processes which were taking place within the entire working class in
accordance with the changes and shifts in the economic and political
situation.

Had there been in Germany in 1918 and 1919 a Communist Party
comparable in strength to that which existed in March 1921, it is
quite probable that the proletariat would have assumed power as early
as January or March 1919. But there was no such party. The proleariat suffered defeat. Out of the experience of this defeat the Communist Party grew up. Once arisen, if it tried in 1921 to act in the
manner that the Communist Party should have acted in 1919, it would
have been battered to pieces. This is exactly what the last World
Congress made clear.

The dispute over the theory of the offensive became closely inter-
woven with the question of appraising the economic conjuncture and
its future evolution. The more consistent adherents of the theory of
the offensive developed the following line of reasoning: The whole
world is in the grip of a crisis which is the crisis of a decomposing
economic order. This crisis must ineluctably deepen and thereby
revolutionize the working class more and more. In view of this it
was superfluous for the Communist Party to keep a watchful eye on
its rear, on its main reserves ; its task was to take the offensive against
capitalist society. Sooner or later the proletariat, under the lash of
economic decay, would come to its support. This standpoint did not
reach the floor of the Congress in such a finished form because the
sharpest edges had been blunted during the sessions of the Commission that took up the economic situation. The mere idea that the
commercial-industrial crisis could give way to a relative boom was
regarded by the conscious and semi-conscious adherents of the theory
of the offensive almost as centrism. As for the idea that the new
commercial-industrial revival might not only fail to act as a brake

upon the revolution, but on the contrary gave promise of imparting new vigor to it—this idea already seemed nothing short of Menshevism.   The pseudo-radicalism of the " Lefts " found a belated and rather innocent expression at the last convention of the German Communist Party where a resolution was adopted in which, let me note in passing, I was singled out for a personal polemic, although I expressed only the views of our party's Central Committee.   I reconcile myself all the more readily with this tiny and harmless revenge of the " Lefts " because, on the whole, the lesson of the Third World Congress did not fail to leave its mark on any one, least of all, our German comrades.

II

There are incontestable signs today of a break in the economic conjuncture.   Commonplaces to the effect that the present crisis is the final crisis of decay, that it constitutes the basis of the revolutionary epoch, that it can terminate only in the victory of the proletariat—such commonplaces cannot, obviously, replace a concrete analysis of economic development together with all the tactical consequences flowing therefrom.   As a matter of fact, the world crisis came to a halt, as has been said, in May of this year.   Symptoms of improvement in the conjuncture became revealed first in the consumer-goods industry.   Thereupon heavy industry too got under way.   Today these are incontrovertible facts which are mirrored by statistics.   I shall not adduce these statistics so as not to make it harder for the reader to follow the general line of thought.*

Does this mean that the decay of capitalist economic life has halted? That this economy has regained its equilibrium?   That the revolutionary epoch is drawing to a close?   Not at all.   The break in the industrial conjuncture signifies that the decay of capitalist economy and the course of the revolutionary epoch are far more complex than certain simplifiers imagine.

The movement of economic development is characterized by two curves of a different order.   The first and basic curve denotes the general growth of the productive forces, circulation of commodities, foreign trade, banking operations, and so on.   On the whole, this curve moves upward through the entire development of capitalism.

* I refer readers interested in these significant statistics to the article of Comrade Pavlovsky, issue No. 10 of " Communist International " and to the articles of Comrade S. A. Faulkner in "Ekonomicheskaya Zhizn" (Nos. 284, 285 and 286).—L.T.

It expresses the fact that society's productive forces and mankind's wealth have grown under capitalism. This basic curve, however, rises upward unevenly. There are decades when it rises only by a hair-breadth, then follow other decades when it swings steeply upward, only in order later, during a new epoch, to remain for a long time on one and the same level. In other words, history knows of epochs of swift as well as more gradual growth of the productive forces under capitalism. Thus, by taking the graph of English foreign trade, we can establish without difficulty that it shows only a very slow rise from the end of the Eighteenth Century up to the middle of the Nineteenth Century. Then in a space of twenty-odd years (1851 to 1873) it climbs very swiftly. In the ensuing epoch (1873 to 1894) it remains virtually unchanged, and then resumes the swift upward climb until the war.

If we draw this graph, its uneven upward curvature will give us a schematic picture of the course of capitalist development as a whole, or in one of its aspects.

But we know that capitalist development occurs through the so-called industrial cycles, which comprise a set of consecutive phases of the economic conjuncture: boom, lag, crisis, cessation of crisis, improvement, boom, lag, and so on. Historical survey shows that these cycles follow one another every eight to ten years. If they were placed on the graph, we would get, super-imposed on the basic curve which characterizes the general direction of capitalist development, a set of periodic waves moving up and down. Cyclical fluctuations of the conjuncture are inherent in capitalist economy, just as heart beats are inherent in a living organism.

Boom follows crisis, crisis follows boom, but on the whole the curve of capitalism has climbed upward in the course of centuries. Clearly the sum total of booms must have been greater than the sum total of crises. However, the curve of development assumed a different aspect in different epochs. There were epochs of stagnation. The cyclical oscillations did not cease. But since capitalist development as a whole kept climbing, it therefore follows that the crises just about balanced off the booms. During epochs in which the productive forces climbed upward swiftly, the cyclical oscillations continued to alternate. But each boom obviously moved economy a greater distance forward than it was thrown back by each succeeding crisis. The cyclical waves might be compared to the vibrations of a wire string, assuming that the line of economic development bears a resemblance to a string of wire under tension: in reality of course this line is not straight but of a complex curvature.

This internal mechanics of capitalist development through the incessant alternation of crisis and boom suffices to show how incorrect, one-sided and unscientific is the idea that the current crisis must, while becoming increasingly graver, endure until the proletarian dictatorship is established, independently of whether this happens next year, or three years or more from now. Cyclical oscillations, we said in refutation in our report and resolution at the Third World Congress, accompany capitalist society in its youth, in its maturity and its decay, just as the beatings of a heart accompany a man even on his deathbed. No matter what the general conditions may be, however profound might be the economic decay, the commercial-industrial crisis acts to sweep away surplus commodities and productive forces, and to establish a closer correspondence between production and the market, and for these very reasons opens up the possibility of industrial revival.

The tempo, scope, intensity and duration of the revival depend upon the totality of conditions that characterizes the viability of capitalism. Today it can be stated positively (we stated it back in the days of the Third World Congress) that after the crisis has leveled the first barricade, in the shape of exorbitant prices, the incipient industrial revival will, under present world conditions, run up quickly against a number of other barricades: the profoundest disruption of the economic equilibrium between America and Europe, the impoverishment of Central and Eastern Europe, the protracted and profound disorganization of the financial systems, and so forth. In other words, the next industrial boom will in no case be able to restore the conditions for future development in any way comparable to pre-war conditions. On the contrary, it is quite probable that after its very first conquests this boom will collide against the economic trenches dug by the war.

But a boom is a boom. It means a growing demand for goods, expanded production, shrinking unemployment, rising prices and the possibility of higher wages. And, in the given historical circumstances, the boom will not dampen but sharpen the revolutionary struggle of the working class. This flows from all of the foregoing. In all capitalist countries the working-class movement after the war reached its peak and then ended, as we have seen, in a more or less pronounced failure and retreat, and in disunity within the working class itself. With such political and psychological premises, a prolonged crisis, although it would doubtless act to heighten the embitterment of the working masses (especially the unemployed and semi-employed), would nevertheless simultaneously tend to weaken their activity because this activity is intimately bound up with the workers' consciousness of their irreplaceable role in production.

Prolonged unemployment following an epoch of revolutionary political assaults and retreats does not at all work in favor of the Communist Party. On the contrary the longer the crisis lasts the more it threatens to nourish anarchist moods on one wing and reformist moods on the other. This fact found its expression in the split of the anarcho-syndicalist groupings[26] from the Third International, in a certain consolidation of the Amsterdam International and the Two-and-a-Half International, in the temporary conglomeration of the Serrati-ites, the split of Levi's group, and so on. In contrast, the industrial revival is bound, first of all, to raise the self-confidence of the working class, undermined by failures and by the disunity in its own ranks ; it is bound to fuse the working class together in the factories and plants and heighten the desire for unanimity in militant actions.

We are already observing the beginnings of this process. The working masses feel firmer ground under their feet. They are seeking to fuse their ranks. They keenly sense the split to be an obstacle to action. They are striving not only toward a more unanimous resistance to the offensive of capital resulting from the crisis but also toward preparing a counter-offensive, based on the conditions of industrial revival. The crisis was a period of frustrated hopes and of embitterment, not infrequently impotent embitterment. The boom as it unfolds will provide an outlet in action for these feelings. This is precisely what the resolution of the Third Congress, which we defended, states:

" But should the tempo of development slacken, and the current commercial-industrial crisis be superseded by a period of prosperity in a greater or lesser number of countries, this would in no case signify the beginning of an ' organic ' epoch. So long as capitalism exists, cyclical oscillations are inevitable. These will accompany capitalism in its death agony, just as they accompanied it in its youth and maturity. In case the proletariat should be forced to retire under the onslaught of capitalism in the course of the present crisis, it will immediately resume the offensive as soon as any amelioration in the conjuncture sets in. Its economic offensive, which would in that case inevitably be carried on under the slogan of revenge for all the deceptions of the war period and for all the plunder and abuses of the crisis, will tend to turn into an open civil war, just as the present offensive struggle does."

III

The capitalist press is beating the drums over the successes of economic " rehabilitation " and the perspectives of a new epoch of capitalist stability. These ecstasies are just as groundless as the complementary fears of the " Lefts " who believe that the revolution must grow out of the uninterrupted aggravation of the crisis. In reality, while the coming commercial and industrial prosperity implies economically new riches for the top circles of the bourgeoisie, all the political advantages will accrue to us. The tendencies toward unification within the working class are only an expression of the growing will to action. If the workers are today demanding that for the sake of the struggle against the bourgeoisie the Communists reach an agreement with the Independents and with the Social Democrats, then on the morrow— to the extent that the movement grows in its mass scope—these same workers will become convinced that only the Communist Party offers them leadership in the revolutionary struggle. The first wave of the flood-tide lifts up all the labor organizations, impelling them to arrive at an agreement. But the selfsame fate awaits the Social Democrats and the Independents: they will be engulfed one after the other in the next waves of the revolutionary flood-tide.

Does this mean—in contrast to partisans of the theory of the offensive—that it is not the crisis but the coming economic revival which is bound to lead directly to the victory of the proletariat? Such a categorical assertion would be unfounded. We have already shown above that there exists not a mechanical but a complex dialectical interdependence between the economic conjuncture and the character of the class struggle. It suffices for understanding the future that we are entering the period of revival far better armed than we entered the period of crisis. In the most important countries on the European continent we possess powerful Communist parties. The break in the conjuncture undoubtedly opens up before us the possibility of an offensive—not only in the economic field, but also in politics. It is a fruitless occupation to engage now in speculations as to where this offensive will end. It is just beginning, just coming into sight.

A sophist may raise the objection that if we grant that the further industrial revival need not necessarily lead us directly to victory, then a new industrial cycle will obviously take place, signifying another step toward the restoration of capitalist equilibrium. In that case wouldn't there actually arise the danger of a new epoch of capitalist restoration? To this one might reply as follows: If the Communist Party fails to grow ; if the proletariat fails to gain experience ; if the proletariat fails to resist in a more and more far-reaching and irreconcilable revolutionary way ; if it fails to pass over at the first opportunity from defense to offense, then the mechanics of capitalist development, supplemented by the maneuvers of the bourgeois state, would doubtless accomplish their work in the long run. Entire countries would be hurled back economically into barbarism ; tens of millions of human beings would perish from hunger, with despair in their hearts, and upon their bones some new sort of equilibrium of the capitalist world would be restored. But such a perspective is sheer abstraction. On the way toward this speculative capitalist equilibrium there are many gigantic obstacles: the chaos of the world market, the disruption of currency systems, the sway of militarism, the threat of war, the lack of confidence in the future. The elemental forces of capitalism are seeking avenues of escape amid heaps of obstacles. But these same elemental forces lash the working class and impel it forward. The development of the working class does not cease even when it retreats. For, while losing positions, it accumulates experience and consolidates its party. It marches forward. The working class is one of the conditions of social development, one of the factors of this development, and moreover its most important factor because it embodies the future.

The basic curve of industrial development is searching for upward avenues. Movement is rendered complex by cyclical fluctuations, which in the post-war conditions resemble spasms. It is naturally impossible to foretell at which point of development there will occur such a combination of objective and subjective conditions as will produce a revolutionary overturn. Nor is it possible to foretell whether this will occur in the course of the impending revival, at its beginning, or toward its end, or with the coming of a new cycle. Suffice it for us that the tempo of development does to a considerable measure depend upon us, upon our party, upon its tactics. It is of utmost importance to take into account the new economic turn which can open a new stage of fusing the ranks and in preparing a victorious offensive. For the revolutionary party to understand that which is, already implies in and of itself an abridgment of all time-intervals and the moving up of dates.

First published in **Pravda,**
Issue No. 292, December 25, 1921.

7

Paul Levi and some 'Lefts'

Dear Comrade,

You ask me to express my views* on the policy of the so-called Communist League of Germany (KAG), and in passing you refer to the fact that Paul Levi, the leader of the Communist League, is abusing my name by claiming me as virtually his co-thinker.

I must candidly confess that following the Third World Congress I have not read a single article by Levi, just as I have not read—to my sincere regret—many other far more important things. To be sure, I have seen in periodicals published by Levi, which I happened to run across by chance, extracts from my report at the World Congress. Some comrades informed me that I had been almost enrolled as a member of Levi's group. And if these happened to be very "leftist" and very young comrades, they mentioned it with holy horror, while those who were somewhat more serious confined themselves to a joke. Inasmuch as I am utterly unable to enroll myself either among the very young (to my sorrow) or among the very "leftist" (for which I am not at all sorry), my reaction to this news was not at all tragic. Let me confess I still see no reason for changing my attitude.

From the nature of the case it seemed to me, as it still does, that the decision concerning Levi adopted by the Congress at Moscow is perfectly clear and requires no extended commentaries. By the decision of the Congress, Levi was placed outside the Communist International. This decision was not at all adopted against the wishes of the Russian delegation, but on the contrary with its rather conspicuous participation, inasmuch as it was none other than the Russian delegation that drafted the resolution on tactics. The Russian dele-

---

* This letter is in reply to a communication sent me by one of the oldest comrades in Germany in connection with the split of Levi's opportunist group. —L.T.

gation acted, as usual, under the direction of our party's Central Committee. And as member of the Central Committee and member of the Russian delegation, I voted for the resolution confirming Levi's expulsion from the International. Together with our Central Committee I could see no other course. By virtue of his egocentric attitude, Levi had invested his struggle against the crude theoretical and practical mistakes connected with the March events with a character so pernicious that nothing was left for the slanderers among the Independents to do except to support him and chime in with him. Levi opposed himself not only to the March mistakes but also to the German Party and the workers who had committed these mistakes. In his fright lest the party train suffer a wreck in rounding a dangerous curve, Levi fell, because of fear and malice, into such a frenzy and devised such a "tactic" of salvation as sent him flying out of the window and down the embankment. The train, on the other hand, although heavily shaken and damaged, rounded the curve without being derailed.

Thereupon Levi decided that the Communist International was unworthy of its name unless it forced the German Communist Party to accept Levi once again as its leader. Levi's letter to the Congress was written in exactly that spirit. There was nothing left for us to do except shrug our shoulders. An individual who talks so heatedly about Moscow's dictatorial rule, demanded that Moscow by a formal decision impose him upon the Communist Party out of whose ranks he had propelled himself with such remarkable energy.

I do not mean to say by this that I considered Levi irretrievably lost to the Communist International as far back as the Congress. I was too little acquainted with him to draw any categorical conclusions one way or the other. I did, however, entertain the hope that a cruel lesson wouldn't pass for nought and that Levi would sooner or later find his way back to the party. When on the second day after the Congress a comrade who was departing abroad asked me what there remained now for Levi and his friends to do, I gave approximately the following reply: "I do not at all feel myself called upon to offer any advice to Levi because Comrade Lenin's letter to the Jena Convention of advice I would suggest his trying to understand that an expulsion of the party's former chairman, approved by a World Congress, is not something subject to correction by fits of hysteria. Unless Levi is prepared to drown himself in the swamp of the Independents, he must silently submit to a decision which is harsh but which he himself has provoked, and, while remaining outside the party, to continue working as a rank-and-file soldier for the party until the latter once again opens its doors to him."

I had all the less reason for issuing any special declarations with regard to Levi because Comrade Lenin's letter to the Jena Convention of the German Communist Party[27] expressed exactly and completely the point of view which I together with Comrade Lenin defended at the World Congress not only during the plenary sessions but especially in commission sessions and during conferences with various delegations.   The German delegation is quite aware of this.   But when I learned—and this happened two or three weeks after the Congress— that Levi instead of patiently climbing up the embankment began noisily proclaiming that the track of the party and the entire International must be switched over to the precise place where he, Paul Levi, had tumbled, and that therewith Levi began building a whole " party " on the basis of this egocentric philosophy of history, I was obliged to say to myself that the Communist movement had no other re- course—deplorable as it may be—except to definitely place a cross over Levi.

Incidentally, I ought to mention that I was on one occasion about to make an attempt to untangle certain alleged " misunderstandings " concerning my position, concocted not only by the followers of Levi but also by some " Lefts."   This was at the time of the Jena Con- vention.   It was not without astonishment that I learned that this Party Convention had differentiated itself with maximum vagueness from certain unspecified views of mine, while at the same time it completely solidarized itself with the resolutions of the Third Congress. But between this Congress and myself, however, there had been no misunderstandings at all.   However, on reflection, I dismissed the matter.   During the Congress itself a group of Lefts, whom the Inter- national had pulled back sharply, tried to camouflage the extent of their retreat: " While we are indeed retreating to the right, we shall never go—heaven forbid! —as far to the right as Trotsky."   To this end the Left strategists, on whose toes I, in the line of party duty, had to step several times at the Congress, tried to represent matters as if my position were in some respects, which they alone comprehended, " to the right " of the position of the Third Congress as expressed, among other things, in the resolution on the economic and interna- tional situation which Comrade Varga and I had written.   This was not an easy thing to prove and no one actually tried to prove it.   The

Central Committee of our own party, even before the opening of the Congress, had to correct certain leftist deviations in our own midst.*

The resolution on the international situation and tactics was painstakingly edited by our Central Committee. On the eve of the World Congress and after its adjournment, I made two reports[28] before our Moscow party organization—the strongest both in the ideological and organizational sense—in which I defended the position of the Central Committee on the questions in dispute at the Congress. The Moscow organization approved our point of view wholeheartedly and completely. Both of my Moscow reports have since been published in the German language as a book: *Die Neue Etappe* (*The New Stage*). If some Leftists continue to chatter that I either recognize or incline to recognize that capitalism has restored its equilibrium and that thereby the proletarian revolution is relegated to the dim future, then I can only shrug my shoulders once again. After all it is necessary to think and to express oneself a little more coherently. For all these reasons I regarded the above-mentioned Jena resolution merely as the last echo of the March confusion and the harmless revenge of the " Lefts " for the severe lesson taught them by the Third Congress.

Two or three times during this period I have had the occasion to acquaint myself—true, very cursorily—with the writings of Comrade Maslow and his closest co-thinkers. I do not know whether a cross must likewise be placed over them, that is, whether one should renounce all hope of these comrades being able sometime to learn something ; but it must be affirmed in any case that they failed to learn anything at the Congress. It is out of the question to consider them as Marxists. They convert Marx's historic theory into automatism and for good measure they add to it unbridled revolutionary subjectivism. Elements of this sort easily pass into their opposite at the very first turn of events. Today they preach that the economic crisis must unfailingly and uninterruptedly worsen up to the dictatorship of the proletariat. But tomorrow, should some improvement of the economic conjuncture give them a fillip on the nose, many of them will become transformed into reformists. The Communist Party of Germany has paid far too dearly for its March lesson to permit a repetition of it, even in a diluted form. It occurs to me, by the way,

---

* These leftist deviations consisted in the failure of certain comrades to consider in advance how dangerous for the development of the proletarian revolution the adventuristic-putschistic tendencies in the Comintern itself might prove.—L.T.

that it is very doubtful that the Lefts still retain the same moods as those with which they entered the March battles and summoned others to follow. They have retained primarily their prejudices and deem themselves honor bound to defend the March phraseology and theoretical confusion. By this stubbornness they hinder the German workers from learning. It is impermissible to allow this.

After everything that has happened since the World Congress, I had no reason to be surprised at Levi's conduct in making public the documents relating to the March battles. The false tactical views that manifested themselves in the March events led naturally to specific practical consequences. The erroneousness of the tactic found its expression in blunders and stupidities committed by a whole number of splendid party workers. The Congress condemned the mistakes and pointed out the correct road. The most important and valuable section of those comrades who in their day had made mistakes or approved of them submitted to the Congress not out of fear but out of conviction. After the accomplishment of this curative and educational work, to pull documents out of one's own pocket or someone else's (it amounts to the same thing)—documents which can no longer teach anyone anything new but can only provide great moral satisfaction to the bourgeois and Social-Democratic scum—to do so is to add a personal transgression to a political sin.

Equally blind in its vengefulness is the belated publication by Paul Levi of Luxemburg's critical article against Bolshevism[29]. In the course of these last few years all of us have had to clear up many things in our own minds and to learn a great deal under the direct blows of events. Rosa Luxemburg accomplished this ideological work more slowly than others because she had to observe events from the side lines, from the pits of German prisons. Her recently published manuscript characterizes only a particular stage in her spiritual development and is therefore of importance biographically but not theoretically. In his day Levi was adamantly opposed to the publication of this booklet. During four years of the Soviet Revolution this manuscript was kept under lock and key. But when Levi, miscalculating the forces of motion, fell out of the party train and down the embankment, he decided to make the same use of the old manuscript as he has of " revealing " documents filched from the pockets of others. Thereby he has merely once again demonstrated that all things—positive and negative alike—acquire meaning for him solely depending upon how they happen to relate personally to Paul

Levi. He is the measure of all things. What a monstrous intellec-
tualistic egocentrism! The person of Levi is Levi's psychologic premise for his political attitude toward the German Communist Party
and toward the entire International.

The organization created by Levi is bound, in the very nature of
things, to attract all those who accidentally fell into the ranks of the
Communist Party and who require, especially after the March upheaval, the first convenient pretext for betaking themselves to the
hills. It would be far too awkward for them to return straightway
to the Independents. For these tired pilgrims Levi has arranged something in the nature of a sanatorium or rest home for critics. Its name
is the KAG. The German working class has no earthly use for this
institution. The German working class already possesses its own
revolutionary party. The latter has still far from overcome all its
growing pains. In store for it still lie heavy trials and tribulations
both external and internal. But it is the genuine party of the German
working class. It will grow and develop. It will conquer.

First published in **Pravda,**
Issue No. 5, January 6, 1922.

8

On the United Front[30]

I. *General Considerations on the United Front*

1. The task of the Communist Party is to lead the proletarian revolution. In order to summon the proletariat for the direct conquest of power and to achieve it the Communist Party must base itself on the overwhelming majority of the working class.

So long as it does not hold this majority, the party must fight to win it.

The party can achieve this only by remaining an absolutely independent organization with a clear program and strict internal discipline. That is the reason why the party was bound to break ideologically and organizationally with the reformists and the centrists who do not strive for the proletarian revolution, who possess neither the capacity nor the desire to prepare the masses for revolution, and who by their entire conduct thwart this work.

Any members of the Communist Party who bemoan the split with the centrists in the name of " unity of forces " or " unity of front " thereby demonstrate that they do not understand the ABC of Communism and that they themselves happen to be in the Communist Party only by accident.

2. After assuring itself of the complete independence and ideological homogeneity of its ranks, the Communist Party fights for influence over the majority of the working class. This struggle can be accelerated or retarded depending upon objective circumstances and the expediency of the tactics employed.

But it is perfectly self-evident that the class life of the proletariat is not suspended during this period preparatory to the revolution. Clashes with industrialists, with the bourgeoisie, with the state power, on the initiative of one side or the other, run their due course.

In these clashes—insofar as they involve the vital interests of the entire working class, or its majority, or this or that section—the working masses sense the need of unity in action, of unity in resisting the onslaught of capitalism or unity in taking the offensive against it. Any party which mechanically counterposes itself to this need of the working class for unity in action will unfailingly be condemned in the minds of the workers.

Consequently the question of the united front is not at all, either in point of origin or substance, a question of the reciprocal relations between the Communist parliamentary fraction and that of the Socialists, or between the Central Committee of the two parties, or between *l'Humanité* and *Le Populaire*[31]. The problem of the united front— despite the fact *that a split is inevitable in this epoch between the various political organizations basing themselves on the working class* —grows out of the urgent need to secure for the working class the possibility of a united front in the struggle against capitalism.

For those who do not understand this task, the party is only a propaganda society and not an organization for mass action.

3. In cases where the Communist Party still remains an organization of a numerically insignificant minority, the question of its conduct on the mass-struggle front does not assume a decisive practical and organizational significance. In such conditions, mass actions remain under the leadership of the old organizations which by reason of their still powerful traditions continue to play the decisive role.

Similarly the problem of the united front does not arise in countries where—as in Bulgaria, for example—the Communist Party is the sole leading organization of the toiling masses.

But wherever the Communist Party already constitutes a big, organized, political force, but not the decisive magnitude; wherever the party embraces organizationally, let us say, one-fourth, one-third, or even a larger proportion of the organized proletarian vanguard, it is confronted with the question of the united front in all its acuteness.

If the party embraces one-third or one-half of the proletarian vanguard, then the remaining half or two-thirds are organized by the reformists or centrists. It is perfectly obvious, however, that even those workers who still support the reformists and the centrists are vitally interested in maintaining the highest material standards of living and the greatest possible freedom for struggle. We must consequently so devise our tactic as to prevent the Communist Party, which will on the morrow embrace the entire three-thirds of the working class, from turning into—and all the more so, from actually being —an organizational obstacle in the way of the current struggle of the proletariat.

Still more, the party must assume the initiative in securing unity in these current struggles. Only in this way will the party draw closer to those two-thirds who do not as yet follow its leadership, who do not as yet trust the party because they do not understand it. Only in this way can the party win them over.

4. If the Communist Party had not broken drastically and irrevocably with the Social Democrats, it would not have become the party of the proletarian revolution. It could not have taken the first serious steps on the road to revolution. It would have for ever remained a parliamentary safety-valve attached to the bourgeois state.

Whoever does not understand this, does not know the first letter of the ABC of Communism.

If the Communist Party did not seek for organizational avenues to the end that at every given moment joint, coordinated action between the Communist and the non-Communist (including the Social-Democratic) working masses were made possible, it would have thereby laid bare its own incapacity to win over—on the basis of mass action— the majority of the working class. It would degenerate into a Communist propaganda society but never develop into a party for the conquest of power.

It is not enough to possess the sword, one must give it an edge ; it is not enough to give the sword an edge, one must know how to wield it.

After separating the Communists from the reformists it is not enough to fuse the Communists together by means of organizational discipline; it is necessary that this organization should learn how to guide all the collective activities of the proletariat in all spheres of its living struggle.

This is the second letter of the alphabet of Communism.

5. Does the united front extend only to the working masses or does it also include the opportunist leaders?

The very posing of this question is a product of misunderstanding.

If we were able simply to unite the working masses around our own banner or around our practical immediate slogans, and skip over reformist organizations, whether party or trade union, that would of course be the best thing in the world. But then the very question of the united front would not exist in its present form.

The question arises from this, that certain very important sections of the working class belong to reformist organizations or support them. Their present experience is still insufficient to enable them to break with the reformist organizations and join us. It may be precisely after engaging in those mass activities, which are on the order of the day, that a major change will take place in this connection. That is just what we are striving for. But that is not how matters stand at present. Today the organized portion of the working class is broken up into three formations.

One of them, the Communist, strives toward the social revolution and precisely *because of this* supports concurrently every movement, however partial, of the toilers against the exploiters and against the bourgeois state.

Another grouping, the reformist, strives toward conciliation with the bourgeoisie. But in order not to lose their influence over the workers reformists are compelled, against the innermost desires of their own leaders, to support the partial movements of the exploited against the exploiters.

Finally, there is a third grouping, the centrist, which constantly vacillates between the other two, and which has no independent significance.

The circumstances thus make wholly possible joint action on a whole number of vital issues between the workers united in these three respective organizations and the unorganized masses adhering to them.

The Communists, as has been said, must not oppose such actions but on the contrary must also assume the initiative for them, precisely for the reason that the greater is the mass drawn into the movement, the higher its self-confidence rises, all the more self-confident will that mass movement be and all the more resolutely will it be capable of marching forward, however modest may be the initial slogans of struggle. And this means that the growth of the mass aspects of the movement tends to radicalize it, and creates much more favorable conditions for the slogans, methods of struggle, and, in general, the leading role of the Communist Party.

The reformists dread the revolutionary potential of the mass movement; their beloved arena is the parliamentary tribune, the trade-union bureaus, the arbitration boards, the ministerial ante-chambers.

On the contrary, we are, apart from all other considerations, interested in dragging the reformists from their asylums and placing them alongside ourselves before the eyes of the struggling masses. With a correct tactic we stand only to gain from this. A Communist who doubts or fears this resembles a swimmer who has approved the theses on the best method of swimming but dares not plunge into the water.

6. Unity of front consequently presupposes our readiness, within certain limits and on specific issues, to correlate in practice our actions with those of reformist organizations, to the extent to which the latter still express today the will of important sections of the embattled proletariat.

But, after all, didn't we split with them? Yes, because we disagree with them on fundamental questions of the working-class movement.

And yet we seek agreement with them? Yes, in all those cases where the masses that follow them are ready to engage in joint struggle together with the masses that follow us and when they, the reformists, are to a lesser or greater degree compelled to become an instrument of this struggle.

But won't they say that after splitting with them we still need them? Yes, their blabbermouths may say this. Here and there somebody in our own ranks may take fright at it. But as regards the broad working masses—even those who do not follow us and who do not as yet understand our goals but who do see two or three labor organizations leading a parallel existence—these masses will draw from our conduct this conclusion, that despite the split we are doing everything in our power to facilitate unity in action for the masses.

7. A policy aimed to secure the united front does not of course contain automatic guarantees that unity in action will actually be attained in all instances. On the contrary, in many cases and perhaps even the majority of cases, organizational agreements will be only half-attained or perhaps not at all. But it is necessary that the struggling masses should always be given the opportunity of convincing themselves that the non-achievement of unity in action was not due to our formalistic irreconcilability but to the lack of real will to struggle on the part of the reformists.

In entering into agreements with other organizations, we naturally obligate ourselves to a certain discipline in action. But this discipline cannot be absolute in character. In the event that the reformists begin putting brakes on the struggle to the obvious detriment of the movement and act counter to the situation and the moods of the masses, we as an independent organization always reserve the right to lead the struggle to the end, and this without our temporary semi-allies.

This may give rise to a new sharpening of the struggle between us and the reformists. But it will no longer involve a simple repetition of one and the same set of ideas within a shut-in circle but will signify—provided our tactic is correct—the extension of our influence over new, fresh groups of the proletariat.

8. It is possible to see in this policy a rapproachement with the reformists only from the standpoint of a journalist who believes that he rids himself of reformism by ritualistically criticizing it without ever leaving his editorial office but who is fearful of clashing with the reformists before the eyes of the working masses and giving the latter an opportunity to appraise the Communist and the reformist on the equal plane of the mass struggle. Behind this seeming revolutionary fear of " rapproachement " there really lurks a political passivity which seeks to perpetuate an order of things wherein the Communists and reformists each retain their own rigidly demarcated spheres of influence, their own audiences at meetings, their own press, and all this together creates an illusion of serious political struggle.

9. We broke with the reformists and centrists in order to obtain complete freedom in criticizing perfidy, betrayal, indecision and the half-way spirit in the labor movement. For this reason any sort of organizational agreement which restricts our freedom of criticism and agitation is absolutely unacceptable to us. We participate in a united front but do not for a single moment become dissolved in it. We function in the united front as an independent detachment. It is precisely in the course of struggle that broad masses must learn from experience that we fight better than the others, that we see more clearly than the others, that we are more audacious and resolute. In this way, we shall bring closer the hour of the united revolutionary front under the undisputed Communist leadership.

II. *Groupings in the French Labor Movement*

10. If we propose to analyze the question of the united front as it applies to France, without leaving the ground of the foregoing theses which flow from the entire policy of the Communist International, then we must ask ourselves: Do we have in France a situation in which the Communists represent, from the standpoint of practical actions, an insignificant magnitude (*quantité négligeable*)? Or do they,

on the contrary, encompass the overwhelming majority of organized workers? Or do they perhaps occupy an in-between position? Are they sufficiently strong to make their participation in the mass movement of major importance, but not strong enough to concentrate the undisputed leadership in their own hands?

It is quite incontestable that we have before us precisely the latter case in France.

11. In the party sphere the predominance of the Communists over the reformists is overwhelming. The Communist organization and the Communist press surpass by far in numbers, richness and vitality the organization and press of the so-called Socialists.

This overwhelming preponderance, however, far from secures to the French Communist Party the complete and unchallenged leadership of the French proletariat, inasmuch as the latter is still strongly under the influence of anti-political and anti-party tendencies and prejudices, the arena for whose operation is primarily provided by the trade unions.

12. The outstanding peculiarity of the French labor movement consists in this, that the trade unions have long served as an integument or cover for a peculiar anti-parliamentary political party which bears the name of syndicalism. Because, however the revolutionary syndicalists may try to demarcate themselves from politics or from the party, they can never refute the fact that they themselves constitute a political party which seeks to base itself on trade union organizations of the working class. This party has its own positive, revolutionary, proletarian tendencies, but it also has its own extremely negative features, namely, the lack of a genuinely definitive program and a rounded organization. The organization of the trade unions by no means corresponds with the organization of syndicalism. In the organizational sense, the syndicalists represent amorphous political nuclei, grafted upon the trade unions.

The question is further complicated by the fact that the syndicalists, like all other political groupings in the working class, have split, after the war, into two sections: the reformists who support bourgeois society and are thereby compelled to work hand in hand with parliamentary reformists; and the revolutionary section which is seeking ways to overthrow bourgeois society and is thereby, in the person of its best elements, moving toward Communism.

It was just this urge to preserve the unity of the class front which inspired not only the Communists but also the revolutionary syndical-

ists with the absolutely correct tactic of fighting for the unity of the
trade union organization of the French proletariat.   On the other
hand, with the instinct of bankrupts who sense that before the eyes of
the working masses they cannot, in action, in struggle, meet the competition of the revolutionary wing, Jouhaux, Merrheim and Co. have
taken the path of split.   The colossally important struggle now unfold-
ing throughout the entire trade union movement of France, the struggle
between the reformists and the revolutionists, is for us at the same time
a struggle for the unity of the trade union organization and the trade
union front.

III.   *The Trade Union Movement and the United Front*

13.   French Communism finds itself in an extremely favorable position precisely with regard to the idea of the united front.   In the
framework of political organization, French Communism has succeeded in conquering the majority of the old Socialist Party, whereupon the opportunists added to all their other political credentials
the quality of " Dissidents," that is, splitters.   Our French Party has
made use of this in the sense that it has branded the social-reformist
organization with the label of Dissidents (splitters), thus singling out
the fact that the reformists are disrupters of unity in action and unity
of organization alike.

14.   In the field of the trade union movement, the revolutionary
wing and above all the Communists cannot hide either from themselves
or their adversaries how profound are the differences between Moscow
and Amsterdam—differences which are by no means simple shadings
within the ranks of the labor movement but a reflection of the profoundest contradiction which is tearing modern society apart, namely,
the contradiction between the bourgeoisie and the proletariat. But at the
same time the revolutionary wing, i.e., first and foremost the conscious
Communist elements, never sponsored, as has been said, the tactic of
leaving the trade unions or of splitting the trade union organization.
Such slogans are characteristic only of sectarian groupings of "local-
ists," of the KAPD, of certain " libertarian " anarchist grouplets in
France, which never wielded any influence among broad working
masses, which neither aspire nor strive to gain this influence but are
content with small churches of their own, each with its rigidly demarcated congregation.   The truly revolutionary elements among the
French syndicalists have felt instinctively that the French working class
can be won on the arena of the trade union movement only by counter-

posing the revolutionary viewpoint and the revolutionary methods to those of the reformists on the arena of mass action, while preserving at the same time the highest possible degree of unity in action.

15. The system of cells in the trade union organizations adopted by the revolutionary wing signifies nothing else but the most natural form of struggle for ideological influence and for unity of front without disrupting the unity of organization.

16. Like the reformists of the Socialist Party, the reformists of the trade union movement took the initiative for the split. But it was precisely the experience of the Socialist Party that largely inspired them with the conclusion that time worked in favor of Communism, and that it was possible to counteract the influence of experience and time only by forcing a split. On the part of the ruling CGT (the French Confederation of Labor) clique we see a whole system of measures designed to disorganize the Left Wing, to deprive it of those rights which the trade union statutes afford it, and, finally, through open expulsion—counter to all statutes and regulations—to formally place it outside the trade union organization.

On the other hand, we see the revolutionary wing fighting to preserve its rights on the grounds of the democratic norms of workers' organizations and resisting with all its might the split implanted from above by appealing to the rank and file for unity of the trade union organization.

17. Every thinking French worker must be aware that when the Communists comprised one-sixth or one-third of the Socialist Party they did not attempt to split, being absolutely certain that the majority of the party would follow them in the near future. When the reformists found themselves reduced to one-third, they split away, nursing no hopes to again win the majority of the proletarian vanguard.

Every thinking French worker must be aware that when the revolutionary elements were confronted with the problem of the trade union movement, they, still an insignificant minority at the time, decided it in the sense of working in common organizations, being certain that the experience of the struggle in the conditions of the revolutionary epoch would quickly impel the majority of the unionized workers to the side of the revolutionary program. When the reformists, however, perceived the growth of the revolutionary wing in the trade unions, they—nursing no hopes of coping with it on a competitive basis—resorted immediately to the methods of expulsion and split.

Hence flow conclusions of greatest importance:

First, the full depth of the differences which reflect, as has been said, the contradiction between the bourgeoisie and the proletariat, becomes clarified.

Secondly, the hypocritical " democratism " of the opponents of proletarian dictatorship is being exposed to the very roots, inasmuch as these gentlemen are averse to tolerating methods of democracy, not only in the framework of the state, but also in the framework of workers' organizations. Whenever the latter turn against them, they either split away themselves, like the Dissidents in the party, or expel others, like the clique of Jouhaux-Dumoulin. It is truly monstrous to suppose that the bourgeoisie would ever agree to permit the struggle against the proletariat to come to a decision within the framework of democracy, when even the agents of the bourgeoisie inside the trade union and political organizations are opposed to solving the questions of the labor movement on the basis of norms of workers' democracy which they themselves voluntarily adopted.

18. The struggle for the unity of the trade union organization and trade union action will remain in the future as well one of the most important tasks of the Communist Party—a struggle not only in the sense of constantly striving to unite ever larger numbers of workers around the program and tactics of Communism, but also in the sense that the Communist Party—on the road to the realization of this goal —both directly and through Communists in the trade unions, strives in action to reduce to a minimum those obstacles which are placed before the workers' movement by an organizational split.

If in spite of all our efforts to restore unity, the split in the CGT becomes sealed in the immediate future, this would not at all signify that the CGT *Unitaire*[32] regardless of whether half or more than half of the unionized workers join it in the next period, will conduct its work by simply ignoring the existence of the reformist CGT. Such a policy would render difficult in the extreme—if not exclude altogether —the possibility of coordinated militant actions of the proletariat, and at the same time would make it extremely easy for the reformist CGT to play, in the interests of the bourgeoisie, the role of *La Ligue Civique*[33] as regards strikes, demonstrations, etc. ; and it would simultaneously provide the reformist CGT with a semblance of justification in arguing that the revolutionary CGTU provokes inexpedient public actions and must bear full responsibility for them. It is perfectly self-evident that in all cases where circumstances permit, the revolutionary CGTU will, whenever it deems it necessary to undertake some campaign, openly address itself to the reformist CGT with specific proposals and demands for a concrete plan of coordinated actions, and bring to bear the pressure of labor's public opinion and expose before this public opinion each hesitating and evasive step of the reformists.

In this way, even in the event that the split of the trade union organization becomes permanent, the methods of struggle for the united front will preserve all their meaning.

19.   We can, therefore, state that in relation to the most important field of the labor movement—the trade unions—the tactic of the united front demands that those methods, by which the struggle against Jouhaux and Co. has already been conducted on our side, be applied more consistently, more persistently and resolutely than ever before.

IV.   *The Political Struggle and the United Front*

20.   On the party plane there is, to begin with, a very important difference from the trade unions in this, that the preponderance of the Communist Party over the Socialist, both in point of organization and the press, is overwhelming. We may consequently assume that the Communist Party, as such, is capable of securing the unity of the political front and that therefore it has no impelling reasons for addressing itself to the organization of the Dissidents with any sort of proposals for concrete actions. This strictly businesslike and legitimate method of posing the question, on the basis of evaluating the relationship of forces and not on the basis of verbal radicalism, must be appraised on its substantive merits.

21.   If we take into account that the Communist Party numbers 130,000 members, while the Socialists number 30,000, then the enormous successes of Communist ideas in France become apparent. However, if we take into account the relation between these figures and the numerical strength of the working class as a whole, together with the existence of reformist trade unions and of anti-Communist tendencies within the revolutionary trade unions, then the question of the hegemony of the Communist Party inside the labor movement will confront us as a very difficult task, still far from solved by our numerical superiority over the Dissidents. The latter may under certain conditions prove to be a much more important counter-revolutionary factor within the working class than might appear, if one were to judge solely from the weakness of their organization and the insignificant circulation and ideological content of their paper, *Le Populaire*.

22.   In order to evaluate a situation, it is necessary to take clear

cognizance of how this situation took shape. The transformation of the majority of the old Socialist Party into the Communist Party came as a result of a wave of dissatisfaction and mutiny engendered in all countries in Europe by the war. The example of the Russian revolution and the slogans of the Third International seemed to point a way out. The bourgeoisie, however, was able to maintain itself throughout 1919-20 and was able, by means of combined measures, to establish on postwar foundations a certain equilibrium, which is being undermined by the most terrible contradictions and which is heading toward vast catastrophes, which meanwhile provides relative stability for the current day and for the period immediately ahead. The Russian revolution, in surmounting the greatest difficulties and obstacles created by world capitalism, has been able to achieve its socialist tasks only gradually, only at the cost of an extraordinary strain upon all its forces. As a result, the initial flood-tide of vague, uncritical, revolutionary moods has been unavoidably superseded by an ebb. Only the most resolute, audacious and youthful section of the world working class has remained under the banner of Communism.

This does not mean naturally that those broad circles of the proletariat who have been disillusioned in their hopes for immediate revolution, for swift radical transformations, etc., have wholly returned to the old prewar positions. No, their dissatisfaction is deeper than ever before, their hatred of the exploiters is fiercer. But at the same time they are politically disoriented, they do not see the paths of struggle, and therefore remain passively expectant—giving rise to the possibility of sharp swings to this or that side, depending on how the situation unfolds.

This big reservoir of the passive and the disoriented can, under a certain combination of circumstances, be widely utilized by the Dissidents against us.

23. In order to support the Communist Party, faith in the revolutionary cause, will to action and loyalty are needed. In order to support the Dissidents, disorientation and passivity are necessary and sufficient. It is perfectly natural for the revolutionary and dynamic section of the working class to effuse from its ranks a much larger proportion of members for the Communist Party than the passive and disoriented section is able to supply to the party of the Dissidents.

The same thing applies to the press. The elements of indifferentism read little. The insignificant circulation and content of *Le Populaire* mirrors the mood of a certain section of the working class. The fact that complete ascendancy of the professional intellectuals over the workers prevails in the party of the Dissidents runs nowise counter to our diagnosis and prognosis. Because the passive and partially disillusioned, partially disoriented worker-masses are an ideal culture medium, especially in France, for political cliques composed of attorneys and journalists, reformist witch-doctors and parliamentary charlatans.

24. If we regard the party organization as an operating army, and the unorganized mass of workers as the reserves, and if we grant that our operating army is three to four times stronger than the active army of Dissidents, then, under a certain combination of circumstances, the reserves may prove to be divided between ourselves and the social-reformists in a proportion much less favorable to us.

25. The political atmosphere of France is pervaded with the idea of the " Left Bloc." After a new period of Poincaré-ism which represents the bourgeoisie's attempt to serve up to the people a warmed-over hash of the illusions of victory, a pacifist reaction may quite likely set in among broad circles of bourgeois society, i.e., first and foremost among the petty bourgeoisie. The hope for universal pacification, for agreement with Soviet Russia, obtaining raw materials and payments from her on advantageous terms, cuts in the burden of militarism, and so on—in brief, the illusory program of democratic pacifism —can become for a while the program of a " Left Bloc," superseding the National Bloc.

From the standpoint of the development of the revolution in France, such a change of regimes will be a step forward only provided the proletariat does not fall prey to any extent to the illusions of petty bourgeois pacifism.

26. Reformist-Dissidents are the agency of the " Left Bloc " within the working class. Their successes will be the greater, all the less the working class as a whole is seized by the idea and practice of the united front against the bourgeoisie. Layers of workers, disoriented by the war and by the tardiness of the revolution, may venture to support the " Left Bloo " as a lesser evil, in the belief that they do not thereby risk anything at all, or because they see no other road at present.

27. One of the most reliable methods of counteracting inside the working class the moods and ideas of the " Left Bloc," i.e., a bloc between the workers and a certain section of the bourgeoisie against

another section of the bourgeoisie, is through promoting persistently and resolutely the idea of a *bloc between all the sections of the working class against the whole bourgeoisie.*

28. In relation to the Dissidents this means that we must not permit them to occupy with impunity an evasive, temporizing position on questions relating to the labor movement, and to use platonic declarations of sympathy for the working class as a cover for utilizing the patronage of the bourgeois oppressors. In other words, we can and must, in all suitable instances, propose to the Dissidents a specific form of joint aid to strikers, to locked-out workers, unemployed, war invalids, etc., etc., recording before the eyes of the masses their responses to our precise proposals, and in this way driving a wedge between them and certain sections of politically indifferent or semi-indifferent masses on whom the reformists hope to lean for support under certain favorable conditions.

29. This kind of tactic is all the more important in view of the fact that the Dissidents are unquestionably bound up intimately with the reformist CGT and together with the latter constitute the two wings of the bourgeois agency inside the labor movement. We take the offensive both on the trade union and political fields simultaneously against this twofold agency, applying the very same tactical methods.

30. The impeccable and agitationally extremely persuasive logic of our conduct is as follows: " You, the reformists of trade unionism and socialism," we say to them before the eyes of the masses, " have split the trade unions and the party for the sake of ideas and methods which we consider wrong and criminal. We demand that you at least refrain from placing a spoke in the wheel during the partial and unpostponable concrete tasks of the working-class struggle and that you make possible unity in action. In the given concrete situation we propose such and such a program of struggle."

31. The indicated method could be similarly employed and not without success in relation to parliamentary and municipal activities. We say to the masses, " The Dissidents, because they do not want the revolution, have split the mass of the workers. It would be insanity to count upon their helping the proletarian revolution. But we are ready, inside and outside the parliament, to enter into certain practical agreements with them, provided they agree, in those cases where one must choose between the known interests of the bourgeoisie and the definite demands of the proletariat, to support the latter in action. The Dissidents can be capable of such actions only if they renounce their

ties with the parties of the bourgeoisie, that is, the ' Left Bloc ' and
its bourgeois discipline."

If the Dissidents were capable of accepting these conditions, then their
worker-followers would be quickly absorbed by the Communist Party.
Just because of this, the Dissidents will not agree to these conditions.
In other words, to the clearly and precisely posed question whether
they choose a bloc with the bourgeoisie or a bloc with the proletariat
—in the concrete and specific conditions of mass struggle—they will
be compelled to reply that they prefer a bloc with the bourgeoisie.
Such an answer will not pass with impunity among the proletarian
reserves on whom they are counting.

V. *Internal Tasks of the Communist Party*

32.   The foregoing policy presupposes, naturally, complete organizational independence, ideological clarity and revolutionary firmness
of the Communist Party itself.

Thus, for example, it would be impossible to conduct with complete
success a policy aimed at making hateful and contemptible the idea
of the " Left Bloc " among the working class, if in our own party
ranks there are partisans of this " Left Bloc " bold enough openly to
defend this projected program of the bourgeoisie.   Unconditional and
merciless expulsion in disgrace of those who come out in favor of
the idea of the " Left Bloc " is a self-understood duty of the Communist Party.   This will cleanse our policy of all elements of equivocation and unclarity ; this will attract the attention of advanced
workers to the acute character of the issue of the " Left Bloc " and
will demonstrate that the Communist Party does not trifle with the
questions which imperil the revolutionary unity in action of the proletariat against the bourgeoisie.

33.   Those who seek to use the idea of the united front for agitating
in favor of unification with the reformists and Dissidents must be mercilessly ejected from our party, inasmuch as they serve as the agency
of the Dissidents in our ranks and are deceiving the workers concerning
the reasons for the split and who is really responsible for it.   Instead
of correctly posing the question of the possibility of this or that coordinated, practical action with the Dissidents, despite their petty-
bourgeois and essentially counter-revolutionary character, they are
demanding that our own party renounce its Communist program and
revolutionary methods.   The ejection of such elements, mercilessly
and in disgrace, will best demonstrate that the tactic of the workers'

united front in no way resembles capitulation to or reconciliation with the reformists. The tactic of the united front demands from the party complete freedom in maneuvering, flexibility and resoluteness. To make this possible, the party must clearly and specifically declare at every given moment just what its wishes are, just what it is striving for, and it must comment authoritatively, before the eyes of the masses, on its own steps and proposals.

34. Hence flows the complete inadmissibility for individual party members to issue on their own responsibility and risk political publications in which they counterpose their own slogans, methods of action and proposals to the slogans, methods of action and proposals of the party. Under the cover of the Communist Party and consequently also inside that milieu which is influenced by a Communist cover, i.e., in a workers' milieu, they spread from day to day ideas hostile to us, or they sow confusion and skepticism which are even more pernicious than avowedly hostile ideologies. Periodicals of this type, together with their editors, must once and for all be placed outside the party and the entire working-class France must learn about this from articles which mercilessly expose the petty-bourgeois smugglers who operate under a Communist flag.

35. From what has been said, it likewise follows that it is completely inadmissible for the leading party publications to carry side by side with articles defending the basic concepts of Communism, other articles disputing these concepts or denying them. Absolutely impermissible is a continuation of a regime in the party press under which the mass of worker-readers find, in the guise of editorials in leading Communist periodicals, articles which try to turn us back to positions of tearful pacifism and which propagate among workers a debilitating hostility toward revolutionary violence in the face of the triumphant violence of the bourgeoisie. Under the guise of a struggle against militarism, a struggle is thus being conducted against the ideas of revolution.

If after the experience of the war and all the subsequent events, especially in Russia and Germany, the prejudices of humanitarian pacifism have still survived in the Communist Party; and if the party finds it advisable for the sake of completely liquidating these prejudices to open a discussion on this question, even in that case, the pacifists with their prejudices cannot come forward in such a discussion as an equal force but must be severely condemned by the authoritative voice of the party, in the name of its Central Committee. After the

Central Committee decides that the discussion has been exhausted, all attempts to spread the debilitating ideas of Tolstoyanism and other varieties of pacifism must unquestionably bring expulsion from the party.

36. An objection might, however, be raised that so long as the work of cleansing the party of ancient prejudices and of attaining internal cohesion remains uncompleted, it would be dangerous to place the party in situations where it would come into close proximity with reformists and nationalists. But such a point of view is false. Naturally it is undeniable that a transition from broad propagandist activity to direct participation in the mass movement carries with it new difficulties and therefore dangers for the Communist Party. But it is completely wrong to suppose that the party can be prepared for all tests without directly participating in struggles, without directly coming in contact with enemies and adversaries. On the contrary, only in this way can a genuine, non-fictitious internal cleaning and fusing of the party be achieved. It is quite possible that some elements in the party and in the trade union bureaucracy will feel themselves drawn more closely to the reformists, from whom they have accidentally split, than toward us. The loss of such camp-followers will not be a liability but an asset, and it will be compensated a hundredfold by the influx of those working men and women who still follow the reformists today. The party will in consequence become more homogeneous, more resolute and more proletarian.

VI. *Party Tasks in the Trade Union Movement*

37. Absolute clarity on the trade union question is a task of first-rate importance, surpassing by far all the other tasks before the Communist Party of France.

Naturally the legend spread by the reformists that plans are afoot to subordinate the trade unions organizationally to the party must be unconditionally denounced and exposed. Trade unions embrace workers of different political shadings as well as non-party men, atheists as well as believers, whereas the party unites political co-thinkers on the basis of a definite program. The party has not and cannot have any instrumentalities and methods for subjecting the trade unions to itself from the outside.

The party can gain influence in the life of the trade unions only to the extent that its members work in the trade unions and carry out the party point of view there. The influence of party members in the trade unions naturally depends on their numerical strength and especially on the degree to which they are able to apply party principles correctly, consistently and expediently to the needs of the trade union movement.

The party has the right and the duty to aim to conquer, along the road above outlined, the *decisive influence* in the trade union organization. It can achieve this goal only provided the work of the Communists in the trade unions is wholly and exclusively harmonized with the principles of the party and is invariably conducted under its control.

38. The minds of all Communists must therefore be completely purged of reformist prejudices, in accordance with which the party is regarded as a political parliamentary organization of the proletariat, and nothing more. The Communist Party is the organization of the proletarian vanguard for the ideological fructification of the labor movement and the assumption of leadership in all spheres—first and foremost in the trade unions. While the trade unions are not subordinate to the party but wholly autonomous organizations, the Communists inside the trade unions, on the other hand, cannot pretend to any kind of autonomy in their trade union activity but must act as the transmitters of their party's program and tactics. To be most severely condemned is the conduct of those Communists who not only fail to fight inside the trade unions for the influence of party ideas but actually counteract such a struggle in the name of a principle of " autonomy " which they apply absolutely falsely. As a matter of fact, they thus pave the way for the decisive influence in the trade unions of individuals, groups and cliques, bound neither by a definite program nor by party organization, and who utilize the formlessness of ideological groupings and relations in order to keep the organizational apparatus in their own hands and secure the independence of their own clique from any actual control by the workers' vanguard.

While the party, in its activity inside the trade unions, must show the greatest attentiveness and caution toward the non-party masses and their conscientious and honest representatives ; while the party must, on the basis of joint work, systematically and tactically draw closer to the best elements of the trade union movement—including the revolutionary anarchists who are capable of learning—the party can, on the contrary, no longer tolerate in its midst those pseudo-Communists who utilize the status of party membership only in order all the more confidently to promote anti-party influences in the trade unions.

39. The party through its own press, through its own propagandists and its members in the trade unions must submit to constant and systematic criticism the shortcomings of revolutionary /syndicalism for solving the basic tasks of the proletariat. The party must tirelessly and persistently criticize the weak theoretical and practical sides of syndicalism, explaining at the same time to its best elements that the only correct road for securing the revolutionary influence on the trade unions and on the labor movement as a whole is the entry of revolutionary syndicalists into the Communist Party: their participation in working out all the basic questions of the movement, in drawing the balance sheet of experience, in defining new tasks, in cleansing the Communist Party itself and strengthening its ties with the working masses.

40. It is absolutely indispensable to take a census of all the members of the French Communist Party in order to determine their social status (workers, civil employees, peasants, intellectuals, etc.) ; their relations with the trade union movement (do they belong to trade unions—do they participate in meetings of Communist and revolutionary syndicalists? do they carry out at these meetings the decisions of the party on the trade unions? etc.) ; their attitude toward the party press (what party publications do they read?), and so on.

The census must be so conducted that its chief aspects can be taken into account before the Fourth World Congress convenes.

March 2, 1922.

9

Resolution of the ECCI on the French Communist Party (March 2, 1922)

The Communist Party of France has since the Tours Convention made major organizational endeavors which kept in its ranks the best forces of the proletariat who have awakened to political action. The Marseilles Convention provided the party with the premise for serious theoretical work from which the revolutionary labor movement will doubtless derive very great benefits.

By breaking with parliamentarian and horse-trading traditions of the old Socialist Party whose conventions set the stage only for the oratorical duels among the leaders, the Communist Party has, for the first time in France, convened a gathering of active workers for a preliminary and deep-going review of the vital problems pertaining to the development of the French revolutionary movement.

The organizational crisis in the French Party, whose importance it would be equally wrong to minimize or exaggerate, constitutes one of the salient moments in the growth of the French Communist Party, its internal cleansing, its internal reconstruction and consolidation upon genuinely Communist foundations.

The split of Tours drew a basic line of demarcation between reformism and Communism. But it was absolutely unavoidable for the Communist Party issuing from this split to retain in some of its segments certain survivals of its reformist and parliamentary past, of which it can divest itself—as it is doing—through internal efforts based on participation in the mass struggle

The survivals of the past—among certain party groups—are expressed in: (1) an urge to restore unity with the reformists; (2) an urge toward a bloc with the radical wing of the bourgeoisie; (3) a sub-

110

stitution of petty-bourgeois humanitarian pacifism for revolutionary anti-militarism ; (4) a false interpretation of the party's relations with the trade unions; (5) a struggle against genuine centralist leadership in the party; (6) efforts to replace international discipline 'in action by a platonic federation of national parties.

Following the split at Tours, tendencies of this sort could not fully disclose themselves and hope to gain a broad influence in the party. Nevertheless under the powerful pressure of bourgeois public opinion, elements inclined toward opportunism tend naturally to gravitate toward each other and are seeking to create their own publications and points of support. However insignificant may be their successes in this direction, it would be a mistake not to assay properly the extent to which their work threatens the revolutionary character and unity of the party. A Communist organization can never serve as an arena for free propaganda of essentially the same views which resulted in the split of the reformist-Dissidents from the working-class party. Any unclarity in this connection is bound unavoidably to hinder the work of revolutionary education among the masses.

The Plenum of the ECCI affirms that the resolutions of the Marseilles Convention, imbued with the spirit of the Communist International, create extremely important points of support for the party's revolutionary activities among the toiling masses of city and country.

Concurrently, the Plenum of the ECCI takes into cognizance with gratification the declaration of the French delegation to the effect that *Journal du Peuple,* the organ which serves as the rallying point for reformist and other vague tendencies, occupies a position directly counter to the program of the International, contrary to the decisions of the Tours and Marseilles Conventions of the French Communist Party, and contrary to the revolutionary irreconcilability of the class-conscious French proletariat, and will therefore shortly be removed from the party.

The ECCI Plenum sees the exceptional importance of the Marseilles Convention in this, that it has posed before the party the most important task of carrying on systematic and correct work in the trade unions in the spirit of the party's program and tactics. Thereby it has condemned in principle the tendencies among those party members who are, under the guise of fighting for the autonomy of the trade unions—which, by the way, no one disputes—in reality fighting to retain their own autonomy in trade union activity, free from the party's control and leadership.

In view of the fact that the statutes of the Communist International and of its sections, founded on the principles of democratic centralism, provide ample guarantees for a correct and normal development of each Communist Party, the Plenum considers as wrong the resignation of several members of the Central Committee who were elected by the Marseilles Convention. This is wrong independently of the political motivations which provoked these resignations. Renunciations of posts delegated by the party can be construed by the broad party circles as a declaration that correct collaboration of different shadings is impossible within the framework of democratic centralism and it can serve as an impulse to the formation of factions within the party.

Expressing its complete assurance that the struggle against the above-cited manifestations of anti-Communist tendencies will be conducted by the overwhelming majority of the party and its leading bodies as a whole, and recognizing that the creation of factions would unavoidably cause the greatest injury to the party's development and its authority among the proletariat, the Plenum of the ECCI notes with satisfaction the declaration of the French delegation to the effect that the Central Committee and the comrades who resigned are ready to take the necessary organizational measures in order to fully realize in life the decisions of the Marseilles Convention and that those who have tendered in their resignations will enter the party's Central Committee to work harmoniously and correctly.

March 2, 1922.

10

The Communists and the Peasantry in France

Our differences of opinion with the French comrades on the question of the united front are far from exhausted. On the contrary, if one were to judge by certain articles published in the French Party press one would get the impression that the differences and misunderstandings —at least among certain party circles—are rooted much more deeply than might have seemed at first. I have before me the article of Comrade Renaud Jean[34] which appeared as an editorial in *l'Humanité* (April 6, 1922). Comrade Jean is an outstanding party activist who made the report on the agrarian question at the Marseilles Convention. With a forcefulness and frankness which we can only welcome, he has expressed himself against the views defended by us which seem to him erroneous. In a caption to his article he refers to the tactic of the united front as a dangerous indiscretion. In the text he speaks flatly of a *catastrophe* which must inescapably result from this tactic in France. "Our country has been debilitated for three-quarters of a century by universal suffrage. Consciousness of class division has permeated only an insignificant minority . . . Bourgeois republican France is the promised land of Babel (confusion)." From all these absolutely correct and established facts Comrade Jean draws a conclusion with which we are in complete accord, namely: "The Communist Party must be more irreconcilable in our country than in any other." And so, from the standpoint of such irreconcilability, Comrade Jean directs his blows against the united front which he continues to regard as nothing else but a combination for inter-party conciliationism. We could say—and we do say—that such an appraisal of a most profound tactical problem is evidence that Comrade Jean has not yet freed himself of the influence of purely parliamentarian traditions of French socialism. There where we see posed the question of conquering broad masses, the question of making a breach in the bourgeois-conciliationist blockade of the proletarian vanguard, Comrade Jean stubbornly refuses to see anything else but a " clever " combination, which can, at best, gain for us a slight increase of seats in parliament (!!), at the price of increasing the disorder and confusion in the political consciousness of the proletariat. And yet France—in this Comrade Jean is absolutely correct — more than any other country stands in need of clarity, precision and resoluteness in political thinking and in party activities. But if Comrade Jean considers that French Communism ought to be the most irreconcilable, then why doesn't he—before taking up arms against the united front—take the trouble to specify that French Communism happens today to be the least irreconcilable, the most tolerant and the most indulgent to all sorts of deviations?

To the clarity and precision which Comrade Jean employs in formulating his criticism we shall likewise reply as precisely and clearly as possible. No other Communist Party would tolerate the articles, declarations and speeches against revolutionary force, in the spirit of vapid and sentimental humanism, that one meets in the French Party press. Renaud Jean is absolutely justified in referring to the " gangrene " of bourgeois-democratic ideology. But, after all, the gravest consequence this has upon the working class is in blunting its revolutionary instinct and its will to offensive action, in dissolving the dynamic tendencies of the proletariat in the fog of hazy democratic perspectives. The humanistic twaddle of "The League of Rights of Man and Citizen " which at every critical hour, as everybody knows, crawls on all fours before French militarism ; the moralistic, Tolstoyan gospel of political vegetarians, etc., etc., however sharply it might differ on the surface from the official policy of the Third Republic, renders the latter, in the final analysis, the best possible services, and is a supplement to it. Vague pacifist agitation, veiled by socialist phraseology, is an excellent tool for the bourgeois regime. This might appear paradoxical to a sincere pacifist, but it is the truth.

Neither Poincaré nor Barthou will be confused or seduced by the pacifist tunes of George Pioch. But these psalmodies do find a fertile soil in the minds of a certain section of the toilers. Hostility toward the bourgeois order and toward military violence does find a sincere but sterile outlet in humanitarian formulas and becomes dissipated without ever crystallizing into action. This is exactly the social function of pacifism. This was most crassly disclosed in America where Bryan's gang[35] gained an enormous influence over the farmers precisely through the slogans of pacifism. Socialists of the Hillquit[36] type and other simpletons, who deem themselves to be super-clever, have fallen completely into the snare of middle-class pacifism and thereby facilitated America's entry into the war.

The task of the Communist Party is to awaken in the working class the readiness to apply force, and this requires teaching others how to differentiate reactionary force whose function is to detain history upon its already accomplished stages, from revolutionary force whose creative function and mission is to clear the path of history of all obstacles heaped up by the past. He who refuses to differentiate between these two types of force, does not know how to differentiate between classes, i.e., remains oblivious of living history. He who declaims against any and all militarism, any and all forms of violence, will ineluctably end up by supporting the violence of the rulers, because the latter is a fact, ratified and sealed by federal legislation, adopted and sanctified by the moral code.

To overthrow it, a different sort of violence is necessary, which must first of all conquer its legitimacy in the minds of the toilers themselves.

The last session of the ECCI[37] called attention to a number of other manifestations in the internal life of the French Party which testify that it is by no means the most irreconcilable party. And yet it must needs be such—this is demanded by the entire political milieu. In one thing we are in accord with Comrade Renaud Jean, namely: the application of the methods of the united front demands complete clarity and precision in the party's political consciousness, streamlined organization, perfect discipline.

Comrade Jean goes on to cite the fact that in the list of demands advanced as a platform for the united front (the struggle against wage taxes, the defense of the 8-hour day, etc.) he fails to find a single demand that might directly interest a good half of the toilers of France, i.e., the peasants. What meaning has the 8-hour day for them? Or taxes on wages?

This argument of Comrade Jean seems to us to be dangerous in the extreme. The question of the small peasants is undoubtedly of great importance to the French revolution. Our French Party has taken a big step forward by advancing an agrarian program and putting the conquest of the peasant masses on the agenda. But it would be dangerous in the extreme and truly fatal if the French proletariat were simply dissolved among the " toilers " or " workers," as a mere half of a single whole.   Today we embrace organizationally as well as politically only a minority of the French working class.   The revolution will become a possibility after we shall have politically conquered the majority.   Only the majority of the French working class, united under the banner of the revolution, can attract and lead behind it the small peasants of France.   In France the question of the united working-class front is the basic one!   Failing a solution of this question, work among the peasantry, no matter how successful, would not bring us closer to the revolution.   Propaganda among the peasantry and a good agrarian program constitute a very important factor for success.   But the peasantry happens to be hard-headed and skeptical; it places no faith in promises, especially in France, where it has been so often deceived.   The French peasant—in the village or in the army barracks—will not be drawn into a serious struggle by programmatic slogans.   He will incur a serious risk only if he sees such conditions as guarantee success, or at least render success extremely probable. He must behold before him a force which instils confidence in him by its massiveness and its disciplined character.   A working class that is split along political and trade union lines cannot loom as such a force in the eyes of the peasantry.   The premise for a victorious revolution in France is the attraction to the side of the working class of the broadest possible section of the peasantry.   But the premise for this attraction still remains the unification of the overwhelming majority of the French working class under the revolutionary banner.   This is the basic task.   It is necessary to win over the workers who today follow Jouhaux and Longuet.   It is futile to object that there are only a few of them.   Naturally the active supporters of Longuet, Blum, and Jouhaux, those who are self-sacrificing, that is, those ready to stake their lives for such a program, are insignificant in number.   But there are still a great many of those who are passive, ignorant, inert, lazy mentally and physically.   They remain on the sidelines, but should events touch them to the quick they will in their present condition sooner rally to the banner of Jouhaux-Longuet than to ours.   Because Jouhaux and Longuet both mirror as well as exploit the passivity, ignorance and backwardness of the working class.

If Comrade Jean, who is in charge of party work among the peasantry, pays disproportionate attention to the peasantry as against the proletariat, then this is vexing, but understandable ; and it is, after all, not so very dangerous because the party as a whole will correct him. But if the party adopted Comrade Jean's standpoint, and were to regard the proletariat as simply one "half" of the toilers, then truly fatal consequences would ensue because the revolutionary class character of the party would become dissolved in a formless " party of toilers ". This danger looms all the more distinctly in the light of Comrade Jean's subsequent line of thought. He flatly rejects such tasks of struggle as do not embrace all of the toilers, or as he puts it: " which do not include demands common to both of the major sections of the proletariat! ". The term " proletariat " here implies not only the proletariat but also the peasantry. This highly dangerous abuse of terminology leads in politics to Comrade Jean's attempt to place the demands of the proletariat (maintenance of the 8-hour day, defense of the wage scale, and so on) under the control of the peasantry!

The peasant is a petty bourgeois who can be drawn more or less closely to the proletariat and who, under certain conditions, can be more or less firmly won over by the proletariat for the revolutionary cause. But to identify the agrarian petty bourgeoisie with the proletariat and to curtail the demands of the proletariat to conform with the views of the small peasantry is to renounce the party's genuine class base and to sow that selfsame confusion for which the soil is so extremely favorable in peasant-parliamentarian France.

While the 8-hour day cannot, as we have heard, become a slogan of the united front in France because it is of " no interest " to the peasant, the struggle against militarism does, from Jean's standpoint, provide a genuine revolutionary program for France. There can be no doubt whatever that the French small peasant, duped by the war, is filled with hatred toward militarism, and responds sympathetically to anti-militarist speeches. Needless to say, we are under obligation to mercilessly expose capitalist militarism in city and country alike. The lesson of the war must be exploited to the utmost. It would, however, be extremely hazardous for the party to beguile itself with illusions about the extent to which peasant anti-militarism can acquire an *independent* revolutionary meaning. The peasant does not want to send his son to the barracks ; he does not want to pay taxes for the army's upkeep ; he sincerely applauds orators who talk against militarism (and even against " all militarisms "). However, peasant opposition to the army has not a revolutionary but a boycottist-pacifist lining. *"Fichez-moi la paix"* (let me alone) — that is the peasant's program! This mood can create a favorable atmosphere for the revolution, but it cannot create the revolution itself, nor assure its success.

Sentimental pacifism in the spirit of Pioch is the very expression of a peasant—but not proletarian—attitude toward the state and toward militarism. The organized and class-conscious proletariat confronted with the state, armed to the teeth, poses the question of how it, the proletariat, can best organize and arm itself for the abolition and destruction of bourgeois violence by means of its own dictatorship. An isolated peasant doesn't go that far; he is simply opposed to militarism, he hates it, he is ready to turn his back upon it—*fichez-moi la paix*! Don't bother me with ALL your militarisms! Such is the psychology of a disgruntled, oppositional peasant, of an intellectual or an urban petty bourgeois. It would be nonsensical not to exploit these moods among our possible petty-bourgeois and semi-proletarian allies but it would be criminal to transmit these moods to the proletariat and to our own party.

The social-patriots, because of their patriotism, find it difficult to reach the peasant. We must profit in every way by this advantage. But this in no case gives us the right to relegate the class proletarian demands to the background—even if we thereby incur the risk of provoking some temporary misunderstandings with our friends, the peasants. The small peasantry must follow the proletariat as it finds it. The proletariat cannot remodel itself after the peasantry. If the Communist Party were to circumvent the vital class demands of the proletariat and follow the line of least resistance, advancing pacifist anti-militarism to the fore, it would run the risk of deceiving the peasants and the workers—and itself.

In France as elsewhere what we need first of all is the united front of the proletariat itself. The French peasantry will not be converted into the proletariat by the fact that Comrade Jean takes the liberty to abuse sociological terminology. But the mere hankering for such an abuse is a dangerous symptom. It is symptomatic of a policy that can sow only the greatest confusion. French Communism more than any other needs clarity, precision and irreconcilability. At all events, on this point we are in accord with our French opponent.

April 29, 1922.

11

The Lessons of May Day

Genoa lays bare the contradiction between Soviet Russia and the rest of the world. Our enemies are convinced that we are today further from capitulation than ever before. But our enemies are still powerful. The danger, too, is great.

Truly monumental in their proportions were the May Day demonstrations not only in Moscow and Petrograd but also in Kharkov and Kiev. Even those in charge did not expect such great numbers of demonstrators. Foreigners, including those very unfavorably inclined toward us, were astounded. One representative of the Amsterdam International remarked under the direct impact of the demonstration that he never saw anything comparable except at the funeral of Victor Hugo[38]. And he had opportunities to witness not a few mass demonstrations in various European countries. The moods among the demonstrators, of course, varied; some marched with enthusiasm, some with sympathy, others out of curiosity, still others out of imitation. But that is always the case in a movement embracing hundreds of thousands. On the whole, the throngs felt themselves part of a common cause. And the tone was naturally set by those who marched with enthusiasm.

A few days prior to May Day, comrades reported from the districts that Genoa[39] had raised to an astonishing degree the political interests and the revolutionary self-confidence of the working masses. Others added that the feeling of revolutionary pride was playing an important part in the prevailing moods; we forced *them* to talk to us almost like human beings!

119

To believe the White Guard and "socialist" publications issued
in Berlin, the Russian working class is completely permeated with
skepticism, with reactionary pessimistic moods and hostility toward
the Soviets. It is quite possible that not all of these reports are
composed in Berlin which is now the center not only of Russian
monarchism but also of yellow socialism. It is quite possible that
some of these reports are even copied from nature. But each one
copies nature as he sees it. The Mensheviks approach everything in
nature from the rear, and that is how they copy it. There is no doubt
that in working-class neighborhoods there is discontent with various
aspects of today's hard life. We can also grant that the slow tempo
of the developing European revolution and the ponderous, full-of-
pitfalls process of our own economic development engender among
isolated, not purely proletarian but rather large circles of the working
class, moods of pessimism and disorientation, verging even on mys-
ticism. During weekdays—and our great epoch, too, has its weekdays
—the consciousness of the class becomes absorbed and distracted by
current cares and concerns ; the differences in the interests and views
among the various groups within the working class come to the forefront. But the very next major events completely reveal the profound
unity of the working class that has passed through the fiery school
of revolution. We had a chance to observe this on more than one
occasion on the long road from the Czechoslovak mutiny in the Volga
to the negotiations in Genoa. Our enemies have said more than once
that the Czechoslovak uprising proved quite beneficial to the Soviet
power. The Mensheviks, the Social Revolutionaries, and their older
brothers, the Cadets of the Miliukov[40] group, keep repeating that
military interventions are harmful precisely because the Soviet power
is strengthened as a result. But what does this mean? It means nothing
else than that all major and serious tests reveal the profound ties
between the Soviets and the toiling masses, despite the disorganization,
the effects of devastation, and the incompetence, despite the exhaustion of some and the discontent of others.

Naturally even a state that is already in conflict with social progress
can sometimes find itself strengthened at a moment of external danger.
We saw this in the case of Czarism during the first phase of the Russo-
Japanese War, and, on a still larger scale, at the beginning of the last
imperialist war. But this held true only for the first phase, i.e., only
until the consciousness of the popular masses was able to assimilate the

new fact. Then came the settling of scores: the obsolete regime lost
far more in stability than it was able to gain during the initial phase of
the war. Why then does this phenomenon, which has the universality
of a law, fail to manifest itself in the destiny of the Soviet Republic?
Why did three years' experience with military interventions impel
our more perspicacious enemies to renounce the idea of further military
assaults? For exactly the same reason that the Genoa Conference
has aroused enthusiasm among the working masses, producing the
unexpected, great demonstrations of May Day.

The Mensheviks and the Social Revolutionaries were, of course,
against the workers' marching, and they issued a call not to march.
All the more clearly was revealed how unanimous the toilers were
with regard to the basic questions involving the life of the Toilers'
Republic. It is of course possible to contend that repressions have
hindered and are hindering the success of the White Guardist and
yellow " Socialist " propaganda. This cannot be denied. But, after
all, the struggle itself comes down to this, that they seek to overthrow
the Soviet power, while the latter refuses to permit them to do it.
We feel positively under no obligation to provide more favorable
conditions for their counter-revolutionary struggle.

After all, the bourgeoisie nowhere strives to facilitate the conditions
for the work of the Communists, nevertheless the revolutionary movement has grown and continues to grow. Czarism had at its disposal
the mightiest apparatus of repressions, but this could not save it
from falling. Moreover, the Mensheviks themselves probably wrote
and said more than once that Czarist repressions only serve to spread
and to temper the revolutionary movement. And this was correct.
During the initial period of the Russo-Japanese imperialist war, Czarism was still able to stage patriotic demonstrations, even if only on a
very limited scale. But very soon the city streets began falling under
the sway of revolutionary crowds. The reference to repressions, consequently, explains nothing, for the question naturally arises: Why
are these repressions successful, while the struggle against them fails
to meet with success? And the answer reads: Repressions fail to
attain their aim whenever they are applied by an obsolete state power
against new and progressive historical forces. In the hands of a
historically progressive power, repressions can prove extremely effective in speeding the removal of out-dated forces from the historical
arena.

But since May Day has laid bare the closest internal bond between the toilers and the Soviet regime and, in passing, also the complete impotence of the parties of White Guards and " socialists," shouldn't one therefore conclude that repressions are unnecessary? Why not legalize impotence, even if it does happen to be mortally hostile to the workers' revolution?

This question, too, merits a completely clear reply. Had May Day been celebrated in the same way throughout the world, then the very question of repressions would never have arisen in Russia. The same thing would apply if Russia existed alone in this world. But, after all, the toilers on May Day come out so unanimously on the streets of Moscow and Petrograd, Kharkov and Kiev and other cities precisely because through Genoa they became more clearly and directly aware of their Workers' and Peasants' Russia standing alone against two-score bourgeois states. Within the national boundaries of Russia the Mensheviks and the S.R.'s are an insignificant magnitude. But on an international scale the relation of forces appears differently, because in power everywhere—in Europe and throughout the world— stand the bourgeoisie, and Menshevism serves as its transmitting political mechanism.

Russian Menshevism is itself insignificant, but it represents a lever of a still mighty system, whose driving force is the stock market in Paris, London, and New York. This was revealed with exceptional clarity in the case of Georgia. The Mensheviks, under Vandervelde's lead, demanded nothing less than the restoration of Menshevik Georgia. M. Barthou, the most reactionary of the French political profiteers, demanded that the former Menshevik Georgian government be invited to Genoa. And this same Barthou has a Wrangel detachment in reserve, in the event of an invasion of the Caucasian shores. And at bottom of it all is the stock market's greed for Caucasian oil.

Within the national boundaries the Mensheviks and the S.R.'s are insignificant. But within the boundaries of capitalist encirclement they were and remain the semi-political, semi-military agencies of imperialism, armed to its teeth. After the long stretch of weekdays, with the silent burrowing by both sides, Genoa has once again dramatically and dazzlingly revealed the contradiction between Soviet Russia and the rest of the world. That is why the toilers of our country have rallied so unanimously to the Soviet banners. This magnificent movement expressed the revolutionary power of the Republic, and also— the power of the dangers surrounding it. Today there are no fronts and no military hostilities, but we still remain a beleaguered fortress.

Our enemies have granted us an armistice and have asked us to send negotiators. Our enemies have probed us and have become convinced that today we are further from capitulation than ever before. But our enemies are still powerful. And this means that the danger is great, too. These are the lessons of May Day. Legitimately proud of our strength, we must not, in the future as well, abate our vigilance by an iota.

First published in **Pravda,**
Issue No. 102, May 10, 1922.

12

From the ECCI to the Central Committee of the French Communist Party (May 12, 1922)

I

Dear Comrades, the ECCI has been following with growing alarm the internal developments inside the French Communist Party and the policy pursued by it among the working masses.

The fact that the party has temporarily stopped growing numerically and has even lost a certain number of members would not in and by itself give rise to alarming conclusions.

The party took shape in the period of postwar revolutionary ferment, a period when hopes were high for a swift development of great revolutionary events. But when the movement proved to be slower in tempo, when the less conscious elements among the masses, i.e., the majority, perceived that the formation of the Communist Party did not imply immediately any drastic changes in the social structure, there was an unavoidable decline in interest in the Communist Party, and a certain section of proletarian and non-proletarian elements, who were swept toward the party by the mounting wave, began to draw away from it.

This lag, conditioned by the logic of events, could and should have aided in cleansing, consolidating and strengthening the party's principles and organizations. But this could have occurred only on one condition, namely, if the party's basic core, first and foremost its Central Committee, had conducted a precise and firm policy. But the ECCI is not cognizant of any such policy. The party is becoming neither more fused nor more homogeneous on the basis of its revolutionary program. On the contrary, it is more amorphous today than ever before. Any weakening of the revolutionary concentration inside the party brings about an increase in the pressure from without, i.e., pressure of bourgeois public opinion. The right wingers, that is, the non-Communist and opportunist party elements, whose actual number is small and who are weak ideologically, tend to acquire under these conditions an ever-growing influence, because through them bourgeois public opinion transmits its pressure upon a party which lacks the necessary unity and firmness to resist external influences.

This alarming situation in the party found crass expression in the case of Fabre and his newspaper. It is clear to every Communist that Fabre's newspaper is absolutely alien and hostile to the spirit of the Communist International. Furthermore this paper is nothing but a private venture by an individual who poses under false pretenses as a member of the Communist Party. Our party's citadel—which is on all sides beleaguered by the bourgeoisie, and such an obdurate and evil one as the victory-flushed French bourgeoisie—has in it a door open to the enemies, through which sneak in spies and other elements who poison and demoralize the party ranks.

As experience has frequently demonstrated, newspapers of this sort find easy access—directly or indirectly—to the party and trade union bureaucracy. Day by day the poison takes effect imperceptibly, all the more so because it is cloaked by the party's banner. And at the decisive moment of the conflict the consciousness and the will of a considerable majority of party organizations, namely, the party cadres, will prove to have been poisoned and paralyzed by the venom of petty-bourgeois skepticism. The party mass, together with the working class as a whole, will find itself rendered impotent and as if beheaded, in the face of great events ; unless attention is paid to this process in time, it can prove fatal to a revolutionary party in the preparatory period.

For these considerations, the enlarged Plenum of the ECCI declared categorically two months ago that the question of *Journal du Peuple*, regardless of its editor's personality, constituted one of the most dangerous and negative aspects in the party's life. And at the present moment we affirm with growing alarm that despite the unanimous warning of the International, the party's leading bodies are still unable to understand this danger and have not resorted to drastic measures to burn out this wound with a red-hot iron. Instead of mercilessly attacking *Journal du Peuple*, the party press simply keeps mum. Instead of posing the question of this newspaper in its full political scope, which would make it possible to dispose of the newspaper in twenty-four hours because the case is perfectly clear politically, the Central Committee of the party, proceeding completely counter to the decisions of the Enlarged Plenum and the pledge made by the French delegation, has reduced the entire question to a purely formal procedural inquiry and has thus prevented the party from getting a clear picture of the case and of the International's demand. To point out to the vanguard of the French proletariat the danger threatening it, the ECCI was compelled first to issue a warning, next to ask compliance with the regulations, and finally to invoke Article 9 of the International's statutes and to expel Fabre and his newspaper from the party, underscoring the full political significance of this step.

II

While the Right Wing has, by exploiting the chronic indecisiveness of the leading party bodies, acquired a disproportionate importance in the life of the French Party, we fail to see these leading party bodies concentrating their attention upon their basic task, namely, the political conquest of the working masses organized in the trade unions or still remaining outside them. We do see that on the pretext of maintaining good relations with the trade unions or the syndicalists, the party keeps systematically making concessions to them on all the basic issues, thus surrendering positions and clearing the way for the most extreme anti-Communist elements among syndicalism and anarchism. We see party members continuing to conduct in the trade union movement an insolent and provocative propaganda against the Communist International. Exploiting the theoretical weakness of syndicalism, they carry out within the trade unions their own private, sectarian policy, and install an irresponsible, oligarchic regime, beyond control and without a program. The party capitulates before each attack of these political opponents who are using the banner of Communism in order to inescapably bring the trade union movement to decomposition and ruin. To continue to ignore this main danger is to permit subversive work against French Communism for many years to come.

Should the party fail to understand that the trade union movement is incapable of solving its main tasks without the aid of Communism, without the party's leading and influencing the Communist members inside the trade unions, then the party will inevitably have to yield its place in the working class and, above all, in the trade unions to the anarchist muddlers and adventurers. The party can win influence over the trade unions only in an open ideological struggle against anarchist muddlers, oligarchic cliques and adventurists. The party must assume the offensive all along the line ; it must expose and criticize all muddling and all muddlers ; it must place all the Communists in the trade unions under its control, educating them in the spirit of strictest discipline, and mercilessly ejecting from its ranks all those who dare use autonomy as a pretext for continuing their debilitating work in the trade union movement.

It is self-evident that in fulfilling this task the party ought to reject forms of agitation and propaganda which are likely to repel syndicalists in whom the revolutionary spirit is becoming imbued, and, all the more so, the broad layers of unionized workers who have not yet rid themselves of political prejudices. It is one thing to take a prudent attitude toward such elements and to educate them ; it is something again to capitulate passively to the anarchists who are exploiting these elements for their own ends. At all events the necessary condition for success in this field is a firm desire to gain success. To this end the party must enforce the strictest control, with all the ensuing consequences, namely, expulsions of those pseudo-Communists who henceforth make so free as not to submit to the decisions of the International and all the more so those who act directly counter to these decisions. In this connection the ECCI expects the Central Committee to take firm and resolute steps which will give the International a genuine guarantee that its decisions are enforced, a guarantee which will free the ECCI of any need of again intervening directly in the organizational tasks and questions, the solution of which ought to be the the business of the Central Committee of our French section.

On the other hand, the ECCI declares that the dilatory tactic of evading and vacillating on life-and-death party questions has already been amply tested and has led only to negative results. For this reason the ECCI will permit no further delays in this sphere.

III

On the question of the united front we see the very same passive and irresolute tendency, but this time masked by verbal irreconcilability. At the very first glance, one is hit between the eyes by the following paradox: the Rightist party elements with their centrist and pacifist tendencies, who overtly or covertly support *Journal du Peuple*, come simultaneously to the forefront as the most irreconcilable opponents of the united front, covering themselves with the banner of revolutionary intransigence. In contrast, those elements who have right up to the Tours Convention held in the most difficult hours the position of the Third International are today in favor of the tactic of the united front.

As a matter of fact, the mask of pseudo-revolutionary intransigence is now being assumed by the partisans of the dilatory and passive tactic. They do not understand that today when the working class is divided into different camps we cannot in any case permit workers to replenish the ranks of the Dissident, reformist, anarchist and other camps. We need politically aggressive initiative in order to disorganize the ranks of our conservative opponents who maintain themselves in the labor movement only thanks to lack of initiative on our part in the sphere of propaganda. The very same traits of indecision and passivity which caused us to suffer big losses in the trade union movement have in recent months cropped up on the question of the united front. It was interpreted and presented in the organs of our French Party in an absolutely false way.

Moreover, although this question was seriously discussed for several weeks, resulting in the adoption of this tactic by the overwhelming majority of the Comintern at the Enlarged Plenum of the ECCI, we nevertheless see the leading body and the organs of the French Party pursuing a tactic absolutely incompatible with both the spirit of the Communist International as well as its statutes. Declarations of " submitting to discipline " seem to serve only as a prelude to more open and systematic violations of this discipline. Despite the specific decisions that have been adopted, the party organs such as *l'Humanité* and *Internationale* carry on, in their official articles, that is, in the party's name, an irreconcilable campaign against the united front. Since both nationally and internationally the issue has passed from the stage of discussion into the stage of action, the polemical articles of the French Communist press constantly supply our enemies with ammunition. This is no longer a discussion, but sabotage of the cause.

The ECCI discerns in these facts the worst vestiges of the spirit of the Second International ; the decisions of the latter's world congresses are purely decorative and are no embarrassment whatever to the tactics of the various national sections who place their " national " considerations above the interests of the revolution and the tasks of the International. A continuation of such impermissible violations of discipline in an international action is unavoidably bound to provoke resolute resistance by the International as a whole as well as by its national sections, who will be compelled to call the French section to order and demand that it submit to discipline.

The ECCI considers that in accordance with the spirit and statutes of the Third International, the Central Committee of the French Party is obliged to assure the leading party organs such a composition and form as will convert them into organs for clarifying, defending and realizing in life the resolutions of the Comintern and not for waging a struggle against them. In this connection the ECCI expects perfectly clear and precise guarantees for the future.

IV

We cannot leave unmentioned the ambiguity which exists in the relations between the Central Committee of the French Party and the ECCI. Not only that single question on which the French delegation voted against at the Third World Congress and at the Enlarged Plenum of the ECCI, but also all the decisions adopted with the complete agreement of all the French delegates, have been depicted as though they have been dictated to the party and imposed upon it from the outside and are being complied with by the party only as a pure formality. For example, all the members of the French delegation agreed in complete unanimity with the Enlarged Plenum that it was indispensable to restore the Central Committee mandates of those comrades who tendered their resignations at the Marseilles Convention. This decision pursued a political aim of the highest importance: the securing of complete unanimity in the functioning of the Central Committee, as well as of the party as a whole. This aim can be achieved only if it is made clear to the party that it is not a question of any sort of personal combinations nor of the personal ambitions of this or that individual, but of creating the organizational premises for complete unanimity in work. The political significance of this question should have been clarified lucidly and precisely in leading articles of the party press and at the party's National Conference. Nothing of the sort was done. Everything was reduced to a pure formality of a show of hands, prepared behind the scenes, that is, behind the party's back, without any explanatory articles or speeches. Had anyone set himself the goal of attaining results diametrically counter to those pursued by the Enlarged Plenum of the ECCI, then such an individual would have behaved exactly as the Central Committee did in this particular instance.

It is perfectly clear that such an approach cannot fail to produce and reinforce among the heterogeneous mass of the French Party an impression that the International or " Moscow " is in the habit of issuing *incomprehensible* and unmotivated ultimatums, political and organizational in character, to which the Central Committee of the French Party submits out of disciplinary considerations while at the same time skillfully making its negative attitude to the International's proposals known to the party rank and file. An atmosphere is thus created which is highly propitious for the intriguers and political horse-traders grouped around *Journal du Peuple*.

V.

Finally, it is of interest to review the history of the relations between the ECCI and the Central Committee. From it we shall see that the misunderstandings and mistakes at no time emanated from the ECCI.

The French Party sent to the Third World Congress at Moscow a delegation of eleven members, representing all the different shadings in the party at the time. This delegation took extensive part in the work of the Congress and of the ECCI. The decisions pertaining to the French Party adopted by the ECCI were discussed with and were unanimously adopted by the French delegation, in particular the decision wherein the ECCI proposed that the French Party institute control over the party press, as is done by all the other Communist parties.

To the surprise of the ECCI, the Central Committee for a long time ignored this decision and the evil which the ECCI had pointed out continued to exist and to grow stronger in the French Party. For this reason the ECCI insisted on the adoption in principle of the control of the party press. After a six months' delay, this principle was finally adopted, but nothing was actually done to carry it out in life.

After the Third World Congress, the ECCI submitted various proposals concerning the French Communist movement to the Central Committee. In addition, Comrades Zinoviev and Trotsky wrote letters to the most prominent members of the French Party in order to facilitate by such friendly correspondence mutual understanding and fraternal collaboration.

In the same spirit the ECCI repeatedly invited Comrades Frossard and Cachin to make a trip to Moscow in order to discuss in person the most important questions of the Communist movement in France.

Unwilling to let slip any opportunity for establishing cordial relations with the leaders of the French Party and in the absence of a favorable reply to its invitations, the ECCI sent a delegate to Paris who was to acquaint himself with the situation and present the viewpoint of the International to the Central Committee.

Toward the end of last year the ECCI managed to get another French comrade assigned to Moscow, and in this way learned the manner in which the Central Committee would like to establish its relations with the International. The ECCI gave its reply in a resolution, which in turn, requested an answer from the Central Committee. This answer was not forthcoming.

The ECCI took advantage of the convening of the Marseilles Convention in order to send an open letter to the French Party, containing among other comments on the state of affairs in the French Party certain critical judgments, made in a friendly and frank spirit, as is customary in International relations among Communists. This letter also requested a precise answer on the questions of discipline and control of party newspapers. Unfortunately the ECCI received no answer either to this letter or to a second and more detailed letter sent to the Central Committee.

Let us also recall that by the time of the Marseilles Convention the ECCI had sent a second delegate to the Central Committee whose stay in France was intended to straighten out all the differences of opinion and to facilitate the establishment of regular connections in the future.

After the Marseilles Convention, for purposes of clarification and of establishing its relations with the French section on a precise basis, the ECCI counted upon Comrade Frossard's coming to Moscow, in accordance with the decision adopted in October by the Central Committee.

The ECCI persistently invited the party secretary to come, in view of the extreme importance of the questions that had to be settled. The ECCI considered, as it still does, that such a direct exchange of opinion is the most expedient way of strengthening the ties between the International and the French section.

The Central Committee never presented objections of a political character to the ECCI, except on the question of the united front. In cases where the decisions of the Enlarged ECCI were carried out in life, this, as we saw on the question of the resignees resuming their posts in the Central Committee, was done in such a purely passive way as if only to underscore a hostile attitude toward the substance of the decision adopted on this question.

The ECCI deems it absolutely impossible to maintain relations of this sort in the future. It proposes that the Central Committee of the French section of the International take clearly into account the motives—unexpressed to this day—which lie at the bottom of such conduct, and also the grave consequences which must necessarily ensue if the tactic of evasion, now practiced in relations between Paris and Moscow, is not replaced by open and revolutionary sincerity.

The Executive Committee
of the Communist International

Moscow, May 12, 1922.

13

French Communism and the Position of Comrade Rappoport

Today the most important question before the entire Communist International is undoubtedly the internal situation in our French Party. Processes that demand the greatest possible attention are taking place within it. Future historians will relate how difficult it was for the proletarian party of an old " republican " and " cultured " country, weighed down by traditions of a parliamentary and opportunist past, to adjust itself to a new historical situation. Those are utterly mistaken who believe or say that because France is a victorious country, no revolutionary situation allegedly exists there and that this is precisely the explanation for the signs of crisis in the French Communist movement. In reality the situation, if one probes deeply enough, is profoundly revolutionary in character. The international position of France is extremely unstable and packed with contradictions. This is the source of inescapable and ever-sharper crises. The country's financial condition is catastrophic and this financial catastrophe cannot be averted except through measures of a sweeping social character, which are positively beyond the powers of the ruling class. France's entire postwar state regime, first and foremost, her militarism and her colonial ambitions, do not correspond to her economic base. One can say that France's position as a great power threatens to crush the country under its weight. The toiling masses are disenchanted in their national illusions; they are discouraged, discontented, angry. The National Bloc, which skimmed the political cream of victory, is running to waste before our very eyes. French Radicalism as well as social-patriotism squandered their basic resources as far back as the war. Should the Radical-Reformist regime (Caillaux-Thomas-Blum) supersede the regime of the National Bloc, it would hardly be for a longer span than that required by the

133

Communist Party for definitively preparing itself to fulfill its basic task.
The objective premises for the revolution and the subjective premises
for revolutionary policy are thus at hand, and if anything does lag
behind, it is the internal evolution of the party.

In this sense the case of Fabre is profoundly symptomatic. Having
broken in principle with nationalistic and reformistic ideology, the
Communist Party keeps extending hospitality in its ranks to one of
the vulgar condottieres of journalism who sets up at his own risk
and for his private profit an unprincipled newspaper enterprise and
after affixing a Communist emblem over his door, he, in turn, extends
the broadest hospitality to reformists, nationalists, pacifists, anarchists,
on this sole condition: that they wage war against the Communist
International. This incredible scandal dates back to the day the Communist Party was founded, and has assumed increasingly open and
demoralizing forms. More than this, the most influential members of
the party's Central Committee have collaborated with Fabre's newspaper; and when the International urged them to cease and desist
from collaboration, they did so in tenderest lyrical terms. There are of
course oracles who have informed us that we "exaggerate" the importance of this fact. We consider these oracles to be simpletons and
dawdlers, if not something worse, and that is, the conscious promoters
of Fabre's clique as a "useful" counterweight to the Left Wing.
The ECCI has shown on this, as on all other internal questions of
French Communism, the greatest caution, offering advice, patiently
waiting for answers and actions, formulating proposals jointly with
the French comrades, waiting for the fulfillment of these proposals,
sending new reminders, and waiting some more, until it finally saw
itself compelled to invoke Article 9 of the statutes and to expel
Fabre from the International. Let us hope that Comrade Rappoport[41],
who is now in Moscow, does not challenge the right and the duty
of the International to decide who can and who cannot hold membership in its ranks. Fabre is not one of us; Fabre has nothing in
common with us; he is an out-and-out enemy. For this very simple
reason, which will be excellently understood by every French worker,
Fabre has been expelled from the International. And anyone who
supports Fabre or solidarizes with him is by this very token automatically liable to expulsion from our ranks. Or does Comrade Rappoport perhaps doubt the expediency of this decision or its time-
liness?

Comrade Rappoport demands in *Izvestia* a prudent attitude toward

the French labor movement. What does this mean? Anyone in the
know will perceive a hint in these words. Unfortunately, only a hint.
We would prefer an open criticism and clear statements of just what
Comrade Rappoport wants and what he does not want. Assuredly
this is not the season for hints and circumlocutions, especially if we
take into account the fact that Comrade Rappoport is a member of
the Central Committee of the French Communist Party.

A few sentences earlier, Rappoport states that it would be incorrect
to draw excessively " pessimistic conclusions " about the French labor
movement. " The revolutionary masses of France," he says, " are
healthy." Again there is a hint. Who is it that draws these pessimistic conclusions and has doubts about the health of the French
revolutionary masses? And who is it that approaches the French
labor movement without sufficient prudence?

The French movement, it must be recognized, has " a right to a
certain independence," says Rappoport. Again, something is left
unsaid. Why only the French movement? Doesn't this apply to all
the national sections of the International as well? Can it really be
that the International illegally impinges—when and where—upon the
independence of the French labor movement? Why hint? Why
make half-statements? Why not better say clearly and positively
wherein the International fails to evince a sufficiently prudent attitude
toward the French labor movement and just where it violated the
necessary independence of French Communism? It is possible to
arrive at agreement only if all the disputed questions are posed
candidly and clearly.

The whole trouble, however, is that Comrade Rappoport's approach
to the question is too sweeping. The rather specific responsibility of
specific party bodies, of specific newspapers, individuals, editors and
leaders is transferred by him to the party as a whole and, finally, to
the labor movement as a whole. No one disputes that the party has
its roots in the movement, while the Central Committee has its roots
in the party. But this does not in the least free the Central Committee and its individual members from responsibility for their own
policies. No one else but the Central Committee of the party has
up to recently evinced an absolutely incomprehensible tolerance
toward a hostile publication, imbedded in the party's body. The
responsibility for this falls upon that very core of the Central Committee of which Comrade Rappoport is a member. In our opinion
—and we want to say this candidly—it is precisely Rappoport and

his co-thinkers who evince an insufficiently prudent attitude toward French Communism and the labor movement as a whole by permitting irresponsible groups to engage in artificially grafting opportunism onto the Communist Party and preparing for the latter's drawing closer to and merging with the opportunist-Dissidents, through the maneuver of isolating its Left Wing. The revolutionary masses of France are healthy ; but this does not at all mean that their health remains unaffected by the errors of the Central Committee, of which Comrade Rappoport is a member. Once again it is necessary to say flatly: Rappoport and his co-thinkers pause irresolutely before Fabre's enterprise not because they deem it too insignificant but, on the contrary, because they fear lest Fabre's expulsion precipitate an unavoidable " crisis " among the leading party circles. But thereby they reveal an extremely pessimistic attitude toward the party ; they assume that the source of and the condition for the party's successes is the preservation of the *status quo* at the top, and not the liberation of the rank and file from cliques they have no need for and which only act as a deterrent.

That the French Communist Party requires independence—on this score the International, to tell the truth, needs no reminders. But this independence is required for action. Yet Comrade Rappoport and his co-thinkers are artificially propping up among the party tops a combination of forces that excludes the possibility of action. Or to put it more accurately, the line of the policy which runs between Rappoport and Verfeuil[42] *is not the line of Communist action.* Herein is the nub of the matter. Hence the ailments, hence the symptoms of a grave crisis.

The blow dealt by the Communist International to the Fabre clique means that the Central Committee must seek to orient itself not through adapting itself to the Right Wing, but through harmonious collaboration with the Left Wing. The combination of forces which will give the resultant for party policy must pass not to the right of Comrade Rappoport but to his left, and moreover, if our guest will permit us, considerably, very considerably to his left. The sooner and more decisively the necessary change of course is achieved at the top, all the more easily will the crisis be overcome, all the less will the rank and file pay for the recovery and consolidation of the party. All the efforts of the ECCI are now being directed to this end. The representatives of all the Communist parties are following the developments in the French Party very closely and in full awareness of their responsibility for each of their steps. And we do not for a moment doubt that the International will succeed in shifting the line of the party leadership to the left, in complete accord with the needs, thoughts and feelings of the party's rank and file. Moreover, we do not doubt that the majority of the leading comrades among the grouping to which Comrade Rappoport himself belongs will support all the latest steps of the International designed to protect the French labor movement against far graver and malignant crises in the future. The revolutionary French working masses are healthy. The party is straightening out its line, entirely and exclusively to be in accord with them.

May 23, 1922.

14

To Comrade Ker

Dear Comrade Ker[45], Your letter of May 27 arrived today on June 3, which is really a record time under the conditions that have persisted since the war of "liberation". Unfortunately I am far from able to solidarize with your appraisal of what is taking place in our French Party, and I consider it my duty to reply to your friendly letter with an equally friendly frankness.

1. The lack of definiteness and the equally inadequate ideological and organizational clarity of French Communism does not emanate from below but from above. The French working class in its dual quality of both *a working class* and *a French* working class is seeking clarity, definitiveness, perfection and resoluteness. To the extent that it failed to find these in the old party, it created a footing for revolutionary syndicalism. To the extent that the leadership of the Communist Party today divests itself too slowly of the heritage of the past, to that extent the French working class is threatened with a relapse into revolutionary syndicalism. As is always the case with historical relapses, the positive features of prewar revolutionary syndicalism wane to zero while its negative features wax in the extreme. Let me repeat, the lack of clarity emanates not from below but from above. Its source is constituted by editors, journalists, deputies, whose mutual relations and whose ties are rooted in the past. Hence flows the extreme indecisiveness of the Central Committee on all questions involving newspapers, newspapermen, and so on (the Fabre incident).

2. I am very much surprised by your reproaches in connection with the expulsion of Fabre. The ECCI intended to expel Fabre as far back as its plenary session. It refrained only because the French delegation assumed responsibility for carrying out the expulsion summarily (in the Commission on which I served as chairman, four weeks were definitely set as the maximum). Subsequently, an amendment was inserted into the text of the resolution which was utterly unex-

138

pected by us: the phrase "*Journal du Peuple* is placed outside the party" was altered to read "*Journal du Peuple* is placed outside the control of the party." This amendment was obviously designed to palliate the expulsion at a time when the Comintern clearly intended to invest the expulsion with an open, demonstrative and sharp political character. Delays and obstructions thereupon ensued which were in direct and flagrant violation of the obligation which had been assumed by the French delegation in the name of the Central Committee. In her report, Comrade Leiciague declared that she had nothing to say concerning the outcome of the Control Commission's findings. *The party press did not carry a single article in this connection.* In particular I cannot conceal from you how surprised I and other comrades were that there appeared no articles *by you,* Comrade Ker, explaining to the French workers the political meaning behind the expulsion from the party of Fabre and his newspaper as a nest of infection. Isn't it an astonishing and at the same time an alarming fact that the leading party publications carry no articles explaining and defending the decisions of the Comintern? Doesn't this convert all speeches about discipline, blood ties, etc., into sheer formality? Modigliani[44] used to say that affiliation with the Comintern meant sending Italian picture post cards from time to time. But precisely for this reason Modigliani has placed himself outside the Communist International. How is it possible to support such conduct as this, that after decisions are adopted with the approval of the French delegation, these decisions are then sabotaged in action and are not even defended formally in the party press?

The Comintern had not only the right but the duty to show the French workers that it is a functioning, centralized organization with a political will of its own. Today the question is posed sharply and clearly. The expulsion of Fabre is a political fact. In spite of the personal insignificance of Fabre, his expulsion is of the greatest significance. The Comintern has by this action signaled to the French Party that it confronts internal dangers and that delays in solving internal problems imply heading for ever sharper crises.

3. Nor am I able to discern any progress in the sphere of the trade union question. On the contrary, we witness here an uninterrupted retreat by the party. Verdier, Quinton[45] and others have exploited the party's authority in order to intrench thmselves in the trade union movement and then they kicked the party aside. Articles in *l'Humanité* defend the Jauresist tendency in the trade union ques-

tion, that is, a tendency directly counter to the tendency which was adopted by the Comintern and which was set down, although not firmly enough, in the resolutions of the Marseilles Convention. Politics, like nature, abhors a vacuum. You are evacuating positions in the trade union movement at a time when the masses are looking for leadership. For this reason, syndicalists and libertarians are automatically occupying positions to which they have no ideological right whatever. And here we discern a dread of precipitating a crisis *among the top circles* of the trade union movement. A few principled, clear and firm leading articles in *l'Humanité* are a hundred times more important than behind-the-scenes agreements with the CGTU. On such questions as the trade union question it is impermissible for leading activists to play the role of prima donnas, each with his own point of view. We have the strict and precise decisions of the Comintern and of the French Party itself. These decisions must be carried out, and whoever violates these fundamental decisions must be expelled from the party, otherwise we shall unavoidably breed adventurers of the Verdier-Quinton type.

4. I cannot at all accept the appraisal made by Comrade Rosmer as too " pessimistic." From Paris I received from him a single letter, which reached Moscow—let me note this in passing in order to forestall any false conclusions—ten days after the ECCI adopted its decisions on the French question. Comrade Rosmer thus did not exert the slightest influence upon the adoption of these decisions. But in Rosmer's letter I found afterward a supplementary confirmation that the unanimously adopted decisions of the ECCI were unconditionally correct.

Let me say in passing that I see no " pessimism " either in Rosmer's views or my own. One the contrary, I detect far more pessimism, dear Comrade Ker, in your own attitude toward the French Party. You apparently consider that it is necessary to employ the same tactic in relation to the French Party as one would in relation to a gravely sick person, namely, speak in whispers, walk only on tiptoe, etc., etc. We, on the other hand, consider that the French Party is, in its basic proletarian core, profoundly healthy, revolutionary, and striving eagerly toward greater definiteness and greater decisiveness in leadership.

5. On the question of the united front I cannot, unfortunately, change my appraisal of the situation either. The hue and cry raised over this question by our French Party press serves only to distract

attention from the truly acute and unpostponable questions of the party's internal life. I cite living proof: Comrade Daniel Renoult[46] publishes the super-opportunistic pacifist articles of Verfeuil, Pioch and Meric, allows Meric to quote sympathetically from *Journal du Peuple*, never criticizes the absolutely treacherous line of the Fabre clique, and expresses constant concern lest Frossard conduct negotiations with Scheidemann and Vandervelde, as power to power[47]. We are all of the impression that for his intransigence Comrade Renoult has a broad arena much closer home, above all his own newspaper. But he prefers to transfer his intransigence to Berlin. The International did not impose upon the French Communist Party any kind of concrete agreement with the Dissidents ; no danger whatever threatened in this connection, but in the meantime the internal Dissidents (the Fabre clique, the cliques *à la* Verdier, Quinton, *et al*) are actually undermining the party, depriving it of its physiognomy, paralyzing its will, and not meeting with any rebuffs.

Certain comrades say that we " over-estimate " the importance of these phenomena. We reply, the fact that leading comrades fail to *estimate properly* the menace implicit in these phenomena is a most dangerous fact.

6. In my opinion the situation inside the French Party is critical. Two paths of future development are possible:

(a). A firm and clear internal course: ejection of the clique of Right-Wing strikebreakers in order to demonstrate that the party has no intention of joking about discipline ; genuine leadership by the party's Central Committee, and a genuine fulfillment of the decisions of the Communist International. This is the healthiest and most desirable path.

(b). A continuation of the indefinite policy by the leading center group, tending toward an isolation of the Left Wing; boundless tolerance toward all manifestations of pacifism, reformism and nationalism inside the party along with an ostensible and fictitious intransigence on questions of international scope, plus the absence of a firm and resolute line on the trade union question. This path automatically leads to a repetition of the Italian experience, that is, to a split in which the Center remains with the Right Wing, while the Left Wing crystallizes into a Communist Party. In Italy this path was produced by the mighty upheaval of the September revolution and its defeat (1920). In France, on the other hand, enriched by the Italian experience, such a path can be produced only by the continued fatalistic passivity of the central leading group. Naturally, even in this least desirable variant, the party will in the long run emerge onto the highway. The inevitable subsequent " regroupings " among the proletariat (to which our French press refers from time to time, but unfortunately very vaguely) will be oriented to the left and not to the right. Politicians who act under the immediate influence of isolated lags and ebbs are impressionists and not revolutionists, and they will be swept aside by the march of events. The party can and must orient itself only upon the further accumulation of revolutionary contradictions. A selection of individuals and their tempering is urgently needed. Events demand of us maximum assurance, maximum concentration of forces, maximum resoluteness. The decisions of the Comintern are dictated by a desire to assist the French Party in attaining these qualities within the shortest time possible.

Let me repeat yet once again. I write with complete frankness because I consider that too much has already been let slip and too much is at stake.

I warmly shake your hand,

L. TROTSKY.

Moscow, June 6, 1922.

Resolution of the ECCI on the French Communist Party (June 11, 1922)[48]

15

(ADOPTED ON THE REPORT OF COMRADE TROTSKY)
Program, Tactics, Statutes.

The most important task before the coming French Party convention is the adoption of a program, tactics and statutes in complete consonance with the party's tasks in the present epoch preparatory to the social revolution. It is necessary to proceed immediately to elaborate corresponding drafts and to publish them both in the organs of the French Party as well as in the organs of the entire International, so that the knowledge and experience of all Communist parties and of the ECCI may be drawn into the discussion and elaboration of basic documents which will assure the complete fusion and combat capacity of the party of the French working class.

The Party's Structure.

The Central Committee. The creation of a homogeneous Central Committee, capable of assuring party leadership on the basis of the decisions of International and national Communist Congresses, must be carefully prepared right now, and then submitted to the next party convention.

It must be recognized as unconditionally indispensable that more than half of the members of the Central Committee be composed of workers really tied up with the masses.

All members of the Central Committee are obliged to devote themselves full-time either to party work or to trade union work ; or they must be workers whose trade binds them with the life of the working masses. Selecting candidates in line with these conditions, checking up on their past, and on their political stability, and making them known in one form or another to local party organizations—all this

143

is the most important part of the preparatory work which naturally falls upon all those members of the present Central Committee who base themselves completely on the resolutions of the Comintern and who want to assure their being carried out organizationally.

In a Central Committee with such a composition, the majority of its members will embody the ties between the Central Committee and the local organizations, the trade unions, the press, etc. At the same time a permanently functioning Political Bureau must be selected from among the personnel of the Central Committee. This body shall reside in Paris; gather in its hands all the threads of leading party work; prepare all the necessary material for elucidating the most principled and important decisions of the full Central Committee; and see to it that these decisions are realized in life by the General Secretary of the Central Committee.

Discipline.

The Central Committee must be empowered to eject from the party any member or any group, in every instance where this is warranted by the situation and by political considerations.

In cases which require a thorough investigation of violation of discipline or other acts and crimes against party interests, the Central Committee may refer the question to the Committee on Conflicts and Grievances.

But in cases where the political character of the question is beyond dispute and where the elementary interests of the party demand expulsion, the Central Committee itself acts on the expulsion and its decision can be appealed only to the party convention.

The Seine Federation.

The Seine organization is of extraordinary importance to the destiny of French Communism and, consequently, to world Communism. Proceeding from this appraisal the International deems it necessary to call upon the Communists in the Seine Federation as well as in our French Party as a whole to make a drastic change in the foundations on which the Seine organization is built today.

The federalistic principle is completely incompatible with the actual interests of the revolutionary organization. References to the federative constitution of the Soviet Republic must be recognized as false to the core, because the organization of the Communist Party cannot be identified with the organization of the Soviet State. In all the

Federated Republics the Communist Party is unified and rigidly centralized. Communists in the Ukraine, in Georgia, in Azerbaijan and elsewhere are linked with Communists in Moscow, Petersburg and so on, not by elements of federalism but by elements of strictest democratic centralism. Only thanks to the unity of this centralized organization of the working class was Soviet Russia able to defend herself in the struggle against her countless enemies. The International categorically warns against the application of the principles of federalism and autonomy inside a revolutionary party which must be the mighty lever of revolutionary action.

To place a committee of a hundred members at the head of party organization is to actually deprive the organization of any consistent and firm leadership.

In consonance with the organizational principles of the Communist International, the Seine organization must have at its head a committee small in number, whose members are elected on the principle of democratic centralism and who are unconditionally responsible for the political and organizational leadership of the Seine organization.

At the same time, in view of the above-mentioned extraordinary importance of the Seine organization, it must be recognized as absolutely necessary for two or three members of the Central Committee to likewise serve as members of the Seine Committee (either by the election to the Central Committee of corresponding workers of the Seine organization or by inclusion of Central Committee members in the Seine Committee by a special decision of the Central Committee). This will assure the necessary ties between the leading party center and its most important organization.

The Trade Union Question.

The International affirms that the greatest danger to the French working class and especially to the trade union movement is represented by individualistic, petty-bourgeois elements, hostile to the spirit of proletarian discipline and artful in dodging all organizational control over their activities. In the person of Verdier, Quinton and others, we see a type of activists who under a smoke screen of phrases about trade union autonomy organize their own tiny cliques inside the unions and seek to seize the leadership of the movement, without offering the organized working class any guarantees not only of a correct leadership but even of ordinary loyalty to the interests of labor. The activity of petty-bourgeois individualists of this type is all the more dangerous since they, like the' Verdiers, Quintons and the rest, worm their way even into the ranks of our party. And while cloaking themselves with its authority, but without submitting to its control, they carry on profoundly demoralizing work, counterposing the trade unions to the party and poisoning the reciprocal relations between them.

Having exploited for their own ends the hospitality of the party, these elements afterward cheerfully leave its ranks because the regime of ideological consistency, of discipline and responsibility, that is, the party regime, is alien to the spirit of these poachers upon the labor movement.

The International considers it the unconditional duty of all the advanced and conscious elements of the working class and, above all, of the leading bodies of the Communist Party, to wage merciless war against this manifestation and its culprits. The party itself must naturally be purged thoroughly and completely of the spiritual brothers of Verdier and Quinton, if any still remain in its ranks.

It is therefore necessary during the Saint Etienne Convention to identify and expose, with the collaboration of the Communist faction and of its bureau, those pseudo-Communists who regard both the party and the trade unions as an arena for the operation of irresponsible cliques. They must be mercilessly ejected from our ranks, lest in the future they cause the working class the same incalculable harm as they did in the past and do today.

*   *   *

Taking into cognizance the fact that there are Communists, members of the party, inside those trade unions which have remained in the CGT, it must be recognized as the unconditional duty of the party to maintain correct organizational ties with these comrades.

Communists inside the reformist trade unions must organize correctly functioning party cells, intimately bound up with the corresponding party bodies.

Independently of how the reciprocal relations between the CGT and the CGTU are finally resolved, and independently of the party's future conduct in its struggle against the reformists, the Communists must wage a struggle from the inside to win all the organs of the CGT.

The United Front.

The International affirms that the press and the leading bodies of the French Communist Party have given completely incorrect information to the party concerning the meaning and importance of the tactic

of the united front. The International simply sweeps aside the superficial judgments of journalists who strive to see a revival of reformism
where there is an enhancement in the method of struggle against
reformism.

The attempt to picture the formation of the Committee of Nine
as the creation of a leading body standing above the three Internationals, stems from a complete misunderstanding of the spirit and
character of the Communist International. To do so is to confound
the Communist International with the old and purely parliamentarian
reformist organizations, whose delegates and representatives climb on
the back of the organized working masses and dictate their will to
them. Given the character of the Communist International and the
spirit of proletarian discipline, the three delegates, assigned to the
Committe of Nine, constituted merely a provisional executive body
with a definite goal and under the unconditional control of the Comintern.

The most glorious page in the history of the French proletariat—
the Paris Commune—was nothing else but a bloc of all the organizations and shadings within the French working class, united against
the bourgeoisie. If, despite the establishment of the united front,
the Commune was quickly crushed, then the explanation for this is
above all to be found in the fact that the united front did not have
at its left flank a genuine révolutionary, disciplined and resolute organization, capable of quickly gaining leadership in the fire of events.

In just this sense the Commune was a workers' government—a bloc
of the working class parties and groupings, counterposed to the bourgeoisie. As a workers' government the Commune represented nothing
else but a stage toward the establishment of the socialist order. The
class conscious French proletariat need only profoundly ponder over
the experience of the Commune, in order to find in its own heroic
past all the necessary arguments in favor of the genuinely revolutionary
tactic of the united front, together with the demand for a workers'
government which flows from this tactic.

*   *   *

The idea of the " Left Bloc " under the present conditions can
corrupt a great many workers who have little or no political experience. The French Communist Party must bear in mind this perspective which represents a very serious danger. To the idea of the
" Left Bloc," in its entire day-to-day propaganda it must systematically
counterpose the idea of a bloc of all workers against the bourgeoisie.

It is self-understood that during elections the party must everywhere run its own Communist ticket, independent of all others.

Only such a tactic, persistently carried out in all spheres (economic, political, municipal, and so on), can reduce to a minimum the number of workers who might be sucked into the orbit of the "Left Bloc"; only such a tactic can extend the influence of the party over the circles of workers left untouched by it.

On the Party Press.

It is possible to raise the political and theoretical level of the mass of the party members only on one condition, namely: provided that the leading party press breaks completely with the habits and customs of bourgeois journalism, leaving its columns not at the disposal of this or that journalist expressing his own personal inclinations but at the disposal of the party which systematically and planfully transmits its own thoughts and its own will through its own journalists. To this end, leading editorials devoted to a principled and consistent elucidation of world events as well as of domestic economic and political life must appear unsigned, i.e., not as the opinion of individuals but as the voice of the party itself. The Central Committee through its corresponding bodies must constantly control and supervise the press, assigning it definite tasks which flow from the political situation; and thus assure complete harmony between the work of its press and its own work both inside the party as well as in the political struggle as a whole. In no case can there or should there appear in the guise of leading editorials, even if signed, articles that criticize decisions of the Communist International or of the French Party which have already been adopted and which must be carried out. If publication of such articles is deemed expedient by the leading party bodies for the sake of completely clarifying a question, then these articles may appear only as discussion articles, accompanied by a precise presentation by the editorial board of the already adopted party decisions on this question, and by a vigorous defense of these decisions in leading editorials.

The Question of Factions.

The International affirms that in the French Party, alongside of other manifestations of the crisis, there are observable symptoms that factions are being revived.

The extreme Right Wing of the party, whose point of concentration is the *Journal du Peuple*, gained an influence among leading party circles and in the party press which did not at all correspond to its actual ideological and political weight. The absence of decisive counter-measures by the Central Committee inexorably led to attempts to revive a Left Wing faction. In its turn, a struggle between these two factions is inevitably bound to drain the party's combat capacity, and it may in the future become a menace to its unity.

The International is profoundly convinced that only the complete consolidation of the crushing majority of the party against the paltry Right Wing and the vigorous enforcement of all the decisions adopted by the present conference will cut the ground from under all factional groupings.

At the same time the International strongly urges the Left Wing, while continuing its defense in the future of the principles of revolutionary Communism, not to crystallize itself in any case into a separate faction but to conduct its work within the framework of the common party institutions and organizations, doing everything in its power to promote collaboration with the central core of the party in all practical work and particularly in the struggle against the reformist, pacifist and anarcho-syndicalist deviations.

The Daily l'Internationale and its Editor Comrade Daniel Renoult.

The editor-in-chief of the Parisian evening daily, l'Internationale, and member of the party's Central Committee, Comrade Daniel Renoult, took a most active part in the work of the February session of the enlarged ECCI; furthermore, on all questions, with the exception of the united front, the ECCI reached complete agreement with all the members of the French delegation, including Comrade Renoult.

On the question of the united front Comrade Renoult, who spoke as the reporter, and who later voted with the majority of the French delegation against the tactic of the united front, declared, nevertheless, most categorically and solemnly that the French Communists will, as loyal soldiers of the revolution, submit without reservations to the decisions adopted after a lengthy and loyal discussion.

The obligations, assumed by the delegation of the Central Committee, remained unfulfilled in their most essential aspects owing to inadequate energy and decisiveness of the Central Committee itself in carrying them out. However, the most important reason for the the failure to fulfil the adopted decision and for the tension between the International and its French section, this conference finds in the conduct of the daily l'Internationale and its editor.

Directly counter to the accepted obligations and to his own solemn pledge, Comrade Daniel Renault, instead of explaining the adopted decisions and instead of calling for their unanimous fulfillment, has engaged in a bitter campaign against the tactic of the united front and against the Communist International as a whole. Not confining himself to a literary polemic, Comrade Daniel Renoult has taken the floor at such authoritative gatherings as the conference of the Seine organization to appeal for a demonstrative vote against the policy of the united front.

In view of the crass violation by Comrade Daniel Renoult of his duties as member of the Communist International and in view of his trampling upon obligations he himself assumed and solemnly pledged to fulfil, the enlarged Plenum votes to censure Comrade Daniel Renoult, in his capacity as delegate of the French Party to Moscow and as editor of the daily *l'Internationale.*

At the same time, the International proposes to the Central Committee and its General Secretary that it adopt all necessary measures to convert the daily *l'Internationale*, during the months still remaining before the party convention, into an organ that actually carries out the decisions of the Communist International.

The Fabre Case.

The expulsion of Fabre and his newspaper from the party constitutes one of the moments in the struggle against the spirit of intellectual anarcho-journalistic bohemia which consistently assumes, especially in France, all the forms and all the colorations of anarchism and opportunism in order invariably to conclude by stabbing the working class in the back. This is the laboratory from which emerged Briand and Herve[49] and hundreds of others. The International firmly expects that the Central Committee and the party press alike will explain to the working masses the political meaning of Fabre's expulsion. On this condition alone will the adopted measure prove to be a death sentence to Fabreism in the party ; and the Communist public opinion will gain the revolutionary tenacity in the face of which journalistic adventures will always and without difficulty be ejected from the ranks of the party.

The Coming Party Convention.

The preparation of the next party convention must be conducted under the banner of struggle for the ideological and organizational consolidation of the party—against the tendencies of petty-bourgeois pacifism, anarcho-syndicalism and verbal revolutionism, against the theories which identify the proletariat with the peasantry and which are thereby directed against the class character of the party, etc. In view of the fact that the foregoing tendencies have already succeeded in introducing extreme confusion into the consciousness of the party, the party press must introduce clarity into all these questions, refreshing the party's memory with the corresponding resolutions of the Communist International, in particular the 21 conditions for parties adhering to the Third International. All these decisions must be illuminated by last year's experience or illustrated by examples of literary and political declarations of a number of prominent party workers, which are obviously incompatible with these resolutions.

The date for the convention call must be fixed by agreement between the Central Committee and the ECCI.

Appeal of the Central Committee.

Taking into consideration the need of a profound shift in the internal policy of the French Party, which can be realized in life only with the conscious cooperation of the overwhelming majority of its members, the International deems desirable the publication of a corresponding solemn appeal by the Central Committee addressed to the entire party. This appeal shall explain the substance of the decisions which the present enlarged Plenum has adopted, and which are designed to inaugurate a new era in the life of the French Communist Party.

16

To Comrade Treint

Dear Comrade Treint[50],

I am very much obliged to you for your extremely interesting letter
which on the whole confirms the information we have received here
both from our French press as well as from letters and interviews.
We have not as yet surmounted in France all the difficulties in the
task of forging the revolutionary proletarian party. The victory at
Tours came too easily. History is now demanding of Communism
that it justify this overall victory and realize it in life through a number
of partial victories. This results in a struggle inside our own party.
This struggle exacts a certain expenditure of forces, a certain transfer
of attention from external enemies to internal impediments and leads
to a deterioration in personal relations, and so on. All this is, in
general, quite unpleasant ; and if all this is considered outside
space and time, then it can furnish a pretext for bitter lamentations about internal party struggles and the like. But sad to
say, there is no other and more economical way for a revolutionary
party to evolve, especially in France.

Sentiments are betimes expressed to the effect that the party ought
to be cleansed and regenerated on the basis of mass actions and then
the very process of cleansing would be less painful. In so general
a form, this idea is correct. But it is far too general and therefore
can become a source of false conclusions. French Communism can
grow stronger as a genuine revolutionary party only on the basis
of mass actions. But on the other hand, the present condition of the
party (conflicting tendencies, lack of leadership, vague character of the
press) provides the worst possible deterrent to its engaging in mass
activities. In this connection I am not even referring to how harmful
is the party's position on the question of the united front. In other

words, there is not a mechanical but a dialectical connection between mass activities and the present condition of the party. The one is thwarted or facilitated by the other. Precisely in order to initiate actions, the party requires a certain minimum of unity of consciousness and unity of will. To secure this internal unity, an expenditure of energy, and a very considerable expenditure at that, becomes imperative. This expenditure of energy, which from a superficial standpoint might appear as so much waste, will be completely recouped during the party's very first serious test in mass action. Conversely, a participation of this sort by the party, which is more united than it is now, will serve further to augment its fusion and dynamism. That is why we are following the internal struggle in the French party without undue alarm. On the contrary, this struggle is evidence of the party's healthy reaction to the bacilli of centrism, pacifism, journalistic individualism, anarcho-syndicalism, and so on. *Le vin est tiré, il faut le boire.* (The bottle has been uncorked, the wine must be drunk.) The struggle must be waged to the very end. It will take place the more painlessly, all the less indulgence is shown by the revolutionary elements of the party, that is, its unquestionable majority, to individualistic journalism and parliamentary oratory whose practitioners lack desire or capacity to reeducate themselves in a revolutionary spirit and to submit to the discipline of a combat party.

The results of the Saint Etienne Convention[51] undoubtedly represent a forward step. It would, however, be brought to nothing unless followed up immediately by the second and third steps. Impunity for anarcho-syndicalist proclivities under the banner of Communism, was, as it remains, the greatest danger. So long as pseudo-Communists, counteracting the influence of Communism in the trade unions, are not automatically expelled from the party, the latter will remain unable to establish correct relations with the trade unions. In this connection I should like to say a few words about the totally false impression which some French comrades labor under, apparently owing to an imperfect presentation by Comrade Frossard of my attitude toward Monmousseau's group and its resolution. An impression might have arisen that I propose to declare war against the *La Vie Ouvrière* group. This is completely wrong. What I, together with all other members of the ECCI, demanded was that the Communists conduct themselves in accordance with the orders of the Communist Party. When the party decides to vote in favor of adhering, without any reservations, to the Profintern (Red Interna-

tional of Labor Unions or RILU), then every Communist who votes
against such a resolution (and, let us say, in favor of Monmousseau)
must be expelled from the party. The whole question is: whether
it is possible in the existing party situation to adopt a binding decision
to vote in favor of adhering (to the RILU) without any reservations.
Comrade Frossard has declared categorically that the relationship of
forces is such as to preclude the party's adopting this decision. In
that case there remains only a bloc with Monmousseau's group. But
here again, the Communists could cast their vote for Monmousseau's
resolution only by the decision of the party. In this case, too, they
are duty-bound to submit to the discipline of their own party and
not that of Monmousseau's faction. Otherwise they face expulsion.
At the same time I strongly stressed that it was imperative for us to
go hand in hand with Monmousseau's group, which represented very
precious elements of the French labor movement. In this there is,
of course, no contradiction. We can and should respect Monatte and
Monmousseau and their co-thinkers, striving at all costs to reach
an agreement with them, while at the same time expelling from the
party those Communists who place the discipline of Monmousseau's
faction above the party discipline.

You ask my opinion of how we envisage here the coalition between
the Lefts and all the revolutionary elements of the Center; and how
we envisage the existence of the Left Wing. One must proceed from
facts. The Left, the Center and the Right exist as tendencies toward
personal groupings, and to a certain extent and under certain conditions, each threatens to become converted into a shut-in faction.
Under the conditions of internal party struggle, it would be the height
of philistinism to demand of co-thinkers that they refrain from meeting,
taking counsel and discussing their line of conduct. Naturally this
also applies to the Left, because the Left Wingers, who are striving
to defend the resolution of the International, have no reason whatever
of depriving themselves of means of struggle at the disposal of all
other groupings. But it seems to me, the following conditions ought
to be observed: 1. Under no circumstances should the Left constitute
itself as an organized faction, that is, it categorically rejects the idea
of split. 2. The Left vigorously strives to draw closer to all revolutionary elements of the Center, without falling into despair because
of individual failures, and all the while defending " the united front "
between the Center and the Left against all anti-Communist elements
and groupings within the party. 3. The Left lays down a correct per-

spective with regard to the various deviations inside the party and sets as its aim to convince the Center to accept this appraisal and perspective.

As touches the appraisal and perspectives of the internal party struggle, they appear to me to be as follows : (a) There are the reformist and pacifist elements, partisans of the " Left Bloc," nationalists, parliamentarian and journalistic individualists ; we must mercilessly settle accounts with this intellectual grouping, burning out once and forever with white-hot irons these running sores of shyster and parliamentarian individualism inside the Communist Party and therewith increase the respect and confidence in the party among revolutionary workers. (b) There are syndicalist elements, that is, workers who belong to the Communist Party but who at the same time follow the tendency of Monatte and Monmousseau, which rests on the mistrust of the party's revolutionary spirit and of its proletarian essence ; required here is a patient and persistent ideological struggle against anti-Communist tendencies, with the aim of winning over to the Communist Party all the healthy elements, i.e., the overwhelming majority of this group. (c) There are the federalist elements, the extreme leftists, and others ; the rank and file of these groupings is unquestionably revolutionary, many of their confusions and blunders flow from youth and inexperience ; required here is a calm, comradely and, in part, even a pedagogical approach. (d) There is (as you put it) the so-called *paysanism* (peasantry-ism); if the party permitted this tendency to develop to its logical conclusion, it would unquestionably lead to the formation of a faction in the spirit of our SR's ; here criticism is absolutely indispensable, but naturally every efforts should be exerted lest such valuable and greatly promising Communists as Renaud Jean be repelled into the camp of the Right from which Renaud Jean is far removed by his revolutionary spirit.

Permit me, dear Comrade, to close my letter on the above note. I am forwarding a copy to Comrade Frossard.

Sincerely yours,

L. TROTSKY

Moscow, July 28, 1922.

17

From the ECCI
to the Seine Federation
of the French Communist Party

Dear Comrades,

During the last session of the enlarged Plenum of the ECCI, the International devoted a considerable part of its labors to analyzing the situation in the French Party and especially in its important organization, the Seine Federation.

Several months earlier, in February, the enlarged Plenum had already discussed this question jointly with a large delegation of the French Party and pointed out to the latter the dangers to which the Seine Federation and the party are being subjected owing to the acceptance of the federalist principle as a basis for a Communist organisation.

Because of the tenacity of federalist prejudices and the failure to straighten out the line of the Paris Communist organization, in consonance with the general structure of the International and all its affiliated Communist parties, the ECCI has been compelled to submit the question of the Seine Federation to a special discussion. In complete agreement with the General Secretary of the French CP and the attending French delegates, the ECCI has, after an exhaustive discussion in the French Commission and in plenary sessions, adopted unanimously a resolution inviting the Seine Federation to set up its organizational structure in accordance with the rules set down by the International in the statutes relating to the structure and organization of Communist parties.

The International is convinced that this resolution will be well received by the overwhelming majority of the French comrades who have been convinced both by the theoretical conclusions drawn by perspicacious Communists and by practical experience whose lessons are reinforced by the existing condition of the Seine Federation. In harmony with the spirit of fraternal revolutionary frankness, which must be the rule among the Communists of various sections, the International insists that this resolution be widely published so that all party members are given an opportunity to discuss and appraise it.

The organizational principles and regulations set down by the International are not the product of intellectual fancy, but are the conclusions drawn from the experience of three-quarters of a century of proletarian liberationist struggles in both hemispheres. In traversing the first stages of its revolutionary road, the working class did not fight and suffer in vain. Both defeats and victories have convinced the working class how indispensable it is for the fighting proletarians to keep their ranks welded together, to preserve the discipline of class organization, and to have a unified leadership. That is why the World Communist Congresses have—in their theses and special resolutions, summarizing succinctly the sum total of the knowledge and experience gained by workers' parties of all countries— advanced the principle of democratic centralism as the main foundation of proletarian political organization.

Centralism—because it is imperative to assure unity in action of all sections of the proletariat and the simultaneity of demonstrations under a single common slogan ; this can be achieved only if there is a genuine concentration of leadership in the hands of responsible central and local bodies, stable in their composition and in their attitude to their political line. *Democracy*—because these leading central and local bodies, which under certain conditions may be very small, must be elected by all party members, controlled by them and accountable to them.

Centralized concentration of leadership is sometimes opposed on the ground that it presumably leads to arbitrary rule by the leaders ; that the membership becomes insufficiently active and an oligarchic regime is created. It is self-understood that centralism, applied falsely, can degenerate into a system of oligarchy. The fault, however, lies not in centralism but precisely in a wrong application of its methods and advantages. But by its very nature a strictly centralized organization promotes the activity of the masses to the highest degree, to the extent that it assures a systematic, stable and continuous political leadership. Those who claim that the working class has no need at all of leaders are simply misleading the workers. Without a careful selection of leaders on a local and national scale, without a constant testing of these leaders in action, the working class can never be victorious. A party organization along federalist lines leads to a turn-over in the leadership, an amorphousness in leadership, and an absence of any definite personal responsibility. Exactly under such circum-stances, groups crystallize within the organization, which are under no one's control, but which have actually gained leadership behind the backs of the membership, lulled by the fictitious superiorities of the federalist structure.

Arguments from the federalist structure of the Soviet Republic must be regarded in this connection as sheer misunderstanding. Federal-ism in state organization is applied by the Soviet Republic in the measure that it is necessary to coalesce enormous territories, popu-lated by different national and tribal groups (Byelo-Russians, Ukrain-ians, Georgians, Armenians, etc.). This type of organization is made necessary by certain national-state functions (state language, national school and so on). But we never applied this federalist principle to the building of the proletarian party. Nor are we doing so now. Ukrainian, Georgian, Armenian and other Communist organizations enter into the framework of the unified party not on federalist prin-ciples but on rigidly centralist ones. Failing this party centralism, the working class of Russia would have never succeeded in defending the Soviet Republic, or even attaining the conquest of power.

To every class conscious worker it is clear that in the face of the strictly centralized and disciplined power of the bourgeoisie there must be a no less centralized and disciplined power of the proletariat. That is why those who oppose the idea of democratic centralism, proclaimed by the International, thereby show that they are alien to the spirit reigning among the enlightened sections of the proletariat and are involuntarily doing harm to the interests of the revolution.

Communist parties are not academic discussion clubs, nor propa-ganda societies. They are combat organizations and must be built as such. The workers' revolutions in modern times, the proletariat's tragic struggle against capitalist oppression, the countless sacrifices made by the best sections of the proletariat—all this is a never-to-be-forgotten lesson for the embattled vanguard of the social revolution. The Seine Federation, the spiritual heir of the Paris Commune, ought to be the last one to ignore the most important reasons for the defeat of the Commune, namely, petty-bourgeois, democratic and federalist principles, the absence of a strong hand to guide the revolution, to unify, discipline and centralize it.

The International is convinced that it has outlined the best path of organization, in consonance with the revolutionary interests of the Seine Federation. It notes with satisfaction that there exists within the French Party a broad tendency inspired by the ideas of the International and capable of unifying all the healthy forces at the coming conference of the Federation.

The ECCI is pleased that the question of Article 9 of the International statutes has been placed on the agenda of the next convention. A discussion of this issue will throw into the limelight the basic distinction between the Third International and the Second, a distinction to which the Comintern largely owes the confidence of broad working masses.

Like each of its component Communist parties, the International is a centralized organization whose leadership is concentrated in the Executive Committee, invested with full powers by a World Congress which convenes annually. In contrast to all other international organizations, steeped in national prejudices, the Comintern is thus not a federation of independent national parties, but a unified and great World Communist Party. The International has the unquestionable right to reject applications for membership and to expel previously admitted parties. In the intervals between World Congresses this right is exercised by the ECCI. That is the meaning of Article 9 of the statutes.

This means that the foregoing Article was not drafted in the heat of a battle, nor under the sway of impressions arising from accidental and temporary circumstances. It flows logically from the organic principle of democratic centralism and can be cancelled out only with cancellation of the very concept of a combat organization, with the proletariat's renunciation of gaining emancipation through intense struggles.

To place a question mark over Article 9 or to interpret it by discarding its revolutionary content, is to place a question mark over the organic principle of the Communist International. Each national section has the right and the duty to demand a reconsideration of any principle which experience shows to be invalid or poorly applied ; and the French section is free to exercise this right at the Fourth World Congress. But the Seine Federation will agree that such an important question must be posed in its full scope and on a correct plane. If it is found necessary to review the very foundations of the International organization, then the question ought to be raised without quibbling over an incident of a disciplinary character.

The International found it necessary to invoke the right granted it by Article 9 in order to expel from its ranks citizen Fabre and all those who solidarize with him. In this decision the ECCI was guided by considerations of revolutionary expediency. In an old bourgeois parliamentarian country such as France the pressure of bourgeois public opinion is especially powerful. This public opinion seeks for instruments by means of which to penetrate inside the revolutionary party in order to split, weaken and poison it. Fabre's periodical is one such instrument of bourgeois public opinion. To ignore manifestations of this kind is to incur the greatest risk for the revolutionary party. For this reason the ECCI deemed it its duty to call the attention of the entire party to the Fabre group. The Dissidents and the bourgeoisie immediately made Fabre's cause their own, precisely because Fabre had previously defended inside the party the cause of the bourgeoisie. The hue and cry over Fabre invests him with a semblance of importance. But the moment the bourgeoisie finds that the Communist Party has drastically purged itself of Fabre-ism, then Fabre and his publication will be of no value whatever to it, and this ideologically barren and parasitic group will burst like a bubble.

The interests of the revolution thus demanded the ejection of Fabre and his co-thinkers from the party ranks. Political interests have priority over any and all formal and juridical considerations. But it is self-understood that attention must be paid to considerations of a formal character which are of secondary importance. However, it is precisely from a purely formal standpoint that Article 9, at the disposal of the Comintern, revealed its full effectiveness in the given instance. The Central Committee of the French Communist Party, whose overwhelming majority recognized the need of expelling Fabre, proved unable to carry out this expulsion owing to certain peculiarities of the French Party's statutes. The Committee on Conflicts and Grievances which plays a very important role in the party's organism is essentially entrusted with the task of reviewing carefully, thoroughly and impartially all individual cases involving the moral character and honor of individual members, specific cases of violations of party discipline, infractions of party morality and so on. But the Fabre case involved not a complex procedural investigation, but a political evaluation of a group completely hostile in spirit to Communism. Such a question must naturally be referred for decision not to a control commission but to the party's Central Committee, the highest leading body in between conventions. Insofar as the Central Committee deemed itself, on the basis of existing statutes, without power to expel the Fabre clique, it was the duty of the ECCI to invoke Article 9 of the International statutes. The conclusion to be drawn from this highly instructive experience is not that Article 9 of the International statutes ought to be eliminated or restricted, but that the statutes of the French Communist Party ought to be amended to fully empower its Central Committee to safeguard the ideological purity and the discipline of the proletarian party.

The experience of all parties shows that unstable, politically shaky and semi-opportunist elements give expression to their tendency as a rule not in open struggle with the revolutionary tendency but in opposing the latter on secondary, formal, legalistic and similar issues. The Seine Federation will teach these vacillating and unstable elements a proper lesson by instructing them to submit to Communist discipline; and to participate in a merciless political struggle against the remnants of Fabreism in the party, instead of indirectly supporting Fabre on formal and obviously false grounds.

The program of the coming Seine Conference must be the consolidation of all the genuinely revolutionary elements. This will meet with the unlimited support of the mass of the worker-members. It is necessary to assure a firm revolutionary leadership in the most important organization of the French proletariat. The Seine Conference must be a worthy prelude to the next party convention scheduled for October which will likewise have the task of consolidating the revolutionary Communist elements, of annihilating the centrist and pacifist tendencies, of instituting a regime of revolutionary discipline in the party, of putting an end to factional struggles inside the party, and assuring a genuine political leadership in the hands of a homogeneous Central Committee.

The process of building a Communist Party is a difficult and complex one, indissolubly bound up with self-criticism and an internal purge. The ECCI is confident that the vanguard of the French proletariat will be able to cope with this task and that in this work the Seine Federation will take the first place which rightfully belongs to it.

The Executive Committee
of the Communist International

From the ECCI to the Paris Convention of the French Communist Party (September 13, 1922)[52]

18

Dear Comrades,

The coming convention of the French Communist Party is of exceptional importance. After a year of profound internal crisis which paralyzed the party's will, this convention must help the party to emerge on the broad highway of revolutionary action. For the convention to successfully fulfil this task it is necessary that the whole party critically review the road that has been traversed, gain a clear conception of the reasons for the severe internal maladies which resulted in political passivity, and apply, at the convention, with a firm hand all the necessary measures for restoring party health and reinvigorating it. This letter is aimed to help the public opinion of the French Party to solve this task.

1. *General Causes of the Party Crisis.*

Official French socialism and official French syndicalism proved in the course of the imperialist war that they were completely poisoned by democratic and patriotic ideology. The columns of *l'Humanité* and of all other party and trade union publications used to preach day in and day out that this was a war to end all wars, that this was a just war, that the Entente headed by France represented the loftiest interests of civilization, that the victory of the Entente would bring a democratic peace, disarmament, social justice, and so forth. After these fantasies, impoisoned with chauvinism, found their embodiment in the foul and revolting reality of the Versailles peace, official French socialism arrived in a blind-alley. Its inner fraud was laid bare starkly and irrefutably. The masses were seized by ideological alarm, the party's leading circles lost their poise and self-confidence. These were the circumstances under which the party went through its transformation at the Tours Convention and adhered to the Communist International. Naturally, the results of this convention were prepared by the tireless and heroic work of the Committee for the Third International. Nevertheless, the speed with which these results were achieved astonished the entire international proletariat at the time. The overwhelming majority of the party, together with its most important publications including *l'Humanité*, were transformed into the French section of the Communist International. The most discredited elements, all of whose interests and thoughts were tied up with bourgeois society, split away from the party. This swift transformation of a Socialist Party into a Communist Party, resulting from the glaring contradiction between the ideology of democratic patriotism and the reality of Versailles, unavoidably also brought negative consequences in its wake. The party recoiled from its own past, but this did not at all mean that it had succeeded, in so brief a span of time, in critically examining and assimilating the theoretical principles of Communism and the proletarian methods of revolutionary policy.

In addition, the revolutionary movement has, during the last two years, assumed a more gradual and protracted character in Europe. Bourgeois society acquired a semblance of new equilibrium. On this soil there ensued a revival inside the Communist Party of the old prejudices of reformism, of pacifism and democratism which the party had formally renounced at Tours. Hence the unavoidable internal struggle which has resulted in the profound party crisis.

Following Tours a considerable number of revolutionary syndicalists joined the party. In and by itself this was a very valuable development. But precisely because there was a total lack of clarity in our party on the question of the interrelations between the party and the trade unions, the syndicalist views, which demand that the party refrain from "meddling" in the trade union movement, tended to reinforce the utterly false idea that the party and the trade unions constitute two absolutely independent powers whose only bond at best is that of mutual and friendly neutrality. In other words, it was not the revolutionary syndicalists who were remoulded in the party's forge, but, on the contrary, it was they who imprinted upon the party their stamp of anarcho-syndicalism, thereby further increasing the ideological chaos.

One might thus say that the Tours Convention only roughly outlined the general framework within which the difficult process of the party's regeneration from a democratic, Socialist Party into a Communist Party continues to take place to this very day.

2. *Internal Party Groupings.*

The most obvious and acute expression of the crisis lies in the struggle of tendencies within the party. These tendencies, reduced to their basic groupings, are four in number:

(a) *The Right Wing.* The revival and consolidation of the Right Wing inside the Communist Party has proceeded along the line of least resistance, that is to say, along the line of pacifism which can always count on scoring superficial successes in a country with such traditions as France, especially after an imperialist war. Humanitarian and tearful pacifism which doesn't contain anything revolutionary provides the most convenient camouflage for all the other views and sympathies in the spirit of reformism and centrism. The party's Right Wing began to gain in confidence and boldness in the same measure as the protracted character of the proletarian revolution became more apparent ; as the European bourgeoisie gained more and more ascendancy over the state apparatus after the war ; as the economic difficulties of the Soviet Republic began to multiply. The Rightist elements knew and felt that they could be assured influence only if the party's consciousness remained formless and confused. For this reason, without always being bold enough to attack Communism openly, they waged all the more bitter a struggle against the demands for clarity and precision in the party's ideas and organization. Under the slogan of " freedom of opinion," they have defended the freedom of petty-bourgeois intellectuals, lawyers and journalistic grouplets to introduce confusion and chaos into the party and thereby paralyze its ability to act. All the violators of party discipline found sympathy among the Right Wing which never fails to discover singular courage each time a deputy or a journalist tramples underfoot the program, tactics or statutes of the proletarian party. Under the slogan of national autonomy they have launched a struggle against the Communist International. Instead of fighting for this or that viewpoint inside the International, which they have formally joined, the Rights have challenged the very right of the International to "interfere" in the internal life of the various parties. They have gone further. By identifying the International with Moscow, they began hinting to the French workers in a covert and therefore all the more pernicious manner that such and such decisions of the Communist International were dictated not by the interests of the world revolution but by the opportunistic state interests of Soviet Russia. If this were actually the case, or if the Right Wing seriously believed it, they would be duty-bound to launch an irreconcilable struggle against the Russian Communists, branding them as the betrayers of the world Communist cause and summoning the Russian workers to overthrow such a party. But the Rights did not even dream of taking this road, which is the only consistent and principled one. They have confined themselves to hints and insinuations, seeking to play on the nationalistic feelings of a certain section of the party and the working class. This flirtation with pseudo-democratism (" freedom of opinion ") and with nationalism (Paris vs. Moscow) was supplemented by lamentations over the split with the Dissidents and with probing the soil in preparation for the policy of the " Left Bloc." In its entire spirit the Right Wing is thus hostile to Communism and to the proletarian revolution. The elementary requirement for the party's self-preservation is to purge its ranks of tendencies of this sort and of those individuals who are conveyors of these tendencies. It is self-understood that party members who have openly announced their adhesion to the Right Wing after the Tours Convention cannot occupy any responsible posts in the Communist Party. This is the first and perfectly clear condition for surmounting the internal crisis.

(b) " *The Extreme Left Wing.*" On the party's opposite flank we observe the so-called Extreme Left, where under fictitious, verbal radicalism there not infrequently lurk—side by side with revolutionary impatience—purely opportunist prejudices on tactical and organizational questions of the working class. Localism, autonomy and federalism, which are completely incompatible with the revolutionary needs of the working class, find their partisans among the so-called Extreme Left. From here have also come on occasion appeals for pseudo-revolutionary actions, obviously not in consonance with the existing situation and incompatible with the realistic policies of Communism. Among the majority of the Extreme Lefts there is splendid revolutionary material as was shown by last year's experience and especially by the experience of the Seine Federation. Under a correct and firm party leadership this majority is ridding itself of pseudo-revolutionary prejudices in favor of genuine Communist politics. But unquestionably there are inside this wing isolated representatives of the anarcho-reformist type who are always eager for a bloc with the Rights against Communist politics. A vigilant and strict control over the future activities of these elements is an indispensable supplement to the pedagogic work among those party circles whose inexperi-

ence is being exploited by the anarcho-syndicalists of the " extreme "
Left Wing.

(c) *The Left Tendency*. Ideologically and largely in point of personal composition, the Left tendency represents the continuation and
development of the Committee for the Third International. The Left
tendency has unquestionably exerted every effort to bring the party's
policy in deeds and not merely words in accord with the principles of
the Communist International. There has been a certain resurgence
in the activity of the Left grouping because of the consolidation of
the Right Wing and the latter's aggressive policy against Communist
principles, policies and discipline. The ECCI, which had in its day
dissolved the Committee for the Third International for the sake of
party unity, took all the necessary measures to avert the resurgence
of a factional situation, the danger of which became perfectly clear
from the moment when the Right Wing, in the absence of the necessary
resistance, became sufficiently emboldened to trample openly upon
the ideas of Communism and upon the statutes of the party and of
the International. The ECCI did not and does not see in the activity
of the Left tendency (*La Gauche*) any indication that the Lefts are
seeking to create a closed faction. On the contrary, in complete harmony with the decisions and directives of the ECCI the Left tendency
is upholding the need of complete unity and fusion of all sincere
Communist elements in cleansing the party of the disruptive and
corrosive vestiges of its past.

(d) The broadest and least defined group is constituted by the *Center*
which mirrors most clearly the evolution of the French Party, as
characterized at the beginning of this letter. The rapid transition from
Socialism to Communism under the pressure of revolutionary moods
among the ranks has resulted in bringing within the party's framework
numerous elements whose regard for the Communist banner is quite
sincere, but who are far from having liquidated their democratic-
parliamentary and syndicalist past. Many of the Center representatives believe quite sincerely that a renunciation of the most discredited
formulas of parliamentarism and nationalism sufficed in and by itself
to convert the party into a Communist Party. In their eyes the issue
was settled by the formal acceptance of the 21 conditions at Tours.
Without being sufficiently cognizant of the profound internal regeneration still in store for the party before it could become the leader of
the proletarian revolution in the main citadel of capitalist reaction

and deeming that the Tours Convention had already resolved the main difficulties, the representatives of the Center frowned upon the raising of tactical and organizational problems in the party and were inclined to regard principled conflicts as personal squabbles and circle clamor. The ideologically insignificant and discredited Right Wing was able to raise its head only because the Center, leading the party, failed to immediately counteract it.   Caught between the more or less crystallized Right and Left groupings, the Center was therewith deprived of any independent political physiognomy. Attempts by various representatives of the Center, like Comrade Daniel Renoult, to create an independent platform resulted in practice to his agreeing on some questions with the Right Wing and on others with the Extreme Lefts, thereby only adding to the ideological confusion. It is beyond doubt that some representatives of the Center gravitate entirely to the Right and remain a deterrent to the party's growth. But the task of the majority of the leading elements of the Center—and we hope that they will fulfil this task—consists in standing four-square upon the decisions of the Communist International and in cleansing the party, shoulder to shoulder with the Left tendency, of all those elements who in political practice have demonstrated, are demonstrating and will continue to demonstrate that they do not belong in Communist ranks, in order in this way to strengthen the party's discipline and turn the party into a reliable instrument for revolutionary action.

Side by side with the representatives of the Left, who have proved their loyalty to the cause of the proletarian revolution during the most difficult days, there must enter into the party Central Committee those representatives of the Center who have shown a genuine readiness to usher in a new era in the life of the French Party.

3. *The Question of the United Front.*

The question of the united front arose before the International in the same measure as the Communist parties of the most important countries began passing from preparatory ideological and organizational work to the road of mass action. For the above-stated reasons the French Party found itself caught off-guard by the question of the united front. This manifested itself in the adoption of wrong party decisions on this question. Yet the policy of the united front, carried out by a homogeneous centralized revolutionary party, can and must assume enormous importance precisely in the French labor movement.

Prior to the war, social relations in France were the most inert of all Europe. The relative stability of economic life in the presence of a numerically large small peasantry was the fountainhead of conservatism in political life, which had its effects upon the working class as well. Nowhere else was there such a tenacious reign of revolutionary and pseudo-revolutionary sects as in the French labor movement. The dimmer were the prospects of the social revolution, all the more did each grouping, faction and sect strive to convert itself into a self-sufficient, shut-in little world. Sometimes these factions fought each other for influence, as did the Guesdeists and the Jauresists; at other times they de-limited their influence on the principle of non-intervention, as did the Jauresists and the syndicalists. Each little grouping, especially its bureaucracy, regarded its very existence as an end in itself. Added to this were the ever present careerist considerations: the press became an end in itself to the journalists ; parliamentary posts to the deputies. These traditions and habits, products of a long democratic past under the conditions of a conservative milieu, remain very strong in the French labor movement to this very day.

The Communist Party did not come into being so as to exist merely as one faction in the proletariat alongside the Dissidents, the anarcho-syndicalists and the rest but rather in order to shake these conservative groupings and factions to their very foundations; to lay bare their complete incompatibility with the needs and tasks of the revolutionary epoch and therewith to impel the proletariat to become aware of itself as a class, all of whose sections are dynamically joined together by the united front against the bourgeoisie and its state. A parliamentary socialist organization or a propaganda sect can remain for decades within one and the same framework which assures it a few parliamentary posts or a certain outlet for pamphlets. But the party of the social revolution is obliged to learn in action how to fuse together the majority of the working class, utilizing to this end every opportunity for mass action that opens up. The outlived groupings and factions are interested in preserving intact and immutable all the barriers dividing the working class into segments. We, on the other hand, have a vital stake in pulling down these barriers of conservatism and in teaching the working class to follow our example. Herein lies the whole meaning of the united front policy, a meaning which derives directly from the social revolutionary essence of our party.

From this standpoint all talk to the effect that we should accept a united front with the masses but not with the leaders is sheer scholasticism. This is like saying that we agree to conduct strikes against the capitalists but refuse to enter into negotiations with them. It is impossible to lead strike struggles without entering at a certain moment into negotiations with the capitalists or their plenipotentiaries. It is just as impossible to summon the organized masses to a united struggle without entering into negotiations with those whom a particular section of the mass has made its plenipotentiaries. What comes clearly to the fore in this intransigence is political passivity, the ignoring of the most important task for the sake of which the Communist Party had been actually created.

We consider it necessary to analyze here some of the objections to the united front which have been recently raised, particularly by Comrade Daniel Renoult, and which are ostensibly based on the experience of the Communist International and its various sections.

We are told that the attempt to convene a world-wide labor congress has not been crowned with success, but, on the contrary, has resulted only in aggravating the struggle waged by the Second and the Two-and-a-Half Internationals against Communism. An attempt is made to draw the same conclusion from the experience with the united front policy in Germany. What we really see there, we are told, is not a united front of the proletariat but a confederation of the Social Democrats and the Independents against the Communists.

No one disputes these facts. But they can be employed as arguments against the united front policy only by those who entertain hopes of attaining, through the policy of the united front, a softening of political antagonisms, or a conversion of Ebert, Scheidemann, Vandervelde, Renaudel, Blum and Longuet into revolutionists. But such hopes can be cherished only by opportunists; and, as we actually see, the standpoint of Comrade Renoult and his co-thinkers represents not the position of revolutionists, but of opportunists fallen into despair. Our task is not at all to re-educate Scheidemann, Blum, Jouhaux and Co., but to blow apart the conservatism of their organizations and to cut a path to action by the masses. In the last analysis the Communist Party stands only to gain from this. Among the masses the urge to unity is great. At a certain moment our agitation forced even the Second and the Two-and-a-Half Internationals to enter into negotiations with us about convening a unified congress of labor. It is absolutely incontestable that the Social Democrats and the Independents did everything in their power to smash united action and in process of struggle on this issue against the Communists, they have drawn still closer to each other. In Germany this has led to preparations for the complete merger of these two parties. Only those who completely lack the understanding of how complex are the paths of the political development of the working class, can see in this the collapse of the united front policy. The merger of the Independents with the Social Democrats will temporarily make it appear as if they have grown stronger in relation to us. But in reality, this merger will prove wholly to our advantage. The Independents will try to hold back the Social Democrats from fulfilling their bourgeois-governmental role; with far greater success the Social Democrats will hold back today's Independents from playing their "oppositional" role. With the disappearance of the shapeless blotch constituted by the Independents, the Communist Party will stand before the working class as the sole force fighting against the bourgeoisie and summoning the working class to a united front in this struggle. This cannot fail to change the relation of forces in our favor. It is quite probable that soon after our growing strength makes itself felt, the United Social Democratic Party will be forced to accept the slogan of the united front in one instance or another. In such a situation, the Communists, who are the most resolute fighters for the partial and overall interests of the working class, stand only to gain favor with the toilers. It therefore follows that as a consequence of this temporary collaboration, the Social Democrats will recoil from the Communists once again and even more sharply, and will launch an even more venomous campaign against them. The Communist Party's struggle for the influence over the working class does not proceed along a straight line, but rather along a complicated curved line, whose general direction is upwards, provided there is homogeneity and discipline in the Communist Party itself.

The unquestionable political successes of the united front policy are already clear, as is attested by a report of Comrade Clara Zetkin[53] which is appended to this letter.

* * *

Certain French comrades, who are even prepared to accept "in principle" the tactic of the united front, consider it inapplicable at the present time in France. We, on the contrary, affirm that in no other country is the united front tactic so unpostponable and imperative as in France. This is determined in the first instance by the state of the French trade union movement.

The split of the French trade union organizations carried out by Jouhaux and Co. out of political motives is a crime no less grave than was the conduct of this clique during the war. Every tendency and doctrine is granted the opportunity to create its own grouping within the working class. But the trade unions are the basic organizations of the working class and the unity of the trade union organizations is dictated by the need to defend the most elementary interests and rights of the toiling masses. A split of the trade union organizations for political motives is simultaneously a betrayal of labor as well as a confession of one's bankruptcy. Only by isolating—through a split—a small section of the working class away from revolutionary groupings, could Jouhaux and Co. hope to retain for a little longer their influence and their organization. But for this very reason the reformist trade unions have ceased to be trade unions, that is mass organizations of the toilers, and have become instead a camouflaged political party of Jouhaux and Co.

There is no doubt that there were partisans of the split also among the revolutionary anarcho-syndicalists. Alien to the broad tasks of the proletarian revolution, these elements in the main limit their program to the creation of a clerico-anarchistic sect, with its own hierarchy and its own congregation. They enter into a "pact" of their own, a secret agreement whereby they pledge to mutually aid each other in capturing leading posts; and in this sense the split in the trade union movement suits the affairs of these cliques in the best possible manner.

On this issue, our position has been, as it remains, absolutely instransigent. Here as in all other things, the interests of our party coincide with the genuine interests of the working class which needs unified trade unions and not splinters. Naturally the revolutionary Confederation of Labor is closer to us than the reformist Confederation. But it is our duty to fight to restore the unity of the trade union organizations, not in the dim future but right now, forthwith, in order to repel the capitalist offensive. The trade union split is the handiwork of the criminal trade union bureaucracy. The rank and file in both groupings did not and does not want split. We must be with the masses against the splitting and treacherous trade union bureaucracy.

The revolutionary Confederation of Labor calls itself united ("*unitaire*"). For the anarcho-syndicalists this is only a hypocritical statement. But for us, Communists, it is a banner. We are obliged, each time an opportunity offers, and especially at every opportunity for mass action, to explain that the existence of the revolutionary Confederation of Labor is not an end in itself, but only a means to

attaining the speediest possible unification of the trade union movement. In connection with the Havre strike did the party turn publicly
to both Confederations with a proposal that they coordinate their
demands in order to aid this strike? It did not; and this was a major
blunder. The circumstance that the CGTU itself was opposed to
this, can in no case serve as an alibi. For we are not obliged to do
only what the CGTU wishes. We happen to have our own Communist views on the tasks of trade union organizations, and when a
union organization commits an error we must. on our own responsibility, correct this error openly, before the eyes of the toiling masses
so as to help the working class avoid similar mistakes in the future.
We were obliged to ask both confederations openly, before the eyes
of the whole proletariat, whether they were willing to get together in
order to elaborate a joint program to aid the Havre strike. Such
concrete proposals, such programs of action elaborated by us in advance must be tirelessly advanced on every suitable occasion, on a
national or local scale depending upon the character of the issues and
the scope of the movement. The CGTU cannot and will not throw
obstacles in the way of such initiative. The CGT will, in order to
keep its followers from coming in contact with the revolution, keep
shying away. So much the worse for the CGT. The united front
policy will become a battering ram that will breach the last fortifi-
cations of Jouhaux and Co.

But this is not enough. As a party, we cannot remain on the side
lines during such major events as the Havre strike. Nor can we
permit the Messrs. Dissidents to sit them out or keep silent on the
side lines. We should have likewise made a direct and public proposal
to them, the Dissidents, for a conference. There is not and there
cannot be a rational, serious argument against such a proposal. And
if, under the influence of the situation and under our pressure, the
Dissidents had taken a half-step forward in the interests of the strike,
they would have thereby rendered the workers a real service, and
the majority of the working masses, including those who follow the
Dissidents, would have understood that it was our pressure that made
them take this political step. Had the Dissidents refused ,they would have
discredited themselves. On the other hand, we would not only have
fulfilled our duty toward a section of the proletariat engaged in active
struggle at the time, i.e., the Havre strikers, but we would also have
raised our authority. Only a tireless, persistent and flexible propaganda in favor of unity, on the soil of the living facts of mass action,

is capable of breaking down the barriers of sectarianism and of shut-in circles within the working class, raising its feeling of class solidarity and thereby necessarily increasing our own influence.

On the basis of all this activity, the slogan of a Workers' Government, raised at a proper time, could generate a powerful attractive force. At a suitable time, prepared for by events and by our propaganda, we shall address ourselves to the working masses who still reject the revolution and the dictatorship of the proletariat or who have simply not yet matured sufficiently for these questions, and speak to them as follows: "You can now see how the bourgeoisie is restoring its own class unity under the sign of the 'Left Bloc' and is preparing its own 'left' government which actually unifies the bourgeoisie as a whole. Why shouldn't we, the workers, belonging to different parties and tendencies, create together with non-party workers our own proletarian bloc in defense of our own interests? And why shouldn't we put forward our own Workers' Government?" Here is a natural, simple and clear statement of the whole issue.

But can we Communists conceivably participate in the same government with Renaudel, Blum and the rest?—some comrades will ask. Under certain conditions this might prove temporarily unavoidable, just as we Russian Communists were willing, even after our October victory, to permit Mensheviks and SR's to enter the government, and we actually did draw in the Left SR's. But at the present time the question does not, unfortunately, arise in France in such a practical manner. At issue is not the immediate or impending formation of a Workers' Government with the participation of Frossard and Blum, but rather the question of counterposing agitationally a workers' bloc to the bourgeois bloc. For matters to reach the point of creating a Workers' Government, it is first necessary to rally the majority of the working class around this slogan. Once we achieve this, that is, the moment when the worker-Dissidents and the members of the General Confederation of Labor demand a united labor government, the stock of Renaudel, Blum and Jouhaux would not be worth much, because these gentlemen are able to maintain themselves only through an alliance with the bourgeoisie, provided the working class is split.

It is perfectly obvious that once the majority of the French working class unites under the banner of a Workers' Government, we shall have no cause whatever to worry about the composition of this government. A genuine success for the slogan of a Workers' Government would already signify, in the nature of things, the prelude to the proletarian revolution. This is what those comrades fail to understand who approach slogans formally and assay them with the yardstick of verbal radicalism, without taking into account the processes occurring within the working class itself.

To put forward the program of the social revolution and oppose it "intransigently" to the Dissidents and the syndico-reformists, while refusing to enter into any negotiations with them until they recognize our program—this is a very simple policy which requires neither resourcefulness nor energy, neither flexibility nor initiative. It is not a Communist policy. We Communists seek for methods and avenues of bringing politically, practically and in action the still unconscious masses to the point where they begin posing the revolutionary issue themselves. The unification of the workers' vanguard under the banner of the social revolution, has already been accomplished in the shape of the Communist Party. This party must now strive to unify the entire working class on the soil of economic resistance to capitalism as well as on the soil of political resistance to the bourgeoisie and its governmental bloc. We shall thus actually bring the social revolution closer and prepare the proletariat for victory.

4. *The Cardinal Political Task of French Communism*

The struggle against the Versailles Treaty and the drawing of ever broader masses into this struggle, while investing it with an ever more resolute character—this is the central political task of the French Communist Party.

The French bourgeoisie is able to maintain the regime instituted by the Versailles peace, which is so monstrous and fatal to Europe, only through straining militarily the energy of the French people and through unremittingly pillaging and ruining Germany. The constant threats to occupy German territory constitute one of the biggest obstacles in the way of the growth of the proletarian revolution in Germany. On the other hand, the material resources stolen from the German people serve to strengthen the position of the French bourgeoisie, which is today the main counter-revolutionary force not only in Europe but the world over.

At the same time, it is unquestionable that the French bourgeoisie is using German reparations to create a privileged position for the largest possible section of the French working class so as to make it easier for French capitalism to crack down on the French proletariat as a whole. We have observed this same policy for decades in Britain, but on a somewhat larger scale. The British bourgeoisie, while pillaging its colonies and exploiting the more backward countries, expended a small fraction of its global booty to create a privileged layer of labor aristocrats who helped the bourgeoisie to exploit the working masses all the more cruelly and with impunity. This was how the utterly corrupt bureaucracy of the British trade unions received its training. Naturally the imperialist efforts of the French bourgeoisie come belatedly in this field as in all others. European capitalism is no longer in the cycle of progressive growth; it is in the cycle of decay. And the struggle of French capitalism to maintain the Versailles regime occurs at the price of the further disorganizatioñ and increasing impoverishment of economic life of Europe as a whole. It is, however, perfectly obvious that the interval during which French capitalism will retain the possibility of continuing its fatal labors depends in large measure on how energetically the Communist Party will be able to foster throughout the country an active struggle against the Versailles peace and its author, the French bourgeoisie.

There is not and there cannot be any doubt that the Dissidents and the syndico-reformists have active and conscious partisans among that tiny section of the working class which has a direct or indirect stake in the robber regime of reparations. The economics and the psychology of these elements is essentially parasitic in character. Messrs. Blum, Jouhaux, *et al.* are the consummate political and trade union expressions of this parasitic spirit which binds certain elements among the labor aristocracy and bureaucracy to the Versailles regime in Europe. These cliques are incapable of waging a serious struggle against the existing thievish hegemony of France, because this struggle would inescapably deal them blows, too.

The struggle for the social revolution in France today confronts the proletariat above all as the struggle against the military hegemony of French capitalism, as the struggle against the continued pillage of Germany, as the struggle against the Versailles peace. The genuinely internationalist and genuinely revolutionary character of the French Communist Party must be demonstrated and unfolded precisely on this issue.

During the war the internationalist character of the proletarian party found its expression in the rejection of the principle of national defense, because at that time this rejection was dynamic in character, denoting the mobilization of the working masses against the bourgeois father-

land. At the present time when the French bourgeoisie is devouring
and digesting unprecedented booty, the rejection by the Communist
Party of the principle of national defense is in and of itself necessary, but it is absolutely insufficient. The bourgeoisie can readily
reconcile itself with a declamatory anti-patriotism up till the outbreak
of a new war. Today only a struggle against the robber fruits of
national defense, a struggle against indemnities and reparations, against
the Versailles peace can acquire actual and genuine revolutionary
content. Only in this struggle will the party be able at one and the
same time to test and temper its membership, ruthlessly sweeping
aside all elements infected with the plague of national parasitism, if
such elements still lurk in some nook and corner of the Communist
Party.

On this question, too, your convention must open a new era of
revolutionary mass struggle against Versailles and against the supporters of Versailles.

5. *Organization Questions.*

From the foregoing consideration the organizational questions flow
automatically. What is at issue is to assure the Communist Party its
character as a genuine proletarian organization, intimately bound up
with all forms of the labor movement, extending its connections into
all workers' associations and groupings, controlling and directing in
equal measure the activity of Communists in parliament, in the press,
municipalities, cantonal councils, trade unions and cooperatives.

From this standpoint the draft amendments to party statutes and
on the regime in the press submitted by the Central Committee unquestionably represent a step forward. It goes without saying that
these statutes and formal organizational changes can acquire meaning
only if the entire activity of the party's leading bodies corresponds to
them in its content. In this connection, the question of the composition of the party's Central Committee is of exceptional importance.
In determining this composition, two criteria are paramount, in our
opinion: First, the Central Committee must personify the unification
of the Left and Center against the Right, i.e., against opportunism
and in favor of centralism, for the sake of promoting revolutionary
political mass activity. Second, the majority of the Central Committee must be composed of workers, and moreover, of workers intimately connected with the trade union organizations. The meaning

of the first criterion has already been explained; concerning the second it is necessary to say a few words.

To assure the party's ties with the masses means in the first instance to assure these ties with the trade unions. It is necessary once and forever to put an end to the view, which is fantastic and suicidal from the standpoint of revolution, that the party has no business in the trade unions or in their functioning. Naturally a trade union organization as such is autonomous, that is, it directs its own policies on the basis of workers' democracy. But the party, too, is autonomous in the sense that no anarcho-syndicalists dare prescribe for it what issues it may or may not touch. The Communist Party has not only the right but the duty to seek the leading position in the trade unions on the basis of the voluntary trust of the union members in the party's slogans and tactics. And end must be put once and for all to a regime where the trade unions have been controlled by anarcho-syndicalist cliques, mutually bound by secret agreements in the spirit of Masonic careerism. The party enters the trade unions with its visor open. All the Communists work in the trade unions as Communists and are bound by party discipline in the Communist cells. On questions involving trade union actions the Communists naturally submit to trade union discipline. From this standpoint an enormous importance attaches to drawing a large number of trade union activists into the personnel of the Central Committee. They will assure the ties between the Central Committee and the mass organizations; and on the other hand, the Central Committee will become for them the highest school of Communist politics; and our French Party is in dire need of educating revolutionary proletarian leaders.

* * *

Such are the main tasks before the coming convention of the French Communist Party. The Communist International will follow its proceedings and results with the greatest attention. The exacting attitude of the International toward the Communist Party of France is actually an exacting attitude toward itself, inasmuch as the French Party constitutes one of its important sections. The profound contradictions inherent in the situation of the Republic of French Capitalism open up before the French proletariat in the near future, we hope, the possibilities for the greatest historical actions. In preparing for them it is necessary that we have the most vigilant and exacting attitude toward ourselves. This letter is inspired by the idea of the great historical mission of the French proletariat. The exacting attitude shown by the International toward its parties rests on a profound confidence in the revolutionary development of the world proletariat and, above all, of the proletariat of France.

The French Communist Party will surmount its internal crisis and will rise to the level of its boundless revolutionary tasks.

(Enclosure) The United Front in Germany*.

The impending merger of the SPG and ISPG[54] is not the product of the united front policy but a caricature of it. The merger has been imposed upon the leaders of these two parties by the need to cover up their bankruptcy by means of a new deception. Taking into cognizance the need of uniting the proletarian forces, a need that is felt by the masses, the reformist leaders in both parties are utilizing it for an evil purpose: For uniting with the bourgeoisie against the Communists. This unification is the natural and unavoidable consummation of the replacing by both of these parties of the program of class struggle by a policy of " national unity," a policy of class collaboration. The whole remaining difference between them comes down only to this, that the followers of Scheidemann have discarded revolutionary phrasemongering while the followers of Ditman still resort to it. Between these two reformist parties there are no principled or tactical differences, and therefore nothing hinders their merger. Indeed they must merge in order to regain some strength or at least an appearance of strength. The Socialist Party of Germany (SPG) lost last year 46,000 members, a huge loss even for its first-rate organization. The Independent Socialist Party of Germany (ISPG) has not yet made public its report, but it is an open secret that this party doesn't know how to meet its deficit and that its central organ *Freheit* is on the rocks. But the main thing is that both these parties must strain all their efforts in order to regain, even if only partially, their former popularity, compromised as they are by their reformist policies which have thrown them into the embraces of Stinnes. And so they have proceeded to make malicious use of the slogan most popular among the masses. But the masses will soon discover how profound and basic is the difference between an organic unity of these two parties and the unification of the proletarian masses for their own struggles.

Side by side with this organic unity of the two reformist parties,

---

* This enclosure consists of the text of a letter written by Clara Zetkin to the Executive Committee of the Comintern.—Ed.

the Communist Party continues its unremitting work for the united front against the leaders of these parties and against the trade union bureaucracy. Successes were already evident in the campaign launched in connection with the assassination of Rathenau[55]. In the Rhine and Westphalian provinces, with their large industrial centers, Committees of Action, in many cities and districts, have been organized, composed of representatives of the two reformist parties, the Communist Party and the trade unions. (In some cases, committees were organized in the *Gewerkschaftliche Kartelle* of particular localities or districts and representatives of the three workers' parties were elected to them.) Under the pressure of the organized masses, the leaders of the reformist parties, particularly the DAGB (Executive Committee of the German Trade Union Alliance), found themselves compelled to establish relations with the Communist Party. Notwithstanding the brief duration of this joint activity, two large demonstrations were held in quick succession in Germany; and thanks to these negotiations and demonstrations the Communist Party made intimate contacts with the working masses in rather large areas. Committees of Action set up for the purpose of disarming counter-revolutionary elements continued to function after the protest movement had waned so quickly owing to the treachery of the reformists.

The idea of the united front is again marching forward with giant strides. It is aided by the current crisis. The economic struggle is driving the workers and employees to unite and to demand that their representatives in the unions and in the political parties work jointly and harmoniously. To illustrate we cite the joint meeting of the factory delegates in Berlin. More than 6,000 of these delegates attended despite the warning by the trade union bureaucracy, by the ISPG and SPG, that it was impermissible for their members to attend this meeting.

This gathering, which was a real event, elected a committee of 15 to arrange an All-German conference of factory and shop delegates. This committee is composed of members from all the workers' parties. It is instructed to call the convention if the Executive Committee of the Trade Union Alliance fails to do so. The aim is to establish "Control Committees" to supervise production, distribution, prices and so on. In many industrial centers such Control Committees have already been formed. There is quite a large number of cities where the workers have called meetings of factory and shop delegates at which committees were organized demanding control over production

Everywhere the Communists were at the head of this movement whose aim is to bring about unity in the struggle.

Certain elements in our party, it is true, hold views opposed to the united front. However these views are aimed chiefly against mistakes that have been made and against the incorrect application of the united front. In the future there will be fewer and fewer mistakes. The party must learn how to maneuver in the new conditions and how to establish a common front, while simultaneously preserving and expressing its own political physiognomy.

The Executive Committee
of the Communist International

Moscow, September 13, 1922.

From the ECCI to the Paris Convention of the French Communist Party (October 6, 1922)

19

On the eve of the Paris Convention of the French Communist Party the situation in Paris has become so complicated that the ECCI feels itself compelled to turn to the Paris Convention with the following supplement to its already published documents:

1. The ECCI *proposes that the Paris Convention take a special roll-call vote on the* 21 *conditions* adopted by the Second World Congress of the Communist International. It would be best both for the French Communist Party and for the Comintern as a whole *to have complete clarity* on this question.

It is self-understood that if the French Communist Party desires to propose any changes in the 21 conditions to the Fourth World Congress of the Communist International, the Paris Convention has the full right to do so. Every proposal of the Paris Convention will be taken up by the Fourth World Congress with the greatest attention and care.

2. In view of the fact that the majority of the old Central Committee has, to the astonishment of the ECCI, failed to expel from the Party Verfeuil and his co-thinkers even after their latest glaring anti-Communist actions—the ECCI is compelled to inform the Paris Convention that it *no longer* considers as members of the Comintern Raoul Verfeuil and all those who signed jointly with him the notorious "Appeal to the Party," beginning with the words *"La situation dans laquelle se trouve le parti . . . ."* (The situation in which the party now finds itself . . . .)

The content of this Appeal completely confirms the prior declaration of the ECCI to the effect that Raoul Verfeuil and his co-thinkers are bitter enemies of Communism who remained in the French Communist Party only to undermine it from within.

Should the Paris Convention disagree with the ECCI on this question, it will be referred for final decision to the Fourth World Congress of the Comintern.

The ECCI once again proposes that the Paris Convention pose point-blank all the most important questions which are at the present in dispute in the French Party. The grave lesson taught to the Italian Socialist Party—which after two years of grave mistakes and vacillations has just found itself compelled to recognize the correctness of the Comintern's demands—should not be allowed to pass in vain.

The Comintern is confident that the Paris Convention will put an end to vacillations and create a genuine Communist Party worthy of leading the heroic proletariat of France.

The Executive Committee
of the Communist International

Moscow, October 6, 1922.

The Fourth

World Congress

Picture: Trotsky addressing the Fourth Congress of the Communist International. Right to left, Marchlewski (Poland), Neurath (Czechoslovakia) and Zinoviev (Russia).

EDITOR'S NOTE: The Fourth—and last Leninist—Congress of the Comintern convened on November 5, 1922 in Petrograd, with the remaining sessions up to December 5, 1922 being held in Moscow. 408 delegates from 61 countries attended; 343 delegates had decisive votes.

The agenda included 24 items. The report of the ECCI was delivered by Zinoviev. Lenin, Zetkin and Bela Kun were the reporters on the Five Years of the Russian Revolution and the Perspectives of the World Revolution. The report on the NEP was given by Trotsky.

The problems of the united front and of the formation of a Workers Government were the most important tactical questions discussed, along with that of trade union tactics.

Internal situations in various parties received particular attention in following order: France, Italy, Czechoslovakia, Norway, Turkey, Denmark, Yugoslavia.

The question of program came up as the fifth point on the agenda, with drafts presented by Bukharin (USSR), Thalheimer (Germany) and Kabakchiev (Bulgaria). No program was adopted.

20

The Fifth Anniversary of the October Revolution and the Fourth World Congress of the Communist International

Delivered Before the Active Membership of the Moscow Organization,

October 20, 1922.

Comrades, the Fourth World Congress of the Communist International will convene during a jubilee for the Soviet power, its Fifth Anniversary. My report will be devoted to these two events. The jubilee is of course a purely formal one; involving a date on the calendar, but events are not regulated by the calendar. The Fifth Anniversary of the Soviet power does not represent any kind of completed historical period, all the less so because in our revolutionary epoch everything is undergoing change, everything is in flux, everything is still far from static, nor will the finished forms be reached soon. Nevertheless it is quite natural for every thinking individual, all the more so a Communist, to strive toward an understanding of what has taken place, and to analyze the situation as it shapes up on this formal date on the calendar, on the Fifth Anniversary of the Soviet power and, therefore, also on the occasion of the Fourth World Congress of the Comintern.

The Tangled Skein of Capitalist Contradictions Is Becoming Unravelled, Beginning with Russia.

Two day ago I happened to attend a party cell meeting at the former Bromley plant. One of the comrades there, a member of the cell, raised the following question: In what country would the proletarian revolution be most advantageous from the standpoint of

Communist interests?   After a moment's reflection I replied that
taking it so abstractly one would have to say that a revolution in
the United States would be the most advantageous.   The reason for
this is quite easy to understand.   This country is the most independent in the world, economically speaking.   Its agriculture and industry
are so balanced as to enable the country to lead, in the event, say, of
a savage blockade, a wholly independent existence.   Moreover it is
the richest country in the world, disposing of the foremost industrial
technology, holding in its hands approximately one-half, perhaps
slightly less, of the visible gold reserve.   It is a country concentrating
in its hands the bigger half of world production in the most important
branches.   Naturally, were the proletariat of this country to take
power into its hands, it would possess unsurpassed material foundations, and organizational and technical premises for socialist construction.   The next country in order is—Great Britain, while Russia would
come on this list if not the very last in the series (because there exists
Asia, there is Africa), then at any rate very low toward the bottom
of the list of countries within the borders of Europe.   Yet history is,
as you know, unravelling this tangled skein from the opposite end,
namely from the end where Russia is located, a country which, in the
cultural and economic sense, is the most backward among the major
capitalist countries, a country which is extremely dependent in the
economic and technological sense, and which, in addition, has been
utterly ruined by the war.   And if we were to ask ourselves today
what are the political premises for the proletarian revolution in the
United States, then naturally one may grant a possible course of events
such as may extraordinarily hasten the conquest of power by the
American proletariat.   But if we take the situation as it stands today,
then we must say that in this strongest, largest, and most decisive
leading capitalist country, the political premises, i.e., premises on the
plane of the creation of systematic party and class organizations, are
the least prepared.   One could devote an entire report to explain
why history began unravelling the skein of revolution from such a weak
and backward country in the economic sense as ours, but in that case
I would be able to speak of neither the Fourth World Congress nor
of the Fifth Anniversary of the Soviet power.   It suffices right now
that we have been compelled for these five five years to pursue the
work of socialist construction in the economically most backward country, while capitalism, mortally hostile to us, has been preserved in
bourgeois countries far superior to us economically.   This is the funda-

mental fact, and from it, naturally, stemmed the fearsome intensity of our Civil War.

The Fundamental Lesson of the Russian Revolution.

Here, if we wish to draw our fundamental conclusion, we must say in praise of our party that it has set a colossal example—for the proletariat of all countries—of how to fight for power and of how, after conquering it, to defend this power by means of the most resolute measures, applying wherever necessary harsh and ruthless methods of dictatorship, without flinching before any decisive measures in trampling upon bourgeois hypocrisy, when at stake is the securing of state power by the revolutionary proletariat. And this text-book of the Russian revolution, which ought to be written, the workers of all countries will study in the course of the next few years or perhaps decades, because it is impossible to say how long the proletarian revolution will endure from its beginning to its termination: It is a question of an entire historical epoch. Whether we did or did not make mistakes during the Civil War (and of course there were mistakes), we nevertheless did on the whole accomplish the most classic part of our revolutionary work. We have more than once spoken of the mistakes which conditioned our need to retreat in the economic sphere, a major retreat which is known among us as the NEP (New Economic Policy). The fact that we marched forward at the very beginning along a certain road, and then retreated and are now fortifying ourselves on certain positions, tends to disrupt in the extreme the perspective not only among our enemies but also among many of our friends. Correspondents sympathetic to us and many Communists, European and American alike, pose as the first question, both during the departure of our delegation to Genoa as well as today, the fact that many things have changed in Moscow (and there were many visitors to Moscow in 1919 and 1920) and that Moscow now resembles too much other European and American cities. And in general where is the guarantee that you Russian Communists will check the further development and head for Communism and not for capitalism? Where is the guarantee?

The general impression at a superficial glance is that the socialist conquests gained in the first period are now spontaneously and automatically melting and crumbling away and there does not seem to be a power capable of retaining them. It is possible, Comrades, to approach the question from the other end and say as follows: Let us for a moment forget that we proceeded along the line of the so-called War Communism and later retreated to the present position. Let us take the situation as it exists today and compare it with what it was on October 25, or on the eve of the 1917 revolution. If our foreign well-wishers or the European and American Communists were to submit us to a cross-examination, we would say: The railways, the mines, the plants and the factories were at that time in the hands of private owners. Enormous areas of the land and the country's natural resources were in the hands of private owners. Today all the railways, the overwhelming majority, or in any case all of the most important plants and factories, all of the most valuable natural resources in the country are in the hands of the state, which is, in turn, the property of the working class, supporting itself upon the peasant masses. This is the fact which we have before us as the product of five years. There was an offensive followed by a retreat, but here is the balance-sheet: As the product of five years, the most important means of industry and production and a considerable sector of agricultural production are under the direct supervision and management of the workers' state. This is a fundamental fact. But what has produced the retreat? This is a very important question, because the very fact of the retreat tends to disrupt the perspective. How did we conceive the successive order, the course of nationalizing the means of industry and of the organization of socialism? In all our old books, written by our teachers and by us, we always said and wrote that the working class, having conquered state power, will nationalize step by step, beginning with the best prepared means of production, which will be transferred to the socialist foundations. Does this rule remain in force today? Unquestionably it does, and we shall say at the Fourth World Congress, where we will discuss the question of the Communist program: Will the working class on conquering power in Germany or in France have to begin by smashing the apparatus for organizing the technical means, the machinery of money economy and replace them by universal accounting? No, the working class must master the methods of capitalist circulation, the methods of accounting, the methods of stock market turnover, the methods of banking turnover and gradually, in consonance with its own technical resources and degree of preparation, pass over to the planned beginnings, replacing accounting by a computation of the profitability or non-profitability of a given enterprise, replacing accounting by taking stock of the centralized means and forces, including the labor force.

This is the fundamental lesson which we must once again teach the workers of the whole world, a lesson we were taught by our teachers. If we violated this lesson, it was owing to conditions of a political character, owing to the pressures brought to bear upon us after our conquest of state power. This is the most important difference between the proletarian revolution as it has occurred in Russia and the revolution which will occur, say, in America. In that country, prior to the conquest of power, the working class will have to surmount the most colossal difficulties but once it has conquered power, the pressure on those fronts on which we were compelled to fight will be far less, because our country with its petty-bourgeoisie, its backward *kulaks* (well-to-do peasants), experienced the revolution in a different way and because our revolution caught the Russian bourgeoisie by surprise. By the very fact of the October Revolution we taught the bourgeoisie to understand just what it has lost when the workers took power and it was only the fact of the revolution itself that impelled the bourgeoisie, the *kulaks* and the officers to organize. We smashed the bourgeoisie not so much prior to October 25 and during the night of October 25-26 as in the three years' interval following October 25, when the bourgeoisie, the landlords and the officers fathomed what was involved and began the struggle against us with the aid of European capitalism. In Europe we have a process differing profoundly from that in our country, because there the bourgeoisie is far better organized and more experienced, because there the petty-bourgeoisie has graduated from the school of the big bourgeoisie and is, in consequence, also far more powerful and experienced; and, in addition, the Russian revolution has taught them a good deal. In these countries therefore the preparation and the arming of counter-revolutionary gangs is now taking place parallel with the preparation and tempering of the Communist Party for this struggle, which will be far more intense prior to their October 25, but not afterwards. Only before. The fact that in our country, the day after the conquest of power, the plants and factories turned out to be the fortresses and citadels of the bourgeoisie, the main base upon which European imperialism was able to depend, this fact compelled us to resort to nationalization, independently of our ability or the extent of our ability to organize these enterprises with our own forces and resources.

And if, for political reasons, we drove the property owners out of the factories, while being ourselves bereft of the possibility of even immediately gaining hold of these factories; if, for political reasons, we brought down the sword of dictatorship and of terror upon the stock market and the banks, it is self-evident that we thereby mechanically destroyed the apparatus in the service of the bourgeoisie and which the bourgeoisie employed for organizing the economy and for distributing the productive forces and commodities in the country. Insofar as we destroyed this apparatus at a single blow, we were, generally speaking, obliged to replace it with another—with the apparatus of centralized accounting and distribution. But such an apparatus had first to be created; we had to have it; but, naturally owing to all the pre-conditions, owing to our entire past, owing to our level of development and knowledge, we could not possibly create it. And so, because of the titanic and ineluctable aspects of the Civil War as such, and because of the impossibility even for an advanced working class and all the more so for us, in a backward country, to create an apparatus of socialist calculation and distribution in the space of twenty-four hours—precisely because of this there arose the entire tragedy of our economy. War Communism, too, was not our program —it was imposed upon us. To the extent that there were fronts in the Civil War, to the extent that we were compelled to destroy the enemy's bases of support behind these fronts, i.e., the private capitalist enterprises of all categories, to that extent we were driven to manage the enterprises in a migratory and warlike manner. This was the epoch of War Communism and I shall not conceal that here, as is always the case, people tended to make a virtue out of necessity, i.e., in the same measure as War Communism was imposed upon us, the party workers and the leading party institutions tended to be carried away by inertia, in the sense of deluding themselves that we had here a complete solution of the tasks of socialist economy. But if we draw the balance-sheet, we must say that the offensive and the retreat in the domain of economy had been dictated by the requirements of the Civil War, which were absolutely imperative, and which cut across our economic conditions and the degree of our economic adaptation, or lack of adaptation. In other words, essentially both our offensive along the line of War Communism as well as our retreat along the line of the NEP were historically unavoidable in part and as a whole; and only on the basis of this historic necessity is it possible and necessary to analyze our subjective errors—both as a party and as a state power.

The Overhead Expenditures of the Revolution.

There remains, Comrades, the most important question of all. As a result of five years, the workers' state, as I said, disposes, after our retreat, of the most important means of production, and wields power. This is a fact. But there also is another fact—namely that we represent today one of the poorest countries in Europe. Yet it is quite obvious that socialism has meaning only to the extent that it assures a higher productivity of labor. Capitalism in its day superseded feudalism, while the latter superseded slave economy. Why? Because each succeeding economic order was more profitable in the socio-technological sense than the order it shunted aside; and socialism will naturally acquire its practical and not theoretical justification only on the condition that it supplies a greater quantity of goods per each unit of labor power for the satisfaction of social needs. And this is the chief argument employed against us. It was made use of even by the French representatives at Genoa; and Colrat, the French economic expert, repeated it in a crude and insolent form: "Don't you dare teach us socialism when your own country is in a state of complete disorganization." We would have preferred to provide in the last five years proofs of empirical character, that is, show Europe an economy superior to the one which we obtained in 1917. This does not happen to be the case, but this is already ascribable entirely to the expenditures incurred by the revolution itself. Not a single revolution was ever accomplished without a lowering of the country's economic level; and one of the conservative bourgeois historians of the French Revolution, Taine, so highly esteemed in the Third French Republic, has affirmed that for eight years following the Great French Revolution, the French people remained poorer than they were on the eve of revolution. This is a fact. Society is so shot through with contradictions, that it is capable of reaching a higher stage of development only through an internal class struggle. Society is so constituted that an internal class struggle in the fully unfolded form of civil war implies a lowering of economic levels. But, at the same time, of course, (every school boy knows this today), it was precisely and exclusively the Great French Revolution that created in France those governmental, juridical and cultural premises which provided the sole basis for the development of capitalism there, with all of its prowess, its technology and its bourgeois culture. In other words, what I wish to say is that the five-year period (and we must say this to all our critics, malicious and well-meaning alike who employ this argument) does not provide a historic scale by means of which it is possible to weigh the economic results of the proletarian revolution. All that we see up to now in our country are the overhead expenditures in the production of the revolution. These are expenditures for the revolution itself. And naturally, since these expenditures had to be covered from inherited capital, which, in turn, had been disorganized and devastated by the imperialist war, it therefore follows that we see in our country many more ruins of capitalism than results of socialist construction. The scale is far too small. This is what we must repeat once again at the Fourth World Congress of the Communist International. Five years in relation to the task of superseding capitalism by socialism, a task of the greatest historical magnitude—five years could not naturally bring about the necessary changes and what is, naturally, most important these five years constituted the period when socialism—as I said in the beginning—was being built or attempts were made to build it in the most backward country. The Great French Revolution, on the other hand, unfolded in the most advanced country on the European continent, a country that had attained a higher level than any other, with the exception of England across the Channel. In our country, the state of affairs assumed a far less favorable turn from the very beginning.

Here, Comrades, are in rough outline, those arguments which we shall develop in our party's name at the Fourth World Congress where we are bound to ask our European and American comrades and at the same time ourselves, too: How do matters really stand with regard to the chances for the development of the European revolution? Because it is perfectly self-evident that the tempo of our future construction will in the highest measure depend upon the development of the revolution in Europe and in America.

European Communism Must Conquer the Working Class.

In order to answer the question concerning the stage that has been reached today by the revolutionary movement of the European and the American proletariat, above all by the former, it is necessary to dwell briefly on the Third World Congress of the Comintern which took place last summer. At that time, too, I was assigned by the Moscow organization to make a report to the Moscow comrades, appraising the Third Congress as a new stage, as inaugurating a new stage in the development of the revolutionary proletarian movement. This stage also began with a certain and very important retreat. And these two retreats of ours, the one, on the economic field and the other, on the political field in Europe are linked intimately with each other, because our War Communism could have unfolded without a retreat into complete socialism and communism on one condition, namely; that the proletariat of Europe seized power in 1920 and 1921. Had that happened, not only would hostile pressure from the outside have ceased, but we would have obtained inexhaustible resources for technical, organizational and cultural assistance. We may say that War Communism objectively imposed upon us essentially by the imperative requirements of the Civil War was at the same time subjectively justified insofar as it was linked up with hopes for a swift flow of the revolution in Western Europe, which would lift us up and propel us forward at a far faster pace than we could attain on our own rather pathetic cultural foundations. The revolution in the West was retarded and the revolution took this into account at the Third Congress last year, some 15 or 16 months ago. The revolution also took into account the nature of its future methods of action. The signal for a review of the international tasks of Communism was given by the March 1921 events in Germany. You will recall what happened. There were calls for a general strike, there were sacrifices by the workers, there was a cruel massacre of the Communist Party, internally there were disagreements on the part of some, and utter treachery on the part of others. But the Comintern said firmly: In Germany the March policy of the Communist Party was a mistake. Why? Because the German Party reckoned that it was directly confronted with the task of conquering power. It turned out that the task confronting the party was that of conquering not power, but the working class. What nurtured the psychology of the German Communist Party in 1921 that drove it into the March action? It was nurtured by the circumstances and the moods which crystallized in Europe after the war. Do you recall the year 1919? It was the year when the entire structure of European imperialism tottered under the impact of the greatest mass struggle of the proletariat in history and when we daily expected news of the proclamation of the Soviet Republic in Germany, in France, in England, in Italy. The word "Soviets" became terrifically popular; everywhere these Soviets were being organized. The bourgeoisie was at its wits' end. The year 1919 was the most critical year in the history of the European bourgeoisie. In 1920 the tremors (we can state this today in retrospect) subsided considerably but still remained extremely turbulent, so much so that it was possible to cherish hopes for a swift liquidation of bourgeois rule, within a few weeks or months. What were the premises for the proletarian revolution? The productive forces were fully mature, so were the class relations; the objective social role of the proletariat rendered the latter fully capable of conquering power and providing the necessary leadership. What was lacking? Lacking was the political premise, the subjective premise, i.e., cognizance of the situation by the proletariat. Lacking was an organization at the head of the proletariat, capable of utilizing the situation for nothing else but the direct organizational and technical preparation of an uprising, of the overturn, the seizure of power, and so forth. This is what was lacking. This became tragically clear in September 1920 in Italy. Among the Italian workers, as workers of a country that had suffered most cruelly from the war, and as a young proletariat without the superiorities of an older proletariat but also without the latter's negative features—conservatism, old traditions, etc.—within this proletariat the ideas and methods of the Russian revolution met with the most powerful response. The Socialist Party of Italy, however, did not clearly take into account the full content of these concepts and these slogans. In September 1920 the working class of Italy had, in effect, gained control of the state, of society, of factories, plants and enterprises. What was lacking? A trifle was lacking—a party was lacking, which would, resting upon the insurrectionary working class, have engaged in an open struggle with the bourgeoisie for those remnants of material forces still in the latter's hands, destroying these forces, seizing power and thus consummating the victory of the working class. In essence the working class had already conquered or virtually conquered, but there was no organization capable of definitively consolidating this victory and so the working class found itself hurled back. The party split into segments, the proletariat was smashed; and since then, throughout 1921 and 1922 we have been witnessing the most frightful political retreat of the working class in Italy under the blows of consolidated bourgeois and petty-bourgeois gangs, known as the Fascists.

Fascism is the revenge, the vengeance exacted by the bourgeoisie for the dread it had experienced during the 1920 September days and at the same time it is a tragic lesson to the Italian proletariat, a lesson on the meaning of a political party that is centralized, unified and knows what it wants; that is cautious in choosing conditions, and resolutely ruthless in applying the necessary means when the hour for it strikes. Comparing events of such a type as the September days in Italy with those in our own country we must and should learn over and over again to value our party which has to function under incomparably more difficult conditions, because it is functioning under the conditions of a backward and low cultural milieu, where the peasantry predominates.

In the March 1921 events of Germany we had a picture diametrically opposite to what happened in Italy. In 1919 the German working class engaged in a number of cruel and bloody battles, the same thing happened in 1920, and during the January and March days of 1920 the German working class became convinced that heroism alone, that readiness to venture and to die was not enough; that somehow the working class was lacking something. It began to take a more watchful and expectant attitude toward events and facts. It had banked in its time upon the old Social Democracy to secure it the socialist overturn. The Social Democracy dragged the proletariat into the war. When the thunders of the November 1918 revolution rolled, the old Social Democracy began to talk the language of social revolution and even proclaimed, as you recall, the German republic to be a socialist republic. The proletariat took this seriously, and kept pressing forward. Colliding with the bourgeois gangs it suffered crushing defeats once, twice and a third time. Naturally this does not mean that its hatred of the bourgeoisie or its readiness to struggle had lessened, but its brains had meanwhile acquired many new convolutions of caution and watchfulness. For new battles it already wants to have guarantees of victory. And this mood began to grow increasingly stronger among the European working class in 1920-1922, after the experiences of the initial assault, after the initial semi-victories and minor conquests and the subsequent major defeats. At that moment, in the days when the European working class began after the war to understand clearly, or at least to sense, that the business of conquering state power is a very complicated business and that bare hands cannot cope with the bourgeoisie—at that moment the most dynamic section of the working class formed itself into the Communist Party. But this Communist Party still felt as if it were a shell shot out of a cannon. It appeared on the scene and it seemed to it that it needed only shout its battle-cry, dash forward and the working class would rush to follow. It turned out otherwise. It turned out that the working class had, upon suffering a series of disillusions concerning its primitive revolutionary illusions, assumed a watch-and-wait attitude by the time the Communist Party took shape in 1920 (and especially in 1921) and rushed forward. The working class was not accustomed to this party, it had not seen the party in action. Since the working class had been deceived more than once in the past, it has every reason to demand that the party win its confidence, or, to put it differently, the party must still discharge its obligation of demonstrating to the working class that it should follow and is justified in following the party into the fires of battle, when the party issues the summons. During the March days of 1921 in Germany we saw a Communist Party—devoted, revolutionary, ready for struggle—rushing forward, but not followed by the working class. Perhaps one-quarter or one-fifth of the German working class did follow. Because of its revolutionary impatience this most revolutionary section came into collision with the other four-fifths; and already tried, so to speak, mechanically, and here and there by force to draw them into the struggle, which is, of course, completely out of question. The party incurred the risk of shattering itself not so much against the resistance of the bourgeoisie, as against the resistance of the four-fifths or two-thirds of the working class itself. But at that moment the International sounded the alarm, proclaiming a new stage. In the course of 1919 and 1920, the period of spontaneous revolutionary movements, the conquest of power was really feasible. Given even a small Communist Party in Germany, say, with one or two hundred thousand Communists, the chances for the conquest of power were there. But following the disillusionment of the working class, once the bourgeoisie succeeded in recovering its wits, in entrenching itself and restoring its state apparatus, and once the working class assumed a more cautious and dilatory position, the appearance of one hundred or two hundred thousand Communists no longer sufficed. And the need instead arose for the Communists to conquer, in experience, in practice, in struggle, the confidence of the working class under the new conditions. And this is exactly what the Third Congress proclaimed. In this connection, we had heated clashes with the German comrades here in Moscow. Later at their own Convention, following the world gathering, they actually shifted over to a new track, and criticized us a little bit, arguing that even granted that a new stage was beginning, it was not at all in accordance with the expectations of the Russian comrades, who were swinging a little too far to the right, and so forth and so on. If we were to ask ourselves: What was, in essence, the beginning of this new stage? Did it begin with the March events in Germany? Then we would have to answer in the negative. No, it began with the criticism of the March events. The March events came as the consummation of the initial epoch of chaotic assault which failed to bring victory because there was no Communist Party in Europe. And the March movement and the March policy came already as an abortion of this epoch. And so, with the criticism of the Communist Party's March policy, a new epoch opened up in the development of the Comintern, an epoch, which at first glance contains much that is, so to speak, prosaic, namely—agitation, propaganda, organization, conquest of the confidence of the workers in the day-to-day struggles. Some comrades told us: And where is the guarantee that this organizational-agitational-educational work will not degenerate into the very same reformism, along the road travelled by the Second International? No guarantees are handed us from the outside. The guarantees arise from our work, our criticism, our self-criticism and our control. But there are objective guarantees—much more serious. They are inherent in the situation of capitalism itself and in the existence of one country under a workers' government.

The Situation of International Capitalism.

The situation of capitalism itself is likewise a question on which we dwelt in detail at the Third Congress and on which we will in all likelihood also dwell at the Fourth Congress in discussing the questions of tactics. The issue comes down to this: Is the European and world capitalism disintegrating, or has it given proof of its viability? Is it restoring its equilibrium? The problem on the whole is a very big one, and I will touch only upon its most general features, which are unconditionally indispensable for understanding the destinies of the revolutionary movement in Europe and throughout the world. In 1920 the world economy experienced a fearsome crisis, such as had never been known in the history of capitalism. This crisis erupted in the spring of 1920 in Japan and in America and then suddenly leaped over into Europe, seizing all of Europe by the middle of 1920 and plummeting to incredible depths and acuteness by the early part of 1921. The Third Congress convened precisely at the moment when the crisis had seized the whole world, when there were five to six million unemployed in the U.S., about two million in England, and so on. Industry and trade declined by comparison with 1913 at different rates in different countries, but, on the whole, the proportions of the decline were enormous. And so, many comrades pictured the situation as follows. Here we have the crisis of capitalism consequent upon the war. And it is the final and fatal crisis which must continue to disintegrate economic life more and more, until as a result of this crisis there issues the proletarian revolution, civil war, and conquest of power. Hence—out of this psychology—sprang the tactic of the March days in Germany. This 1920 crisis was regarded as the final and decisive and fatal crisis of capitalism. On this question there occurred among us an ideological struggle not only with European comrades but also a flurry in our own ranks. When I made a chance remark to the effect that this crisis, like every other crisis, is bound to be superseded by a revival, I recall that a certain number of comrades, first and foremost, N. I. Bukharin and Comrade Sokolnikov vehemently rose up in arms against me. Today, however, Comrades, the Comintern has issued as an official document for the Fourth World Congress, an economic report by Comrade Varga, which is based entirely on this, that the breaking point of the economic conjuncture took place in the latter part of 1921 and terminated in the first half of 1922. And how could it have been otherwise? Those comrades who denied that an economic revival was unavoidable, were taking their point of departure from a purely economic outlook with regard to the decay of capitalism. At this point it is necessary for me to recall in the most general way two or three theoretical truths indispensable for our understanding of the situation as it has arisen.

The productive forces of capitalism have developed, one may say, from the infancy of capitalism up to the World War. The lines of development tend, from a certain standpoint, to diverge, the productive forces expand, rising to ever higher and higher levels; and as we learned from Marx, from his *Capital*[56] (this fact was also known to the pre-Marxist bourgeois economists but it was Marx who explained it) the development of capitalism takes place not along a straight line or evenly, but through oscillations, crises and revivals, with all the intermediate transitional phases. Every eight or nine or ten years world capitalism and together with it the respective national capitalisms pass through stages of boom, lag, depression, crisis, cessation of crisis, revival, boom, and so on. This line charting the ascent of capitalism and of its productive forces thus represents not a straight but a wavy line and each wave embraces a span of approximately nine years on the average for the last 150 years. First comes a boom, and then a crisis follows. What does this mean? We say that the crisis destroys the superfluous productive forces while the boom regenerates the productive forces, increasing them. And what is the end result? The end result, say for 150 years of capitalism, is that all of the countries have become richer. What does this mean? It means that, on the whole, the boom of the productive forces surpasses the crisis, i.e., that the sum-total of booms produced a surplus which was not destroyed by crises. Or else capitalism could not have developed. But does an identical boom follow each given crisis? No. The curve of capitalist development does not represent a uniformly rising graph, but a rise which occurs as follows: In the beginning, it is virtually horizontal. The productive forces show almost no growth, say, for a period of 50 years, if we take the interval up to 1849. Next, beginning with 1849 the curve begins to move sharply upwards, up till the early Seventies. From 1873 to 1895-96 there is retardation—the productive forces develop very gradually.

Then from 1896 to 1913 the curve whirls violently upwards almost up to the eve of the last war. Further, this curve vibrates up and down all the time, like a tightly strained string. These are the periodic waves in each decade. When capitalism develops on the same level, i.e., remains almost unchanged, it means that the booms are approximately balanced off by the crises. When capitalism develops stormily upwards, the productive forces expand, the nation grows richer—it means that the booms by far surpass the crises, the booms become more prolonged, the crises are more in the nature of transitory and brief retardations. In the epoch of capitalist decline, the productive forces are decomposing, as has been by and large the case in the epoch which began after the war, which has endured to this very day and which will continue to endure for a long time to come.

This means that in the epoch of decline the crises strike deeper than the booms: the crises surpass the booms. Can capitalism develop without cyclical fluctuations, without the transitions from boom to crisis? No. Just as the human organism (I have repeated this tens of times) continues to breathe until death, so the heart-beats of capitalism continue—in the infancy and in maturity and on the death-bed alike. Its heart continues to beat but the heart-beats are not the same. When a man is dying his heart beats in an entirely different way from a healthy man's, and from this, by taking the pulse, it is possible to determine his condition. Similarly it is possible to determine whether capitalism is ascending, or resting on one and the same level, or disintegrating. In 1920, and even earlier in 1913, there occurred an unmistakable breaking point. I have already said that in the course of 17 to 18 years, from 1896 to 1913, capitalism made an extraordinary upward leap but it was then stymied by the struggle of capitalist countries on the world market; it became constricted in the national states and hence arose the imperialist war of 1914. The governments, the diplomatic staffs, the bourgeoisie, the military circles became all the more jittery and precipitated the conflict through the sanguinary deed in 1914 because of the lag that occurred, beginning with 1913, on the world market. This lag signified a profound breaking point and had there been no war, capitalist stagnation would have set in anyway in 1914; the development of capitalism would have started its downward plunge, continuing to fluctuate all the while. The imperialist war was the product of the stormy development of capitalist forces in the course of these 17 most remarkable years in the history of capitalism. The war created an artificial market and seemed to sweep the crisis away. The war laid the basis for utilizing the engines of destruction; it opened up the method of ruining all nations. After the war, in 1919, during the most critical period, the bourgeoisie continued its wartime policy. Throwing all caution to the wind, it kept issuing paper currency, and continued the system of piling up national debts. It supplemented the workers' wages either with cheap rents or with an assortment of privileges; it accepted the 8-hour working day. All this flowed not from the position of capitalism, but from the political position of the bourgeoisie as a class. This economic strategy saved the bourgeoisie in 1919, for it bribed the labor aristocracy, splitting the proletariat into a democracy and an aristocracy of labor. The bourgeoisie artificially extended prosperity into 1919, disorganized its state finances and its economic foundation but paralyzed the revolution. However, the laws of economic development, which could be checked only temporarily, made themselves felt by 1920. A crisis ensued which assumed monstrous forms, with millions of unemployed in Europe and America. To some comrades it seemed that this crisis, which began in 1920, was the final crisis of capitalism; and that on the basis of this crisis the working class was bound to come to power through an insurrection. Hence flowed the March events in Germany. We fought against this view. We knew that the crisis would be followed by a revival and there was the greatest danger that the Communists, upon bumping their heads against this revival, might say that the soil for the revolution had been exhausted since a revival had set in and capitalism was restoring its equilibrium.

We fought against such a mechanical point of view, and I hope that there will be no need for us to fight any longer at the Fourth World Congress. If we are told: "And where are the guarantees (we once again meet up with the demand for guarantees)—where are the guarantees that capitalism will not restore its equilibrium through cyclical oscillations?" then I would say in reply: "There are no guarantees and there can be none." If we cancel out the revolutionary nature of the working class and its struggle and the work of the Communist Party and of the trade unions, that is, if we cancel out that for the sake of which we exist and act, and take instead the objective mechanics of capitalism, then we could say: "Naturally, failing the intervention of the working class, failing its struggle, its resistance, its self-defense and its offensives—failing all this, capitalism will restore its own equilibrium, not the old but a new equilibrium; it will establish the domination of the Anglo-American world in which the entire economy will pass into the hands of these countries and there will be a temporary alliance between the United States and Great Britain, but presently this equilibrium will once again be disrupted." The automatic interplay of capitalist forces, inherent in its nature, operates in this direction wherever there are superfluous forces. Take the Central European theater—Czechoslovakia. The latter has preserved her industry almost intact. In old Austria-Hungary this industry supplied 60,000,000 people and today it is supplying Czechoslovakia— 8,000,000 Czechoslovaks and 3,000,000 Germans. At all events, this highly integrated industry serves a small number of people—a dozen million or so and what was once the main section of Austria-Hungary's industry has remained virtually intact. And so, Czechoslavakia, precisely because she has preserved her old integrated industry, is unable to emerge from conditions of crisis. This means that a destruction of the superfluous productive forces is taking place. When will the crisis in Czechoslovakia cease? When it has brought industry into equivalence with the market, with the buyer, if no market is found in the neighboring countries.

Therefore the restoration of equilibrium does not always represent growth but sometimes a decline as well, and one way or another an equilibrium is reestablished which has been disrupted by the spontaneous growth of capitalist forces and, in addition, by wartime and political events. Within ten or fifteen years some sort of new political equilibrium will be thus created on the bodies and bones of hundreds of thousands and millions of working men and women, if the latter continue to docilely submit to the elemental interplay of capitalism. In other words, Czechoslovak capitalism must, in order to conquer the foreign market, pay wages as low as possible to the workers. And should the workers tolerate this, then Czechoslovak capitalism will restore its equilibrium within such and such limits; but if the workers resist, they will thereby disrupt the action of capitalism toward the restoration of economic equilibrium. In other words, we have here action and reaction; we have here the dialectic of historical forces and the outcome will be determined by the correlation of these contending historical forces.

And so, our viewpoint was, that we need have no fears of an economic revival, nor be fearful lest it terminate the revolutionary epoch. We said that if we do not succeed in achieving the revolution prior to a new economic revival—not some kind of blossoming of capitalism, of which, assuredly, there cannot even be talk—but a new oscillation of the conjuncture within the framework of this minor ten-year cycle —if we do not succeed in achieving the proletarian revolution in Europe, the industrial revival will not come as a blow hurling us back but as an impulse propelling us forward. Why? Because, we argued, following the initial defeats suffered by the working class (and the war itself was the greatest of defeats), and afterwards in 1918—1920—1921 in face of the huge reserve army of unemployed, moods of apathy and exhaustion must unavoidably set in among the working class. But an economic revival, even such a small one as would make factory owners add out of the reserve army a single worker to each thousand workers would, on the contrary, make itself felt. Because the thousand workers employed in this factory begin to feel more secure and already begin to press forward. A tiny change in the conjuncture tends to alter the situation. Naturally, this does not take place mechanically. In Europe we witness during the initial stages, seemingly just the opposite phenomenon, but this falls wholly within this same historical framework. As a matter of fact, we are now witnessing in Europe the continued offensive of capitalism. In America this offensive is already slackening, and even giving way to concessions. In European industry the revival is very feeble. In England, in France and in Italy it is hardly perceptible, or altogether imperceptible. On the other hand, owing to the peculiarities of her economy and of her international position, Germany is experiencing market phenomena whose sign is negative. When a bourgeois crisis raged throughout the world, in Germany there was to be observed a feverish revival, which signified only a different form of the country's ruination. Germany was being sold on the auction block at cheap prices. Germany was compelled to throw her commodities on foreign markets at a loss for her national wealth, even though the upper capitalist crust coined profits. This riddle is very easily explained economically. I shall not dwell upon it. Today, on the contrary, when other countries—Japan, England, France—are in the midst of a revival, Germany is confronted with the threat of growing unemployment for reasons that are perfectly clear. In 1919, 1920 and 1921, and especially in 1920 when the crisis was frightful, and the danger of the proletarian revolution was still very great, the bourgeoisie did not dare, for political reasons, to take the offensive against the workers, and for economic reasons the situation was so desperate that wage cuts of 10 or 15 or 20 percent made little change in the basic market conditions. But when substantial stability became manifest and the first symptoms of a break in the conjuncture arrived and when the crisis ceased to unfold, then the bourgeoisie began immediately to pass over to the offensive. In the competition on the world market a difference of 5 to 20 percent is of great moment. For this very reason the workers were driven to resist. And so, the initial effect of a certain feeble improvement in the economic conjuncture found its expression in an offensive, in an intensified pressure of capitalism upon the workers, but concurrently the resistance of the workers likewise increased, because the class struggle had become aggravated extensively and intensively. In America capitalism is out-running the others on the road of concessions and thereby it indicates to us the path of the movement's future development, i.e., not a defensive struggle by the workers but an offensive by them on the basis of this altered conjuncture. But, Comrades, how does this altered situation affect the revolution? Does it mean that the proletariat will conquer power on the basis of this improved conjuncture? It would be absolutely false to make such predictions. This is possible, but there are no guarantees other than the correlation of forces, which keep constantly changing, because these living forces are in conflict, because they grow, group, regroup, merge, and so on. It is quite possible for the industrial revival to last a year or two—a very pathetic revival which does not correspond to the general decline of economy owing to its lack of equilibrium, owing to the currency chaos, owing to high tariffs and tariff walls with which all the states even the United States are surrounded, and owing to the diplomatic instability of militarism. All this does, of course, correspond to the decaying state of capitalism. Hence the pathetic nature of the revival. But there is a difference between a pathetic revival and a most profound crisis and the former affects the organization and the struggle of the working class. The impulse has already been given by this revival. It is an impulsion toward a mass movement —and this is especially apparent in France. In that country there was almost complete stagnation, but today one strike after another is tending to become stubborn in character.

The Future Tactic of the Communist Parties.

Whether or not this impulsion will lead to the seizure of power, we cannot tell. This depends upon innumerable factors, above all, naturally, insofar as the question is posed politically, it depends upon tactics, the future political tactic. And it is with this future political tactic, that I shall now deal, once again in briefest outline. The Third Congress centered its attention upon the German Party with its March policy which compelled the International to review all the circumstances and to issue new slogans, fix new signposts and proclaim that the task of the European Communists did not consist in conquering power today or tomorrow but in winning over the majority of the working class and thereby creating the political premise for the conquest of power. The German Communist Party has assimilated this lesson very well. Hence sprang the tactic of the united front. What does "hence sprang" mean? The meaning is quite plain. If we consider that the party is on the eve of the conquest of power and the working class will follow it, then the question of the united front simply doesn't exist. But if we have a situation in which the Communist Party calls for a general strike, as was the case in March 1921 in Germany, and the party is followed by one-fifth or one-sixth of the entire working class, while the other four-fifths remain partly passive and partly profoundly hostile; and if we become convinced that a certain interval must elapse, perhaps several years, before the conquest of power. . . . Let me recall parenthetically that at the Third World Congress Comrade Lenin remarked: "Comrades, our own position is of course bad, but if you require another year or two, we can wait." And at that time the German comrades and a number of Italian comrades regarded this as almost a betrayal of the proletarian revolution. Yet almost two years have since elapsed and we shall be obliged to extend another moratorium for two more years, or in any case until the next Congress. . . . To resume, if the situation is such as to require two or three years of preparatory work for the conquest of power, it is then necessary to ponder over what will happen in the interim to the working class, which has its own immediate tasks: the struggle against the offensive of capitalism, the onset of reaction, and so on. But the working class is divided. It would of course be splendid if the working class were ready to instantly follow the Communists. But such is not the case. And in the current struggle we witness a split among the labor organizations and the old organizations place the blame for this split on the Communists. And so, the Communists reply, "So far as we are concerned we are ready for the conquest of power, but insofar as you Independents, and you non-party workers pose such and such tasks for yourselves, to that extent we are willing to enter with you into a united front for the struggle against the bourgeoisie." In Germany, after the March events, this tactic was adopted by the Communist Party as a whole; and it has been applied successfully. The dialectic of history, however, sometimes acts to turn our own slogans against ourselves. The slogan of the united front, raised by the Comintern in Germany, has unquestionably gained great popularity among the German workers. But with what results? It immediately produced the unification of the Scheidemannists and the Independents against us; and the picture you see in Germany is that of the united Social-Democrats supporting the government's savage onslaught upon the Communists, who are being virtually converted into an illegal party. There occur street clashes and attacks in which the monarchist counter-revolution employs a united front against the Communist minority of the proletariat. And some French Communists, like Daniel Renoult, see in all this an argument against the united front, claiming that we had allegedly helped the Scheidemannists unite with the Independents. Let us not deceive ourselves. At the beginning the unification signifies an influx of material forces for the Social Democracy. But if we approach this unification from a longer range view, then it constitutes a colossal political gain for us because the intermediate formation in the shape of an Independent Party and of the Two-and-a-Half International, which served as a buffer between the worker-Communists and the Social Democrats, muddled up the real relations and tended to direct the minds of a certain section of workers along pseudo-oppositional channels. When we have, on the one side, only the Social Democracy tied up with the bourgeois state, and on the other side only the Communists remaining in the opposition, then the attractive power of the Communist Party must increase to the maximum; and we shall unquestionably witness in the next period the growth of the German Communist Party's ideological influence, after the working class has taken the unification of the Social Democrats and the Independents into account, even if roughly. In France we undoubtedly lag politically behind Germany. I am referring to the Communist Party itself. This lag found its expression in the fact that the French Communist Party, the vanguard of the working class, repeated only recently, only last month, the March mistakes of the German Communist Party, even though on a smaller scale.

In general, Comrades, the International is a wonderful institution. And the training one party gives to another is likewise irreplaceable. But generally speaking, one must say that each working class tends to repeat all the mistakes at the expense of its own back and bones. The International can be of assistance only in the sense of seeing to it that this back receives the minimum number of scars, but in the nature of things scars are unavoidable. We saw this almost the other day in France. In the port of Havre there occurred a strike of 15,000 workers. This strike of local importance attracted the nation-wide attention of the working class, by its stubborness, firmness and discipline. It led to rather large contributions for the benefit of the strikers through our party's central organ, *l'Humanité;* there were agitational tours, and so on. The French government through its police-chief brought the strike to a bloody clash in which three workers were killed. (It is quite possible that this happened through some assistance by anarchist elements inside the French working class who time and again involuntarily abet reaction.) These killings were of course bound to produce great repercussions among the French working class. You will recall that the March 1921 events in Germany also started when in Central Germany the chief of police, a Social Democrat, sent military-police gangs to crush the strikers. This fact was at the bottom of our German party's call for a general strike. In France we observe an analogous course of events: a stubborn strike, which catches the interest of the entire working class, followed by bloody clashes. Three strikers are killed. The murders occurred, say, on Friday and by Saturday there already convened a conference of the so-called unitarian unions, i.e., the revolutionary trade unions, which maintain close relations with the Communist Party; and at this conference it is decided to call the working class to a general strike on the next day. But no general strike came out of it. In Germany during the (so-called) general strike in March there participated one-quarter, one-fifth or one-sixth of the working class. In France even a smaller fraction of the French proletariat participated in the general strike. If one follows the French press to see how this whole affair was carried out, then, Comrades, one has to scratch one's head ten times in recognizing how young and inexperienced are the Communist parties of Western Europe. The Comintern had accused the French Communists of passivity. This was correct. And the German Communist Party, too, had been accused prior to March of passivity. Demanded of the party was activity, initiative, aggressive agitation, intervention into the day-to-day struggles of the working class. But the party attempted in March to recoup its yesterday's passivity by the heroic action of a general strike, almost an uprising. On a lesser scale this was repeated the other day in France. In order to emerge from passivity they proclaimed a general strike for a working class which was just beginning to emerge from passivity under the conditions of an incipient revival and improvement in the conjuncture. How did they motivate this? They motivated it by this, that the news of the murder of the three workers had produced a shocking impression on the party's Central Committee and on the Confederation of Labor. How could it have failed to produce such an impression? Of course, it was shocking! And so the slogan of the general strike was raised. If the Communist Party were so strong as to need only issue a call for a general strike, then everything would be fine. But a general strike is a component and dynamic part of the proletarian revolution itself. Out of the general strike there arise clashes with the troops and the question is posed of who is master in the country. Who controls the army—the bourgeoisie or the proletariat? It is possible to speak of a protest general strike, but this is a question of utmost importance. When a dispatch comes over the wires that three workers have been killed at Havre and when it is known that there is no revolution in France but, instead, a stagnant situation, that the working class is just beginning to stir slightly out of a condition of passivity engendered by events during the war and postwar period—in such a situation to launch the slogan for a general strike is to commit the greatest and crudest blunder which can only undermine for a long time, for many months to come, the confidence of the working masses in a party which behaves in such a manner. True enough, the direct responsibility in this case was not borne by the party; the slogan was issued by the so-called unitarian, that is, revolutionary trade unions. But in reality what should the party and the trade unions have done?

They should have mobilized every party and trade union worker who was qualified and sent them out to spread this news from one end of the country to the other. The first thing was to tell the story as it should have been told. We have a daily paper, *l'Humanité*, our central organ. It has a circulation of approximately 200,000—a rather large circulation. But France has a population of not less than 40 million. In the provinces there is virtually no circulation of the daily newspapers. Consequently, the task was to inform the workers, to tell them the story agitationally, and to touch them to the quick with this story. The second thing needed was to turn to the Socialist Party, the party of Longuet and Renaudel with a few questions—no occasion could have been more propitious—and say: "In Havre three worker strikers have been killed; we take it for granted that this cannot be permitted to go unpunished. We are prepared to employ the most resolute measures. We ask, what do you propose? "

The very posing of these questions would have attracted great attention. It was necessary to turn to Jouhaux's reformist trade unions which are much closer to the strikers. Jouhaux feigned sympathy for this strike and gave it material aid. It was necessary to put to him the following question: "You of the reformist trade unions, what do you propose? We, the Communist Party, propose to hold tomorrow not a general strike but a conference of the Communist Party, of the unitarian revolutionary trade unions and of the reformist trade unions in order to discuss how this aggression of capitalism ought to be answered." It was necessary to touch to the quick the hearts of the broadest working masses who yesterday refused to listen to us and who followed Jouhaux, Renaudel and the others. It was necessary to swing the working masses into motion. Perhaps a general strike might have come out of it, I do not know; maybe a protest strike, maybe not. In any case it was far too little simply to announce, to cry out that my indignation had been aroused, when I learned over the wires that three workers had been killed. It was instead necessary to touch to the quick the hearts of the working masses. After such an activity the whole working class might not perhaps have gone out on a demonstrative strike but we could, of course, have reached a very considerable section. However, instead there was a mistake, let me repeat, on a smaller scale than the March events. It was a mistake on a two by four scale. With this difference that in France there were no assaults, no sweeping actions, no new bloody clashes but simply a failure; the general strike was a fiasco and by this token—a minus on the Communist Party's card, not a plus but a minus. This is quite obviously and largely connected, Comrades, with the fact that our French Communist Party has generally been lagging behind in its internal life. It adhered to the Comintern at the Tours Convention in 1920, but the heritage of the old Socialist Party, the heritage of extensive parliamentary culture, of French republican conditions, of the tradition of the Great French Revolution—all this cannot be shaken off easily. I will not, Comrades, go into those complex interrelations which have existed during the past period between the Comintern and the French Communist Party; and whose task it was to reduce the number of scars on the backs of the vanguard section of the French workers. As a result of these relations and interventions, discussions over here and experiences on the spot over there—five grouping have crystallized inside the French Communist Party. These groupings are now convening in Paris at the Convention of the French Communist Party. We still don't know the results. However, to characterize the gist of what we should like to achieve, I must say a few words about the groupings themselves. The Left grouping consists of those elements who held the revolutionary standpoint during the war, and played a major role in the French Party's adhesion to the Comintern. Next there is the Center which probably embraces the majority of the workers because the latter have not yet received a full Communist education and they joined the Comintern together with their old local and national leaders. Then there is the Right Wing. These are the avowed enemies of the Comintern. Their leader is Verfeuil, who was expelled from the party by the Seine Federation and by the Comintern.

There is also an Extreme Left Wing which is a conglomeration of anarchist and reformist prejudices among two or three leading members; its worker followers are simply affected by revolutionary impatience. These are splendid elements who need education. The task consists in compelling the Center to break with the Right Wing, to unite with the Lefts, on the basis of the program and tactics of revoluionary Communism, and create a Central Committee capable and desirous of guiding the party in this spirit. And therewith it is necessary to secure in this Central Committee, a majority of workers connected with the mass trade union movement, something which has never existed in France. In France the field of the trade union movement is one thing and the field of high politics is something else again. And when the Comintern demanded that these two fields be closely interlinked, the Communist Ernest Lafont[57], a lawyer, a deputy and a party member, declared: "This is a silly demand. What can we lawyers tell the workers about the field of trade union movement?" But if you lawyers have nothing to tell the workers in the field of the trade union movement, then we must tell you that, generally speaking, you have the wrong address. For the legal profession there are other institutions outside the Comintern. If you do find yourselves here, it means that you must decide questions of the labor movement and a labor movement without the trade unions is no labor movement at all. To us this is so elementary that it is embarrassing to mention it at a workers' gathering, all the more so at a party meeting. But in France it is necessary to wage a struggle against prejudices, left over from the old democratic culture. At the Fourth Congress we shall have in the case of the French Party, in the shape of several different and still contending tendencies, approximately the same thing that we faced at the Third Congress in the case of the German Communist Party. At that time, last year, the Comintern played a major role insofar as it accelerated the process of restoring party unity, and rendering the greatest service to the party's capacity for action. I think that the French Communist Party proposes after approximately a year and a quarter's delay, to do what was done in March by the German Communist Party.

In Italy the situation is even more acute. Following the September 1920 events the Communist wing, approximately one-third of the old Socialist Party, split away, while the old Socialist Party consisting of the then Center and Right Wing continued its existence. Under the onslaught of the bourgeoisie which placed the executive power in the hands of the fascist gangs, the reformists shifted more and more to the right, seeking to enter the government, whose executive organ was and remains the fascist gangs. This led to a split in the Socialist Party between the Right Wing and the so-called Serrati group, wherewith Serrati's party announced at its Convention that it adheres to the Comintern. We shall have at the Congress two parties: our Italian Communist Party and the party of Serrati—who having made a wide circle—now wants to join the Communist International. The majority of this party is undoubtedly striving for genuine revolutionary activity. Here we have a certain similarity with the French situation. In France the prospect is to effect a unification of the Left Wing and the Center, but both the Left Wing and the Center belong formally to the same party. They are merely two tendencies, not to say two factions, whereas in Italy they are two different parties. It will of course be no simple matter to amalgamate them, for the task is to amalgamate the proletarian rank and file of these two parties and at the same time to assure a firm revolutionary Communist leadership. It therefore follows that both in France and Italy the task today is largely internal, organizational, preparatory and educational in character, whereas the German party can and must now pass over, as it is doing, to an agitational counter-offensive, taking advantage of the fact that the Independents and the Social Democrats have united and that the Communist Party now remains the sole opposition party.

The Situation in England and France.

A few words on England. Here our Communist Party still remains a successfully functioning educational and propaganda society but not a party, capable of directly leading the masses.

In England, however, the situation is taking shape or tending in a direction favorable to us, outside of the Communist Party's framework —within the working class as a whole. Today we received a cable that Lloyd George's government has resigned.

This was the only government older than ours. (*Laughter.*) We were considered to be the least stable among all the governments. This is Lloyd George's polite gift to our jubilee, so as not to hurt our feelings. (*Laughter.*) It obviously means new elections in England. And new elections imply a struggle between the three basic groupings, which are: the Tories, the Unionists, and the Independent Liberals. What Lloyd George does personally is a subsidiary question. He may go either with the Tories or with the Independent Liberals, clasping the Labor Party's right hand. His personal career is all that is involved here. Essentially the struggle will occur between the three groupings, and therewith chances are by no means excluded that a coalition of the Labor Party and the Independent Liberals may turn up in power. What this means hardly requires comment. The appearance of the working class in power will place the entire responsibility for the government's actions upon the Labor Party; and will give rise to an epoch of English Kerenskyism in the era of parliamentarianism, providing a favorable environment without parallel for the Communist Party's political work. Should the Tories win (I hesitate to weigh the odds, but let us here assume they are favorable), it would only signify a worsening of the country's domestic situation; it would tend to sharpen the Labor Party's opposition and would thereby bring about new elections very quickly, because elections in England can take place within a month or a few months, as has happened more than once in the past. In other words, the stability of the domestic political situation, which had been enhanced by the coalition headed by Lloyd George, is relegated to the museum with Lloyd George's departure; and England is experiencing shocks and oscillations which can play only into our hands.

In France the policy of the National Bloc headed by Poincaré resembles that of Lloyd George and doesn't differ from the latter by an iota, although one London correspondent informed me today that the opinion in England is that Lloyd George's policy is as far removed from Poincaré's as heaven is from earth; and that unlike Lloyd George who enjoys a great popularity in Russia, Poincaré enjoys a great animosity. To this my answer was that Lloyd George justifiably vies with Poincaré for animosity so far as our working masses are concerned. He was extremely astonished and promised to make this discovery known in the English press. (*Laughter.*) In France the bloc headed by Poincaré has two more years to run before its formal demise; and it is unquestionable that power in France will then be assumed by the "Left Bloc" whose leader Herriot[58] paid us a visit here in Moscow. He will be the Prime Minister. There is no other candidate except Caillaux whom Clemenceau exiled from France as a traitor because Caillaux wanted to terminate the war. Caillaux has to be first pardoned which can be done only by a new parliament and then he may owing to his influence turn up at the head of the government. But the most likely candidate at the present time is Herriot who is preparing the background and the conditions for a new policy, for French Kerenskyism, because the assumption of power by the "Left Bloc" signifies a government of Radicals and Socialists, who will undoubtedly enter the Bloc. Once again the situation is exceptionally favorable for the Communist Party because today the Socialists and the Radicals and Jouhaux are fighting the National Bloc, but on the morrow only one party will fight the new Bloc. If a "Left Bloc" materializes because the ancient hulk of the National Bloc has become decrepit, then the Communist Party will appear as the sole opposition party and, in consequence, such a change will be most advantageous to us. In the two main countries of Europe— England and France—a change of regimes is now in process; England is in the midst of, while France is preparing for, a liquidation of the regime that grew out of the war and the victory won by these countries; and there is now taking place an internal gyration, the most violent disruption of the stability of these states that had to be reconstituted or semi-reconstituted after the war and this opens up broader perspectives for the Communist Party. All these are the positive factors which we are taking into account. Nevertheless, Comrades, everything I said leads to the conclusion that we still remain in Europe in the period of preparation, the period of organizing an internal review of the Communist parties, the period of their tempering and their struggle for influence over the working masses. This means that we, the Soviet Republic, must allow the Communist parties of Europe another year or two or three for preparatory work toward the conquest of power. This preparatory work is more difficult than in our country because the enemy there is more expert and intelligent; and we witness in all European countries the creation of counter-revolutionary Fascist gangs, which we did not have in our country. Fascism is a duplicate, unofficial government, which is ceded place and honor by the official government. This unofficial government is not hampered by any fictitious democratic norms; it stages massacres, it kills. Fascism has ceased to be a purely Italian phenomenon. Fascism is spreading in all countries. In Germany it is constituted by the *Orgesch* organization and gangs, who merely employ a different label. In France Fascism bears the Royalist label. As you know, in France there is a Royalist Party headed by Leon Daudet, son of the novelist Alphonse Daudet. Leon Daudet is a malicious buffoon. What does he want? He wants to restore, by the grace of God, one of the Capets[59]. This is an archaic program for the French Republic but the whole point is that Daudet fights the Republic as a royalist, and has no need of respecting the norms of the republic, the norms of democracy. He organizes gangs that are at his disposal for pogroms, and the bourgeoisie says: "Here is my man."

Daudet's party differs from other parties in not being bound even by the superficial prejudices or fictions of democracy. Daudet knows how to prepare incendiary attacks, killings, bloodlettings and so on. Unless my memory fails me, the French press has, since the war reported on five or ten occasions rumors about appointing Leon Daudet —this malicious buffoon, this French Purishkevich[60]—as Minister of Internal Affairs. And this is no joke at all. Today this is premature, but we have here a figure around whom the corresponding elements are rallying, selected elements who will play the chief role for the Republic on the other side of the barricades. Similarly in all other countries. I leave aside England, the English parliament and the

French parliament. What are the churches in England alone worth! Not for nothing has Lloyd George said that the Church is the central power station of all parties, holding in its grip all the leaders of the working class. And, in addition, you have the auxiliary storm-troop gangs for purposes of direct assault. This gives you some inkling of the colossal difficulties amid which the Communist parties will have to pick their way even after they conquer the majority of the working class. But they have not yet conquered this majority. They must still conquer it. Consequently we are facing a protracted process. The struggle of the European and world proletariat for power is very arduous and spun-out but—with a correct policy—it is absolutely assured, absolutely certain. Parallel with the struggle there will occur the grandiose process of our socialist accumulation, our socialist construction at home.

From Hit-and-Miss Work To Systematic Construction.

From this standpoint we must make a transition in all relations from a migratory way of life to stable and settled forms, from hasty hit-and-miss work to systematic and methodic work. We have all sinned on this score. We must pass from our absolute universality—and in this I am in complete agreement with Comrade Bukarin—over to specialization. We must start to perfect our knowledge in all fields and most important of all we must wage war against a type created by our history during the last five years. It is the type of individual who is capable of everything, knows everything, supervises from the sidelines, and issues directives to everybody. I lived in emigration in Vienna for several years and the Viennese have a word which I believe is not to be found in any other language. This word is "kibitzer." Make note of it. It will come in handy. It applies to a man who when, for example, two others are playing a game of chess, will unfailingly sit himself down and always knows the best move that ought to be made; but when you sit down to play with him, he turns out to be a first class botcher. This, of course, applies not alone to chess but to anything you please, to questions of technology, as well as to tool shops and so forth.

Among us this "kibitzer" disease is very widespread. And it flows, I repeat, from our entire situation. All of us were thrown hither and thither becoming jacks of all trades but masters of none. And we had to put up with this nomadic way of life. It was unavoidable. But to the extent that a prolonged preparatory work is under way in the West to attain discipline and to conquer confidence while we in our country are at work conquering the economic life, to the same extent the transition to systematic and methodical work plays a colossal role and there comes to the fore the crucially important question of reproducing our party, of replenishing and regenerating its ranks, of making good the losses.

Education of the Youth—A Life-and-Death Question For Our Party.

In that very same nucleus of the former Bromley factory where I spent several hours, I was struck by the fact that the party there was held together chiefly by the older cadres, that is, by workers of the older generations. The fact is that the generation that grew up in 1916-17 is apparently hardly attracted to us. The Bromley workers told me that young proletarians who have now reached the age of 21 or 22 or 23, and especially the 24-year old show little interest in politics. Among them there is apathy, a certain indifference — drunkenness and card playing are more prevalent than among the older and younger generations, and the youngest generation which is now 17 or 18 or 19 years old constitutes the most auspicious and responsive element. This new generation has matured already within the framework of a stable Soviet power. As a whole it thinks of itself only in Soviet terms; it seeks leadership, it is more cultured, it tends to group around our clubs, it gravitates toward culture. This is the generation that the party can completely take into its own hands.

It is a new generation which has grown up under the conditions of the Soviet regime, and it mirrors these conditions. And so we must assure the restoration of our party's basic capital. I say this not at all for the sake of turning a high-sounding phrase. I say that the question of educating the youth is now a life-and-death question for our party.

At the Fourth Congress of the Comintern where we shall once again assay the international situation, where we shall once again have to grant a deferment to the European revolution, we shall say that during the year and a half that has elapsed since the Third World Congress, we have kept firmly on our own feet, and we shall maintain ourselves because, in the first place, we have learned how to wield state power, how to maneuver with it and manipulate it; and secondly, because we have learned and are learning how to dispose of our party's basic capital.

The purge proved most beneficial. This is perfectly clear and indisputable today. It has restored the party's political confidence in itself, but at the same time it has restricted and pared down our party by eliminating the stray elements and thereby diminishing the party cadres. Meanwhile the task of our country still remains gigantic. A new state power will not appear on the European horizon before a certain and rather considerable number of months have elapsed, and maybe even a certain, though not large, number of years. And our work will of course proceed under better conditions than those of the last five years. Nevertheless we are not insured against new relapses of capitalist fury against us up to and including the restoration of the war fronts. All this flows precisely from the dialectic of the class struggle. Right now the intensification of the revolutionary movement in Europe might prove to be a signal for an assault against Soviet Russia. In practice the incipient proletarian power in Germany —and history will still apparently unravel its tangled skein from Russia through Germany to the West—has posed before us tasks which go far beyond the limits of our domestic construction. To this end it is imperative for us to renew our party cadres, create a mighty reserve of youth. And while we shall once again say to the Communist parties: "You, European Communists must go to the masses before the question of conquering power confronts you pointblank; you must learn to correct your mistakes; you must learn to conquer the masses," then to our own party, we say: "Before us is a young party which we must conquer in order to hold the Soviet fortress in our own hands until the proletarian revolution conquers Europe, and later the whole world."

21

Speech in Honour of the Communist International

Comrade delegates to the World Congress, working men and working women of Moscow, Red Army soldiers, Red sailors, commander and commissars!

Once again within the walls of Red Moscow we greet our dear guests, the elected and chosen representatives of the world working class. It is five years since the gates of Moscow have been opened wide for the delegates of the world proletarian revolution. Five years of struggle. Five years of suffering and sacrifice. Five years of struggle for our right to exist as a Workers' and Peasants' Government. Five years of assaults, blows and treachery by the enemy; five years of fraternal support by our friends. And even today, on the Fifth Soviet Anniversary we have normal relations with only one major power—defeated Germany. We remain unrecognized to this very day. But we have received recognition from history. We have been adopted and accepted with enthusiasm into the family of the world working class. Today this class sends us its exalted greetings, sealed by the bonds of complete solidarity.

Surveying your ranks, we can with calm assurance say to the journalists, the politicians and all representatives of the other camp: Cast your experienced eyes over Red Moscow today. Examine whether there is so much as a crack between the Soviet power, the Red Army and the toiling people—that crack which our enemies would like to magnify into a gulf and an abyss

Never were the Soviet government and the working class so much in harmony as they are today, after five years of struggle and suffering. Messrs. Politicians of the other camp, if your governments entertain doubts concerning the strength of the Soviet regime—cast your eyes attentively over the ranks of Red warriors, workers and peasants marching today across this Square.

If Messrs Capitalists hope that capitalism will be reborn again in our country, they will be disappointed. For the resurrection of capitalism in our country, they would have to wait until the second coming of Christ.

We shall today address the delegates who have come to us from fifty countries in all parts of the world, the representatives of the toilers of all Europe, of America, of the peoples of the East, of Africa and Australia, all of whom are represented at the Congress and whose eyes, Red Army, are fixed upon you. And we shall tell them and show them by our today's celebration that we are not only patiently and confidently awaiting the termination of the struggle for the emancipation of the toilers, but that we have not been sitting with our hands folded. We have improved our organization both in military and civilian pursuits; we have tirelessly sought the path to the hearts of the working class, not only the advanced workers but also the ignorant, feebly class-conscious and downtrodden workers. We shall say to our brothers and guests: We know how hard it is to struggle against capitalist Europe armed to its teeth; we know what your conditions are in this struggle and we are ready to stand by under our Red Banner, guarding the fortress of the Soviet Republic, knowing full well that your policy is correct and will lead to victory.

There are still many difficult hours in store for the working class of Soviet Russia; there are many tasks still unsolved by the Soviet power; but in struggle we have conquered peace for ourselves for a long time to come, and all of us to the last man are ready to put aside the implements of war in order to engage in peaceful labors—to heal the heavy wounds on the body of the Soviet Republic's economy. We wanted peace and we hope that during this same month there will convene in Moscow a conference of those states that have warred against us to discuss disarmament. Wherever collaboration is needed in order to secure peace, there the Soviet power will be the first to raise its hands.

If we receive a sincere and honest response from those whom we are inviting to make peace, all of us to the last man would with gladness in our hearts reduce our Army to one-half, one-third, and even one-tenth of its present size. And meanwhile we wait, without renouncing hopes that peace will be attained. We wait without letting the rifles slip out of the hands of the workers and peasants.

We have watched a procession of many governments and many Ministers who from their lofty thrones regarded the Soviet power as something ephemeral, something injected into history on the crest of an accidental wave. Not so long ago, in Genoa, when our delegates proposed the establishment of peaceful relations and a reduction of armaments, Lloyd George, the representative of capitalist England, replied haughtily: "Let us first take a look at what sort of passengers you are and then perhaps we shall take you aboard ship." He kept looking at us so long that he stubbed his toe and fell overboard himself.

This is why I say: Many difficult hours are still ahead; more than once will the clouds gather over the heads of the working class, but we know that when the time comes, these clouds will scatter. Two days before this celebration, the fogs had colored all of Moscow white, but the Soviet calendar reads true. We now see red banners flying here beneath a clear blue sky. Even the sun has put in its appearance on the holiday of the Fifth Anniversary of the October Revolution. We know that soon will come the dawn of the bright unquenchable sun of human brotherhood, of peaceful labor and superior culture. Foreseeing this we gather new inspiration. We will not surrender our banners and the Soviet Republic will grow mighty.

In its name and in the name of all the participants in today's demonstration I propose that we greet our guests with unanimous and fraternal cheer. Hurrah!

(At the conclusion of Comrade Trotsky's speech, thunderous cheers kept rolling over the Red Square, cheers in which the voices of all the military detachments and the endless columns of demonstrators joined.)

22

The New Economic Policy of Soviet Russia and the Perspectives of the World Revolution

Delivered at the November 14th, 1922 Session of the Fourth World Congress of the Comintern

The Course of the Civil War.

The chief task of every revolutionary party is the conquest of power. To use the philosophical terminology of idealism, in the Second International this task was regarded as merely a "regulative idea," which means an idea having little relation to practice.

It is only within the last few years that we have been learning on an international scale to make the conquest of political power a practical revolutionary aim. The Russian revolution aided in this. The fact that we in Russia can name a definite date—October 25 (November 7) 1917—on which the Communist Party, leading the working class, wrested political power from the hands of the bourgeoisie proves more decisively than any arguments that the conquest of power is not a "regulative idea" for revolutionists, but a practical task.

On November 7, 1917 our party assumed power. As was soon disclosed quite clearly, this did not signify the end of the Civil War. On the contrary, the Civil War actually began to unfold on a large scale in our country only after the October overturn. This is not only a fact of historical interest but also a source of the most important lessons for the Western European proletariat.

Why did events follow this course? The explanation must be sought in the cultural and political backwardness of a country that had just cast off Czarist barbarism. The big bourgeoisie and the nobility had gained some political experience, thanks to the municipal Dumas, the *zemstvos*, the state Duma, etc. The petty bourgeoisie had little political experience, and the bulk of the population, the peasantry, still less. Thus the main reserves of the counter-revolution— the well-to-do peasants (*kulaks*) and, to a degree, also the middle peasants—came precisely from this extremely amorphous milieu. And it was only after the bourgeoisie began to grasp fully what it had lost by losing political power, and only after it had set in motion its counter-revolutionary combat nucleus, that it succeeded in gaining access to the peasant and petty-bourgeois elements and layers; and therewith the bourgeoisie had, of necessity, to yield the leading posts to the most reactionary elements among the ranking officers of noble birth. As a result, the Civil War unfolded fully only after the October overturn. The ease with which we conquered power on November 7, 1917, was paid for by the countless sacrifices of the Civil War. In countries that are older in the capitalist sense, and with a higher culture, the situation will, without doubt, differ profoundly. In these countries the popular masses will enter the revolution far more fully formed in political respects. To be sure, the orientation of individual layers and groups among the proletariat, and all the more so among the petty-bourgeoisie, will still continue to fluctuate violently and change but, nevertheless, these changes will occur far more systematically than in our country; the present will flow much more directly out of the past. The bourgeoisie in the West is preparing its counterblow in advance. The bourgeoisie more or less knows what elements it will have to depend upon and it builds its counter-revolutionary cadres in advance. We witness this in Germany; we witness this, even if not quite so distinctly, in France; and finally we see it in its most finished form in Italy, where in the wake of the incompleted revolution there came the completed counter-revolution which employed not unsuccessfully some of the practices and methods of the revolution.

What does this mean? This means it will hardly be possible to catch the European bourgeoisie by surprise as we caught the Russian bourgeoisie. The European bourgeoisie is more intelligent, and more farsighted; it is not wasting time. Everything that can be set on foot against us is being mobilized by it right now. The revolutionary proletariat will thus encounter on its road to power not only the combat vanguards of the counter-revolution but also its heaviest reserves. Only by smashing, breaking up and demoralizing these enemy forces will the proletariat be able to seize state power. But by way of compensation, after the proletarian overturn the vanquished bourgeoisie will no longer dispose of powerful reserves from which it could draw forces for prolonging the civil war. In other words, after the conquest of power, the European proletariat will in all likelihood have far more elbow room for its creative work in economy and culture than we had in Russia on the day after the overturn. The more difficult and gruelling the struggle for state power, all the less possible will it be to challenge the proletariat's power after the victory.

This general proposition must be dissected and concretized with regard to each country depending upon its social structure and its order of succession in the revolutionary process. It is perfectly obvious that the larger is the number of countries where the proletariat overthrows the bourgeoisie, all the briefer will be the revolutionary birth pangs in the other countries, and all the less inclined will the vanquished bourgeoisie be to resume the struggle for power—especially if the proletariat shows that on such questions it doesn't like to be trifled with. And the proletariat will, of course, do just that. And to this end, it will be able to utilize fully the example and experience of the Russian proletariat. We made mistakes in various fields, including, of course, politics as well. But by and large we did not set the European working class a poor example of resoluteness, of firmness and, when need arose, of ruthlessness in revolutionary struggle. This ruthlessness is nothing but the highest revolutionary humanitarianism, if only because, by assuring success, it shortens the arduous road of the crisis. Our Civil War was not simply a military process—of course it was that, saving the presence of esteemed pacifists, including those who through misunderstanding still keep wandering into our Communist ranks. The Civil War was not only a military process, but something more. It was also—and even above all—a political process. Through the methods of war, the struggle unfolded for the political reserves, that is, in the main, for the peasantry. After vacillating for a long time between the bourgeois-landlord bloc, the "democracy" serving this bloc, and the revolutionary proletariat, the peasantry invariably—at the decisive moment when the final choice had to be made—cast in their lot with the proletariat, supporting it—not with democratic ballots but with food supplies, horses, and force of arms. Just this decided the victory in our favor.

The peasantry thus played a gigantic role in the Russian revolution. It will also play a great role in other countries, for example, in France where the peasantry still constitutes a bigger half of the population. But those comrades are mistaken who assume that the peasantry is capable of playing an independent, leading role in the revolution, on equal rights, so to speak, with the proletariat. If we conquered in the Civil War, it was not solely and not so much because of the correctness of our military strategy. It was rather because of the correctness of our political strategy on which our military operations were invariably based throughout the Civil War. We did not forget for a moment that the basic task of the proletariat consisted in attracting the peasantry to its side. However, we did not do it after the S.R. fashion. The latter, as is well known, enticed the peasants by dangling an independent democratic role before them and then betrayed them hand and foot to the landlords. We were positive that the peasantry constitutes a vacillating mass which is as a whole incapable of an independent, and all the less so, leading revolutionary role. By being resolute in our actions we made the peasant masses understand that there was only one choice open to them—the choice between the revolutionary proletariat on the one side, and the officers of noble birth at the head of the counter-revolution, on the other. Failing this resoluteness on our part in tearing down the democratic partition, the peasantry would have remained confused, continuing to vacillate between the different camps and the different shades of "democracy"—and the revolution would have ineluctably perished. The democratic parties, with the Social Democracy in the van—and there is no doubt that the same situation in Western Europe, too, will arise—acted invariably as the bellwethers of the counter-revolution. Our experience on this score is conclusive in its character. You know, Comrades, that a few days ago our Red Army occupied Vladivostok[61]. This occupation liquidates the last link in the long chain of the Civil War fronts during the last half of a decade. Apropos of the occupation of Vladivostok by the Red troops, Miliukov, the well known leader of the Russian Liberal Party, has written in his Paris daily a few historico-philosophic lines, which I am prepared to term classical. In an article dated November 7, he sketches briefly the imbecilic and ignominious, but steadfast role of the party of democracy. I quote:

"This sad history—it has always been a sad history (*laughter*)—begins with a solemn proclamation of the complete unanimity of the anti-Bolshevik front. Merkulov[62] (he was the chief of the counter-revolution in the Far East) acknowledged that the "non-socialists" (that is, the Black Hundred elements) owed their victory in great

measure to the democratic elements. But the support of democracy,"
continues Miliukov, "was used by Merkulov only as a tool for overthrowing the Bolsheviks. Once this was achieved, the power was
seized by these elements who in the main regarded the democrats as
concealed Bolsheviks."

This passage which I have just called classic may seem trite. As
a matter of fact, it only repeats what has more than once been said
by Marxists. But you must recall that this now is being said by the
liberal Miliukov—six years after the Revolution. It ought to be borne
in mind that he is here drawing the balance sheet of the political role
of the Russian democracy on a vast arena—from the Finnish Gulf
to the shores of the Pacific. This is what happened in the case of
Kolchak, next with Denikin, and then with Yudenich. This is what
happened during the English, French and American occupations.
That is how it was during Petlura's reign in the Ukraine. All along
our frontiers the one and the same wearisomely monotonous phenomenon kept recurring. The democracy—the Mensheviks and the
S.R.'s—drove the peasantry into the arms of reaction, the latter seized
power, unmasked itself completely, thrust the peasants aside, whereupon the victory of the Bolsheviks followed. Among the Mensheviks
there ensued the chapter of repentance. But not for long—till the next
temptation. And thereupon, the same history was repeated in the same
sequence in some other theater of the Civil War. First, betrayal, and
discredited as it appears to be, we can nevertheless be sure that it will
be repeated by the Social Democrats in all countries whenever the
proletariat's struggle for power becomes fierce. The primary task of
the proletarian revolutionary party in all countries is to be implacably
then semi-repentance. Yet, extremely simple as this mechanics is, and
resolute once the issue is transferred to the arena of civil war.

The Conditions For Socialist Construction.

Once power has ben conquered, the task of construction, above all
in economy, becomes posed as the key and, at the same time, the
most difficult task. The solution of this task depends upon factors
of different orders and varying scope: First, the level to which the
productive forces have been developed and in particular the reciprocal
relation between industry and agriculture. Second, the general cultural
and organizational level of the working class which has conquered
state power. Third, the political situation internationally and nationally, namely—whether the bourgeoisie has been defeated decisively or

still continues to resist; whether foreign military interventions are under-
way; whether the technological intelligentsia engages in sabotage, and
so forth.

The relative importance of these factors for socialist construction
is in the order that I have enumerated. The most fundamental of
these factors is the level of the productive forces; next comes the cultural level of the proletariat; and, finally, the political or military-
political situation in which the proletariat finds itself consequent upon
the conquest of power. But this is a rigidly logical order. In practice, the working class upon assuming power collides first of all against
political difficulties. In our country these were the White Guard
fronts, the interventions, and so on. Secondly, the proletarian vanguard runs up against difficulties that stem from the inadequate cultural level of the broadest working masses. And only then—and
thirdly—does the economic construction collide with the limits set by
the existing level of the productive forces.

Our party when in power had to carry on its work almost invariably
under the pressure of needs dictated by the Civil War; and the history
of economic construction during the five years of Soviet Russia's
existence cannot be understood if approached solely from the standpoint of economic expediency. It must be approached, first of all,
with the gauge of military-political necessity and, only in the second
place with the gauge of economic expediency.

What is rational in economic life does not always coincide with what
is necessary in politics. If in the course of war I am menaced by a
White Guard invasion, I blow up a bridge. From the abstract standpoint of economic expediency it is barbarism, but from a political
standpoint it is a necessity. I would be a fool and a criminal not to
blow up a bridge in time. We are reconstructing our economy as a
whole primarily under the pressure of the need to secure militarily the
power of the working class. We have learned in the elementary school
of Marxism that it is impossible to jump from capitalism into the
socialist society at one leap. Nor has any of us ever interpreted so
mechanically Engels' famous words· concerning the leap from the
kingdom of necessity into the realm of freedom. None of us ever
believed that upon conquering power a new society could be built
overnight. What Engels really had in mind was an entire epoch of
revolutionary transformations which on a world historical scale would
indeed signify a "leap." From the standpoint of practical work,
however, it is not a leap but a whole system of intermeshing reforms,

transformations and sometimes very detailed undertakings. It is perfectly obvious that from the economic standpoint the expropriation of the bourgeoisie is justified to the extent that the workers' state is able to organize the exploitation of enterprises upon new beginnings. The wholesale, overall nationalization which we carried through in 1917-18 was completely out of harmony with the condition I have just now outlined. The organizational potentialities of the workers' state lagged far behind total nationalization. But the whole point is that under the pressure of Civil War we had to carry this nationalization through. Nor is it difficult to demonstrate and to understand that had we sought to act more cautiously in an economic sense, i.e., to carry through the expropriation of the bourgeoisie at a "rational," gradual pace, it would have been the height of political irrationality and the greatest folly on our part. Such a policy would not have enabled us to celebrate our Fifth Anniversary in Moscow in the company of Communists of the whole world. We must reconstruct mentally all the peculiarities of our position as it shaped up on the day after November 7, 1917. Indeed, had we been able to enter the arena of socialist development after the victory of the revolution in Europe, our bourgeoisie would have quaked in its boots and it would have been very simple to deal with it. They would not have dared to so much as stir a little finger upon the seizure of power by the Russian proletariat. In that case, we could have tranquilly taken hold only of the large-scale enterprises, leaving the middle-sized and small ones to exist for a while on the private capitalist basis; later we would have reorganized the middle-sized enterprises, rigidly taking into account our organizational and productive potentialities and requirements. Such an order would unquestionably have been in harmony with economic "rationality," but unfortunately the political sequence of events failed to take it into consideration this time, either. Generally speaking, we must bear in mind that the revolutions are in and of themselves an outward expression of the fact that the world is by no means ruled by "economic rationality;" it is still the task of the Socialist revolution to install the rule of reason in the domain of economic life and thereby in all other domains of social life.

When we assumed power, capitalism still straddled the whole world (as it continues to straddle the world to this very day). Our bourgeoisie refused to believe, come what may, that the October overturn was something serious and durable. After all, throughout Europe, throughout the world, the bourgeoisie remained in power. But in our country, in backward Russia it was—the proletariat!   Hating us, the Russian bourgeoisie refused to take us seriously.   The initial decrees of the revolutionary power were greeted with scornful laughter; they were flouted; they remained unfulfilled.   Even the newspapermen —as cowardly a set as you can find—even they refused to take seriously the basic revolutionary measures of the workers' government.   It seemed to the bourgeoisie as if it all was just a tragic joke, a misunderstanding.   How else was it possible to teach our bourgeoisie and its flunkies to respect the new power, except by confiscating its property?   There was no other way.   Every factory, every bank, every office, every little shop, every lawyer's waiting room became a fortress against us.   They provided bellicose counter-revolution with a material base, and an organic network of communications.   The banks at the time almost openly supported the saboteurs, paying out salaries to striking functionaries.   For exactly this reason we did not approach the question from the standpoint of abstract economic "rationality" (as do Kautsky, Otto Bauer, Martov and other political eunuchs), but from the standpoint of the revolutionary war needs.   It was necessary to smash the enemy, to deprive it of its sources of nourishment, independently of whether or not organized economic activity could keep up with this.   In the sphere of economic construction we were compelled in those days to concentrate all our efforts on the most elementary tasks — to provide material support, even if on semistarvation levels, for the maintenance of the workers' state, for feeding and clothing the Red Army defending this state at the fronts, for feeding and clothing (this already came second in the order of importance) the section of the working class which remained in the cities.   This primitive state economy which solved these tasks for better or for worse was subsequently given the name of War Communism.

War Communism.

To define War Communism, three questions are most pertinent: How were the food supplies obtained?   How were they apportioned? How was the operation of state industries regulated?

The Soviet power did not meet up with free trade in bread grains but with a monopoly resting on the old commercial apparatus.   The Civil War shattered this apparatus. Nothing remained for the workers' state except to improvise hastily a substitute state apparatus for siphoning the grain from the peasants and concentrating the supply in its own hands.

Provisions were distributed virtually without regard to labor productivity. And it could not have been otherwise. In order to establish a correspondence between work and wages, one must dispose of a far more perfected apparatus of economic administration, and far larger food resources. During the first years of the Soviet regime, however, it was primarily a question of keeping the urban population from starving to death. This was achieved by fixed food rations. Both the confiscation of grain surpluses from the peasants and the apportioning of rations were essentially measures of a beleaguered fortress and not of socialist economy. Under certain conditions, namely, with an early outbreak of the revolution in the West, the transition from the regime of a beleaguered fortress to the socialist regime could, naturally, be facilitated and speeded up for us in the highest degree. But we shall speak of this presently.

What was the gist of War Communism in relation to industry? Every economy can exist and grow only provided a certain proportionality exists between its various sectors. Different branches of industry enter into specific quantitative and qualitative relations with one another. There must be a certain proportion between those branches which produce consumer goods and those which produce the means of production. Proper proportions must likewise be preserved within each of these branches. In other words, the material means and living labor power of a nation and of all mankind must be apportioned in accordance with a certain correlation of agriculture and industry and of the various branches of industry so as to enable mankind to exist and progress.

How is this achieved? Under capitalism it is achieved through the market, through free competition, through the mechanism of supply and demand, the play of prices, the succession of periods of prosperity and periods of crisis. We call this method anarchistic, and correctly so. It is bound up with the squandering of a huge quantity of resources and values through periodic crises and it inevitably leads to wars which threaten to destroy human culture. Nevertheless this anarchistic capitalist method establishes, within the limits of its historical action. a relative proportionality between the various branches of economy, a necessary correlation owing to which bourgeois society is alone able to exist without choking to death.

Our prewar economy had its own internal proportionality that became established as a result of the interplay of capitalist forces in the market. Then came the war, and with it a vast reshuffling of the correlation between the different branches of economy. War industries sprouted like poisonous mushrooms at the expense of industries of the usual type. Next came the revolution and the Civil War with its havoc and sabotage, with its secret sapping. But what did we inherit? An economy retaining faint traces of proportionality among the various sectors which had existed under capitalism, which were afterwards deformed by the imperialist war and were then completely mangled by the Civil War—this was our heritage. What methods could we use to find our way to the highway of economic development?

Under socialism economic life will be directed in a centralized manner, and therefore the necessary proportionality among its different branches will be achieved through a meticulous plan observing all proportions—and of course allowing for the greatest possible autonomy to each sector, which, however, in its turn would remain subject first to all-national, and later, international control. This overall envelopment of the entire economy, this purely Socialist method of accounting that we are talking about, cannot be created *a priori*, through cogitation, or within four office walls. It can grow only out of a gradual adaptation of an existing practical economic accounting with regard to the available material resources together with the latent possibilities as well as the new needs of the socialist society. A long road lies ahead. Where, then, could and should we have started in 1917-18? The capitalist apparatus—with its market, its banks, its exchanges—was destroyed. The Civil War was at its peak of intensity. There could not even be talk of coming to terms economically with the bourgeoisie or even a section of it, in the sense of granting it certain economic rights. The bourgeois apparatus of economic management was destroyed not only on a national scale but within each individual enterprise. Hence arose the elementary burning task: to create a substitute apparatus, even if only a crude and temporary one, in order to extract from our chaotic industrial heritage the most indispensable supplies for the warring army and for the working class. In the nature of things this was not an economic task in the strict sense of the word, but rather the task of producing for war. With the aid of the trade unions the state took physical possession of the industrial enterprises and set up an extremely cumbersome and unwieldy centralized apparatus, which despite all its defects nevertheless enabled us to provide the armies in the field with supplies and military equipment, the volume of which was extremely inadequate but which nevertheless sufficed for our emerging from the struggle not as the vanquished but as the victors.

The policy of confiscating the surpluses of the peasants led inescapably to a contraction and decline in agricultural production. The policy of paying equal wages led inescapably to the lowering of labor productivity. The policy of a centralized bureaucratic management of industry excluded the possibility of a genuine centralized management, of fully utilizing technical equipment along with the available labor force. But this entire policy of War Communism was imposed upon us by the regime of a fortress under seige, a fortress with a disorganized economy and spent resources.

You might ask whether we had expected to make the transition from War Communism to socialism without making major economic turns, without experiencing convulsions, without executing retreats, i.e., effecting the transition more or less along a steadily rising curve. Yes, it is true that at this period we did actually think that the revolutionary development in Western Europe would proceed more swiftly. This is undeniable. And had the proletariat in Germany, in France, in Europe as a whole, conquered power in 1919, our entire economic development would have assumed a completely different form. In 1883 Marx, writing to Nicholas Danielson[63], one of the theoreticians of Russian populism (*Narodnikism*), that should the proletariat assume power in Europe before the Russian *obschina* (communal village agriculture) had been completely abolished by history then even this *obschina* could become one of starting points for Communist development in Russia. And Marx was absolutely right. We had even more reason to assume that if the European proletariat had conquered power in 1919, it could have taken our backward country in tow—backward in the economic and cultural sense—could have come to our aid technically and organizationally and thus have enabled us, by correcting and modifying our methods of War Communism, to move straight toward a genuine socialist economy. Yes, admittedly, such were our hopes. We have never based our policy on the minimizing of revolutionary possibilities and perspectives. On the contrary, as a living revolutionary force we have always striven to expand these possibilities and exhaust each one to the very end. It is only the Messrs. Scheidemanns and Eberts who on the eve of the revolution deny it, have no faith in it, and make ready to become His Imperial Majesty's Ministers. The revolution catches them by surprise, engulfs them; they flounder helplessly and later at the first opportunity become converted into the tools of the counter-revolution. As regards the gentlemen of the Two-and-a-Half International, they made special efforts in those days to demarcate themselves from the Second International; they proclaimed the inception of a revolutionary epoch and they recognized the dictatorship of the proletariat. Naturally, it was only empty talk so far as they were concerned. At the very first sign of an ebb, all of this nondescript human rubbish returned under Scheidemann's roof. But the very fact that the Two-and-a-Half International was formed is evidence that the revolutionary perspective of the Communist International and of our party in particular was not at all "Utopian"—not alone from the standpoint of the general tendency of historical development but also from the standpoint of its actual tempo.

After the war what the revolutionary proletariat lacked was the revolutionary party. The Social Democracy saved capitalism, that is postponed its hour of doom for several years, or more accurately, prolonged its death agony because the life of the capitalist world today is nothing but a long drawn out death agony.

But at all events, this fact created the least favorable conditions for the Soviet Republic and for its economic development. Workers' and Peasants' Russia found herself caught in the vise of economic blockade. From the West we received not technical and organizational assistance, but one military intervention after another. And after it became clear that we would emerge as victors in the military sense it likewise became clear that in the economic sense we were compelled to continue for a long while to depend upon our own resources and forces.

"The New Economy Policy" (The NEP).

Hence—out of War Communism, i.e., out of emergency measures designed to sustain the economic life of a beleagured fortress—arose the need of changing over to a system of measures that would assure a gradual expansion of the country's productive forces, even without the collaboration of Socialist Europe. The military victory which would have been excluded if not for War Communism, permitted us, in turn, to pass over from measures dictated by military necessity to measures dictated by economic expediency. Such is the origin of the so-called New Economic Policy. It is frequently called a retreat, and we ourselves—for good and substantial reasons— call it a retreat. But in order to correctly appraise exactly what this retreat involves, in order to understand how little this retreat resembles "capitulation" it is first necessary to have a clear picture of our present economic situation and of the tendencies of its development.

In March 1917 Czarism was overthrown. In October 1917 the working class seized power. Virtually all of the land, nationalized by the state, was handed over to the peasants. The peasants cultivating this land are now obliged to pay the state a fixed tax in kind, which forms the main fund for socialist construction. All the railways, all the industrial enterprises became state property and with a few minor exceptions, the state operates these enterprises for its own benefit. The entire credit system is in the hands of the state. Foreign trade is a state monopoly. Anyone capable of evaluating soberly and without preconceptions the result of the five years' existence of the workers' state would have to say: Yes, indeed, for a backward country there has been a very notable socialist advance.

The main peculiarity, however, lies in the fact that this advance has not been effected through a steady upward movement but through zigzags. First we had the regime of " Communism," followed by our opening the gates for market relations. The bourgeois press has declared this turn in policy to be a renunciation of Communism, marking the beginnings of a capitulation of capitalism. Needless to say, the Social Democrats are expounding this theme, elaborating it and adding commentaries to it. It is inadmissible, however, not to recognize that here and there even a few of our friends have fallen into doubt: Isn't there actually a masked capitulation to capitalism here? Isn't there really a danger that capitalism might, by basing itself on the free market we restored, begin to develop more and more, and gain the upper hand over the beginnings of socialism? To answer this question it is first necesary to clear away the basic misunderstanding. The contention that Soviet economic development is travelling from Communism to capitalism is false to the core. We never had Communism. We never had socialism, nor could we have had it. We nationalized the disorganized bourgeois economy, and during the most critical period of life-and-death struggle we established a regime of "Communism" in the distribution of articles of consumption. By vanquishing the bourgeoisie in the field of politics and war, we gained the possibility of coming to grips with economic life and we found ourselves constrained to reintroduce the market forms of relations between the city and the village, between the different branches of industry, and between the individual enterprises themselves.

Failing a free market, the peasant would be unable to find his place in economic life, losing the incentive to improve and expand his crops. Only a mighty upsurge of state industry, enabling it to provide the peasant and agriculture with all its requirements, will prepare the soil for integrating the peasant into the general system of socialist economy. Technically this task will be solved with the aid of electrification, which will deal a mortal blow to the backwardness of rural life, the mouzhik's barbaric isolation, and the idiocy of village life. But the road to all this is through improving the economic life of our peasant-proprietor as he is today. The workers' state can achieve this only through the market, which stimulates the personal and selfish interests of the petty proprietor. The initial gains are already at hand. This year the village will supply the workers' state with more bread-grains as taxes in kind than were received by the state in the period of War Communism through confiscation of the grain surpluses. At the same time, agriculture is undoubtedly on its way up. The peasant is satisfied—and in the absence of normal relations between the proletariat and the peasantry, socialist development is impossible in our country.

But the New Economic Policy does not flow solely from the inter-relations between the city and the village. This policy is a necessary stage in the growth of state-owned industry. Between capitalism, under which the means of production are owned by private individuals and all economic relations are regulated by the market—I say, between capitalism and complete socialism, with its socially planned economy, there are a number of transitional stages; and the NEP is essentially one of these stages

Let us analyze this question, taking the railways as a case in point. It is precisely railway transportation that provides a field which is prepared in the maximum degree for socialist economy, because the railway network in our country had been for the most part national-ized already under capitalism and it has been centralized and to a certain extent normalized by the very conditions of technology. The bigger half of the roads we obtained from the state, the remainder we confiscated from the private companies. A genuine socialist man-agement must of course approach the entire network as a unit, that is, not from the standpoint of an owner of this or that railway line, but from the standpoint of the interests of the entire transport system and the country's economy as a whole. It must apportion locomotives or freight cars among the various lines to meet the requirements of economic life as a whole. But a transition to such an economy even in the centralized field of railway transport is not so simple. A whole number of intermediate economic and technical stages is involved. Locomotives happen to be of various types, because they were constructed at different periods, by different companies, and in different plants, and, furthermore, different types of locomotives are simultaneously repaired in one and the same set of railway shops and, conversely, locomotives of the same type—in different shops. Capitalist society wastes, as is well known, a huge amount of labor power, by its super-diversification, and the anarchistic kaleidoscopy of the component parts of its productive apparatus. It is, consequently, necessary to sort the locomotives according to type and allot them to the various railway lines and shops. This will be the first serious step on the road toward normalization, that is, the institution of technological homogeneity with regard to locomotives and locomotive parts. Normalization, as we have said more than once, and correctly so, is socialism in technology. Failing normalization technology cannot reach its fullest flowering. And where should we start the normalization if not with railways? We did actually tackle this task but immediately ran up against major obstacles. The railway lines, not only those privately owned, but also the state-owned lines, settled their accounts with all the other economic enterprises through the medium of the market. Under the particular system this was economically unavoidable and necessary because the equipment and development of a particular line depends upon how far it justifies itself economically. Whether a particular railway is beneficial to the economy can be ascertained only through the medium of the market—so long as we have not yet elaborated the methods of overall statistical calculations of a socialist economy; and these methods, as I have said, can become available only as the result of an extensive practical experience gained on the basis of nationalized means of production.

And so, in the course of the Civil War the old methods of economic control were eliminated before it was possible to create new methods. Under these conditions the entire railway network was formally unified but each individual line in this network lost contact with the rest of the economic milieu and remained suspended in mid-air. By approaching the network as a self-sufficient technical entity, by consolidating railway carriages and the freight car stock of the entire network, by centralistically fixing uniform types of locomotives, and by centralizing the repair work, that is, by following an abstract

technico-socialist plan, we ran the risk of completely losing all control over what was necessary and what was not, over what was profitable and what was not in the case of each individual railway and the
network as a whole.   Which line should be expanded and which one
should be contracted?   What rolling stock and what personnel should
a given line have?   How much freight could the state transport for
its own needs and what share of the carrying capacity should be
allotted for the needs of other organizations and private individuals?
All these questions—at the given historical stage—cannot be resolved
except by fixing rates for transportatation, by correct bookkeeping, and
exact commercial calculation.   Only by maintaining a profit and loss
balance between the various sections of the railway network, coupled
with the same sort of balance among other branches of economy,
will we be able to elaborate methods of socialist calculation and the
methods for a new economic plan.   Hence flows the necessity—even
after all the railways have become state property — of permitting
individual railway lines or groups of lines to retain their economic
independence, in the sense of their being able to adjust themselves
to all the other economic enterprises upon which they depend or
which are serviced by them.   In and of themselves abstract plans
and formal socialist aims do not suffice to switch the operation of
railways from the capitalist over to the socialist track.   For a certain
and rather long period of time, the workers' state shall have to
utilize capitalist methods, that is, methods of the market, in operating
the railway network.

The foregoing considerations apply even more obviously to industrial enterprises which were not any way nearly so centralized and
so normalized under capitalism as the railway lines.   With the liquidation of the market and of the credit system each factory resembled
a telephone whose wires had been cut.   War Communism created
a bureaucratic surrogate of economic unity.   The machine-building
factories in the Urals, in the Donets Basin, Moscow, Petrograd and
elsewhere were consolidated under a single Central Commissariat,
which centralistically allotted them fuel, raw materials, technical
equipment and working forces, maintaining the latter through a system
of equal rations.   It is perfectly self-evident that such a bureaucratic
management completely levelled off the peculiarities of each individual enterprise and cancelled out any possibility of verifying its productive capacity and its gainfulness, even if the bookkeeping entries
of the Central Commission had been distinguished by a greater or

lesser degree of precision, which in reality has been out of the question.

Before each enterprise can function planfully as a component cell of the socialist organism, we shall have to engage in large-scale transitional activities of operating the economy through the market over a period of many years. And in the course of this transitional epoch each enterprise and each set of enterprises must to a greater or lesser degree orient itself independently in the market and test itself through the market. This is precisely the gist of the New Economic Policy: while politically it has meant that concessions to the peasantry have taken the limelight, it is of *no lesser* importance as an unavoidable stage in the development of state-owned industry during the transition from capitalist to socialist economy.

And so, in order to regulate industry the workers' state has resorted to methods of the market. A market must have a universal equivalent. In our case, as you know, this universal equivalent is in a rather sorry condition. Comrade Lenin has already dealt with our efforts to secure a more or less stable ruble; and he has pointed out that our attempts in this direction have not been entirely unsuccessful. It is very instructive to note that together with the restoration of the market, there has likewise occurred a revival of fetishistic manifestations in the domain of economic thought. Among those affected by it are many Communists in so far as they speak not as Communists but as traders on the market. Our enterprises, as you well know, suffer from a lack of resources. Where can we get them? Why, that's obvious—from the printing presses. We need only, it is argued, increase our currency emissions in order to set in motion a number of factories and plants now shut down. "In exchange for your paltry pieces of paper, which you issue in such miserly amounts," some comrades say, "we could in a few months supply you with linen, shoes, screws and other beautiful things." The utter falsity of such reasoning is perfectly obvious. The scarcity of the means of circulation is simply evidence of our poverty; and it signifies that in order to expand production we must first pass through a stage of primitive socialist accumulation. Our poverty in bread, in coal, locomotives, apartments, and so on today assumes the form of scarcity in the means of circulation because we have shifted our economic life over to the foundations of the market. Thereupon heavy industry has been pointing enviously to the successes of light industry. What does this mean? This means, that with the incipient revival of economy, the available resources are being directed in the main where they are most urgently needed—that is, into those branches that produced goods for personal or productive consumption of workers and peasants.   Business is now booming in enterprises of this type. Further, the state-owned enterprises are competing with one another on the market, and, in part, they have to compete with private enterprises, which, as we know, are very small numerically.   Only in this way will nationalized industry learn to function properly.   There is no other way of our reaching this goal.   Neither *a priori* economic plans hatched within heremetically sealed four office walls, nor abstract Communist sermons will secure it for us.   It is necessary for each state-owned factory, with its technical director and with its commercial director, to be subjected not only to control from the top— by the state organs—but also from below, by the market which will remain the regulator of the state economy for a long time to come. In proportion as the state-owned light industry, by consolidating itself on the market, starts to provide the state with income, we shall acquire the means of circulation for heavy industry.   Naturally this is not the only source at the disposal of the state.   It has other sources, too: there is the tax in kind, coming from the peasant, there are the taxes on private industry and private trade, income from tariffs, and so on.

The financial difficulties of our industry are not, therefore, self-limited in character but derive from the entire process of our economic revival.   If our Financial Commissariat were to accede to the demands of each industrial enterprise by increasing its currency emissions, the market would regurgitate the superfluous paper money, before the impatient factories succeeded in throwing new products into the markets.   In other words, the value of the ruble would drop so catastrophically that the purchasing power of this doubled or tripled emission would be less than the purchasing power of the money now in circulation.   Our state of course does not renounce new currency emissions, but these must come in consonance with the actual economic process and must in each case be so calculated as to increase the state's purchasing power and thereby aid in the primitive socialist accumulation.   Our state, for its part, does not renounce planned economy *in toto*, that is, of introducing deliberate and imperative corrections into the operations of the market.   But in so doing our state does not take as its point of departure some *a priori* calculation, or an abstract and extremely inexact plan-hypothesis, as was

the case under War Communism. Its point of departure is the actual
operation of this very same market; and one of the instruments of
regulating the market is the condition of the country's currency and
of its centralized governmental credit system.

The Forces and Resources of the Two Camps.

Whither is the NEP leading us :   Toward capitalism or toward
socialism? This is, of course, the central question. The market, the
free trade in grain, competition, leases, concessions—what will be
the upshot of all this? If you give the devil a finger, mightn't it be
necessary to give him next an arm and then a shoulder, and, in the
end, the whole body, too? We are already witnessing a revival of
private capital in the field of trade, especially along the channels
between the city and the village. For the second time in our country
private merchants' capital is passing through the stage of primitive
capitalist accumulation, while the workers' state is passing through
the period of primitive socialist accumulation. No sooner does private
merchants' capital arise than it seeks ineluctably to worm its way into
industry as well. The state is leasing factories and plants to private
business men. The accumulation of private capital now goes on,
in consequence, not merely in trade but also in industry. Isn't it then
likely that Messrs. Exploiters—the speculators, the merchants, the
lessees and the concessionaires—will wax more powerful under the
protection of the workers' state, gaining control of an ever larger
sector of the national economy, draining off the elements of socialism
through the medium of the market, and later at a propitious moment,
gaining control of state power, too? For we are as well aware as
Otto Bauer that economics constitutes the social foundation, while
politics is its superstructure. So doesn't all this really signify that
the NEP is a transition to capitalist restoration?

In answering abstractly a question posed in so abstract a manner,
no one can of course deny that the danger of capitalist restoration
is by no means excluded, no more than, in general, danger is excluded
of a temporary defeat in the course of any struggle. When we fought
Kolchak and Denikin, who were backed by the Entente, we incurred
the likely danger of being defeated as Kautsky benignly expected
from one day to the next. But, while taking into consideration the
theoretical possibility of defeat we oriented our policy in practice upon
victory. We supplemented this relation of forces with a firm will
and a correct strategy. And in the end we conquered. Once again

there is war between the self-same enemies: the workers' state and capitalism. But this time the hostilities occur not on the military arena but in the field of economy. Whereas during the Civil War there was a duel for influence over the peasants between the Red Army on the one side and the White Army on the other, so today the struggle between state capital and private capital is for the peasant market. In a struggle it is always necessary to have the fullest and most accurate estimate possible of the forces and resources disposed by the enemy and at our own disposal. How do matters stand on this score?

Our most important weapon in the economic struggle occurring on the basis of the market is—state power. Reformist simpletons are the only ones who are incapable of grasping the significance of this weapon. The bourgeoisie understands it excellently. The whole history of the bourgeoisie proves it.

Another weapon of the proletariat is that the country's most important productive forces are in its hands: the entire railway system, the entire mining industry, the crushing bulk of enterprises servicing industry are under the direct economic management of the working class.

The workers' state likewise owns the land, and the peasants annually contribute in return for using it, hundreds of million of puds (one pud equals 36 lbs.) in taxes in kind.

The workers' power holds the state frontiers: foreign commodities, and foreign capital generally can gain access to our country only within limits which are deemed desirable and legitimate by the workers' state.

Such are the weapons and means of socialist construction.

Our adversaries gain of course the opportunity to accumulate capital even under the workers' power—exploiting above all the free trade in grain. Merchants' capital may infiltrate and is already infiltrating industry, leasing enterprises, making profit on them and growing. All this is absolutely incontestable. But what are the reciprocal quantitative relations between these contending forces? What is the dynamic of these forces? In this sphere as in all others quantity passes into quality. If the country's most important productive forces were to fall into the hands of private capital, then there could not naturally even be talk of socialist construction and the days of workers' power would be numbered. How great is this danger? How close is it? Only facts and figures can give an answer to this question. I shall cite the most important and indispensable data.

Our railway system extends for 63,000 versts, employs more than 800,000 persons, and is wholly in the hands of the state. No one would deny that the railway system is a very important factor in economic life, and in many respects a decisive factor; and we do not propose to let it slip out of our hands.

Let us now consider the field of industry. Even now under the New Economic Policy all industrial enterprises without a single exception remain the property of the state. True enough, some of these enterprises are leased out. But what is the correlation between the industries which the state continues to operate itself and those which it has leased?

This correlation may be gauged from the following figures: There are more than 4,000 state-owned and state-operated enterprises, employing approximately one million workers; there are a little less than 4,000 leased enterprises employing all told about 80,000 workers. This means that in the state enterprises the average number of workers is 207 workers per enterprise, whereas in the leased enterprises the average is 17 workers. The explanation for this is to be found in the fact that under lease are secondary and, for the most part, tertiary enterprises in the light industry. But even of the leased enterprises only a little more than half (51 percent) are exploited by private capitalists: the remaining enterprises are operated by individual commissariats and distributive cooperative societies who rent them from the state and run them on their own account. In other words, there are about 2,000 of the smallest enterprises employing 40,000 to 50,000 workers under the exploitation of private capital as against 4,000 of the most powerful and best equipped enterprises, employing approximately one million workers, which are operated by the Soviet state. It is laughable and ridiculous to talk of the triumph of capitalism " in general " in the face of these facts and figures. Naturally the leased enterprises compete with the state-operated enterprises and from an abstract standpoint, one may say that if the leased enterprises are run very well while the state enterprises are run very poorly, then over a period of many years private capital would devour state capital. But we are still very far removed from this. Control over the economic process remains in the hands of the state power; and this power is in the hands of the working class. In reestablishing the market, the workers' state naturally introduced a number of juridical changes indispensable for obtaining a market turnover. Insofar as these legal and administrative reforms open up the possibility of capitalist accumulation they constitute indirect but very important concessions to the bourgeoisie. But our neo-bourgeoisie will be able to exploit these concessions only in proportion to its economic and political resources. We know what its economic resources are. They are less than modest. Politically its resources are equal to zero. And we shall do everything in our power to see to it that the bourgeoisie does not " accumulate capital " in the *political* field. You ought not to forget that the credit system and the tax apparatus remain in the hands of the workers' state and that this is a very important weapon in the struggle between state industry and private industry.

True enough, private capital plays a more extensive role in the field of trade. No exact figures on this score are as yet available. According to very rough approximations made by statisticians of our distributive cooperatives, private trading capital comprises 30 percent of the trading turnover in the country, while the state and the cooperatives have 70 percent. Private capital plays in the main the role of middleman between agriculture and industry, and in part, between the different branches of industry. But the most important industrial enterprises belong to the state; the key to foreign trade is likewise in its hands; the state is the chief buyer and chief seller on the market. Under these conditions the distributive cooperatives can compete quite successfully with private capital, with time working in favor of the former. Further, let us repeat once again that the pruning knife of taxation is a very important instrument. With it the workers' state will be able to clip the young plant of capitalism, lest it thrive too luxuriously.

In point of theory, we have always maintained that the proletariat would, upon conquering power, be compelled for a long while to tolerate along side the state enterprises the existence of those private enterprises which are technologically less advanced and least suited for centralization. Therewith we never had any doubt that the relations between the state enterprises and private enterprises, as well as the reciprocal relations among individual state enterprises or groups, would be regulated by the market through monetary calculations. But for this very reason we consequently recognized that parallel with the process of socialist economic reorganization there would still recur the process of private capitalist accumulation. It never entered our minds, however, to fear that private accumulation would outstrip and devour the growing state economy. Whence and why, then, all this talk about the inevitable victory of capitalism or of our alleged "capitulation" to it? It arises for no other reason save this, that we didn't at first simply leave the small enterprises in private hands but nationalized them and even attempted to run a number of them on the state's own account, but leased them later on. But, however you evaluate this economic zigzag—whether as an exigency arising out of the entire situation or as a tactical blunder—it is perfectly clear that this turn in policy or this "retreat" alters nothing in the relation of forces between the state industry and privately leased sectors. On the one hand you have, the state power, the railway system and one million industrial workers; and on the other, approximately 50,000 workers exploited by private capital. Where then is the slightest justification for claiming that under these conditions capitalist accumulation is assured the victory over socialist accumulation?

Clearly we hold the trump cards, all except one, which is indeed very important, namely: Private capital now operating in Russia is backed up by world capital. We are still living in a capitalist encirclement. For this reason, one can and should raise the question whether our incipient socialism, which still has to employ capitalist methods, may not in the end be bought up by world capitalism.

There are always two parties to a transaction of this kind: the buyer and the seller. But we hold the power—it is in the hands of the working class. It decides what concessions to make, their object as well as their scope. Foreign trade is a monopoly. European capital seeks to make a breach in this monopoly. But they will be sadly disappointed. The monopoly of foreign trade is of principled importance to us. It is one of our safeguards against capitalism which, of course, would not at all be averse under certain conditions *to buy up* our incipient socialism, after failing to snuff it out by military measures.

So far as concessions are concerned today, Comrade Lenin has here remarked: "Discussions are plentiful, concessions are scarce." (*Laughter.*) How explain this? Precisely by the fact that there is not and there will not be any capitulation to capitalism on our part. To be sure, those who favor the resumption of relations with Soviet Russia have more than once contended and written that world capitalism, in the throes of its greatest crisis, is in need of Soviet Russia; England needs an outlet for her goods in Russia, Germany needs Russian grain, and so forth and so on. This seems perfectly true, if one surveys the world through pacifist spectacles, that is, from the standpoint of "plain horse sense" which is invariably quite pacifistic. (*Laughter.*) And that is why it is invariably bamboozled. One would then imagine that the English capitalists would try with might and main to invest their funds in Russia; one would then imagine that the French bourgeoisie would orient German technology in this same direction so as to create new sources whereby German reparations could be paid. But we see nothing of the sort. Why not? Because we are living in an epoch when the capitalist equilibrium has been completely upset; because we live in an epoch when economic, political and military crises instantly criss-cross; an epoch of instability, uncertainty and unremitting alarm. This militates against the bourgeoisie's conducting any long-range policy, because such a policy immediately becomes transformed into an equation with too many unknowns. We finally succeeded in concluding a trade agreement with England. But this happened a year and a half ago; in reality, all our transactions with England are still on a cash-and-carry basis; we pay with gold; and the question of concessions is still in the phase of discussion.

If the European bourgeoisie and above all the English bourgeoisie believed that large-scale collaboration with Russia would bring about *immediately* a serious improvement in Europe's economic situation, then Lloyd George and Co. would have undoubtedly brought matters in Genoa to a different conclusion. But they are aware that collaboration with Russia cannot *immediately* bring any major and drastic changes. The Russian market will not eliminate English unemployment within a few weeks or even months. Russia can be integrated only gradually, as a constantly increasing factor, into Europe's and the world's economic life. Because of her vast extent, her natural resources, her large population and especially because of the stimulus imparted by her Revolution, Russia can become the most important economic force in Europe and in the world, but not instantaneously, not overnight, but only over a period of years. Russia could become a major buyer and supplier provided she were given credits today and, consequently, enabled to accelerate her economic growth. Within five or ten years she could become a major market for England. But in the latter event, the English government would have to believe that it could last ten years and that English capitalism would be strong enough ten years hence to retain the Russian market. In other words, a policy of genuine economic collaboration with Russia can only be a policy based on very broad foundations. But the whole point is that the postwar bourgeoisie is no longer capable of conducting long-range policies. It doesn't know what the next day will bring and, still less, what will happen on the day after tomorrow. This is one of the symptoms of the bourgeoisie's historical demise.

To be sure this seems to be in contradiction with Leslie Urquhart's[64] attempt to conclude an agreement with us for not less than 99 years. But this contradiction is truly only an apparent one. Urquhart's motivation is quite simple and, in its own way, unassailable; should capitalism survive in England and throughout the world for the next 99 years then Urquhart will keep his concessions in Russia, too! But what if the proletarian revolution erupts not 99 years or even 9 years from now but much earlier? What then? In that case, naturally, Russia would be the last place where the expropriated proprietors of the world could retain their property. But a man who is about to lose his head, has little cause to shed tears over his mop of hair . . . .

When we first made the offer of long-term concessions, Kautsky drew the conclusion that we had lost hope in the early coming of the proletarian revolution. Today he ought to conclude flatly that we have postponed the revolution for at least 99 years. Such a conclusion, quite worthy of this venerable put somewhat shabby theoretician, would, however, be groundless. As a matter of fact, in signing a particular concession, we assume obligations only for our legal code and administrative procedure with regard to this concession, but in no case for the future course of the world revolution. The latter will have to hurdle several major obstacles other than our concession agreements.

The alleged "capitulation" of the Soviet power to capitalism is deduced by the Social Democrats not from an analysis of facts and figures, but from vague generalities, as often as not from the term "state capitalism" which we employ in referring to our state economy. In my own opinion this term is neither exact nor happy. Comrade Lenin has already underscored in his report the need of enclosing this term in quotation marks, that is, of using it with the greatest caution. This is a very important injunction because not everybody is cautious enough. In Europe this term was interpreted quite erroneously even by Communists. There are many who imagine that our state industry represents genuine state capitalism, in the strict sense of this term as universally accepted among Marxists. That is not at all the case, If one does speak of state capitalism, then this is done in very big quotation marks, so big that they overshadow the term itself. Why?

For a very obvious reason. In using this term it is impermissible to ignore the class character of the state.

It is not unhelpful to bear in mind that the term itself is socialist in its origin. Jaures and the French reformists in general who emulated him used to talk of the "consistent socialization of the democratic republic." To this we Marxists replied that so long as political power remained in the hands of the bourgeoisie this socialization was not socialization at all and that it would not lead to socialism but only to state capitalism. To put it differently, the ownership of various factories, railways and so on by diverse capitalists would be superseded by an ownership of the totality of enterprises, railways and so on by the very same bourgeois firm, called the state. In the same measure as the bourgeoisie retains political power, it will, as a whole, continue to exploit the proletariat through the medium of state capitalism, just as an individual bourgeois exploits, by means of private ownership, "his own" workers. The term "state capitalism" was thus put forward, or at all events, employed polemically by revolutionary Marxists against the reformists, for the purpose of explaining and proving that genuine socialization begins only after the conquest of power by the working class. The reformists, as you know, built their entire program around reforms. We Marxists never denied socialist reforms. But we said that the epoch of socialist reforms would be inaugurated only after the conquest of power by the proletariat. There was a controversy over this. Today in Russia the power is in the hands of the working class. The most important industries are in the hands of the workers' state. No class exploitation exists here, and consequently, neither does capitalism exist although its forms still persist. The industry of the workers' state is a socialist industry in its tendencies of development, but in order to develop, it utilizes methods which were invented by capitalist economy and which we have far from outlived as yet.

Under a genuine state capitalism, that is, under bourgeois rule, the growth of state capitalism signifies the enrichment of the bourgeois state, its growing power over the working class. In our country, the growth of Soviet state industry signifies the growth of socialism itself, a direct strengthening of the power of the proletariat.

We observe more than once in history, the development of economic phenomena, new in principle, within the old integuments, and moreover this occurs by means of the most diverse combinations. When industry took root in Russia, still under the laws of feudalism, in the days of Peter the Great and thereafter, the factories and plants, while patterned after the European models of those times were nevertheless built upon feudal beginnings, that is, serfs were attached to them in the capacity of the labor force. (These factories were called manorial factories). Capitalists like the Strogonovs, Demidovs[65] and others, who owned these enterprises, developed capitalism within the integuments of feudalism. Similarly, socialism must unavoidably take its first steps within the integuments of capitalism. It is impossible to make a transition to perfected socialist methods by trying to leap over one's own head, especially if it happens to be a head that is not very clean nor well combed, as happens to be the case with our own Russian heads. This remark, I hope, will not be taken amiss, it is not meant personally. We must still learn and keep on learning.

Criterion of the Productivity of Labor.

There remains, however, a question which is important and fundamental for determining the viability of a social regime which we have not touched upon at all. This is the question of the economy's productivity, not alone the productivity of individual workers, but the productivity of the economic regime as a whole. The historical ascent of mankind consists in just this, that a regime which assures a higher productivity of labor supersedes regimes with a lower productivity. If capitalism supplanted ancient feudal society it was only because human labor is more productive under the rule of capital. And the main and sole reason why socialism will vanquish capitalism completely and definitely is because it will assure a far greater volume of products per each unit of human labor power. Can we already say that our state enterprises are operating more productively than under the capitalist regime? No, we have yet to attain this. Not only are the Americans, the English, the French or the Germans in their capitalist factories working better, more productively than we do—this was the case even before the Revolution—but we ourselves used to work better before the Revolution than we do today. This circumstance might at first glance appear very damnable from the standpoint of appraising the Soviet regime. Our bourgeois enemies and echoing them, naturally, also our Social Democratic critics make every possible use of the fact that our economy's productivity is so low. At the Genoa Conference the French delegate Colrat[66] in reply to Chicherin announced with typical bourgeois insolence that the Soviet delegation had generally no right to say a word about economic affairs in view of Russia's actual economic condition. This argument appears at first glance crushing. But, as a matter of fact, it is merely evidence of abysmal historical and economic ignorance. Of course it would be splendid if we were able right now to prove the superiorities of social- ism not by theoretical arguments drawn from past experience, but by material facts. That is to say, if we could show that our plants and factories assure thanks to their greater centralization and efficiency, higher productivity of labor than similar enterprises before the Revolu- tion. But we haven't attained this yet. Nor is it possible to attain it so soon. What we have now is not socialism as opposed to capital- ism, but the laborious process of accomplishing the transition from one to the other, and, moreover, only the initial and most painful steps of this transition.

Paraphrasing the famous words of Karl Marx, one may say that we are suffering from the fact that our country still retains massive vestiges of capitalism amid only the rudiments of socialism.

Indeed, the productivity of labor in our country has declined and so have the living standards. In agriculture, last year's crops were approximately three-fourths of the average prewar yield. The situ- ation is even sadder in industry; our production this year is about one- fourth of the prewar period. Our transportation system is operating at about one-third of its prewar capacity. These are very sad facts. But how did matters stand during the transition from feudalism to capitalism? Was there a different situation at this time? Capitalist society, so rich and so boastful of its wealth and culture, also sprang from revolution, and a very destructive one at that. The objective historical task of creating the conditions for a higher productivity of labor was in the last analysis solved by the bourgeois revolution, or more accurately by a number of revolutions. But how did this take place? Through the most widespread devastation and through a temporary decline in material culture. Let us take as an illustration the case of France herself. Naturally M. Colrat, in his capacity of bourgeois Minister, is under no obligation to be acquainted with the history of his own passionately beloved fatherland. But we, on the other hand, are familiar with the history of France and the history of her revolution. It is immaterial, whether we turn to the writings of the reactionary Taine[67] or the socialist Jaures[68]; in either case we can ascertain many graphic facts characterizing the horrible condition of France following her revolution. So vast was the devastation that after the Ninth of Thermidor[69], that is, five years after the outbreak of the revolution, the impoverishment of France did not abate but on the contrary became progressively worse. In the tenth year of the Great French Revolution when Napoleon Bonaparte was already First Consul, Paris with a population of 500,000 at that time received a daily supply of flour ranging from 300 to 500 sacks, whereas the minimum subsistence requirement of the city was 1,500 sacks. One of the main concerns of the First Consul was to keep a daily check on the flour deliveries. This was the situation—please note! —ten years after the beginning of the Great French Revolution. By that time the population of France had declined—because of famine, epidemics and wars—in 37 out of the 58 departments. Needless to say, the English Colrats and Poincarés of that day looked down upon the ruined France with the greatest contempt.

What does all this mean? It simply means that revolution is a very harsh and costly method of solving the question of society's economic transformation. But history has not invented any other method. The revolution throws open the doors for a new political order, but does so through a wide-wasting catastrophe. In our country, moreover, the revolution has been preceded by war. We are not in the tenth year of our revolution—please note this, too! —but just at the beginning of the sixth year and our revolution goes far deeper than the Great French Revolution, which merely replaced one form of exploitation by another, whereas we are replacing a society resting on exploitation of man by man, by a society that rests on human solidarity. The shocks have been very severe, causing great havoc and breaking many dishes—and what first strikes the eyes are the overhead expenses of the revolution. So far as the greatest conquests of the revolution are concerned these are realized in life only gradually over a period of years and decades.

Just the other day I chanced to run across a speech pertaining to this question which interests us. This speech was delivered by a French chemist Berthelot, son of the more celebrated chemist Pierre Berthelot, speaking as a member of the Academie des Sciences. Here is the idea put forward by him, and I cite from the text reported by the *Temps*:

" In all epochs of history and in the domain of sciences, in that of politics and in that of social phenomena alike, it has been the splendid and terrible privilege of armed conflicts to speed with blood and iron the birth of new times."

Of course, M. Berthelot was thinking principally of war. Essentially he is nevertheless correct; for wars, to the extent that they served the cause of revolutionary classes, have also greatly stimulated historical development. To the extent, however, that wars served the cause of oppressors—which has been most frequently the case—they have often given an impulse to the movement of the oppressed. Berthelot's statement applies even more directly to revolution: "Armed conflicts" between classes that entail vast havoc simultaneously entail "the birth of new times." From these considerations we infer that the overhead costs of revolution are not at all wasteful expenditures (*faux frais* as the French put it). But dividends cannot be demanded before the payments fall due. And we have to ask our friends to give us another five years. Then in the tenth year of the revolution, that is, in the year when Napoleon used to keep a strict tally of the sacks of flour for starving Paris, we shall be in a position to prove the superiority of socialism to capitalism in the economic field, not by theoretical arguments merely, but by hard facts. And we trust that by then eloquent facts will already be at hand.

But aren't there, en route to these future successes, still dangers that our regime may suffer capitalist degeneration—precisely because of the extremely sorry state of our industry at the present time? The peasantry has harvested this year, as I have already said, about three-quarters of the prewar crop; on the other hand, industry produced all told one-fourth of the prewar output. Thereby the reciprocal relation between the city and country has been upset in the extreme, and greatly to the city's detriment. Under these conditions state industry will be unable to supply the peasant with an equivalent product for his grain and the peasant surpluses thrown into the market will provide the basis for private capitalist accumulation. Naturally, at bottom such reasoning is correct; market relations have a logic of their own, regardless of what goals we may have in mind in restoring them. But here it is once again important to establish correct quantitative correlations. If the peasantry were to throw its entire crop into the market this would, in view of the fourfold weakening of our industry, entail the direst consequences for socialist development. But in reality the peasantry is producing in the main for its own personal consumption. Over and above this the peasantry must pay the government this year more than 350 million puds for the tax in kind. The peasant will throw into the market only the surpluses after his personal needs are met and the tax in kind is paid. This will hardly amount to more than 100 million puds in the current year; and further, an important,

if not the decisive part of this surplus of 100 million puds will be pur-
chased by the distributive cooperatives or by state institutions. The
state industry thus stands counterposed not to the peasant economy
as a whole, but only to one section of it, still insignificant, which is
throwing its produce into the market. This section of the peasantry
alone (or more accurately, only a fraction of this section) becomes a
source for private capitalist accumulation. In the future this fraction
will undoubtedly grow. But parallel with it there will also grow the
productivity of the unified state industry. And there is absolutely no
ground for concluding that the growth of state industry will lag behind
the prosperity in agriculture. As we shall presently see the sagacious
and profound criticisms of the gentlemen of the moribund Two-and-a-
Half International are based principally either on ignorance or on misunderstanding of elementary economic relations in Russia, as they
are shaping up in the concrete conditions of time and space.

On the Social-Democratic Criticism.

On our Fourth Anniversary, that is, one year ago, Otto Bauer
devoted a whole pamphlet to our economy. In this pamphlet Bauer
recapitulates in a polite and oily way all that our more temperamental
enemies in the Social-Democratic camp have been accustomed to say,
frothing at the mouth, concerning our New Economic Policy. In the
first place, he tells us, the New Economic Policy is " capitulation to
capitalism," but that's precisely what is good and realistic about it,
according to Bauer. (These gentlemen invariably see realism in falling
on their knees before the bourgeoisie at the very first suitable occasion.) Bauer goes on to lecture us that the final upshot of the Russian
revolution could not possibly be anything else than the establishment
of a bourgeois democratic republic, and he, Bauer, tells us that this
is what he predicted as far back as the year 1917. Yet we seem to
recall that in 1919 the "predictions" of these scrubby heroes of the
Two-and-Half International were couched in a somewhat different
tone. At that time they talked of the collapse of capitalism and the
inception of a social revolutionary epoch. But the biggest fool in the
world will refuse to believe that if capitalism were approaching its
doom throughout the world, its blossoming time would be at hand
in revolutionary Russia where the working class is in power !

And so in 1917 when Otto Bauer still retained his virginal Austro-
Marxist faith in the durability of capitalism and of the Hapsburg
monarchy, he wrote that the Russian revolution must end in the estab-

lishment of a bourgeois state. Socialist opportunism, however, is always impressionistic in politics. Startled by the revolution and gasping for breath in its waves, Bauer admitted in 1919 that capitalism was collapsing and the social revolutionary epoch was at hand! But inasmuch as now, God be praised, the tide of revolution is once again ebbing, therefore our oracle hastily falls back upon his prophecy of 1917; for, as we already know, he has fortunately two sets of prophecies on tap and can turn on whichever seems to suit the occasion. (*Laughter*.) Bauer goes on to reason as follows:

"What we see being restored (in Russia) is thus a capitalist economy, dominated by a new bourgeoisie, resting upon millions of peasant households—a capitalist economy to which legislation and state administration are willy-nilly compelled to adapt themselves." Do you realize now what our Soviet Russia represents? A year ago this gentleman was already proclaiming that Soviet economy and the Soviet state were dominated by a new bourgeoisie. This leasing of enterprises, poorly equipped and employing, as I said, about 50,000 workers —as against the million workers in the best state enterprises—this, according to Bauer, is "a capitulation of the Soviet power to industrial capital! "

In order to back up these assertions, silly as they are cynical, with the necessary historical justification, Bauer asserts: "After prolonged hesitation, the Soviet government has at length (!!) decided to recognize the Czarist foreign debts."

In brief, one capitulation after another!

Since many comrades will, not unnaturally, be hazy about the details of our history, let me remind you that as far back as February 4, 1919 we made the following proposals by radio to all the capitalist governments:

1.—We offered to recognize foreign debts incurred by Russia.

2.—We offered to pledge our raw materials, as guarantees for payment of debts and interest.

3.—We offered to grant concessions—at their convenience.

4.—We offered territorial concessions in the shape of military occupation of certain areas by Entente troops or by those of its Russian agents.

All this we offered by radio on February, 4, 1919 to the capitalist world in return for their leaving us in peace. And in April of the same year we repeated our proposals in even greater detail to the unofficial American plenipotentiary — what was the fellow's name?

(*Laughter.*) Yes, Bullitt, that was the fellow. Well, Comrades, if you compare these proposals with those which our representatives rejected at Genoa and at the Hague, you will see that our trend has not been toward enlarging concessions, but rather toward more firmly defending our revolutionary conquests. Today we do not recognize any debts; we neither pledge nor are willing to pledge raw materials as guarantees; we are quite chary on the question of concessions; and on no account are we willing to tolerate occupation troops on our territories! There have been a few changes since the year 1919.

We have already been informed by Otto Bauer that the trend of this entire development is toward " democracy." This pupil of Kautsky and this teacher of Martov lectures us as follows: "It has been once again confirmed that an overturn in the economic foundation must be followed by another overturn in the entire political superstructure."

It is perfectly true that between the economic foundation and the political superstructure there exists in part and on the whole precisely the interrelationship indicated by Bauer. But in the first place, the economic foundation of Soviet Russia is by no means altering in the manner pictured by Otto Bauer, nor even in the manner desired by Leslie Urquhart, whose exactions on this matter, we must acknowledge, bear far more weight than Bauer's. And secondly, to the extent that the economic basis is really changing in the direction of capitalist relations, these changes are occurring at such a rate and such a scale as to exclude the danger of our losing political control of this economic process.

From a purely political standpoint the issue still boils down to this, that the working class in power offers such and such important concessions to the bourgeoisie. But this is still a far cry from " democracy," that is, from the transfer of power into the hands of the capitalists. To attain this goal the bourgeoisie would require a successful counter-revolutionary overturn. And for such an overturn it must dispose of corresponding forces. In this respect we have learned a little from the bourgeoisie itself. Throughout the Nineteenth Century the bourgeoisie did nothing else except alternate between repressions and concessions. It made concessions in favor of the petty bourgeoisie, in favor of the peasantry and the upper layers of the working class, while at the same time mercilessly exploiting the toiling masses. These concessions were either political or economic or a combination of both. But at all times these were concessions made by a ruling class which kept firm hold on state power. Some of the bourgeoisie's experiments in this field seemed at first quite venturesome—the introduction of universal suffrage for instance. Marx designated the legal limitation of the working day in England as the victory of a new principle. Whose principle? The principle of the working class. But as we are well aware, there still remained a long road to travel from a partial victory for this principle to the conquest of political power by the English working class.

The ruling bourgeoisie doled out concessions, retaining all the while complete control over the debit and credit sides of the state ledger. Its ruling politicians decided which concession could be granted not merely without endangering its secure hold on power, but on the contrary, for the sake of strengthening bourgeois rule. We Marxists have said more than once that the bourgeoisie has exhausted its historical mission. Meanwhile it still retains power in its hands to this very day. This means that the interrelation between the economic foundation and the political superstructure by no means proceeds along a straight line. We observe a class regime maintaining itself for a number of decades after it had come into an obvious conflict with the needs of economic progress.

What theoretical grounds are there for asserting that concessions granted by the workers' state to bourgeois relations must automatically entail the replacement of the workers' state by a capitalist state? If it is true that capitalism has exhausted itself on a world scale— and this is unquestionably true—then this goes to prove the progressive historic role of the workers' state. Concessions granted by the workers' state to the bourgeoisie simply represent a compromise dictated by the difficulties of development, but this development itself is predetermined and assured by history. Naturally if our concessions were to grow boundlessly, multiplying and accumulating; if we began leasing ever newer and newer groups of nationalized industrial enterprises; if we began granting concessions in the most important branches of the mining industry or railway transport; if our policy were to continue sliding downward on the gravity chute of concessions for a number of years, then a time would inevitably arrive when the degeneration of the economic foundation would bring with it the collapse of the political superstructure. I speak of collapse and not of degeneration because capitalism cannot wrest power from the hands of the Communist proletariat otherwise than through a fierce and merciless civil war. But whoever poses this question thereby presupposes that the rule of the world and the European bourgeoisie will remain virile and ever-lasting. This is what it all boils down to in the end. By recognizing, on the one hand, in their Sunday articles that capitalism, especially in Europe, has outlived itself and has become a brake upon historical progress; and by expressing, on the other hand, assurance that the evolution of Soviet Russia must inevitably end up in the triumph of bourgeois democracy—the Social-Democratic theoreticians fall into a most wretched and banal contradiction, quite worthy of these dull and pompous muddleheads. Our New Economic Policy is calculated for specific conditions of space and time : it is the maneuverist policy of a workers' state still living in a capitalist encirclement and banking firmly on revolutionary developments in Europe. To operate with absolute categories of capitalism and socialism and with "adequately" corresponding political superstructures—in deciding the destiny of the Soviet Republic—shows an utter inability to understand the conditions of a transitional epoch. It is the hallmark of a scholastic and not of a Marxist. One must never exclude from political calculations the factor of time. If you grant that capitalism will continue to exist in Europe for another century or half a century and that Soviet Russia will be driven to adjust herself in her economic policy to capitalism, then the question resolves itself automatically. For by granting this you presuppose in advance the collapse of the proletarian revolution in Europe and the inception of a new epoch of capitalist renascence. On what possible grounds? Since Otto Bauer has been able to discover miraculous symptoms of capitalist resurrection in the life of present-day Austria, then it goes without saying that Soviet Russia's doom is predestined. But we still fail to see any miracles, nor do we believe in miracles. From our standpoint the perpetuation of the European bourgeoisie's rule for a number of decades would under existing world conditions signify not a new blossoming of capitalism but the economic decay and cultural disintegration of Europe. That such a variant of historical development could drag Soviet Russia also into the abyss cannot, generally speaking, be denied. In that case, whether our country would pass through the stage of democracy or suffer decay in some other form—is a second-rate question But we see no reason whatever to enroll under the banner of Spengler's[70] philosophy. We firmly count upon the revolutionary development of Europe. The New Economic Policy is simply our adaptation to the tempo of this development.

Otto Bauer himself, apparently senses uneasily that the regime of capitalist democracy by no means follows quite so directly from the changes which have occurred in our economy. For this reason he very touchingly pleads with us to assist the capitalist tendency of development as against the socialist tendency. Bauer writes, "The reconstruction of capitalist economy cannot be effected under the dictatorship of the Communist Party. The new course in economics demands a new course in politics." Isn't this touching to the point of tears? The same individual who has rendered such wonderful economic and political assistance to the flowering of Austria . . . (*Laughter.*) This man urges us: "Take notice, for God's sake, capitalism cannot possibly flourish under the dictatorship of your party." Just so. And it is precisely for this reason, saving the presence of all the Bauers, that we maintain the dictatorship of our party! (*Loud laughter. Applause.*)

In our country concessions to capitalism are doled out by the Communist Party, as the leader of the workers' state. At the present time our press is conducting an extensive discussion on the question of granting a concession to Leslie Urquhart. Should it be made or should it be withheld? This discussion is intended to clarify both the concrete material provisions of the contract as well as to appraise this contract from the standpoint of its role in the overall system of Soviet economy. Perhaps the concession is too sweeping? Mightn't capitalism sink its roots, through this concession, too deeply into the very heart of our industrial economy? These are the pros and cons. Who decides them? The workers' state. Naturally, the NEP contains an enormous concession to bourgeois relations and to the bourgeoisie itself. But it is we who determine the limits of this concession. We are the masters. The key to the door is in our hands. The state is in and of itself a factor of huge importance in economic life. And we haven't the slightest intention of letting this factor slip out of our hands.

The World Situation and the Revolutionary Perspectives

Let me repeat: The Social-Democratic prophecy concerning the consequences of our New Economic Policy derives entirely from the conception that the proletarian revolution in Europe is hopeless for the next historical period. We cannot prevent these gentlemen from remaining pessimists at the expense of the proletariat and optimists for the benefit of the bourgeoisie. This happens to be the historical calling of the epigones of the Second International. As for ourselves, we see no reason to cast doubt on or to modify the analysis of the

world situation as formulated by us in the theses adopted by the Third
Congress of the Communist International.   In the eighteen months
that have since elapsed capitalism has not moved a step closer to
restoring its equilibrium, completely upset by the war and the consequences of war.   Lord Curzon, the English Minister for Foreign
Affairs, speaking on November 9, the birthday of the German Republic gave a rather good summary of the world situation.   I don't know
how many of you have managed to read this speech and so I propose
to quote a passage from it, which merits citation.   Says Curzon:

"All the powers have emerged from the war with weakened and
broken energies.   We (English) are ourselves suffering from a heavy
burden of taxation which weighs upon the industry of our country.
We have a great number of unemployed in all branches of work . . . .
As regards France, her indebtedness is immense and she is not able
to obtain the payment of the war indemnities . . . .   Germany is in
a condition of political instability and her economic life is paralyzed
by an appalling currency crisis . . . Russia still remains outside the
family of European nations.   It is still under the Communist flag"—
Curzon, it appears, is not at all in agreement with Otto Bauer
(*laughter*)—"and continues to carry on constant propaganda all over
the world"—which is entirely untrue (*laughter*)—" Italy," continues
Curzon, "has passed through a number of shocks and governmental
crises"—has far from passed through!   I would say, Italy is still
passing through (*laughter*)—"The Near East is in a condition of
absolute chaos.   The situation is a terrible one."

Even we, Russian Communists, would be hard put to it to carry
on better propaganda than Curzon all over the world.   "The situation
is a terrible one."   On the Fifth Anniversary of the Soviet Republic,
this is the assurance we get from one of the most authoritative representatives of the strongest European power.   And he is right: the
situation is terrible.   And—let us add—it is necessary to find a way
out of this terrible situation.   The one and only way out is *revolution*.

An Italian correspondent recently asked me to appraise the present
world situation.   I gave the following and, incidentally, rather banal
answer: "The bourgeoisie is no longer capable of ruling"—which
is. as we have just heard, confirmed in the main by Lord Curzon—
"while the working class is still incapable of seizing power.   This
is what determines the ill-starred character of our epoch."   Such
was the gist of my remarks.   Three or four days ago a friend sent
me from Berlin a clipping from one of the latest issues of the *Freiheit*

just prior to its demise. Its heading is "Kautsky's Victory Over Trotsky." (*Laughter*.) It states that the *Rote Fahne* cannot summon up sufficient courage to speak up against my capitulation to Kautsky —although, as you know, Comrades, *Rote Fahne* has not usually been backward in attacking me, even when I was right. Still, that story pertains to the Third World Congress and not to the Fourth. (*Shouts of approval and laughter*.) Well, I had said to the Italian journalist: "The capitalists are already incapable of ruling, while the workers are not yet capable of ruling. This is the character of our epoch." Whereupon the *Freiheit*, of blessed memory, commented as follows: "What Trotsky advances here as his *own* view is the opinion earlier expressed by *Kautsky*." And so I am virtually guilty of plagiarism. This is a high price to pay for a banal interview. I am obliged to tell you that giving interviews is not a very pleasant occupation, and that here in Russia we are never interviewed of our own free will but always upon the strict orders of friend Chicherin. You will note that in the era of the New Economic Policy, wherein we have renounced excessive centralism, a few things have nevertheless remained centralized in Russia. At all events, all the orders for interviews are centralized in the Commissariat for Foreign Affairs. (*Laughter*.) And since interviews are obligatory, one naturally trots out his choicest and stalest stock of commonplaces. Let me confess that in this particular case I never regarded the statement that our epoch was transitional in character to be an original invention of my own. Now I learn, if *Freiheit* can be trusted, that the spiritual father of this aphorism is none other than Kautsky. If this were actually so it would be a punishment too severe for my interview. For everything that Kautsky is now saying or writing has the one and manifest purpose of demonstrating that Marxism is one thing while a quagmire is something else again. Yes, I did say and I now repeat that the European proletariat, in its present state, is incapable of conquering power, right now, at this given moment. This is an incontestable fact. But why is this so? Precisely because the broad working class circles have not as yet rid themselves of the decomposing influence of ideas, prejudices and traditions, whose quintessence is Kautskyanism. (*Laughter*). This is exactly and even exclusively the reason for the political division within the proletariat and for its inability to conquer power. This was the simple idea expounded by me to the Italian correspondent. To be sure, I did not mention Kautsky's name. It should have been obvious to any intelligent person just against whom and against what my remarks were directed. Such is my "capitulation" to Kautsky.

The Communist International has not and cannot have any reason for capitulating to anybody, either in point of theory or in point of practice. The Third Congress theses on the world situation characterized the basic traits of our epoch quite correctly as those of the greatest historical crisis of capitalism. At the Third Congress we stressed how indispensable it was to distinguish sharply between the major or historical crisis of capitalism and the minor or conjunctural crises, each of which is a necessary stage of a commercial-industrial cycle. Let me recall that there was an extended discussion on this topic both in the commissions of the Congress and especially during the plenary sessions. As against a number of comrades we defended the viewpoint that in the historical development of capitalism we must differentiate sharply between two types of curves: the *basic* curve which graphs the development of capitalist productive forces, growth of the productivity of labor, accumulation of wealth, and so on; and the *cyclical* curve which depicts a periodic wave of boom and crisis, repeated on the average every nine years. The correlation of these two curves has not been elucidated up to now in Marxist literature—nor to my knowledge, in general economic literature. Yet the question is of utmost importance both theoretically and politically.

In the middle Nineties the basic curve of capitalist development climbed steeply upwards. European capitalism passed its pinnacle. In 1914 a crisis broke out, which marked not merely a periodic cyclical oscillation, but the beginning of an epoch of prolonged economic stagnation. The imperialist war was an attempt to break out of the impasse. The attempt failed and the profound historical crisis of capitalism became aggravated. However, within the framework of this historical crisis, cyclical ups and downs are inevitable, that is, an alternation of booms and crises—but with this profound difference that, in contrast to the prewar period, the cyclical crises are extremely acute in character, while the booms are far more superficial and feeble. In 1920 there ensued—on the basis of universal capitalist decay—an acute cyclical crisis. Some comrades among the so-called "Lefts" held that this crisis must uninterruptedly deepen and sharpen up till the proletarian revolution. We, on the other hand, predicted that a break in the economic conjuncture was unavoidable in the more or less near future, bringing a partial recovery. We insisted, further, that such a break in the conjuncture would tend not to weaken the revolutionary movement but, on the contrary, to impart new vitality to it. The cruel crisis of 1920, coming in the wake of several years of revolutionary ferment, weighed heavily upon the working masses, temporarily engendering in their ranks moods of passive expectation and even hopelessness. Under these conditions an improvement in the economic conjuncture would certainly raise the self-confidence of the working masses and revive the class struggle. Some of the comrades seriously thought at that time that this prognosis mirrored a deviation toward opportunism and a tendency to find excuses for postponing the revolution indefinitely. The minutes of the Jena Convention of our German party bear clear imprints of the echoes of these naive views.

Let us try, Comrades, to realize where we would be today had we accepted and sponsored a year and a half ago this purely mechanical "leftist" theory, the theory of a commercial-industrial crisis growing steadily worse! Today, no one of sober mind would deny that a break has occurred in the conjuncture. In the United States, the most powerful of all capitalist countries, there is an obvious industrial boom. In Japan, Britain, and France the improvement of the economic conjuncture is much more feeble, but here, too, there has been a break.

How long this boom will last and what heights it will reach—that is another question. We must not for a moment forget that the improvement of the conjuncture takes place amid the decay of international and especially of European capitalism. The root causes of this decay are not affected by conjunctural changes of the market. But on the other hand, the decay does not cancel out the conjunctural changes. We should have been compelled today to re-examine theoretically our fundamental conception as to the revolutionary character of our epoch, had we made a year and a half ago a concession to the "Lefts" who lumped together the historical crisis of the capitalist economic system with the conjunctural cyclical oscillations of the market; and who demanded that we adopt a purely metaphysical outlook to the effect that a crisis, is under any and all conditions, a revolutionary factor. Today however, we have no reason to revise or modify our position. We did not judge our epoch to be revolutionary because the sharp conjunctural crisis of 1920 swept away the fictitious boom of 1919. We adjudged it to be revolutionary because of our general appraisal of world capitalism and its conflicting basic forces. Lest this lesson be wasted, we ought to reaffirm the theses of the Third Congress, as fully applicable at this very hour.

The basic idea underlying the decisions of the Third Congress was as follows. After the war the masses were seized by revolutionary moods and were eager to engage in open struggle. But there was no revolutionary party capable of leading them to victory. Hence the defeat of the revolutionary masses in various countries; hence the depressed moods, the passivity. Today revolutionary parties exist in all countries, but they rest directly only upon a fraction of the working class, to be more precise, a minority of the working class. The Communist parties must conquer the confidence of the crushing majority of the working class. Upon becoming convinced through experience of the correctness, firmness and reliability of Communist leadership, the working class will shake off disillusionment, passivity and dilatoriness—and then the hour for launching the final assault will sound. How near is this hour? We make no predictions on this score. But the Third Congress did fix the task of the hour as the struggle for influence over the majority of the working class. A year and a half has elapsed. We have unquestionably scored major successes, but our task still remains the same: We must conquer the confidence of the overwhelming majority of the toilers. This can and must be achieved in the course of struggle for the transitional demands under the general slogan of the proletarian united front.

Today the world labor movement is confronted with an offensive by capitalism. At the same time, even in countries like France where the labor movement a year or some eighteen months ago was passing through a period of utter stagnation, we now clearly witness increasing readiness of the working class to offer resistance. Despite the extremely inadequate leadership, strikes are becoming more frequent in France. They tend to assume an extremely intense character which is evidence of the growing fighting capacity of the working masses. The class struggle is thus gradually deepening and sharpening. The capitalist offensive finds its complement in the concentration of state power in the hands of the most reactionary bourgeois elements. Simultaneously we witness, however, that while heading for sharper class struggles, the bourgeois public opinion with the tacit semi-approval of the ruling cliques, is paving the way for a new orientation—an orientation to the left, in the direction of reformist and pacifist deceptions. In France, where the ultra-reactionary Nationalist Bloc, headed by Poincaré is in power, there is being simultaneously and systematically prepared the victory of the "Left Bloc" which will naturally include the Messrs. Socialists. In Britain, the general elections are now taking place.

Because of the collapse of Lloyd George's coalition government they came sooner than expected. The outcome is still unknown.

There is a likelihood that the previous ultra-imperialistic grouping will be returned to power.* But even if they do win, their reign will be short. A new parliamentary orientation of the bourgeoisie is being clearly prepared both in Britain and France. The openly imperialist, aggressive methods, the methods of the Versailles Treaty, of Foch, Poincaré, and Curzon, have obviously run into a blind alley. France cannot extract from Germany what Germany hasn't got. France in turn is unable to pay her debts. The rift between Britain and France keeps widening. America refuses to renounce collecting payments on the debts. And among the intermediate layers of the population, especially among the petty bourgeoisie, reformist and pacifist moods are growing stronger and stronger: an agreement ought to be reached with Germany, and with Russia; the League of Nations should be expanded; the burden of militarism should be lightened; a loan from America should be made, and so forth and so on. The illusions of war and defensism, the ideas and slogans of nationalism and chauvinism, together with the subsequent hopes in the great fruits that victory would bring—in brief, the illusions which seized a considerable section of the working class itself in the Entente countries are giving way to more sober reactions, and disillusionment. Such is the soil for the growth of the "Left Bloc" in France, and of the so-called Labor Party and the Independent Liberals in England. Naturally, it would be false to expect any serious change of policy consequent upon the reformist-pacifist orientation of the bourgeoisie. The objective conditions of the capitalist world are today least suited to reformism and pacifism. But it is quite probable that the foundering of these illusions in practice will have to be experienced before victory of the revolution becomes possible.

Thus far we have dealt solely with the Entente. But it is perfectly evident, that if the Radicals and Socialists assume power in France while the Laborite opportunists and the Independent Liberals form the government in Britain, this would provoke in Germany a new influx of conciliationist and pacifist hopes. It would seem plausible that an agreement could be reached with the democratic governments of Britain and France; that a moratorium on and even a cancellation of payments could be obtained; that a loan from America might be arranged with the cooperation of Britain and France, and so on.

* The Tories were victorious.—L.T.

And who is better qualified, than the German Social Democrats for reaching an agreement with the French Radicals and Socialists and the British Laborites?

Of course, the events may take a sharper turn. It is not excluded that the reparations problem plus French imperialism, plus Italian Fascism may drive matters to a revolutionary culmination, depriving the bourgeoisie of the opportunity to move its left flank to the fore. But there are too many indications that the bourgeoisie will be driven to resort to a reformist and pacifist orientation, before the proletariat feels itself prepared for the decisive assault. This would signify an epoch of European Kerenskyism. Of course it would be preferable to skip over it. Kerenskyism, and on a world scale at that, is none too tasty a dish. But the choice of historical paths depends upon us only up to a limited extent. Under certain conditions we shall have to accept European Kerenskyism too, just as we accepted Russian Kerenskyism in its day. Our task will then consist in transforming the epoch of reformist and pacifist deception into a prelude to the conquest of power by the revolutionary proletariat. In our country Kerenskyism lasted about nine months all told. How long will it last in your countries, if it is destined to arise at all? It is of course impossible to reply to this question at the present time. It depends on how quickly the reformist and pacifist illusions are liquidated, that is to say, it depends to a large measure on how skillfully your Kerenskies are able to maneuver, for in contrast to our breed they at least know how to add and multiply. But it also depends on the energy, resoluteness and flexibility with which our own party is able to maneuver.

It is perfectly obvious that the epoch of reformist-pacifist governments would be the season for a growing pressure by the working masses. Our task would then consist in mastering this pressure, getting to the head of it. But to achieve this, our party must enter the epoch of pacifist deception completely purged of pacifist and reformist illusions. Woe to the Communist Party which finds itself to a greater or lesser extent engulfed by the pacifist wave! The inevitable shipwreck of pacifist illusions would at the same time signify the shipwreck of such a party. The working class would find itself compelled once again as in the year 1919 to look around for a party which never tried to deceive it. That is why the inspection of our ranks and cleansing them of alien elements is a cardinal task for us in this epoch of revolutionary preparation. A French comrade, Frossard by name, once said : *"Le parti c'est la grande amitié."* (The party is a great friendship.) This phrase has been frequently repeated. And it is of course impossible to deny that the phrase itself is quite attractive and in a limited sense each one of us is ready to accept it. But one must firmly bear in mind that the party does not spring full-born as a great friendship, but becomes transformed into a great collaboration through profound struggle, externally and, if need be, internally, through the cleansing of its ranks; through a careful and, if need be, ruthless selection of the best elements among the working class who are devoted heart and soul to the cause of the revolution. In other words, before it can become a great collaboration the party must pass through a great selection! *(Ovation.)*

23

The Economic Situation of Soviet Russia from the Standpoint of the Socialist Revolution (Theses)*

1. The question of the direction taken by the economic development of Soviet Russia must be appraised and understood by the class conscious workers of the whole world from a twofold standpoint : Both from the standpoint of the destinies of the first workers' republic in the world, its stability, its strength, its enhanced wellbeing and its evolution toward socialism, as well as from the standpoint of those lessons and conclusions to be drawn from the Russian experience by the proletariat of other countries for their own constructive economic work, upon their conquest of state power.

2. The methods and tempo of economic construction by the victorious proletariat are determined : (a) by the level of development attained by the productive forces in economy as a whole as well as in its separate branches, and especially the reciprocal relation between industry and agriculture; (b) by the cultural and organizational level of the proletariat as the ruling class; (c) by the political situation consequent upon the conquest of power by the proletariat (resistance of the overthrown bourgeois classes, the attitude of the petty bourgeoisie and the peasantry, the extent of the civil war and its consequences, military interventions from outside, and so forth).

It is perfectly clear that the higher the level of the productive forces of a country, the higher the cultural organizational level of the proletariat, all the weaker will be the resistance of the deposed classes, the more regularly, systematically, rapidly and successfully can the

---

* These theses are a summary for the report delivered by me at the Fourth Congress of the Communist International on the economic position of Soviet Russia and the perspectives of the world revolution.—L.T.

transition from capitalist to socialist economics be carried out by the victorious proletariat.

Owing to a peculiar combination of historical conditions, Russia is the first country to enter the path of socialist development, and this, although Russia, despite the high concentration of the most important branches of her industry, is economically backward; although Russia's worker and peasant masses, despite the extraordinarily superb revolutionary political qualities of the proletarian vanguard, are backward in culture and organization.

These contradictions in the economic, social and political structure of Russia, coupled with the fact that the Soviet Republic has been, as it remains, encircled by capitalism during the whole of its existence, determine the fate of the economic construction by the workers' and peasants' power; determine the turns made in this construction and the reasons for adopting the present so-called New Economic Policy.

3. The wholesale expropriation not only of the big and middle bourgeoisie but also of the petty bourgeoisie in city and country was a measure dictated not by economic expediency but by political necessity. The continued rule of capitalism over the rest of the world resulted in this, that not only the Russian big bourgeoisie but also the petty bourgeoisie refused to believe in the stability of the workers' state; and this tended to convert the petty bourgeoisie into a reservoir for the landlord-bourgeois counter-revolution. Under these conditions the resistance of the landlords and the bourgeoisie could be broken and the Soviet power maintained by no other means than the complete expropriation of the bourgeoisie and the exploiting upper layers in the villages. Victory for the workers' state was secured only by this resolute and ruthless policy which forced the vacillating peasant masses to choose between the restoration of landlords and the workers' state.

4. The workers' state, as soon as it began functioning, thus came into possession of all the industrial enterprises down to the very smallest ones. The internal reciprocal relations among the various branches of the industry, including, above all, the basic branches, had already been completely disrupted and distorted by the conversion of industry for the war. The personnel of the main apparatus of economic administration had either emigrated or flocked to the White Guard fronts. As for those who remained in Soviet service, they served in the capacity of saboteurs.

The conquest and maintenance of power by the working class was paid for by a swift and ruthless destruction of the entire bourgeois apparatus of economic administration from top to bottom, in every enterprise and all over the country.

These were the conditions under which the so-called "War Communism" originated.

5. The new regime had as its most unpostponable task to secure food for the cities and for the army. The imperialist war had already forced the change from free trade in grain to monopoly. The workers' state, having destroyed all the organizations of trading capital, under the pressure of the civil war was naturally unable to make a beginning by reestablishing free trade in grain. It was compelled to replace the destroyed trade apparatus by a state apparatus, which operated on the basis of compulsory confiscation of the peasant grain surpluses.

The distribution of foodstuffs and other articles of consumption took the form of issuing uniform state rations, almost completely without regard to the skill and productivity of the workers. This "communism" was rightly called *War Communism* not only because it replaced economic methods by military ones but also because it served military purposes above all others. It was not a question of assuring a systematic development of economic life under the prevailing conditions but of securing the indispensable food supply for the army at the fronts and of preventing the working class from dying out altogether. War Communism was the regime of a beleaguered fortress.

6. In the field of industry, a crude centralized apparatus was created, based on the trade unions and aided by them. This apparatus pursued the immediate aim of at least extracting from industry —totally ruined by the war, by the revolution and by sabotage—the minimum of products necessary to enable the Civil War to be carried on. Something resembling a unified plan was obtained only by utilizing the existing productive forces to a very limited extent.

7. Had the victory of the Western European proletariat followed shortly upon the victory of the Russian proletariat, this would not only have very much shortened the Civil War in Russia, but would have also opened up new possibilities of organization and technology for the Russian proletariat by firmly coupling Soviet Russia's economy to the more advanced economies of other proletarian countries. In that case the transition from "War Communism" to genuine

socialism would doubtless have taken place in a much shorter time and without the convulsions and retreats which isolated proletarian Russia has had to endure during these five years.

8. The economic retreat, or more accurately the political retreat on the economic front became absolutely unavoidable as soon as it became finally established that Soviet Russia was confronted with the task of building her economy with her own organizational and technical forces and resources during the indefinite period required to prepare the European proletariat for the conquest of power.

The counter-revolutionary events[71] of February 1921 showed that it was absolutely impossible to postpone any longer a major adjustment of economic methods of socialist construction to the needs of the peasantry. The revolutionary events in March 1921 in Germany showed that it was absolutely impossible to postpone further a political "retreat," in the sense of preparing the struggle for winning over the majority of the working class. Both of these retreats, which coincided in point of time, are, as we have seen, most intimately connected. They are retreats in a qualified sense, for what they demonstrated most graphically was the necessity, in Germany as in Russia, of our passing through a certain period of preparation: a new economic course in Russia; a fight for transitional demands and for the united front in the West.

9. The Soviet state has shifted from the methods of War Communism to the methods of the market. The compulsory collections of grain surpluses have been replaced by taxes in kind, enabling the peasantry to freely sell its surpluses on the market; monetary circulation has been restored and a number of measures taken to stabilize the currency; the principles of commercial calculation have been reintroduced into the state-owned enterprises and the wages again made dependent on skill and output of workers; a number of small and medium industrial enterprises have been leased to private business. The gist of the New Economic Policy lies in the revival of the market, of its methods and of its institutions.

10. On the Fifth Anniversary of the Soviet Republic, its economy may be roughly outlined as follows:

(a) All land belongs to the state. Approximately 95 percent of the arable land is at the disposal of the peasantry for cultivation in return for which the peasantry has during the current year made payments in taxes in kind amounting to more than 300 million puds of rye from a crop approximately three-fourths of the average prewar yield.

(b) The entire railway network (more than 63,000 versts) is state property. Staffed by more than 800,000 employees and workers, the railroads are now fulfilling about one-third of the work done before the war.

(c) All industrial enterprises belong to the state. The most important of these (more than 4,000 enterprises), employ about a million workers, and are operated by the state on its own account. Up to 4,000 enterprises of second and third rank, employing about 80,000 workers, are leased. Each state enterprise employs on an average 207 workers each; each leased enterprise averages 17 workers. But of the leased enterprises only about one half are in the hands of private businessmen; the others have been leased by various state institutions or cooperative organizations.

(d) Private capital accumulates and operates at the present time chiefly in the sphere of trade. According to initial estimates which are very rough and unreliable, about 30 percent of the total trade turnover falls to private capital, with the remaining 70 percent consisting of sums owned by the state organizations and the cooperatives closely connected with the state.

(e) Foreign trade, amounting during the current year to one-quarter of the prewar import and a twentieth of the prewar export, is completely concentrated in the hands of the state.

11. The methods of War Communism, that is, the methods of an extremely crude centralized registration and distribution are superseded under the new policy by market methods: by buying and selling, by commercial calculation and competition. But in this market the workers' state plays the leading part as the most powerful property owner, and buyer and seller. Directly concentrated in the hands of the workers' state are the overwhelming majority of the productive forces of industry as well as all means of railway traffic. The activity of the state organs is thus controlled by the market and to a considerable extent also directed by it. The profitability of each separate enterprise is ascertained through competition and commercial calculation. The market serves as the connecting link between agriculture and industry, between city and country.

12. However, insofar as a free market exists, it inevitably gives rise to private capital which enters into competition with state capital —at first in the sphere of trade only, but attempting later to penetrate

into industry as well. In place of the recent Civil War between the proletariat and the bourgeoisie there has come the competition between proletarian and bourgeois industry. And just as the contest in the Civil War involved in the main which side would succeed in attracting the peasantry politically, so today the struggle revolves chiefly around the peasant market. In this struggle the proletariat has mighty advantages on its side : the country's most highly developed productive forces and the state power. On the side of the bourgeoisie lies the advantage of greater proficiency and to a certain extent of connections with foreign capital, particularly that of the White Guard emigres.

13. Special emphasis must be laid on the taxation policy of the workers' state and the concentration of all the credit institutions in the hands of the state. These are two powerful mediums for securing the ascendancy of state forms of economy, that is, of forms socialist in their tendency, over private capitalist forms. The taxation policy provides the opportunity for siphoning off increasingly greater portions of private capital incomes for the purposes of state economy, not only in the sphere of agriculture (taxes in kind) but also in the sphere of commerce and industry. Thus under the proletarian dictatorship private capital (the concessions !) is compelled to pay tribute to primitive socialist accumulation.

On the other hand the commercial-industrial credit system concentrated in the hands of the state supplies—as is proved by the statistical data of the last few months—the state enterprises, to the extent of 75 percent, the cooperatives, 20 percent and the private enterprises, 5 percent at the most.

14. The assertion of the Social Democrats to the effect that the Soviet state has "capitulated" to capitalism is thus an obvious and crass distortion of the reality. As a matter of fact the Soviet government is following an economic path which it would doubtless have pursued in 1918-1919 had not the implacable demands of the Civil War obliged it to expropriate the bourgeoisie at one blow, to destroy the bourgeois economic apparatus and to replace the latter hastily by the apparatus of War Communism.

15. The most important political and economic result of the NEP is our obtaining a serious and stable understanding with the peasantry who are stimulated to expand and intensify their work by gaining access to the free market. Last year's experience, especially the increase of winter sowing, affords every reason to expect a continued systematic rehabilitation of agriculture. There is thus being created

not only a reserve of foodstuffs for Russia's industrial development but also a highly important reserve of commodities for foreign trade. Henceforward Russian grain will appear in ever increasing quantities in the European market. The significance of this factor for the social- ist revolution in the West is self-evident.

16. The branches of industry working for immediate consumption, and especially for the peasant market, have already made undoubted and quite noticeable progress during the first year of the NEP. Heavy industry is admittedly still in an extremely difficult situation, but the reasons for this lag in heavy industry, stemming entirely from the conditions during the last few years, are likewise to be found in the conditions for the incipient reconstruction of a commodity economy: Only after the first successes have been gained in the agricultural field and the field of light industry can a real impetus be given to the proper development of machine building, metallurgy and coal, oil and other fuel production, which are naturally assured of receiving the utmost attention from the state. The state will constantly expand its field of operations, concentrate in its hands an ever-increasing volume of turnover capital, and later likewise renew and increase its basic capital by way of state accumulation ("*primitive socialist accumulation*"). There is no ground whatever for assuming that state accumulation will proceed more slowly than private capitalist accumulation and that private capital will thus be likely to emerge from the struggle as the victor.

17. As touches foreign capital (mixed companies, concessions, etc.), separate and apart from its own super-hesitant and super- cautious policy, its role on Russian territory is determined by con- siderations and calculations of the workers' state, which grants indus- trial concessions and enters into commercial agreements only within such limits as will safeguard the foundations of its state economy from being undermined. The monopoly of foreign trade is in this respect an extrordinarily important safeguard of socialist development.

18. The workers' state, while shifting its economy to the founda- tions of the market, does not, however, renounce the beginnings of planned economy, not even for the period immediately ahead. The single fact that the whole railway system and the overwhelming majority of industrial enterprises are already being operated and financed by the state directly for its account renders inevitable that the centralized state control over these enterprises will be combined with the automatic control of the market. The state is centering its

attention more and more on heavy industry and transport, as the foundations of economic life, and adjusts its policy with regard to finances, revenues, concessions and taxes to a great degree to the requirements of heavy industry and transport. Under the conditions of the present period the state economic plan does not set itself the utopian task of substituting omniscient prescience for the elemental interplay of supply and demand. On the contrary, taking its starting point from the market, as the basic form of distribution of goods and of regulation of production, our present economic plan aims at securing the greatest possible preponderance of state enterprises in the market by means of combining all the factors of credit, tax, industry and trade; and this plan aims at introducing in the reciprocal relations between the state enterprises the maximum of foresight and uniformity so that by basing itself on the market, the state may aid in eliminating the market as quickly as possible, above all in the sphere of the reciprocal relations between the state-owned enterprises themselves.

19. The inclusion of the peasantry in planned state economy, that is, socialist economy, is a task far more complicated and tedious. Organizationally the way is being paved for this by the state-controlled and state-directed cooperatives, which satisfy the most pressing needs of the peasant and his individual enterprise. Economically this process will be speeded up all the more, the greater is the volume of products which the state industry will be able to supply to the village through the medium of cooperative societies. But the socialist principle can gain complete victory in agriculture only through the electrification of agriculture which will put a salutary end to the barbaric disjunction of peasant production. The electrification plan is therefore an important component part of the overall state economic plan; and because its importance will doubtless increase in proportion to the growing productive forces of Soviet economy, it is bound to gain in ascendancy in the future, until it becomes the basis for the overall socialist economic plan as a whole.

20. The organization of economy consists in a correct and expedient allocation of forces and means among the various branches and enterprises; and in a rational, that is, the most efficient utilization of these forces and means within each enterprise. Capitalism attains this goal through supply and demand, through competition, through booms and crises.

Socialism will attain the same goal through the conscious upbuilding first of the national and later of the world economy, as a uniform whole. This upbuilding will proceed on a general plan, which takes as its starting point the existing means of production and the existing needs, and which will be at one and the same time completely comprehensive and extraordinarily flexible. Such a plan cannot be made *a priori*. It has to be worked out by departing from the economic heritage bequeathed to the proletariat by the past; it has to be worked out by means of systematic alterations and recastings, with increasing boldness and resoluteness in proportion to the increase of economic "know-how" and technical powers of the proletariat.

21. It is perfectly clear that a lengthy epoch must necessarily elapse between the capitalist regime and complete socialism; and that during this epoch the proletariat must, by making use of the methods and organizational forms of capitalist circulation (money, exchanges, banks, commercial calculation), gain an ever increasing control of the market, centralizing and unifying it and thereby, in the final analysis, abolishing the market in order to replace it by a centralized plan which stems from the whole previous economic development and which supplies the premise for the administration of economic life in the future. The Soviet Republic is now following this path. But it still is far nearer to its point of departure than to its ultimate goal. The mere fact that the Soviet state, after being compelled by domestic conditions to adopt War Communism, found itself driven by the delay of the revolution in the West to execute a certain retreat—a retreat, by the way, more formal than substantial in character—this fact has tended to becloud the picture and has afforded the petty bourgeois opponents of the workers' state a pretext for discerning a capitulation to capitalism. In reality, however, the development of Soviet Russia proceeds not from socialism to capitalism but from capitalism—temporarily pressed to the wall by the methods of so-called War Communism—to socialism.

22. Completely untenable and historically absurd is the contention that the decline of Russia's productive forces is a product of the irrationality of socialist or communist economic methods. In point of fact this decline came above all as a result of the war and then as a result of the revolution, in the form it assumed in Russia, that of a bitter and protracted civil war. The Great French Revolution which created the premises for the mighty capitalist development of France and the whole of Europe had for its immediate result the greatest devastation and decline in economic life. Ten years after the start of her Great Revolution, France was poorer than before the revolu-

tion.   The circumstance that the Soviet Republic's industry did not produce last year more than a quarter of the average prewar output does not go to prove the bankruptcy of socialist methods.   Because it has not even been possible to apply these methods as yet.   All this shows is the extent of economic disorganization unavoidably attendant on revolution as such.   But so long as class society exists, among mankind, every great advance will ineluctably be paid for by the sacrifice of human lives and material wealth—whether the transition be from feudalism to capitalism or the incomparably more far-reaching transition :   from capitalism to socialism.

23.   In and by itself the foregoing answers the question of the degree to which the economic policy designated as *new* in Russia forms a necessary stage of every proletarian revolution.   In the New Economic Policy two elements must be distinguished: (a) the element of "retreat" already characterized above; and (b) of economic management by the proletarian state on the basis of the market, with all its methods, processes and institutions.

(a) As regards the "retreat," it may also occur in other countries owing to purely political causes, that is, owing to the necessity, in the heat of civil war, of wresting from the enemy a far greater number of enterprises than the proletariat is able to organize economically. Partial retreats consequent upon this are not excluded in every single country.   But in other countries such retreats are not likely to bear so severe a character as in peasant Russia where the civil war, moreover, did not actually start until after the seizure of power by the proletariat.   Today we can no longer entertain doubts that in the majority of capitalist countries the proletariat will come to power only after a fierce, stubborn and lengthy civil war.   In other words the proletariat of Europe will have to crush the main forces of the enemy before conquering power and not after this conquest.   At all events, the resistance of the bourgeoisie—militarily, politically and economically—will be the weaker all the greater is the number of countries in which the proletariat succeeds in wresting power.   And this means that the moment of military seizure of industry and the following moment of economic retreat will in all likelihood play a far lesser role elsewhere in the world than in Russia.

(b) As regards the second element :   the utilization of methods and institutions created by capitalism for regulating economic life, all workers' states will, in a greater or lesser degree, have to pass through this stage, on the road from capitalism to socialism.   In other words, every new workers' government—after unavoidably destroying to a greater or lesser degree the capitalist economic organs during the civil war—the exchanges, banks, trusts, syndicates—will find itself compelled to restore these institutions again, subordinating them politically and organizationally; and after linking them up with the entire mechanism of the proletarian dictatorship, will have to master them by creative work in order to carry out gradually with their aid the reconstruction of economic life on socialist beginnings.   The greater the number of countries in which the proletariat is already in power; and the more powerful is the proletariat seizing the power in any country, all the more difficult will it be for capital, or even the individual capitalists to emigrate, all the less and all the weaker will be the support afforded for sabotage on the part of administrative-technical intellectuals, and, in consequence, all the slighter will be the destruction of the material and organizational capitalist apparatuses—and all the easier the work of restoring them.

24.   The speed with which the workers' state traverses this stage, during which socialism while under construction still lives and develops in a capitalist integument—this speed, as already indicated will depend, separate and apart from the military and political situation, upon the level of organization and culture and the conditions of the productive forces existing when the workers' state comes into power. It is absolutely clear that the higher both of these levels are, all the more rapidly will the workers' state accomplish the transition to socialist economy and from this to complete Communism.

December 1, 1922.

24

Resolution on
the French question[72]

The Crisis in the Party and the Role of Factions

The Fourth Congress of the Communist International takes note that the evolution of our French party from parliamentary Socialism to revolutionary Communism is proceeding with extreme sluggishness. The explanation for this can by no means be sought exclusively in the objective conditions, traditions, in the national psychology of the working class, and so forth. On the contrary, it stems principally from the direct and betimes extremely stubborn resistance of non-Communist elements who still remain very strong in the party's leading circles especially in Center, the faction that has been for the most part in the leadership of the party since the Tours Convention.

The fundamental cause of the present acute party crisis lies in the extremely indecisive, vacillating and dilatory policy of the Center's leading elements. Confronted with unpostponable organizational needs of the party, they try to gain time and thereby provide a cover for the policy of directly sabotaging the trade union question, the united front issue, that of party organization, and so on. The time thus gained by the leading elements of the Center has been time lost for the revolutionary development of the French proletariat.

The World Congress instructs the ECCI that its duty is to follow with the utmost attention the internal life of the French Communist Party; and by relying on the party's unquestionably revolutionary proletarian majority, to rid the party of the influence of those elements who have provoked the crisis and who invariably aggravate it.

The World Congress rejects the very idea of split. There is nothing in the party's situation to call for split. The party members in their crushing majority are sincerely and profoundly devoted to the cause of Communism. Only a lack of clarity in the party's consciousness has permitted its conservative centrist and semi-centrist elements to introduce this waspish confusion and to engender factional groupings. A firm and persistent elucidation of the gist of the controversial issues before the whole party will consolidate the overwhelming majority of the party members, and above all its proletarian base, around the decisions of this World Congress. As regards those elements who hold membership in the party while remaining captives to the morals and customs of bourgeois society by their entire mode of thinking and living; and who are incapable of understanding genuine proletarian policy or of submitting to revolutionary discipline, the continued purge of such elements from the party is the necessary condition for preserving its health, cohesiveness and capacity for action.

The Communist vanguard of the working class has, of course, need of those intellectuals who bring to its organization their theoretical knowledge, their agitational or literary gifts. But it needs them on one condition, i.e., provided that these elements break completely and irrevocably with the morals and customs of the bourgeois milieu, burning behind them all the bridges to the camp they left and do not demand any exemptions or privileges for themselves but submit to party discipline on par with its rank and file. The intellectuals, so many of whom in France join the party as amateurs or careerists, have caused the party the greatest harm, distort its revolutionary physiognomy, discredit it in the eyes of the proletarian masses and hinder it from conquering the confidence of the working class. It is necessary at all costs to ruthlessly purge the party of all such elements and to bar their entry in the future.

The best way of accomplishing this is to carry out a re-registration of the party membership under the supervision of a special commission composed of workers of irreproachable party morality.

The Congress affirms that the ECCI's attempt to mitigate the organizational manifestations of the crisis by setting up a leading body on the basis of parity between the two chief factions of the Center and Left, was nullified by the Center under the unquestionable influence of its most conservative elements. These invariably gain the upper hand in the Center each time the Center has opposed itself to the Left.

The Congress deems it necessary to explain to all members of the French Communist Party, that the efforts of the ECCI to obtain a prior agreement among the leaders of the chief factions were designed to facilitate the work of the Paris Convention but did not at all infringe upon the rights of the Convention as the supreme body of the French Communist Party.

The Congress deems it necessary to affirm that whatever partial mistakes the Left might have committed, it essentially tried, before and during the Paris Convention, to carry out the policy of the Communist International; and that on the most important issues of the revolutionary movement—on the united front question and on the trade union question—the Left held a correct position as against the Center and the Renoult group.

The Congress earnestly urges all genuine revolutionary and proletarian elements who undoubtedly constitute the majority of the Center faction to put an end to the obstructive course of the conservative elements and to unite with the Left for joint work. The same thing applies to the faction which is the third largest numerically and which has waged the sharpest struggle against the policy of the united front.

The Extreme Left Wing

By liquidating the federalistic character of its organization, the Seine Federation has thereby rejected the crassly erroneous position of the so-called Extreme Left Wing. However, the latter, in the person of Comrades Heine and Lavergne found it possible to give an imperative mandate to Citizen Delplanque[73]—a mandate which obligated him to abstain from voting on all questions and to accept no obligations. This conduct of the above-named representatives of the Extreme Left testifies to how completely they misconceived the meaning and essence of the Communist International.

The principle of democratic centralism which forms the basis of our organization excludes entirely any possibility of imperative mandates for federal, national or international congresses alike. A convention has meaning only to the extent that the collective decisions of the organizations—local, national or international—are arrived at through a free discussion and decision by all the delegates. It is perfectly obvious that discussion, exchange of experiences and of arguments at conventions becomes devoid of all meaning if the delegates are bound beforehand by imperative mandates.

The violation of the International's fundamental organizational principles is made worse in the given instance by this group's refusal to assume any "obligations" whatever toward the International, as if the very fact of adherence to the International did not devolve upon all its members the unconditional duty of discipline and of carrying out in practice all of the adopted decisions.

The Congress invites the Central Committee of our French section to investigate this entire incident on the spot and to draw from it all the necessary political and organizational conclusions.

The Trade Union Question

The decisions adopted by the Congress on the trade union question contain certain organizational and formal concessions which are designed to make it easier for the party to draw closer to the trade union organizations and the masses of organized workers who do not yet accept the Communist point of view. But the meaning of these decisions would be completely distorted by any attempt to interpret them as an approval of the policy of trade union abstentionism, syndicalist in origin, which prevailed in the party and which is still being propagated by many of its members.

The tendencies represented in this question by Ernest Lafont are in a complete and irreconcilable contradiction with the revolutionary tasks of the working class and with the entire conception of Communism. The party has neither the intent nor the desire to infringe upon the autonomy of the trade unions, but it is obliged to implacably unmask and punish those of its own members who demand autonomy for their own disorganizing and anarchistic activities inside the trade unions. In this cardinal question the International will tolerate far less than in any other sphere any further deviations from the Communist path, the only one which is correct both from the standpoint of theory as well as from the standpoint of international policy.

The Lessons of the Havre Strike

The Havre strike, despite its local character, is irrefutable evidence of the growing militancy of the French proletariat. The capitalist government answered the strike by murdering four workers, as if it were in a rush to remind the French workers that they will be able to conquer power and overthrow capitalist slavery only through intensest struggle, heroism, self-sacrifice and many victims. If the French proletariat has given a completely inadequate answer to the Havre murders, then the responsibility for this falls not only upon the betrayal, which has long since become the rule with Dissident and reformist trade unionists, but also on the obviously erroneous course of action pursued by the leading bodies of the CGTU and of the (French) Communist Party. The Congress deems it necessary to dwell on this question because it offers us a striking example of a radically wrong approach to the tasks of revolutionary action.

By severing, in a manner false in principle, the class struggle of the proletariat into two allegedly independent spheres—economic and political—the party failed to evince, on this occasion too, any independent initiative, confining its activities to backing up the CGTU, as if the murder of four proletarians by the capitalist government were actually an economic act and not a political event of first-rate importance. As regards the CGTU, under the pressure of the Parisian Construction Workers' Union, it called, on the day after the Havre murders, on Sunday, for a demonstrative general strike set for Tuesday. The workers of France did not have the time in many places to learn not only about the call for a general strike but also about the very fact of the murders. Under these conditions the general strike was doomed in advance to failure. It is beyond doubt that this time, too, the CGTU adjusted its policy to those anarchist elements who are congenitally incapable of understanding revolutionary action nor how to prepare it, and who substitute revolutionary appeals of their little circles for revolutionary struggle, without ever bothering about realizing these appeals in life. The party, in its turn, silently capitulated to the obviously false step of the CGTU, instead of trying in a friendly but firm manner to convince the latter to postpone the protest strike, with a view to launching a large-scale mass agitation campaign.

The first duty of the party and the CGTU alike when confronted by the vile crime of the French bourgeoisie was to mobilize immediately thousands of the best party and union agitators in Paris and in the provinces for the purpose of explaining to the more backward elements of the working class the meaning of the Havre events, and of preparing the popular masses to protest and resist. The party was under obligation on such an occasion to issue an appeal, in millions of copies, concerning the Havre crime to the French working class and the peasantry. The party's central organ should have daily confronted the conciliationists, the Socialists and the syndicalists with the question : What course of struggle do you propose in answer to the Havre murders? For its part, the party should have, together with

the CGTU, advanced the idea of general strike, without fixing beforehand its date or duration, but regulating itself by the course of the
agitation and of the movement in the country. Attempts should have
been made in each factory and plant or each neighborhood, district
and city to set up provisional protest committees, into which the
Communists and the revolutionary syndicalists should have drawn
representatives of local conciliationist organizations Only a campaign of this type, systematic, concentrated, all-sided, intense and
tireless—could have been, within a week or more, crowned by a
major success—crowned by a powerful and imposing movement in
the shape of mass protest strikes, street demonstrations and the like.
Such a campaign would have brought as its lasting result an increase
in the mass connections, prestige and influence of the party and the
CGTU alike; it would have drawn them closer together in revolutionary work and it would have drawn both of them closer to those
sections of the working class that still follow the conciliators. The
so-called general strike of May 1, 1921 which the revolutionary elements did not have the time to prepare and which was criminally
broken by the conciliators, marked a turning point in the internal
life of France, enfeebling the proletariat and strengthening the bourgeoisie. The demonstrative "general strike" of October 1922 was
at bottom another treachery by the Right coupled with new mistakes
by the Left. The International most urgently calls upon the French
comrades, whatever branch of the proletarian movement they are
working in, to pay the utmost attention to the problems of mass action,
to study minutely the conditions and the methods; to submit the
mistakes of their organization in each concrete instance to a careful
critical analysis; to prepare down to the last detail the very possibility of mass action by means of large-scale and intense agitation;
and to fit the slogans to the readiness and ability of the masses to act.

The conciliationist leaders base themselves in their acts of treachery
upon the advice, suggestions and directives of bourgeois public opinion
as a whole, with which they are indissolubly bound up. Revolutionary
trade unionists, who are perforce a minority within the trade union
organizations, will commit all the fewer mistakes, the more the party
as such devotes its attention to all the questions of the labor movement, minutely studying the circumstances and the situation, and
offering to the trade unions, through the party members, specific
proposals in consonance with the entire situation.

Freemasonry, the League of Rights of Man and Citizen and the Bourgeois Press

The incompatibility between Freemasonry and Socialism was generally recognized by most of the parties in the Second International. The Italian Socialist Party expelled the Freemasons from its ranks in 1914, and this measure was doubtless one of the reasons why this party was able to conduct an oppositional policy in wartime, inasmuch as the Italian Freemasons functioned as tools of the Entente in favor of Italy's intervention in the war.

The Second Congress of the Communist International did not include among the conditions of admission to the International a special point on the incompatibility between Communism and Freemasonry solely because this was deemed self-evident. And, as the minutes of this Congress show, it rejected the idea that it was possible to hold membership in the party of the proletarian dictatorship while simultaneously belonging to a purely bourgeois organization, which masks its electoral-careerist machinations with the formulas of a mystical brotherhood. The fact—unexpectedly disclosed at the Fourth World Congress—that a considerable number of French Communists belong to Masonic lodges, constitutes in the eyes of the International the most striking evidence that our French party has preserved not merely the psychologic heritage of French reformism, parliamentarism and patriotism, but also its connections, purely material and highly compromising to the party leadership, with the secret institutions of the radical bourgeoisie. And, at a time when the Communist vanguard is rallying in the name of the proletarian dictatorship the forces of the proletariat for an implacable struggle against all the groupings and organizations of bourgeois society, a whole slew of prominent party workers—deputies, journalists, right up to members of the Central Committee, retain intimate ties with the secret organizations of the class enemy. Especially deplorable is that neither the party as a whole nor a single one of its tendencies raised this question after the Tours Convention, although it was so clear to the whole International; and that it required a factional struggle inside the party to lay this question bare before the Intertional in its full and dire meaning.

The International considers it urgent to put an end once and for all to these compromising and demoralizing connections between a leadership of the Communist Party and the political organizations of the bourgeoisie. The honor of the revolutionary proletariat demands that all its class organizations be purged of those elements who desire to hold membership simultaneously in the two warring camps.

The Congress instructs the Central Committee of the French Communist Party to liquidate prior to January 1, 1923 all the connections between the party, in the person of its individual members or groups, with the Freemasons. Every Communist, belonging to a Masonic lodge who fails prior to January 1 to openly announce to his party and to make public through the party press his complete break with Freemasonry is thereby automatically expelled from the Communist Party and is forever barred from membership in it. Concealment by anyone of his membership in the Masonic order will be regarded as an act of penetration by an enemy agent into the party ranks and will brand the individual involved with ignominy in the eyes of the whole proletariat.

Mere fact of membership in the Masons, whether or not material, careerist or other corrupt aims were pursued in a given case, denotes extreme immaturity in Communist consciousness and in class dignity. The Fourth Congress therefore considers that those comrades who have up till now belonged to the Masons and who have just broken with them cannot hold any responsible party posts for a period of two years. Only through intense activity for the revolutionary cause, as rank and file members of the Communist Party, can these comrades regain the full measure of confidence and restore their rights to hold corresponding posts in the party.

Taking cognizance of the fact that the "The League for the Defense of the Rights of Man and Citizen" (*Ligue pour la défense des Droits de l'Homme et du Citoyen*) is at bottom a radical bourgeois organization; that it utilizes its sporadic actions against particular "injustices" in order to sow illusions and prejudices of bourgeois democracy; and what is most important, that in every decisive and major case, as for example during the war, it throws all its support behind capitalism organized as a political state, the Fourth Congress of the Communist International holds membership in this League to be absolutely incompatible with the calling of a Communist and contrary to the elementary conceptions of the Communist world outlook; and it calls upon all party members who hold membership in the League to leave the League's ranks before January 1, 1923, informing their organization and making their step public in the press.

The Congress proposes to the Central Committee of the French Communist Party :

(a) To issue immediately to the entire party an appeal explaining the meaning and significance of this resolution.

(b) To take all the measures implicit in the resolution which will assure that the party is purged of Freemasonry and all ties are severed with the "League of Rights" without remission or omission by January 1, 1923. The Congress expresses its assurance that in this cleansing and salutary work the Central Committee will be supported by the overwhelming majority of party members, whichever faction they may belong to.

The Central Committee must draw up lists of all comrades in Paris or in provinces who while belonging to the Communist Party and occupying various party posts, including the most responsible ones, continued at the same time to collaborate with the bourgeois press; and it must invite these elements to make by January 1, 1923 a definitive and irrevocable choice between the bourgeois vehicles for the corruption of the popular masses and the revolutionary party of the proletarian dictatorship.

Party Candidates

In order to give the party a genuine proletarian character and in order to eliminate from its ranks such elements as regard the party only as an ante-chamber to the Parliament, the municipal councils, the general councils and so on, it is necessary to fix as an inviolable rule that nine out of ten candidates on the slates presented by the party during elections be worker-Communists, still at the bench, and peasants; representatives of the liberal professions must be rigidly restricted in number, allowing them not more than one-tenth of the total number of electoral posts which the party occupies or hopes to occupy through its members; therewith special care must be paid to the selection of candidates belonging to the liberal professions (a minute check-up by special proletarian commissions of their previous political records, their social ties, their loyalty and devotion to the cause of the working class). Only under such a regime will Communist parliamentarians, municipal councilors, general councilors, mayors and the like cease to constitute a professional caste which for the most part has little contact with the working class; and will become instead one of the instruments of the revolutionary mass struggle.

Work in the Colonies

The Fourth Congress once again calls attention to the exceptional importance for the Communist Party to carry on correct and systematic work in the colonies. The Congress categorically condemns the position of the Communist section in Sidi-bel-Abbès (Algiers) which employs pseudo-Marxist phraseology in order to cover up a purely slaveholder's point of view, essentially in support of the imperialist rule of French capitalism over its colonial slaves. In the opinion of the Congress our work in the colonies must not be based on elements so completely infected with capitalist and nationalist prejudices, but rather on the best elements among the natives themselves, and in the first place, on the native proletarian youth.

Only an irreconcilable struggle waged by the Communist Party at home against colonial slavery coupled with systematic revolutionary work carried on by the party in the colonies themselves can weaken the influence of ultra-nationalist elements among oppressed colonial peoples over their toiling classes and attract them to the cause of the French proletariat and thereby prevent French capitalism, in the epoch of the revolutionary rise of the proletariat, from making use of colonial natives as the last reserves of the counter-revolution.

The World Congress invites the French party and its Central Committee to pay far more attention and allot far greater forces and resources than it has up till now to the colonial question and to propaganda in the colonies; and, in particular, to set up a permanent bureau attached to the Central Committee, in charge of the work in the colonies, drawing into this bureau representatives of the native Communist organizations.

25

A Militant Labour Programme for the French Communist Party[74]

1. The party's most pressing task is to organize the resistance of the proletariat against the capitalist offensive which is under way in France as in every other major industrial country. The defense of the 8-hour working day, the maintenance and increase of prevailing wage-scales, the struggle for all the immediate economic demands— all this is the best possible platform for reuniting the disorganized proletariat and restoring its confidence in its own strength and future. The party must immediately take the initiative in every united mass action that is capable of halting the offensive of capitalism and instilling the working class with the spirit of unity.

2. The party must undertake a campaign to show the workers the interdependence of maintaining the 8-hour working day and of wages, as well as the inevitable effect of one of these demands upon the other. In its agitation the party must make use not only of the forays of the employers, but also of every attack by the state against the immediate interests of the workers, as for instance the tax on wages, and every economic issue which especially concerns the working class such as the increase in rents, sales taxes, social security, and so on. The party must carry on an active agitation campaign among the workers for the creation of factory and shop committees, embracing all the workers in each enterprise, irrespective of whether they are already organized politically and into unions or not. The aim of these factory and shop committees is to introduce workers' control over the conditions of work and production.

3. The fighting slogans for the vital material demands of the proletariat must serve as a means of realizing in life the united front against economic and political reaction. The tactic of the workers'

united front must be our governing rule for every mass action.
The party must create the favorable conditions for the success of
this tactic; and to this end it must undertake seriously the education
of its own members and sympathizers by every means of propaganda
and agitation at its disposal. The press, the pamphlets, meetings of
all sorts, everything must be used in this work of education which
the party must carry on in every proletarian group where there are
Communists. The party must issue appeals to the important rival
political and economic organizations of labor. Therewith it must
from time to time publicly explain both its own proposals and those
of the reformists, and give reasons for its acceptance of some proposals and the rejection of others. In no case can the party renounce
its unconditional independence, its right to criticize all the participants in a joint action. It must always seek to take and keep the
initiative of these movements as well as to influence the initiative of
the others in the spirit of its own program.

4. To be able to participate in the action of the workers in all
its forms, to help in orienting this action or, in certain circumstances,
to assume the leading role in the action, the party must, without
losing a single day, proceed to organize its work in the trade unions.
The formation of trade union committees in the federations and the
sections (decided upon at the Paris Convention) and of Communist
cells in every factory and large private or state-owned enterprise
will permit the party to penetrate the masses of workers and enable
it to spread its slogans and increase Communist influence in the
proletarian movement. The trade union committee, in each party
or union body, will maintain connections with the Communists who
have, with the permission of the party, remained inside the reformist
CGT and will guide their opposition to the policy of the official leaders.
They will register every trade union member of the party, control
his activities and transmit to him the instructions of the party.

5. The activities of Communists in all trade unions without exception shall consist primarily in seeking to reestablish trade union unity,
indispensable for the victory of the proletariat. The Communists
must take advantage of every opportunity in order to explain the
harmful effects of the existing split and to advocate unity. The party
must combat every tendency inclining toward organizational exclusive-
ness, circle-group atmosphere — in trade unions or localities — and
anarchistic ideology. It shall defend the necessity of a centralized
movement, of forming broad organizations on an industrial basis, and

of coordinating isolated strikes in order to substitute unified mass actions, which will instill the workers with confidence in their own strength, for localized and partial actions that are doomed to failure. In the CGTU the Communists must combat every tendency opposed to the adhesion of the French trade unions to Red Trade Union International (RILU). In the reformist CGT they must expose the Amsterdam International and the manipulations of its leaders in favor of class collaboration. In both federations they must fight for joint actions, demonstrations and strikes, for the united front, for organic unity and for the program of the Red Trade Union International (RILU) as a whole.

6. The party must utilize every large-scale mass movement—spontaneous and organized alike—to show the political character of every class conflict. It must take advantage of every opportunity to spread as widely as possible its slogans of political struggle such as political amnesty, the annulment of the Versailles Treaty, the evacuation of the left bank of the Rhine, and so on.

7. The struggle against the Versailles Treaty and its consequences must remain in the forefront of the party's entire activity. We must effect the union of the proletariat of France and Germany against the bourgeoisies of both countries who profit by this treaty. In view of this it is the pressing task of the French party to inform the workers and the soldiers of the tragic plight of their German brothers, crushed by the intolerable living conditions resulting primarily from this peace treaty. To satisfy the demands of the Allies the German government keeps increasing the burdens of the German working class. The French bourgeoisie spares the German bourgeoisie, engages in negotiations with it to the detriment of the workers, helps it to take possession of the state-owned public utilities and guarantees it aid and protection against the revolutionary movement. The bourgeoisies of both countries are ready to accomplish the merger of French iron and German coal interests; and they are coming to an understanding on the question of the occupation of the Ruhr, which signifies the enslavement of the Ruhr coal miners. But the exploited workers of the Ruhr basin are not the only ones menaced; the French workers will not be in a position to withstand the competition of German production because the latter will be reduced by the depreciation of the mark to a very cheap price for the French capitalists. The party must explain this situation to the French working class and warn it against the danger which menaces it. The party press must constantly

describe the sufferings of the German proletariat, the real victim of the Versailles Treaty, and show the impossibility of carrying out the treaty. Special propaganda must be carried on in the occupied and war-wrecked regions to expose the bourgeoisies of both countries as responsible for the sufferings of these regions, and to develop the spirit of solidarity among the workers of the two countries. The Communist slogan must call for the fraternization of the French and German workers and soldiers on the left bank of the Rhine. The party shall maintain close ties with its sister party in Germany in order successfully to conduct this struggle against the Versailles Treaty and its consequences. The party shall combat French imperialism, and, furthermore, not only its policy in Germany but all over the world : special attention must be paid to the peace treaties of St. Germain, Neuilly, Trianon and Sevres[75].

8.   The party must undertake systematic penetration of the army. Our anti-militarist propaganda must differ radically from the hypocritical pacifism of the bourgeoisie. The principle of arming the proletariat and disarming the bourgeoisie must permeate our propaganda. In their party press or in the parliament, and on all favorable occasions the Communists shall give support to the demands of the soldiers, insist upon the recognition of their political rights, and so on. Our revolutionary anti-militarist agitation must be intensified each time a new levy is called up for draft, each time there is a threat of another war. This propaganda must be carried on under the supervision of a special party body, in which the Communist youth must participate.

9.   The party must make its own the cause of the colonial peoples, exploited and oppressed by French imperialism. It must support their national demands which constitute stages on the road of their liberation from the yoke of foreign capital. It must defend without any reservations their right to autonomy and independence. The unconditional fight for the political and trade union liberties of the natives, and against the native levies, the fight for the demands of the native soldiers—this fight is the immediate task of the party. It must combat implacably every reactionary tendency, existing even among certain working class elements, that favors limiting the rights of the natives. It shall create a special body attached to the Central Committee, to carry on party work in the colonies.

10.   Our propaganda among the peasantry to win over the agricultural laborers, tenant farmers and poor peasants to the revolu-

tionary movement and gain the sympathies of the small landholders must be accompanied by the struggle to ameliorate the living and working conditions of agricultural laborers who hire out or work for the big landowners. Such a struggle demands that the party organizations in the provinces elaborate and propagate programs of immediate demands corresponding to the special conditions in each locality. The party must foster those agricultural associations and cooperatives which go to meet the individual needs of the peasantry. It must pay special attention to building and developing trade unions among the agricultural workers.

11. Party work among women is of first-rate importance and requires a special organization. A Central Commission, attached to the Central Committee, with a permanent secretariat, and with more and more numerous local commissions and a periodical devoted to propaganda among the women must be created. The party must insist that the economic demands of the men and women workers be unified : it must demand equal pay for equal work without distinction of sex, and the participation of exploited women in all the actions of the workers.

12. The party must make far more systematic and persistent efforts than in the past in the development of the Communist Youth movement. In every department and institution of both organizations the closest reciprocal relations must be established between the party and the youth. It ought to be accepted as a principle that the youth must be represented on every Commission attached to the Central Committee. The propaganda departments and the sections of the party must help the existing youth groups, and help to create new ones. The Central Committee must follows the youth press and allot to the youth organization special pages in the central party publications. In the trade unions the party must back up the demands of the young workers in accordance with its program.

13. In the cooperatives the Communists shall defend the principle of a unified national organization and create Communist groups attached to the cooperative section of the Communist International through a commission functioning under the Central Committee. In every federation a special commission must be created to carry on party work in the cooperatives. The Communists will exert every effort to utilize the cooperatives as an auxiliary force in the labor movement.

14. Our members in parliament, in the municipal councils, etc., must conduct an energetic struggle intimately bound up with the struggles of the workers and the campaigns undertaken by the party and the trade union organizations outside parliament. In accordance with the theses of the Second Congress of the Comintern, the Communist deputies, controlled and directed by the party's Central Committee, together with the municipal and district councilors, controlled and directed by the sections and the federations must serve the party as agents of agitation and propaganda.

15. The party must perfect and strengthen its organization following the example of the large Communist parties of other countries and in accordance with the statutes of the Communist International, in order that it may rise to the level of the tasks outlined in its program and by the national and international Congresses, and be in a condition to realize these tasks in life. It must fight for a strict centralization, an inflexible discipline, the subordination of every party member to the corresponding party body, of each party body to the organization immediately above it. Moreover, we must develop the Marxist education of our militants by systematically increasing the number of theoretical courses in the sections, by opening party schools; and these courses and schools must be placed under the supervision of a Central Commission attached to the Central Committee.

26

Resolution of the French Commission[76]

(a) *Central Committee*—As an exception, owing to the acute crisis provoked by the Paris Convention, the Central Committee shall be constituted on a proportional basis, in accordance with the voting at the Convention for members of Central bodies.

The proportional representation of the various factions shall be as follows :

Center :   10 members and 3 candidates.

Left :   9 members and 2 candidates.

Renoult Tendency :   4 members and 1 candidate.

Renaud Jean Minority :   1 member.

Youth :   2 representatives with consultative votes.

The Political Bureau shall be formed on the same basis; the different factions being represented as follows :   Center—3; Left—3; Renoult Tendency—1.

In order to avoid all disputes of a personal character which might tend to aggravate the crisis, the members of the Central Committee, as well as those of the Political Bureau and other important Central bodies will be nominated by the various factions now present in Moscow. The slate of candidates is to be submitted by the French delegation to the Fourth World Congress, and the delegation will undertake to support this slate before the party. The Fourth Congress accepts this declaration in the conviction that this slate is the only possible one for solving the existing party crisis. The slate of the new Central Committee drawn up by the various factions is as follows:

The Center

Members :

Frossard, General Secretary of the party and delegate to the ECCI.

Louis Sellier[77], Acting Secretary.

291

> *Marcel Cachin.*
> *Jacob,* Secretary of the Textile Federation.
> *Garchery,* Municipal Councilor of Paris.
> *Lucy Leiciague,* Stenographer.
> *Marrane,* Mechanic, Secretary of the Seine Federation.
> *Gourdeaux,* Employed in the Paris Post Office.
> *Laguesse,* Discharged Teacher; Secretary of the Seine-et-Marne Federation.
> *Paquereaux,* Turner; Secretary of the Seine-et-Oise Federation.
> Candidates :
> *Pierpont,* Textile Worker.
> *Dupillet,* Treasurer of the Unitarian Federation of Miners (reserved for confirmation in Paris).
> *Plais,* Telephone Worker.

The Left
> Members :
> *Rosmer,* Employee.
> *Treint,* Retired Teacher.
> *Vaillant-Couturier*[78], Deputy.
> *Sauvarine*[79], Journalist.
> *Tommasi*[80], Aviation Construction Worker.
> *Christen,* Mechanic.
> *Amédée Dunois*[81], Journalist.
> *Cordier,* Barber.
> *Bouchez,* Mechanic.
> Candidates :
> *Salles,* Metal Worker.
> *Departer,* Filer.

Renoult Faction
> Members :
> *Barberet,* Metal Worker.
> *Fromont,* Carriage Builder.
> *Dubus,* Miner from Pas-de-Calais.
> *Werth,* (usually called *Rogen Gerald*), Metal Worker.
> Candidates :
> *Lespagnol,* Employee.

A national conference with the powers of a party convention shall ratify this slate not later than the last two weeks in January.

Until that time the provisional Central Committee appointed by the Paris Convention will continue to function.

(b) *The Press*—The Congress confirms the regime that has already been decided : (1) the direction of the newspapers shall be turned over to the Political Bureau; (2) there shall be a daily unsigned leading editorial giving the readers the position of the party; (3) party journalists are prohibited from contributing to the bourgeois press.

Editor of *l'Humanité* : Marcel Cachin.

General Secretary : Amédée Dunois.

Both of these comrades have equal powers; in other words, any disagreement between them must be brought before the Political Bureau and settled by it.

Editorial Secretariat : one representative from the Center and one from the Left.

The editorship of the *Bulletin Communiste* will be given to a comrade of the Left.

The editors who resigned will resume their posts.

In preparation for the national conference, " The Party Page," will be reestablished, in which each tendency will have the right to express its point of view.

(c) *The General Secretariat*—It shall be constituted on a parity basis : one comrade from the Center and one from the Left; all disagreements to be settled by the Political Bureau.

Member : Frossard. Substitutes : Louis Sellier and Treint.

(d) *Delegates to the ECCI*—The congress considers it absolutely necessary, in order to establish normal and cordial relations between the ECCI and the French party, that the two most important tendencies in the party be represented in Moscow by those comrades best qualified and authorized by their respective factions, namely — by Comrades Souvarine and Frossard who shall be delegated for at least three months, that is, until the termination of the crisis within the French party.

The fact that the French party will be represented in Moscow by Frossard and Souvarine will completely assure that every suggestion of the ECCI, arrived at in agreement with these two comrades, will receive the support of the whole party.

(e) *Salaries of Party Functionaries*—As regard the salaries of party functionaries, editors, etc., the party will set up a special commission to regulate this question on the basis of the following two rules : (1) All possibility must be eliminated of excessive salaries which provoke legitimate indignation among the mass of workers adhering to the party. (2) Those comrades whose work is absolutely indispensable for the party must be placed in a position which will permit them to devote all their energies to party work.

(f) *Committees*—(1) Administrative Committee of *l'Humanité*: Center—6 representatives; Left—5; Renoult Tendency—2.

The French Commission finds it acceptable, as an exceptional measure, that proportional representation should likewise be applied to the most important committees.

(2) *Trade Union Secretariat*:   One Secretary from the Center and one from the Left; all disputes to be referred to the Political Bureau.

(g) *Disputed Questions*—Disputes that might arise in connection with the organizational decisions taken in Moscow and over their application shall be settled by a special commission composed of one representative of the Center, one representative of the Left, with the delegate of the ECCI presiding.

(h) *Positions from Which Former Masons Are Barred*—Involved here are those posts whose holders have the power of representing more or less independently and on their own responsibility the ideas of the party before the working masses, by voice or by pen.

In case differences of opinion arise between the two factions concerning such posts, the question must be referred for decision to the above-mentioned commission.

In case of technical difficulties that might possibly arise in reinstating those editors who have resigned, these are to be referred for decision to the same commission.

All decisions that do not involve the formation of the Central Committee are immediately applicable.

In addition to these decisions, the Renoult Tendency has asked to have a substitute at the ECCI along with Comrades Frossard and Souvarine, for a period for three months.   The French Commission has unanimously granted this request of the Renoult Tendency.

After the

Fourth
World
Congress

Picture: Young workers enrol at Sverdlov University — the 'mass
reserves' of the party.

27

Political Perspectives

I welcome the opportunity that Comrade Friedlander's[82] article once again affords me to oppose—most resolutely—the mechanical, fatalistic and non-Marxist conception of revolutionary development which continues, despite the truly salutary work of the Third World Congress, to find a haven in the minds of some people, obviously convinced that they are Lefts.

At the Third World Congress we were told that the economic crisis would endure without interruption and get worse until the proletariat seized power. This mechanistic outlook was at the bottom of the revolutionary optimism of certain "Lefts." When we explained that conjunctural ups and downs are inevitable in world economy, and that it is necessary to forsee them and take them into account tactically, these comrades imagined that we were engaged in a revision of well-nigh the entire program and tactic of the International. In reality we were engaged only in a "revision" of certain prejudices.

In the article of Comrade Friedlander, in the speech of the Dutch Comrade Ravenstein[83] and in statements made by other speakers, we now meet with a transplantation of this same mechanistic, anti-Marxist conception from the economic field into the field of politics. Capitalism, we are told, is on the offensive politically and economically; the capitalist offensive is gaining momentum, and the proletarian uprising will come at a certain moment in reply to the intensifying offensive of capitalism—where then could a new, even if brief, pacifist and reformist period possibly originate?

To lay bare at once the mechanistic conception of Comrade Friedlander, let us take the example of Italy, where the counter-revolution has reached its apogee. What is the political prognosis for Italy? If one assumes that Mussolini[84] will be able to retain power long enough for the workers of city and country to close their ranks against him, to regain their lost confidence in their class strength and rally around the Communist Party, then it is not excluded that Mussolini's regime will be swept away directly by the regime of the proletarian dictatorship.

But there is another variant which is at least just as probable, namely : if Mussolini's regime were to founder because of the internal contradictions within its own social base and because of the difficulties in the domestic and international situation before the Italian proletariat is able to reach the condition attained by it in September 1920 but this time under a firm and resolute revolutionary leadership—in that case it is perfectly clear that an interim regime will once again be established in Italy, a regime of phrases and of impotence, a cabinet headed by Nitti[85] *or* by Turati, or by Nitti *and* Turati : in brief, a regime of Italian Kerenskyism whose ineluctable and wretched bankruptcy will pave the way for the revolutionary proletariat. Does this second variant, by no means less probable than the first, signify a "revision" of the program and tactics of the Italian Communists ? Nothing of the sort ! The Italian Communists will continue today as tomorrow to wage their struggle on the soil of the regime created by Mussolini's victory. The dispersed condition of the Italian proletariat precludes for our Italian comrades the possibility of their posing as an immediate task the overthrow of fascism by force of arms. While carefully preparing the elements for the future armed struggle, the Italian Communists must, to begin with, develop the struggle through broad political channels. Their immediate and preparatory task, which is, moreover, a task of enormous importance, is to begin to disintegrate the plebeian and especially the working class sector of fascist support and to fuse together ever broader proletarian masses under the partial and general slogans of defense and offense. By means of a dynamic and flexible policy the Italian Communists can accelerate in the extreme the downfall of the fascists and thereby drive the Italian bourgeoisie to seek salvation from the revolution by playing its left trump cards : either Nitti or Turati at once. What would such a change signify ? It would signify a further disintegration of the bourgeois state, the further growth of the proletariat's offensive powers, the growth of our combat organization, the creation of conditions for the seizure of power.

How do matters stand in France ? As early as June 16 of last year in my speech at a session of the enlarged ECCI Plenum, I put forth the idea that *unless revolutionary events intervened in Europe and in France,* the entire parliamentary-political life of France would unfailingly begin crystallizing along the axis of the "Left Bloc" as against the present-day ruling "National Bloc". In the year and a half that elapsed the revolution did not materialize. And no one who has followed the life of France would deny that except for the Communists and the revolutionary syndicalists, French politics is actually following the path of preparations for the replacement of the National Bloc by the "Left Bloc". Admittedly France is wholly under the aegis of a capitalist offensive, of constant threats to Germany, and so on. But parallel with this we witness the growth of confusion among the bourgeoisie, especially among the middle classes—their growing disillusionment with the policy of "reparations," their attempts to ameliorate the financial crisis by reducing the expenditures for imperialism, their hopes of resuming relations with Russia, etc., etc. These moods likewise imbue a considerable section of the working class, through the medium of the reformist Socialists and trade unionists. More than this, these moods infect certain elements inside our own party, as illustrated, for example, by the conduct of the recently expelled Barabant[86], who engaged, while a member of the Central Committee of the Communist Party, in propagating the "Left Bloc". There is thus no contradiction whatever between the continued offensive of French capitalism and of French reaction and the obvious preparations of the French bourgeoisie for a new orientation.

In Britain the situation is no less instructive. The rule of the Liberal-Tory coalition has been replaced, as a result of the recent elections, by a pure Tory government. Clearly, a step " to the right" ! But on the other hand, the figures of the last election precisely go to show that bourgeois-conciliationist Britain has already fully prepared a new orientation--in the event of a further sharpening of contradictions and growing difficulties (which are inevitable). The Tories obtained less than $5\frac{1}{2}$ million votes. The Labor Party together with the independent Liberals, almost 7 million. Thus the English electorate has, in its majority, already swung from the lush illusions of imperialist victory to the emaciated illusions of reformism and pacifism. It is noteworthy that the "League for Democratic Control". a radical-pacifist organization, has elected its entire committee to Parliament. Are there serious grounds for believing that the incumbent

Tory regime may bring Britain *directly* to the dictatorship of the proletariat ? We see no such grounds. On the contrary, we assume that the insoluble economic, colonial and international contradictions of the present-day British Empire will tend more and more to swell the plebeian and petty-bourgeois opposition in the person of the so-called Labor Party. From all indications, in Britain more than in any other country on the globe, the working class will, before passing over to the dictatorship, have to pass through the stage of a labor government in the person of the reformist-pacifist Labor Party which has already received in the last elections about 4¼ million votes.

But, objects Comrade Friedlander, such a perspective completely obliterates the question of Germany. Why so ? Revolutionary Germany is one of the most important factors of European and world development, but it is not the only factor. We all follow with the utmost attention the successes of our German Party, whose development entered a new stage after the March events of last year. The previous era was brought to a close by the March events. *The new era began with the criticizm of the March events*, and whoever fails to this day to understand the meaning and content of this new stage is beyond hope and not worth being taken seriously. The German Communist Party has, in its crushing majority, assimilated the lessons of the Third World Congress and is growing surely and firmly. At the same time the disintegration of German economy proceeds apace. At what moment will the criss-crossing of these and other factors bring the German working class to the seizure of power ? A year from now ? Or six months from now ? Or two years hence ? It is very difficult to guess dates. If Germany were isolated, or if only Soviet Russia stood by her side, we would, in the field of prognosis, favor half a year as against one year, and one year as against two years. But there happens also to exist France and Marshal Foch; there is Italy, crowned by Mussolini; there is Britain headed by Bonar-Law[87] and Curzon; there is the continued capitalist offensive—and all these factors exercise a powerful influence on the development of the revolution in Germany. This, of course, does not mean that the German Communist Party is obliged to postpone offensive revolutionary actions until the revolution erupts in France. Our German comrades are far removed from this vile type of opportunism which desires a revolution provided it is wholly guaranteed, fully insured by Paris and London. But it is absolutely self-evident that the threat of military occupation from the West will have a deterring effect upon the development of the German revolution until such time as the French Communist Party shows that it is capable and ready to check-mate this danger.

It is by no means excluded that the German revolution may erupt before the present-day aggressive imperialist governments are replaced in France, Britain and Italy. No one disputes that the victory of the German proletariat would give a mighty impetus to the revolutionary movement in every country in Europe. But just as the impact of the Russian revolution brought within a year Scheidemann and not Liebknecht to power in Germany, so the impact of the victorious proletarian revolution in Germany might bring Henderson or Clynes[88] to power in Britain; and Caillaux in an alliance with Blum and Jouhaux, in France. Such a Menshevik regime in France would, under the given historical conditions, be only a very brief interlude in the death-agony of the bourgeoisie. There is even a possibility that in such a case the Communist proletariat in France might come to power directly over the heads of the (French) Mensheviks. In Britain this is less likely. In any case, such a perspective presupposes the victory of the revolution in Germany during the next few months. Is victory certain so soon ? Scarcely anyone would seriously maintain this. At all events it would be the crassest blunder to restrict our prognosis to such a one-sided and conditional perspective. On the other hand, without a prognosis it is generally impossible to arrive at a far-reaching revolutionary policy. But our prognosis cannot be mechanistic. It must be dialectical. It must take into account the interaction of objective and subjective historical forces. And this opens up the possibility of several variants—depending on how the relation of forces shapes up in the course of living historical action.

And so there is hardly any ground for a categoric assertion that the proletarian revolution in Germany will triumph before the domestic and foreign difficulties plunge France into a governmental parliamentary crisis. This crisis would mean new elections and new elections would result in the victory of the "Left Bloc". This would deal a heavy blow to the Conservative government in Britain; it would strengthen the Labor Party opposition and in all likelihood produce a parliamentary crisis, new elections and the victory of the Labor Party as such or in an alliance with independent Liberals. What would be the effects of such events upon Germany's internal situation ? The German Social Democrats would immediately drop their semi-oppositional status in order to offer "the people" their services in restoring peaceful, normal, etc., relations with the "great Western democracies." This was the sense of my remarks to the effect that a swing in the domestic policy in France and Britain, should it occur prior to the victory of the Communists in Germany, could for a while lend wings to the German Social Democracy. Scheidemann could once again come to power—but this would already signify the open prelude to the revolutionary culmination. For it is perfectly obvious that under the existing European conditions, the impotence of the reformist-pacifist regime would be laid bare not over a number of years but in the course of a few months or weeks. In his speech on the draft program (of the Comintern) Comrade Thalheimer quite correctly reminded us once again about those basic causes which exclude the possibility of a turn in capitalist policy toward Manchesterism, pacifistic liberalism and reformism. In power, Clynes or Caillaux-Blum or Turati would not be able to pursue a policy essentially different from the policy of Lloyd George, Bonar-Law, Poincaré and even Mussolini. But when they come to power the position of the bourgeoisie will be rendered even more difficult, even more inextricable than it is today. Their complete political bankruptcy—provided, naturally, we pursue correct tactics i.e., revolutionary, resolute and at the same time flexible tactics—can become laid utterly bare in a very brief span of time. In a ruined and completely disorganized capitalist Europe after the illusions of war and of victory, the pacifist illusions and the reformist hopes can come only as the ephemeral illusions of the death agony of the bourgeoisie.

Comrade Ravenstein is apparently willing, with a reservation here and there, to recognize all this so far as the plebeian capitalists are concerned, but not as touches the capitalist aristocrats, i.e., the colonial powers. In his opinion the perspective of reformist-pacifist prologue to the proletarian revolution is as inappropriate for Great Britain, France, Belgium and Holland as the slogan of a workers' government. Comrade Ravenstein is perfectly correct in linking up the slogan of a workers' government with the fact that the bourgeoisie still disposes of a reformist-pacifist resource, not a material but an ideological resource in the shape of the influence still retained by the bourgeois-reformist and the Social Democratic parties. But

Comrade Ravenstein is absolutely wrong in offering exemptions to the colonial powers. Before bringing her armed might upon the Russian revolution, Britain sent her Henderson to assist Buchanan[89] in steering the revolution on to a "correct" path. And it must be said that during the war Russia was one of Britain's colonies. The British bourgeoisie followed exactly the same course in relation to India : it first sent well-intentioned and liberal Viceroys and then on their heels, squadrons of bombing planes. The growth of the revolutionary movement in the colonies would doubtless accelerate the assumption of power by the British Labor Party despite its invariable and repeated betrayals of the colonies to British capitalism. But it is equally unquestionable that the further growth of the revolutionary movement in the colonies, parallel with the growth of the proletarian movement at home, would once and for all topple petty-bourgeois reformism and its representative, the Labor Party, into the grave of history.

Most unstable and untrustworthy is revolutionary radicalism, which finds it necessary to keep up its morale by ignoring the dialectic of living forces in economics and politics alike and by constructing its prognosis by means of a pencil and a ruler. A swing in the economic or political conjuncture suffices for such radicals to lose their bearings. At bottom this leftism secretes pessimism and mistrust. It is not for nothing that one of these critical voices comes from an Austrian Communist, and the other from a Dutch Communist, neither of these countries being as yet the hearth of revolution. The dynamic optimism of the Communist International stems from far broader and deeper foundations. For us the bourgeoisie is not a stone dropping into an abyss but a living historical force which struggles, maneuvers, advances now on its right flank, now on its left. And only provided we learn to grasp politically *all* the means and methods of bourgeois society so as to each time react to them without hesitation or delay, shall we succeed in bringing closer that moment when we can, with a single confident stroke, actually hurl the bourgeoisie into the abyss.

First published in *Bolshevik*,
organ of the Fourth World Congress.

28

Report on the Fourth World Congress

Delivered December 28, 1922 at a Meeting
of the Communist Fraction of the Tenth
All-Union Congress of the Soviets with
Non-Party Delegates Attending.

Comrades,

You have invited me to make a report on the recent World
Congress of the Communist International. I take this to mean that
what you want is not a factual review of the work of the last Congress,
since in that case it would be much more expedient to turn to the
minutes of its sessions, already available in printed bulletins, rather
than listen to a report. My task, as I understand it, is to try to give
you an evaluation of the general situation of the revolutionary movement and its perspectives in the light of those facts and issues that we
faced at the Fourth World Congress.

Naturally this presupposes a greater or lesser familiarity with the condition of the international revolutionary movement. Let me remark
parenthetically that our press, unfortunately, does far from everything
it should in order to acquaint us as intimately with facts of the world
labor movement, epecially the Communist movement, as our press
does, say, with facts relating to our economic life, to our Soviet
construction. Yet to us these are manifestations of equal importance.
For my part, I have resorted more than once (contrary to my habits)
to guerrilla actions in order to get our press to utilize the exceptional
opportunities at our disposal in order to provide our party with a
complete, concrete and precise picture of what is taking place in the

sphere of revolutionary struggle, doing this from day to day without lectures, homilies or generalizations (for we need generalizations only from time to time), but simply supplying facts and material from the internal life of each Communist Party.

I think that on this point the pressure of the party public opinion ought to be brought to bear on our press, whose editors read the foreign papers and who proffer on the basis of this press generalizations from time to time, but virtually no factual material. But inasmuch as gathered here is the fraction of the Soviet Congress and, consequently, highly qualified party elements, I shall assume for the purpose of my report a general acquaintance with the actual condition of the Communist parties and of the other parties which still wield influence in the labor movement. My task is to submit to verification our general criteria, our views on the conditions for and the tempos of development of the proletarian revolution from the standpoint of new facts, particularly those facts which were supplied us by the Fourth Congress of the Comintern.

Comrades, I wish to say at the very outset that if our aim is not to become confused and not to lose our perspective, then in evaluating the labor movement and its revolutionary possibilities we ought to bear in mind that there exist three major spheres which, although interdependent, differ profoundly from one another. First, there is Europe; second, America; and third, the colonial countries, that is, primarily Asia and Africa. The need of analyzing the world labor movement in terms of these three spheres flows from the nature of our revolutionary criteria.

Marxism teaches us that in order for the proletarian revolution to become possible there must be given, schematically speaking, three premises or conditions. The first premise is the conditions of production. Productive technique must have attained such heights as to provide economic gains from the replacement of capitalism by socialism. Secondly, there must be a class interested in effecting this change and sufficiently strong to achieve it, that is, a class numerically large enough and playing a sufficiently important role in economy to introduce this change. The reference here is of course to the working class. And thirdly, this class must be prepared to carry out the revolution. It must have the will to carry it out, and must be sufficiently organized and conscious to be capable of carrying it out. We pass here into the domain of the so-called subjective factors and subjective premises for the proletarian revolution. If with these three criteria—productive-technological, social-class and subjective-political—we approach the indicated three spheres, then the difference between them becomes strikingly apparent. True enough, we used to view the question of mankind's readiness for socialism from the productive-technological standpoint much more abstractly than we do now. If you consult our old books, even those not yet outdated, you will find in them an absolutely correct estimate that capitalism had already outlived itself 15 or 20, 25 or 30 years ago.

In what sense was this intended? In the sense that 25 years ago and more, the replacement of the capitalist mode of production by socialist methods would have already represented objective gains, that is, mankind could have produced more under socialism than under capitalism. But 25 to 30 years ago this still did not signify that productive forces were no longer capable of development under capitalism. We know that in all parts of the world, including and especially in Europe which has until comparative recent times played the leading economic and financial role in the world, the productive forces still continued to grow. And we are now able to fix the year up to which they continued to grow in Europe : the year 1913. This means that up to that year capitalism represented not an absolute but a relative hindrance to the development of the productive forces. In the technological sense, Europe developed with unprecedented speed and power from 1894 to 1913, that is to say, Europe became economically enriched during the 20 years which preceded the imperialist war. Beginning with 1913—and we can say this positively —the development of capitalism, of its productive forces, came to a halt one year before the outbreak of the war because the productive forces ran up against the limits fixed for them by capitalist property and the capitalist form of appropriation. The market was split up, competition was brought to its intensest pitch, and henceforward capitalist countries could seek to eliminate one another from the market only by mechanical means.

It is not the war that put a stop to the development of productive forces in Europe, but rather the war itself arose from the impossibility of the productive forces to develop further in Europe under the conditions of capitalist management. The year 1913 marks the great turning point in the evolution of European economy. The war acted simply to deepen and sharpen this crisis which stemmed from the fact that further economic development within the conditions of capitalism was absolutely impossible. This applies to Europe as a whole. Consequently, if before 1913 we were conditionally correct in saying that socialism is more advantageous than capitalism, it therefore follows that since 1913 capitalism already signifies a condition of absolute stagnation and disintegration for Europe, while socialism provides the only economic salvation. This renders more precise our views with respect to the first premise for the proletarian revolution.

The second premise is the working class. It must become sufficiently powerful in the economic sense in order to gain power and rebuild society. Does this condition obtain today? After the experience of our Russian revolution it is no longer possible to raise this issue, inasmuch as the October Revolution became possible in our backward country. But we have learned in recent years to evaluate the social power of the proletariat on the world scale in a somewhat new way and much more precisely and concretely. Those naive, pseudo-Marxist views which demanded that the proletariat comprise 75 or 90 per cent of the population before taking power, these views appear as quite infantile. Even in countries where the peasantry comprises the majority of the population the proletariat can and must find access to the peasantry in order to achieve the conquest of power. Absolutely alien to us is any sort of reformist opportunism in relation to the peasantry. But at the same time, no less alien to us is dogmatism. The working class in all countries plays a social and economic role sufficiently great to be able to find a road to the peasant masses, to the oppressed nationalities and the colonial peoples, and in this way assure itself of the majority. After the experience of the Russian revolution this is not a speculation, not a hypothesis, not a deduction, but an incontestable fact.

And, finally, the third requirement : the working class must be ready for the overturn and capable of accomplishing it. The working class not only must be sufficiently powerful for it, but must be conscious of its power and must be able to apply this power. Today we can and must resolve into its elements and render more precise this subjective factor. During the postwar years, we have observed in the political life of Europe that the working class is ready for the overturn, ready in the sense of striving subjectively toward it, ready in terms of its will, moods, self-sacrifices, but still lacking the necessary organizational leadership. Consequently the mood of the class and its organizational consciousness need not always coincide. Our revolution, thanks to an exceptional combination of historical factors, afforded our backward country the opportunity to effect the transfer of power into the hands of the working class, in a direct alliance with the peasant masses. The role of the party is all too clear to us and, fortunately, it is today already clear to the West European Communist parties. Not to take the role of the party into account is to fall into pseudo-Marxist objectivism which presupposes some sort of purely objective and automatic preparation of the revolution, and thereby postpones the revolution to an indefinite future. Such automatism is alien to us. It is a Menshevik, a Social-Democratic world outlook. We know, we have learned in practice and we are teaching others to comprehend the enormous role of the subjective, the conscious factor that the revolutionary party of the working class represents.

Without our party the 1917 overturn would not, of course, have taken place and the entire fate of our country would have been different. It would have been thrown back to vegetate as a colonial country; it would have been plundered by and divided among the imperialist powers of the world. That this did not happen was guaranteed historically by the arming of the working class with the incomparable sword, our Communist Party. This did not happen in postwar Europe.

Two of the three necessary premises are extant. Long before the war the relative advantages of socialism, and since 1913 and all the more so after the war, the absolute necessity of socialism have been established. Failing socialism, Europe is decaying and disintegrating economically. This is a fact. The working class in Europe no longer continues to grow. Its destiny, its class destiny, corresponds and runs parallel to the development of economy. To the extent that European economy, with inevitable fluctuations, suffers stagnation and even disintegration, to that extent the working class, as a class fails to grow socially, ceases to increase numerically but suffers from unemployment, from the terrible swellings of the reserve army of labor, etc., etc. The war roused the working class to its feet in the revolutionary sense. Was the working class, because of its social weight, capable of carrying out the revolution before the war? What did it lack? It lacked the consciousness of its own strength. Its strength grew in Europe automatically, almost imperceptibly, with the growth of industry. The war shook up the working class. Because of this terrible and bloody upheaval, the entire working class in Europe was imbued with revolutionary moods on the very next day after the war ended. Consequently, one of the subjective factors, the desire to change this world, was at hand. What was lacking? The party was lacking, the party capable of leading the working class to victory.

Here is how the events of the revolution unfolded within our own country and abroad. In 1917, in Russia we have : the February-March revolution; and within nine months—October. The revolutionary party guarantees victory to the working class and peasant poor. In 1918—revolution in Germany, accompanied by changes at the top; the working class tries to forge ahead but is hurled back time and again. The proletarian revolution in Germany does not lead to victory. In 1919, the eruption of the Hungarian proletarian revolution : its base is too narrow and the party too weak. The revolution is crushed in a few months in 1919. By 1920, the situation has already changed and it continues to change more and more sharply.

In France there is a historical date—May 1, 1920. It marks a sharp turn that took place in the relation of forces between the proletariat and the bourgeoisie. The mood of the French proletariat had been on the whole revolutionary but it took too light a view of victory. It was lulled by that party and those organizations which had matured in the preceding period of peaceful and organic development of capitalism. On May 1, 1920, the French proletariat declared a general strike. This should have been its first major clash with the French bourgeoisie.

Entire bourgeois France trembled. The proletariat which had just emerged from the trenches struck terror into its heart. But the old Socialist Party, the old Social Democrats, who dared not oppose the revolutionary working class and who issued the call for the general strike, at the same time did everything in their power to blow it up; on the other hand, the revolutionary elements, the Communists, were too weak, too scattered and too lacking in experience. The May 1st strike failed. And if you consult the French newspapers for 1920 you will see in the editorials and news stories already a swift and decisive growth of the strength of the bourgeoisie. The bourgeoisie at once sensed its own stability, gathered the state apparatus into its hands and began to pay less and less attention to the demands of the proletariat and the threats of revolution.

In that same year, in August 1920, we experienced an event closer to home which likewise brought about a change in the relation of forces, not in favor of the revolution. This was our defeat below Warsaw[90], a defeat which from the international standpoint is most intimately bound up with the fact that in Germany and in Poland at that moment the revolutionary movement was unable to gain victory because there was lacking a strong revolutionary party enjoying the confidence of the majority of the working class.

A month later, in September 1920, we lived through the great movement in Italy. Precisely at that moment in the autumn of 1920 the Italian proletariat reached its highest point of ferment after the war. Mills, plants, railways, mines are seized. The state is disorganized, the bourgeoisie is virtually prostrate, its spine almost broken. It seems that only one more step forward is needed and the Italian working class will conquer power. But at this moment, its party, that same Socialist Party which had emerged from the previous epoch, although formally adhering to the Third International but with its spirit and roots still in the previous epoch, i.e., in the Second International—this party recoils in terror from the seizure of power, from the civil war, leaving the proletariat exposed. An attack is launched upon the proletariat by the most resolute wing of the bourgeoisie in the shape of Fascism, in the shape of whatever still remains strong in the police and the army. The proletariat is smashed.

After the defeat of the proletariat in September, we observe in Italy a still more drastic shift in the relationship of forces. The bourgeoisie said to itself : "So that's the kind of people you are. You urge the proletariat forward but you lack the spirit to take power." And it pushed the fascist detachments to the fore.

Within a few months, by March 1921, we witness the most important recent event in the life of Germany, the celebrated March events. Here we have a lack of correspondence between the class and the party developing from a diametrically opposite direction. In Italy, in September, the working class was eager for battle. The party shied back in terror. In Germany the working class had been eager for battle. It fought in 1918, in the course of 1919 and in the course of 1920. But its efforts and sacrifices were not crowned by victory because it did not have at its head a sufficiently strong, experienced and cohesive party; instead there was another party at its head which saved the bourgeoisie for the second time, after saving it during the war. And now in 1921 the Communist Party of Germany, seeing how the bourgeoisie was consolidating its positions, wanted to make a heroic attempt to cut off the bourgeoisie's road by an offensive, by a blow, and so it rushed ahead. But the working class did not support it. Why not? Because the working class had not yet learned to have confidence in the party. It did not yet fully know this party while its own experience in the civil war had brought it only defeats in the course of 1919-1920.

And so in March 1921 a situation occurred which impelled the Communist International to say : The relations between the parties and the classes, between the Communist parties and the working classes in all countries of Europe are still not mature for an immediate offensive, for an immediate battle for the conquest of power. It is necessary to proceed with a painstaking education of the Communist ranks in a twofold sense : First, in the sense of fusing them together and tempering them; and second, in the sense of their conquering the confidence of the overwhelming majority of the working class. Such was the slogan advanced by the Third International at a time when the March events in Germany were still fresh.

And then, Comrades, after the month of March, throughout the year 1921 and during 1922 we observed the process, at any rate on the surface, of the strengthening of the bourgeois governments in Europe; we observed the strengthening of the extreme right wing. In France the National Bloc headed by Poincaré still remains in power. But Poincaré is considered in France, that is within the National Bloc, as a "leftist" and looming on the horizon is a new and more reactionary, more imperialist ministry of Tardieu[91]. In England, the government of Lloyd George, this imperialist with his stock of pacifist preachments and proverbs, has been supplanted by the purely conservative, openly imperialist Ministry of Bonar Law. In Germany, the coalition ministry, i.e., one with an admixture of Social Democrats, has been replaced by an openly bourgeois ministry of Kuno[92]; and finally in Italy we see the assumption of power by Mussolini, the open rule of the counter-revolutionary fist. In the economic field, capitalism is on the offensive against the proletariat. In every country of Europe the workers have to defend, and not always successfully, the scale of wages they had yesterday and the 8-hour working day in those countries where it had been gained legally during or after the last period of the war. Such is the general situation. Clearly, the revolutionary development, that is, the struggle of the proletariat for power beginning with the year 1917, does not represent a uniform and steadily rising curve.

There has been a break in the curve. Comrades, in order to picture more clearly the situation through which the working class is now passing it might not be amiss to resort to an analogy. Analogy—historical comparison and juxtaposition—is a dangerous device because time and again people try to extract from an analogy more than it can give. But within certain limits, employed for the purpose of illustration, an analogy is useful. We began our revolution in 1905, after the Russo-Japanese War. Already at that time we were being drawn toward power by the logic of things. 1905 and 1906 brought stagnation, and the two Dumas; 1907 brought the 3rd of June and the government coup—the first victories of reaction which met almost no resistance—and then the revolution rolled back. 1908 and 1909 were already the black years of reaction; and then only gradually beginning with 1910-1911 was there an upswing, which the war then intersected. In March 1917, came the victory of bourgeois democracy; in October —the victory of workers and peasants. We have therefore two key points : 1905 and 1917, separated by an interval of 12 years. These twelve years represent in a revolutionary sense a broken curve, first declining and then rising.

In an international sense, first and foremost in relation to Europe, we now have something similar. Victory was possible in 1917 and 1918 but we did not gain it—the ultimate condition was lacking, the powerful Communist Party. The bourgeoisie succeeded in restoring many of its political and military-police positions but not the economic ones, while the proletariat began building its Communist Party brick by brick. In the initial stages this Communist Party tried to make up for lost opportunities by a single audacious leap forward, as in March 1921 in Germany. It burned its fingers. The International issued a warning : "You must conquer the confidence of the majority of the working class before you dare summon the workers to an open revolutionary assault." This was the lesson of the Third Congress. A year and a half later the Fourth World Congress convened.

In making the most general appraisal it is necessary to say that at the time the Fourth Congress convened, a turning point had not yet been reached in the sense that the International could say : "Now the hour of open assault has already sounded." The Fourth Congress developed, deepened, verified and rendered more precise the work of the Third Congress, and was convinced that this work was basically correct.

I said that in 1908-09 on a much narrower arena at the time, we lived through in Russia the moment of the lowest decline of the revolutionary wave in the sense of the prevailing moods among the working class—both in the sense of the then triumphant Stolypinism and Rasputinism[93], as well as in the sense of the disintegration of the advanced ranks of the working class. What remained as illegal nuclei were terribly small in comparison to the working class as a whole. The best elements were in jails, serving hard-labor terms in penitentiaries, or in exile. 1908-09—this was the lowest point of the revolutionary movement Then came a gradual upswing. For the last two years and, in part, right now we are living through a period undoubtedly analogous to 1908 and 1909, i.e., the lowest point in the direct and open revolutionary struggle.

There is still another point of similarity. On June 3, 1907 the counter-revolution gained a victory (Stolypin's coup) on the parliamentary arena almost without meeting any resistance in the country. And toward the end of 1907 another terrible blow descended—the industrial crisis. What influence did this have on the working class ? Did it impel the workers to struggle ? No. In 1905, in 1906 and the first half of 1907 the working class had already given its energies and its best elements to the open struggle. It suffered defeat, and on the heels of defeat came the commercial-industrial crisis which weakened the productive and economic role of the proletariat, rendering its position even less stable. This crisis weakened it both in the revolutionary and political sense. Only the commercial and industrial upswing which began in 1909-1910 and which reassembled the workers in factories and plants, again imbued the workers with confidence, provided a major basis of support for our party and gave the revolution an impulsion forward.

Here too, I say, we can draw a certain analogy. In the spring of 1921 a fearsome commercial crisis broke out in America and in Japan after the proletariat had suffered defeats : the defeat in France on May 1, 1920; in Italy, in September 1920. in Germany, throughout 1919 and 1920 and especially in the March days of 1921. But precisely at this moment in the spring of 1921 there ensued the crisis in Japan and in America and in the latter part of 1921 it leaped to Europe. Unemployment grew to unheard of proportions, especially, as you know, in England. The stability of the proletariat's position dropped still lower, after the losses and disillusionments already suffered. And this does not strengthen, but on the contrary in the given conditions of crisis weakens the working class. During the current year and since the end of last year there have been signs of a certain industrial revival. In America it has reached the proportions of a real upswing while in Europe it remains a small uneven ripple. Thus here, too, the first impulse for the revival of an open mass movement came, especially in France, from a certain improvement in the economic conjuncture.

But here, Comrades, the analogy ceases. The industrial upswing of 1909 and 1910 in our country and in the entire prewar world was a full-blooded, powerful boom which lasted until 1913 and came at a time when the productive forces had not yet run up against the limits of capitalism, giving rise to the greatest imperialist slaughter.

The industrial revival which began at the end of last year denotes only a change in the temperature of the tubercular organism of European economy. European economy is not growing but disintegrating; it remains on the same levels only in a few countries. The richest of European countries, insular England, has a national income at least one-third or one-quarter smaller than before the war. They engaged in war, as you know, in order to conquer markets. They ended by becoming poorer at least by one-fourth or one-third. The improvements this year have been minimal. The decline in the influence of the Social Democracy and the growth of the Communist parties at the expense of the Social Democrats is a sure symptom of this. As is well known, social reformism grew thanks to the fact that the bourgeoisie had the possibility of improving the position of the most highly skilled layers of the working class. In the nature of things, Scheidemann and everything connected with him would have been impossible without this, for after all Scheidemann does not represent simply an ideological tendency, but a tendency that grows out of certain economic and social premises. It represents a labor aristocracy which profits from the fact that capitalism is full-blooded and powerful and has the possibility of improving the condition of at least the upper layers of the working class. That is precisely why we witness in the prewar years from 1909 to 1913, the most powerful growth of the bureaucracy in the trade unions and in the Social Democracy, and the strongest entrenchment of reformism and nationalism among the top circles of the working class which led to the terrible catastrophe of the Second International at the outbreak of the war.

And now, Comrades, the gist of the situation in Europe is characterized by this, that the bourgeoisie has no longer the possibility of fattening up the summits of the working class because it is not able even to feed the entire working class normally, in the capitalist sense of the word, "normal." The lowering of working class living standards is today the same kind of law as the decline of the European economy. This process started in 1913, the war introduced superficial changes into it : after the war it has become revealed with especial ferocity. The superficial fluctuations of the economic conjuncture do not alter this fact. This is the first and basic difference between our epoch and the one prior to the war.

But there is a second difference and it is the existence of Soviet Russia as a revolutionary factor. There is also a third difference : the existence of a centralized International Communist Party.

And we observe, Comrades, that at the very time when the bourgeoisie is scoring one superficial victory after another over the proletariat, the growth, strengthening and systematic development of the Communist Party is not being retarded but advances forward. And herein lies the most important and fundamental difference between our epoch and the one from 1905 to 1917.

What I have said relates, as you see, primarily to Europe. It would be incorrect to apply it wholly to America. In America, too, socialism is more advantageous than capitalism; and it would be even more correct to say that especially in America socialism would be more advantageous than capitalism. In other words, were the present-day American productive forces organized along the principles of collectivism a fabulous flowering of economy would ensue.

But in relation to America it would be incorrect to say, as we do say in relation to Europe, that capitalism already represents the cessation of economic development. Europe is rotting, America is thriving. In the initial years or more correctly in the initial months, in the first twenty months after the war it might have seemed that America would be immediately undermined by the economic collapse of Europe inasmuch as America used and exploited the European market in general and the war market in particular. This market has shrivelled and dried up, and having been deprived of one of its props, the monstrous Babylonian tower of American industry threatened to lean over and to fall down altogether. But America, while having lost the European market of the previous scope (in addition to exploiting its own rich internal market with a population of 100 million), is seizing and has seized all the more surely the markets of certain European countries —those of Germany and to a considerable measure those of Britain. And we see, in 1921-1922, American economy passing through a genuine commercial and industrial upswing at a time when Europe is experiencing only a distant and feeble repercussion of this upswing.

Consequently, the productive forces in America are still developing under capitalism, much more slowly, of course, than they would develop under socialism but developing nevertheless. How long they will continue to do so is another question. The American working class in its economic and social power has, of course fully matured for the conquest of state power, but in its political and organizational traditions it is incomparably further removed from the conquest of power than the European working class. Our power—the power of the Communist International—is still very weak in America. And if one were to ask (naturally this is only a hypothetical posing of the question) which will take place first : the victorious proletarian revolution in Europe or the creation of a powerful Communist Party in America, then on the basis of all the facts now available (and naturally all sorts of new facts are possible such as, say, a war between America and Japan; and war, Comrades, is a great locomotive of history)—if one were to take the present situation in its further logical development, then I would venture to say that there are far more chances that the proletariat will conquer in Europe before a powerful Communist Party rises and develops in America[94]. In other words, just as the victory of the revolutionary working class in October 1917 was the premise for the creation of the Communist International and for the growth of the Communist parties in Europe, so, in all probability, the victory of the proletariat in the most important countries of Europe will be the premise for swift revolutionary developments in America. The difference between these two areas lies in this, that in Europe the economy decays and declines with the proletariat no longer growing productively (because there is no room for growth) but awaiting the development of the Communist Party; while in America, which exploits the disintegration of Europe, the economic advancement is still proceeding.

The third sphere is constituted by the colonies. It is self-understood that the colonies—Asia and Africa (I speak of them as a unity), despite the fact that they, like Europe, contain the greatest graduations—the colonies, if taken independently and isolatedly, are absolutely not ready for the proletarian revolution. If they are taken isolatedly, then capitalism still has a long possibility of economic development in them. But the colonies belong to the metropolitan centers and their fate is intimately bound up with the fate of these European metropolitan centers.

In the colonies we observe the growing national revolutionary movement. Communists represent there only small nuclei implanted among the peasantry. So that in the colonies we have primarily petty- bourgeois and bourgeois national movements. If you were to ask concerning the prospects of the Socialist and Communist development of the colonies then I would say that this question cannot be posed in an isolated manner. Of course, after the victory of the proletariat in Europe, these colonies will become the arena for the cultural, economic and every other kind of influence exercised by Europe, but for this they must first of all play their revolutionary role parallel with the role of European proletariat. In this connection the European proletariat, particularly that of France and in the first instance that of Britain, are doing far too little. The growth of the influence of Socialist and Communist ideas, the emancipation of the toiling masses of the colonies, the weakening of the influence of the nationalist parties can be assured not only by and not so much by the role of the native Communist nuclei as by the revolutionary struggle of the proletariat of the metropolitan centers for the emancipation of the colonies. Only in this way will the proletariat of the metropolitan centers demonstrate to the colonies that there are two European nations, one the oppressor, the other the friend; only in this way will the proletariat give a further impetus to the colonies which will topple down the structure of imperialism and thereby perform a revolutionary service for the proletarian cause.

Comrades, until recently we failed to differentiate adequately between Europe and America. And the slow development of Communism in America might have inspired some pessimistic ideas to the effect that so far as revolution is concerned Europe must wait for America. Not at all !

Europe cannot wait. To put it differently, if the revolution in Europe is postponed for many decades, it would signify the elimination of Europe generally as a cultural force. As you all know, the philosophy now fashionable in Europe is that of Spengler : the philosophy of the decline of Europe. In its own way this is a correct class premonition on the part of the bourgeoisie. Ignoring the proletariat which will replace the European bourgeoisie and wield power, they talk about Europe's decline. Of course, if this actually happened the inevitable result would be, if not a decline, then a prolonged economic and cultural decay of Europe and then, after a lapse of time, the American revolution would come and take Europe in tow. But there are no serious grounds for such a prognosis, pessimistic from the standpoint of time-intervals. To be sure, speculations concerning time-intervals are quite untrustworthy and not always serious, but I want to say that there is no reason for thinking that between the year 1917—the inception of the new revolutionary epoch in Europe—and the major victories in Western Europe, there must be a lapse of many more years than passed between our 1905 and our 1917. Twelve years elapsed in our country from the beginning of the revolution, the initial experience, to the victory. We do not of course know just how many years will pass between 1917 and the first major, stable victory in Europe. It is not excluded that less than twelve years may pass.

In any case, the greatest advantage today lies in the existence of Soviet Russia and of the Communist International, the centralized organization of the revolutionary vanguard and, intimately linked with this, the systematic organizational strengthening of Communist parties in various countries. This does not always signify their numerical growth. Naturally in 1919-20, when the first hopes of the proletariat were still fresh, the ranks of the Communist parties were flooded—as is always the case in time of high tide—and the Communist organizations became filled with unstable elements. Some of these elements have now withdrawn, but there has been no cessation of the growth of the party in terms of its becoming tempered, in terms of higher ideological clarity, in terms of international centralization and ties.

This growth is undeniable and finds its expression both in the fact that the Fourth World Congress made a start toward the drafting of an international program—for the first time in the history of the proletariat—as well as in the fact that the Fourth Congress in electing the Executive Committee created for the first time a centralist organ not on federalistic principles, not on the basis of delegated representatives from various parties, but as a body elected by the Fourth Congress itself. And this Executive Committee has been entrusted with the destinies of the Communist International until the next Congress.

The Communist International is confronted after the Fourth Congress with two intimately interrelated tasks. The first task is to continue the struggle against the Centrist tendencies which express the repeated and persistent attempts of the bourgeoisie through the medium of its left wing to utilize the protracted character of the revolutionary development by sinking its own roots inside the Communist International. The struggle against Centrism within the Communist International and the further purging of this world party—this is the first task. The second is the struggle for influence over the overwhelming majority of the working class.

These two problems were raised very sharply at the Third Congress, especially in connection with our French party which came to the Congress represented by two factions—the Center and the Left. Following the events of 1920, our Italian party split. By the summer of 1921 the Italian Center, the so-called Maximalists headed by Serrati, were no longer present at our Congress (the Third) and they were declared expelled from the International. In the French party these same two tendencies became delineated on the eve of the Fourth Congress. The parallelism in many respects between the Italian and French movements has been previously remarked upon. And here is a fact of the greatest symptomatic significance : despite the triumph of the counter-revolution in Italy as in Europe generally, to which I have already referred, we observe precisely in Italy, where Communism has suffered its worst defeat, not disintegration, not a recoil from, but on the contrary, a new impulsion toward the Communist International. The Maximalists led by Serrati whom we had expelled (and correctly so, for conduct that was truly treacherous), these Maximalists, having split with the reformists during the September 1920 movement, began knocking at the doors of the International on the eve of the Fourth Congress. What does this signify ? It signifies a new revolutionary impulsion to the left on the part of a section of the proletarian vanguard.

There were many indications that the French Centrists would repeat the course of the Italian Maximalists, that is, split with us. We would of course have been reconciled even to such an outcome in the knowledge that the Left Wing would have in the end gained the upper hand. However, the French Centrists, with Cachin and Frossard at the head, have learned something from the experience of the Italian Maximalists who arrived in Moscow with heads bowed in repentance after having split with Moscow. You should all acquaint yourselves with the resolution on the French party adopted by the Fourth Congress. These resolutions are in their own way quite Draconic, especially if one takes into account the morals and customs of France and of its old Socialist Party. A demand for a complete break with all the institutions of the bourgeoisie is something that seems self-evident to us. But in France where hundreds upon hundreds of Communist Party members belonged to Masonic lodges, bourgeois - democratic Leagues for the Defense of the Rights of Man, etc., etc.—there the demand for a complete break with the bourgeoisie, for the expulsion of all Freemasons and the like represents a complete overturn in the party's life.

At the Congress we adopted a demand to the French party that nine-tenths of the candidates for all electoral posts, the parliament, the municipal councils, the cantonal councils, etc., be selected from among workers and peasants directly from the workbench or the plough. In a country where entire legions of intellectuals, lawyers, careerists flock to the gates of various parties whenever they sniff the scent of a mandate, and all the more so a prospect of power, etc., those acquainted with the existing conditions in the French party will understand that a demand for advancing workers and peasants directly from the workbench and the plough to nine-tenths of the electoral posts represents the greatest possible unheaval in the life of the French party. The Left Wing which is approximately as strong numerically as the Center was in favor of this. The Center vacillated a great deal.

We understood that this issue was a very touchy one and that our Moscow boots had stepped on a very sensitive corn and we awaited how Paris would react to the prodding of Moscow. The latest telegrams testify that a break with Moscow was attempted. Morizet is named as the initiator of this attempt. He paid us a visit in Moscow and then wrote a very sympathetic book. (It is one thing to write in Paris a sympathetic book about the Russian revolution; it is something else again to prepare the French revolution). This Morizet together with Soutif[95]—both members of the Central Committee—proposed to split and to proclaim the formation of an independent party without waiting for the return of the French delegation from Moscow. But there was such great pressure from the ranks, the readiness of the rank and file to accept the decisions of the Fourth Congress was so clear and manifest, that they were forced to beat a retreat. And while they abstained—only abstained—the incumbent

Central Committee consisting entirely of Centrists, with not a single Left Winger on it and perhaps without any general enthusiasm among all the members of the Central Committee, nevertheless voted to submit to the Moscow decisions.

I repeat, comrades, this fact may appear secondary from the standpoint of world perspectives. But if we had followed the life of the French working class and its Communist vanguard from day to day —and we must learn to do this through our press—then all of us would have said that only now, only after the Fourth Congress, has French Communism turned the helm in such a way as will guarantee it a swift progress in conquering the confidence of the broad working masses of France. This is all the more true because there is not another working class in this world that has been deceived so often, so shamelessly and vilely as the French working class. Since the end of the Eighteenth Century it has been duped during all the revolutions by the bourgeoisie in all its colorations. Among all the parties of the Second International, the French Socialists of the prewar and war epochs elaborated the most refined technique and virtuosity of treachery. And this is why the French working class with its superb revolutionary temperament inevitably reacted with the greatest mistrust even toward the new Communist Party. It had seen "Socialists" under all sorts of labels; it had seen organizations, no matter how they changed their skins, remain passageways for careerists, deputies, journalists of all sorts, ministers, etc. Briand, Millerand, and all the rest, after all, stem from the old Socialist Party. No other proletariat in the world has passed through such a school of deception and political exploitation. Hence mistrust; hence political indifference: hence syndicalist influences and prejudices.

What we need is for our Communist Party to come before the working class and demonstrate in action that it is not a party like other parties but the revolutionary organization of the working class; that there is no room in its ranks for careerists, Freemasons, democrats and grafters. For the first time this demand has been presented and accepted. Furthermore a date has been fixed : January 1, 1923 is the deadline. Not a single Freemason, not a single careerist—by January 1, 1923. They have only a few days left. Comrades, these are facts of utmost importance. (*Applause.*)

Another question likewise in connection with France was posed very sharply—the question of the united front. As you know, the slogan of the united front arises from two causes. In the first place, we

Communists are still a minority in France, in Germany, in every country of Europe with the exception of Bulgaria and perhaps Czechoslovakia we influence and control less than one-half of the proletariat. Concurrently, the revolutionary development has started to lag; the proletariat wants to live and fight but finds itself split. It is under these conditions that the Communists must conquer the confidence of this working class. On what basis ? On the basis of the struggle in its full scope. On the basis of current day-to-day struggles, on the basis of every demand, at every strike, at every demonstration. The Communist must be in the forefront. The Communist must conquer the confidence of those who still do not trust him today. Hence the slogan of the united front; hence the internal cohesion, the expulsion from our ranks of everything alien to us in spirit and a simultaneous struggle to win over those proletarian elements that still trust these careerists, opportunists, Freemasons and the like. This is a twofold but closely related task. The French Communists, especially the Centrists who, under the pressure of the Dissidents, that is, of the French Socialists, had tolerated Freemasons in their ranks and rejected the tactic of the united front, have proposed to apply the tactic of the united front in connection with the demand for political amnesty. I cite France because these questions found their sharpest expression in that country.

When Frossard, Secretary of the French party, proposed in the name of the Communists to the Dissidents, i.e., Socialists, patriots, reformists, that they engage in joint action in order to obtain amnesty for worker-revolutionists clapped in jail during the war or in the postwar period—as soon as this offer was made, the shrewdest—leaders of the Dissidents immediately replied in a way that is typical and instructive in the highest degree. We have met and we shall meet this answer elsewhere. The Dissidents said : "You Communists have turned to us and consequently you thereby acknowledge that we are not betrayers of the working class. But we want time to think your offer over; and see whether or not you are hiding a brickbat in your sleeves; or are perchance preparing to discredit us." I gather from the papers that in The Hague, Comrade Radek wrote reportedly a very impolite article about Vandervelde and Scheidemann and at the same time offered the local Social Democrats and followers of Amsterdam a united front against militarism and the war danger.

Knowing the irascible temper of Comrade Radek I am ready to allow that his article was not very polite. But the reaction of Messrs.

Amsterdamists was quite typical : "See here," they said, "this means one of two things. Either you must admit that we are not traitors in view of your proposing a united front to us or we shall become firmly convinced that you are hiding not only disrespectful articles, but brickbats, and something worse in your sleeves."

Comrades, this position of course constitutes a most sweeping admission of bankruptcy. Upon reading this I was reminded of the comments of certain Parisian wits in the period of our emigration when the Social Democrats proposed to debate with Burtsev[96]. They pointed out that Burtsev's reply in rejecting the debate amounted to his saying : "I'm a wise old bird and you can't trap me. What you seek by a discussion is to expose my feeble mentality but I refuse to fall for such bait."

The gentlemen of the Second International are shrewder than Burtsev but they fall into the self-same trap. For what is the content of the brickbat in our sleeves ? It is this, that we say that these people are incapable of struggle, incapable of defending the interests of the proletariat. And we address ourselves to their army, that is, those workers who still follow and trust them and say to them : "We are proposing to your leaders a certain way of fighting jointly with us for the 8-hour working day, for political amnesty, and against wage cuts. What is our brickbat ? Why this, that if you Amsterdamists and Social Democrats expose yourselves in this struggle as cowards and traitors, a section of your workers will come over to us. But if contrary to expectations you turn out to be revolutionary tigers and lions, then so much the better for you. Try it."

This is the content of our bait. Our trap is simple. It is so simple, but at the same time it is unassailable. It is impossible to squirm away from it. It does not matter whether a Burtsev agrees or refuses to discuss for fear of revealing that he is no good. In either case he remains no good, and can't remedy the situation. In other words, the slogan of the united front which is already playing an enormous role in all European countries in educating the working masses about the Communists and posing before the workers who do not yet trust the Communists the following proposition :

"You do not believe in revolutionary methods and in the dictatorship. Very well. But we Communists propose to you and your organization that we fight side by side to gain those demands which you are advancing today."

This is an unassailable argument. It educates the masses about

the Communists and shows them that the Communist organization
is the best for partial struggles as well. I repeat that we have gained
major successes in this struggle. And alongside the growing internal
cohesion of the Communist parties we observe the growth of their
political influence and their increased ability to maneuver, really
maneuver. This is something that they have especially lacked.

From the united front flows the slogan of a workers' government. The
Fourth Congress submitted it to a thorough discussion and once again
confirmed it as the central political slogan for the next period. What
does the struggle for a workers' government signify? We Communists of course know that a genuine workers' government in Europe
will be established after the proletariat overthrows the bourgeoisie
together with its democratic machinery and installs the proletarian
dictatorship under the leadership of the Communist Party. But in
order to bring this about it is necessary for the European proletariat
in its majority to support the Communist Party.

But this does not obtain as yet and so our Communist parties say
on every appropriate occasion :

"Socialist workers, syndicalist workers, anarchists and non-party
workers ! Wages are being slashed; less and less remains of the 8-hour
working day; the cost of living is soaring. Such things would not
be if all the workers despite their differences were able to unite and
install their own workers' government."

And the slogan of a workers' government thus becomes a wedge
driven by the Communists between the working class and all other
classes : and inasmuch as the top circles of the Social Democracy,
the reformists, are tied up with the bourgeoisie, this wedge will act
more and more to tear away, and it is already beginning to tear
away the left wing of Social Democratic workers from their leaders.
Under certain conditions the slogan of a workers' government can
become a reality in Europe. That is to say, a moment may arrive
when the Communists together with the left elements of the Social
Democracy will set up a workers' government in a way similar to ours
in Russia when we created a workers' and peasants' government
together with the Left Social-Revolutionaries. Such a phase would
constitute a transition to the proletarian dictatorship, the full and
completed one. But right now the significance of the slogan of a
workers' government lies not so much in the manner and conditions
of its realization in life as in the fact that at the present time this
slogan opposes the working class as a whole politically to all other

classes, i.e., to all the groupings of the bourgeois political world.

At the Fourth Congress we were confronted concretely with the question of a workers' government with respect to Saxony. There the Social Democrats together with the Communists comprise a majority as against the bourgeoisie in the Saxon Landtag. I believe there are 40 Social Democratic deputies and 10 Communist deputies while the total bourgeois bloc numbers less than 50. And so the Social Democrats proposed to the Communists the joint formation of a workers' government in Saxony. There were some doubts and vacillations on this issue in our German party. The question was reviewed here in Moscow and a decision was reached to reject the proposal. What do the German Social Democrats really want ? What were they aiming at with this proposal ? You all know that the German republic is headed by a Social Democrat, Ebert. Under Ebert is a bourgeois ministry, called to power by Ebert. But in Saxony, one of the most highly proletarianized sections of Germany, it is proposed to institute a coalition labor ministry of Social Democrats and Communists. The result would be: a genuine bourgeois government in Germany, over the country as a whole, while in the Landtag of one of the sections of Germany there would be acting as a lightning rod, a coalition Social Democratic and Communist government.

In the Comintern we gave the following answer : If you, our German Communist comrades, are of the opinion that a revolution is possible in the next few months in Germany, then we would advise you to participate in Saxony in a coalition government and to utilize your ministerial posts in Saxony for the furthering of political and organizational tasks and for transforming Saxony in a certain sense into a Communist drillground so as to have a revolutionary stronghold already reinforced in a period of preparation for the approaching outbreak of the revolution. But this would be possible only if the pressure of the revolution were already making itself felt, only if it were already at hand. In that case it would imply only the seizure of a single position in Germany which you are destined to capture as a whole. But at the present time you will of course play in Saxony the role of an appendage, an impotent appendage because the Saxon government itself is impotent before Berlin, and Berlin is—a bourgeois government. The Communist Party of Germany was in complete accord with this decision and the negotiations were broken off. The proposal of the Social Democrats to the Communists—much weaker than the Social Democrats and hounded by these Social Democrats—

to share power with them in Saxony[97] is of course a trap. But in this trap was expressed the pressure of the working masses for unity. This pressure has been evoked by us; and this pressure, insofar as it operates to tear the working class away from the bourgeoisie, will in the last analysis work in our favor.

Comrades, I said that there is a tide of concentrated reaction now sweeping over Europe and her governmental upper stories; the victory of the Tories in England; Poincaré's national bloc with a prospect of Tardieu in France; in Germany which is still called a Socialist Republic today (it was thus hastily labelled in November 1918), there is a purely bourgeois government; and finally in Italy there is the assumption of power by Mussolini.

Mussolini is a lesson being given to Europe with regard to democracy, its principles and its methods. In some respects this lesson is analogous—from the opposite extreme, of course—to the one which we gave Europe in the beginning of 1918 by dispersing the Constituent Assembly. Mussolini is a lesson to Europe that is instructive in the highest degree.

Italy is an old cultured country, with democratic traditions, with universal suffrage, etc., etc. When the proletariat frightened the bourgeoisie to death but proved unable, owing to the treachery of its own party, to deal it the death blow, the bourgeoisie set in motion all of its most active elements, headed by Mussolini, a renegade from socialism and the proletariat. A private party army was mobilized and it was equipped from one end of the country to the other with funds allegedly drawn from mysterious sources but which come principally from governmental resources, partly from the secret Italian funds, and to a considerable measure from French subsidies to Mussolini. Under the aegis of democracy the storm-troop organization of the counter-revolution was organized and in the course of two years it conducted assaults upon workers' districts and threw a ring of its troops around Rome. The bourgeoisie hesitated because it was not sure that Mussolini was capable of coping with the situation. But when Mussolini proved his ability, they all bowed before him.

The speech made by Mussolini in the Italian parliament ought to be posted and placarded in all the workers' institutions and houses in Western Europe. What he said amounts to the following :

"I could chase all of you out of here and turn this (Parliament) into a camp for my fascists. But I don't need to do it because you will lick my boots away." And they all answered, "Hear ! hear !"

And the Italian democrats thereupon requested to know : "Which boot is it your pleasure that we begin with—the right or the left? "

Comrades, this is a lesson of exceptional importance to the European working class which in its top layers is corroded by its traditions, by bourgeois democracy, by the deliberate hypnosis of legality.

I have said that the centralized Communist organization of the Comintern and the existence of the Soviet Republic constitute the greatest conquests of the European and world working class in this epoch of the death-bed triumphs of the European bourgeoisie, in this epoch of a break in the rising curve of the revolution. The gist of the matter is not that we, Russia, conduct internationalist propaganda. It of course happens that Russian comrades like Radek and Lozovsky[98], for example, manage, to our surprise, to reach The Hague, and there write disrespectful articles, and arouse the ire of pacifists of both sexes, etc., etc. This, Comrades, is of course very valuable and very gratifying, but it is still of secondary importance.

Nor is the gist of the matter in the fact that we in Moscow extend hospitality to the Congresses of the Comintern. It is of course a good thing, but our propaganda does not consist in welcoming our comrades from Italy, Germany and elsewhere and assigning them rooms in the Lux Hotel[99] (poorly heated, of course, inasmuch as we have not yet learned to operate heating systems efficiently). The gist lies in the very existence of the Soviet Republic. We have become accustomed to this fact. The entire world working class appears, in a certain sense, to have become accustomed to it. On the other side, the bourgeoisie, too, makes a pretense to a certain extent of having grown accustomed. But in order to understand the significance for the revolution of the existence of the Soviet Republic, let us imagine for a moment that this Republic no longer exists. With Mussolini in Italy, Poincaré in France, Bonar Law in England, a bourgeois government in Germany, the downfall of the Soviet Republic would signify the postponement of the European and world revolution for decades ; it would signify the genuine decay of European culture. Socialism would then arise perhaps from America, from Japan, from Asia. But instead of speculating in terms of decades, what we are striving for is to bring this issue to its consummation in the next few years. (Applause.) For this there is the greatest and most ample opportunity.

Once it establishes a correct relationship with the peasantry, what is the proletariat—of even so backward a country as ours ? We have already seen what it is with our own eyes, and our All-Union Soviet Congress, now convening in Moscow, is demonstrating just what is signified by the power of the proletariat, encircled and blockaded by the whole world, but nevertheless leading the peasantry behind it. The European and world working class draws its strength and energy from this source, from Soviet Russia. We hold the power. In our country the means of production are nationalized. This is a great trump card in the hands of the toiling masses of Russia and at the same time this is a pledge of an accelerated development of the revolution in Europe.

Should (working-class) America lag behind we shall nevertheless gain the upper hand. During the imperialist war the American bourgeoisie warmed its hands at the European bonfire. But, Comrades, once the revolutionary conflagration starts sweeping Europe the American bourgeoisie will not be able to maintain itself long. It is nowhere written that the European proletariat must keep waiting until the American proletariat learns not to succumb to the lies of its triply depraved bourgeoisie. Nowhere is this written. At the present time the American bourgeoisie is deliberately keeping Europe in a condition of decay. Glutted with European blood and gold the American bourgeoisie issues orders to the whole world, sends plenipotentiaries to conferences who are bound by no commitments. These emissaries say nothing but render their own decisions, and from time to time they plant their American foot on the table and the diplomats of the European countries cannot fail to note that this foot is shod in an excellent American boot. And with this boot America dictates her own laws to Europe. The European bourgeoisie, not only of Germany and France but also Britain, begs on its hind legs before the American bourgeoisie which drained Europe in wartime by its support, by its loans, by its gold, and which now keeps Europe in the throes of death-agony. The American bourgeoisie will be repaid by the European proletariat. And this vengeance shall come the sooner, all the firmer our Soviet successes are.

Whether our propaganda is good or bad, it remains in either case a third-rate or fourth-rate factor, but our economy is a first-rate factor. Comrade Peasants!—and unless I am mistaken there are non-party peasant comrades present in this hall—I can categorically assure you that each additional sheaf of grain is another small weight placed on the scales of the European revolution. What does the working class of Britain dread? What does the German working class dread ? Hungry Europe survived for three war years and in the postwar years on American grain. The American bourgeoisie naturally threatens openly that in the event of new revolutionary convulsions in Europe it will starve the continent by a grain blockade just as Britain and France once threw an industrial blockade around Soviet Russia. This is a very important matter in the calculations of the European working class and above all of the German workers. And we, Soviet Russia, must say—and prepare this in action—that the European proletarian revolution will eat grain supplied by Soviet Russia.

And these words, Comrade Peasants, are not hollow syllables, not empty phrases. The fate of all Europe depends upon the solution of this question. Two courses are possible : *either* the European proletariat remains terrorized by the American boot, *or* the European proletariat is backed by the Russian workers and peasants, and thus assured of grain during the difficult days and months of revolution. That is why each economic success in agriculture is a revolutionary deed. And that is why every peasant in Soviet Russia—even those who do not know for sure just where Germany, France, or Britain are located on the map—who seeks to grow his crops, who tries to start things rolling again, to help the city and the industry—this peasant is today a better aid to the world, in the first instance, the European, revolution than are all of us old and experienced propagandists put together.

This, Comrades, applies with equal force to our industry. Miserable indeed would be the revolutionary party of Europe that said to itself —no Communist would ever say it—"I shall bide my time until the Soviet Republic shows me just how the condition of the working class can be improved under socialism." No one has the right to bide his time ; everybody has the duty to fight side by side with us. But, on the other hand, it is incontestable that each of our economic successes, to the extent that it simultaneously enables us to improve the condition of the working class in Russia while the condition of the working class in Europe is dropping lower rung by rung—yes, it is incontestable that each economic success of ours is the weightiest of arguments, the weightiest propaganda in favor of accelerating the proletarian revolution in Europe. Power is in our hands ; the means of production are in our hands. We hold the frontiers. This, too, is no minor circumstance.

That same American billionaire with his first-class boots could buy up all of our Russia with his billions were our frontiers left open to him. That is why the monopoly of foreign trade is just as much our inalienable revolutionary conquest as is the nationalization of the means of production. That is why the working class and the peasants of Russia will not permit any violation of the monopoly of foreign trade no matter how much pressure is exerted upon us from all the five continents of this globe still under the capitalist yoke. These are our trumps. Only with a correct organization of production can we preserve them, multiply them and not waste them. From this standpoint, Comrades, there must be no self-deception concerning the difficulties of our tasks. This is what we said at the Fourth Congress which took up our New Economic Policy as a special point on its agenda, in connection with the world perspectives. We have listed our big trump cards : state power, transport, the primary means of production in industry, natural resources, nationalization of land, taxes in kind which flow from this nationalized land, and the monopoly of foreign trade. These are first-class trumps. But if one does not know how to use them, it is possible to lose with even better trumps. Comrades, we must learn. At the Congress Comrade Lenin in his brief speech laid particular stress upon this, that not only they but we, too, must learn. We must learn how to organize industry correctly, for this correct organization still lies ahead and not behind us. It is our tomorrow and not our yesterday, nor even today.

We are making efforts to stabilize our currency. This was also taken up at the Fourth Congress. Such efforts are indispensable and, naturally, the greater our relative successes in this field, all the easier will be our administrative labors in industry. But we all understand only too clearly that all efforts in the field of finances unaccompanied by genuine material successes in the field of industry must remain mere child's play. The foundation is our industry ; the Soviet state rests upon this foundation, thrives with it and secures from it the assurance of the future victories of the working class.

Finally, there is one more trump, one more machine, one other organization that is likewise in our hands. We talked about it more than once at the Fourth Congress. It is our party. I am speaking here first of all before the Communist fraction of the Soviet Congress and it is necessary in closing to say a few words about our party. From the general analysis it follows that, on the European scale, we are living through a period of recession in the direct revolutionary struggle, and simultaneously through a period of educational work and strengthening of the Communist Party. The development has assumed a retarded and protracted character. This means that we must wait longer for the assistance of the European and, later, of the world proletariat ; this means that our party is destined for a long span of time, perhaps for several years, to remain the vanguard of the world revolution.

This is a very great honor. But it is also a great responsibility, a very great burden. We would prefer to have alongside us Soviet Republics in Germany, Poland and other countries. Our responsibility then would have been less and the difficulties of our position would not have been so great. Our party has old cadres with pre-revolutionary, underground tempering, but they are in the minority. We have in our party hundreds of thousands who in terms of human class material are in no way inferior to the old timers. These hundreds of thousands who poured into our ranks after the revolution possess the advantage of youth but are handicapped by a lesser experience. Comrade Lenin told me (I did not happen to read it myself) that some physician, either a Czech or a German, has written that the Communist Party of Russia consists of a few thousand oldsters and the rest, youth. The conditions of the NEP, he thinks, will tend to reshape our party, and if the old generations—a few thousand strong—depart from activity, the party will be imperceptibly transformed by the elements of the NEP, the elements of capitalism. Here, as you see, is a subtle political and psychological calculation. This calculation is of course false to the core. But at the same time it demands of our party that it give itself an accounting of the protracted character of the revolutionary development and of the difficulties of our position; and that our party double and triple its efforts for the education of its new generations, for attracting the youth and for raising the qualifications of the party mass. In the present conditions this is a life-and-death question for us.

Comrades, I want to refer to still another episode—a very major episode for all of us—and that is the illness of Vladimir Ilyich. Most of you here have not had the opportunity of following the European press. There have been many wild campaigns abroad concerning us and against us, but I do not recall—not even in the days of Kerensky when we were hounded as German spies—such a concentrated campaign of malevolence, of viciousness, and fiendish speculation as the current campaign around the illness of Comrade Lenin. Our enemies of course hoped for the worst outcome, the worst possible personal outcome. At the same time they said that our party is beheaded, split into warring groups, falling apart, and that an opportunity is opening up for their laying hands on Russia. The White Guard scum has talked about it openly, of course. The diplomats, the capitalists of Europe, have hinted about it, understanding each other with half-phrases.

Comrades, in this way they, against their own will and wishes, showed, on the one hand, that they have been able in their own way to appraise the significance of Comrade Lenin to our party and to the revolution; and, on the other hand that they neither know character nor understand—all the worse for them—the nature of our party. It is superfluous for me to talk before the Communist fraction of the Soviet Congress about the significance of Comrade Lenin to the movement in our country and in the world. But there is, Comrades, a kind of bond that is not only physical but spiritual, an internal, indissoluble bond between the party and the individual who expresses it best, the most fully, and in a way that a genius does. And this has found its expression in the fact that when Comrade Lenin was torn from his work by illness, the party (which knew something about the howling of the bourgeois jackals the world over) awaited, with tense expectation, news and bulletins of Comrade Lenin's condition, but at the same time not a single muscle in our party trembled, there was not a single vacillation, not a hint of the possibility of internal struggle, and all the less so of split. When Comrade Lenin withdrew from work by order of his physicians, the party understood that now a double and treble responsibility had fallen upon every rank-and-file member; and the party waited in unanimity and with closed ranks for the leader's return.

Not so long ago I was engaged in conversation by a foreign bourgeois politician who said to me : "I get around a good deal in your party circles and in Soviet circles. Of course, there are personal and group conflicts among you but one must give you your due. Whenever the external world, or an external danger, or general tasks are involved, you always straighten out your front." The last part of his declaration about our straightening out our front gratified me, but the first part, I admit, annoyed me somewhat. To the extent that in such a big party as ours, with such colossal tasks as ours, and under the greatest conceivable difficulties, and with the old timers unquestionably wearing out (as is in the nature of things)—to the extent that some internal dangers could arise in our party, there is not and cannot be any remedy against them other than the raising of the qualification of the entire party and the strengthening of its public opinion so that each member in each post feels the increased pressure of this party public opinion.

These are the conclusions we draw from the overall international situation. The hour of the European revolution will not perhaps strike tomorrow. Weeks and months will pass, maybe several years, and we shall still remain the only workers'-peasants' state in the world. In Italy Mussolini has triumphed. Are we guaranteed against the victory of German Mussolinis in Germany ? Not at all. And it is wholly possible that a much more reactionary ministry than Poincaré's will come to power in France. Before squatting down on its hind legs and pushing its Kerensky to the fore, the bourgeoisie is still quite capable of advancing its last Stolypins, Plehves, Sipyagins[100]. This will be the prologue to the European revolution, provided we are able to maintain ourselves, provided the Soviet state remains standing, and, consequently, provided above all that our party is able to maintain itself to the end. We shall perhaps have to pass through more than one year of this preparatory economic, political and other kinds of work.

Therefore we must draw closer to our mass reserves. More youth around our party and within it ! Raise its qualifications to the maximum ! Given this condition of complete cohesion and with the raising of our party's qualifications, with the transfer of experience from the old to the new generation, no matter what storms—these heralds of the final proletarian victory—may break over our heads, we shall stand firm in our knowledge that the Soviet frontier is the trench beyond which the counter-revolution cannot pass. This trench is manned by us, by the vanguard of Soviet Russia, by the Communist Party, and we shall preserve this trench inviolate and impregnable until that day when the European revolution arrives, and over the whole of Europe there shall wave the banner of the Soviet Republic of the United States of Europe, the threshold to the World Socialist Republic.

(*Long and stormy ovation.*)
(*Shouts*: *Long Live the Leader of the Red Army, Comrade Trotsky!*
Long Live Comrade Lenin!)

29

Preface to *The Communist Movement in France*[101]

Imperialist France is today the ruling power of the European continent and a major force outside the continent. This single circumstance imparts immense importance to the French proletariat and its party. The European revolution will triumph decisively and irrevocably only after it is the master of Paris. The victory of the proletariat on the European continent will almost automatically seal the fate of British capitalism. And finally, revolutionary Europe, which will be immediately joined by the enslaved peoples of Asia and Africa, will be in a position to speak a few convincing words to the capitalist oligarchy that rules America. The master-key of the European situation, and in a large measure also to the world situation, is thus entrusted to the French working class.

The Communist International has followed with the closest attention the internal life of the French party precisely because the CI had, as it still has, a very high estimate of the historical role of the French party. The French workers have been deceived, throughout history, far more often than any other working class. For this reason the French Communist Party must be all the more self-exacting and intransigent. In this respect major successes have been recently attained, which may in a certain sense be called decisive. Behind the shell of the internal factional struggles, or circle strifes, splits and expulsions, the French proletariat has during the last two years cut its real revolutionary teeth, and with these teeth it will have to bite through the armor of a mighty military state. The successes won along this road, still preparatory at present, are in a sense personified in Frossard's departure from the party, and in the adherence of Monatte and Barbusse[102].

Frossard, the party's former General Secretary and at least to a

334

certain point the chief inspirer of its official policy, headed that wing of its parliamentary past which made an attempt to adapt itself to the resolute shift to the left made by the proletarian vanguard. Not bereft of a certain mental agility and elasticity, resourcefulness, and eloquence — valuable traits which are highly useful to everybody, including revolutionists, but which are of self-sufficient significance for a parliamentary politician—Frossard apparently imagined in all seriousness that with the aid of these assets he would be able till the end of time to maneuver between the Communist International and its enemies; that he would be able to cover himself with the authority of Communism in his relations with the workers and at the same time safeguard the French working class from the "excesses" of Moscow. But when Frossard opposed his diplomatic improvisations, his masterpieces of evasion, equivocation, ambiguity, etc., to the principled line of the Communist International, he was bound to lose his bearings at the very first step. The position of this individual may best be characterized by the fact that a few hours before his departure from the Communist Party he did not himself know whether he would take a trip to Moscow in order to participate in guiding the policy of the Communist International as a member of the ECCI or whether he would take a walk into the camp of the enemies of the Comintern.

Frossard's individual peculiarities must not, however, blind us to what is typical in Frossardism. In Italy we came, as everybody knows, into conflict with Comrade Serrati who placed himself and his faction outside of the Communist International for a long time. The exceptionally stormy character of Italy's political development has now once again forced the Maximalist faction with its leaders back to the side of the Communist International. Our hope is that the merger will be more permanent this time.

In Germany we had the classical episode of Paul Levi who began by opposing the obviously erroneous tactic of the German Communist Party in March 1921 and who ended by proving within a few weeks that he had only been seeking a convenient pretext for crossing over into the camp of the enemies of the proletarian revolution. In a less clear and finished form, sometimes with bare hints only, we have experienced similar manifestations in the Czechoslovakian, Norwegian and other parties.

At first glance it is particularly surprising to note that in all these conflicts, the splitters or the vacillators are headed by the most eminent "leaders," that is, by those individuals who appeared at least on the surface as leaders of the movement "for Moscow" and "for the Third International." Serrati was the undisputed leader of the Italian party until September 1920; Paul Levi was the Chairman of the German party; his emulator Friesland[103] was General Secretary of the same party; Frossard was General Secretary of the French party, and so forth. This recurrence shows in and by itself that what rules here is not chance, but lawful necessity. And in the last analysis it is not so very difficult to explain this lawfulness. In the old capitalist countries, possessing old Social-Democratic traditions, the very formation of the Communist Party implied a break with the enormous and ancient deposits of reformism, nationalism, parliamentarianism. But the upper layer of Socialists, those with famous names, great authority, etc., had their roots sunk deeply into this past. And even those Social Democrats who in prewar days or during the war belonged to the extreme left wing of the party and were therefore in opposition to the official Social-Democratic course, were in their overwhelming majority political captives of the Social Democracy. And their opposition to Scheidemannism and Renaudelism was merely the opposition of orators and journalists, formal and literary, but not revolutionary and dynamic in character.

After the war, an irresistible leftward movement set in among the working masses, a movement to settle accounts with the bourgeoisie; and then the Social-Democratic oppositionists imagined that *their* day had come, that the masses intended to justify *their* criticism and were ready to follow *their* instructions. The position and policy of these gentlemen bear a strong resemblance to the position and policy of moderate liberals in times of revolution. The liberals invariably regarded the first awakening of the people as proof of their own strength and of the correctness of their own policy. But by the second day following the revolution they became convinced in horror that the masses, at least their revolutionary section, did not draw any fine line of distinction between the overlords of yesterday and those who had been in a loyal and moderate opposition to these overlords. At this point the liberals invariably threw themselves into the arms of reaction.

That it was possible for the fence-straddling leaders of the Social-Democratic opposition to place themselves at the head of the Communist Party is explained by the circumstance that the genuine revolutionary section of the working class was unable in the space of a few months either to find or educate new leaders. And it must be recognized as a fact that during its initial years, the Communist International had many sections headed by some leaders who were revolutionary but inexperienced or not firm enough; and by others who were semi-revolutionary and eternally vacillating, but possessing considerable authority and political aptitude. Although the situation has greatly improved in this respect, this has been, as it remains today, the source of internal difficulties, friction and strife within the Communist International. The greatest fear of the semi-Centrist leaders was to find themselves pulled out of the groove of legality, decorated with formal radicalism. For this reason they took cover behind the Chinese screens of "national autonomy" as a safeguard against the revolutionary posing of political questions and against the methods involving actual preparations for a rising of the proletariat. But the qualitative sameness of the politics of Paul Levi, of Frossard and the rest shows that involved here are not at all peculiarities inherent in any specific national situation—which of course must be carefully taken into account—but a wholly internationalist tendency, in the spirit of Left Centrism, which is prepared to adopt the external ritual of the Communist International, to swallow 21 and more conditions without a grimace, but all on the sole condition that everything go on exactly as before. Frossard is a perfect representative of this type. That he and his co-thinkers have left the party is therefore a most significant sign-post on the road to the creation of the revolutionary party of the French proletariat.

Although Frossard himself, as we have been, was by no means a unique national peculiarity, the reasons that enabled him so long to deceive himself and others about his actual political destination are nevertheless to be found in the peculiarities of the French political situation. In contrast not only to defeated Germany but even to the half-defeated Italy, victorious France was able to pass through the highly critical postwar years without any profound political upheavals. And although the basic tendencies leading the country toward revolutionary catastrophe are the same in France as in Germany or Italy, they have been much less sharply expressed in France, much milder and more veiled in form. The formation of the revolutionary proletarian vanguard has for this reason been correspondingly slow in France, at any rate until a few months ago. For a time it seemed on the surface as if the old Socialist Party was gradually evolving along Communist lines, after throwing all the openly discredited ballast overboard at Tours. But in reality there were many co-thinkers of Renaudel and Longuet at Tours who parted with them with "heavy hearts," hoping by this sacrifice to purchase the right of holding a leading position in the Communist Party which would then, out of gratitude, refrain from interfering with their good old habits. In consequence of the general sluggishness and conservatism of political life in France since the war, even the left wing, as it took shape in the Committee for the Third International inside the Socialist Party, was distinguished by political amorphousness and heterogeneity. And it was precisely this fact—which was not sufficiently clear to all the comrades—that restrained the International for a time from taking more resolute measures against the policy of Frossard and Co.

As early as 1921 and during the first half of 1922, this group furnished ample grounds for an open split. But at that time such a split would not have been understood by the mass of party members; the split in the party would have occurred along somewhat accidental lines, and, finally, the International would have acquired in the person of the left faction an extremely variegated group which was itself in need of an internal cleansing. The first necessity was therefore to give the left elements an opportunity to clearly grasp their own tasks, to become fused ideologically, to rally an important section of the party around them. It was not until this preparatory ideological, self-critical and educational work had been accomplished that the International could proceed to supplement it on a large scale by more decisive organizational and "surgical" measures. And so in this sense, the lag in the political development of France has had also its positive side for the Communist Party. The left wing was not confronted with major political tests before it had the opportunity to seriously prepare itself for them. In Italy the moment of split in the Socialist Party was not determined by any tactical considerations, but was imposed by the appalling capitulation of the leading circles of the party during the events of September 1920. In France the moment of split with the Left Centrists depended to a large extent on the Communist International. Certain comrades, principally in the French party itself, admittedly tried to force the events, under the impression that the tactics pursued by the ECCI on the French question were too irresolute, far too patient, even erroneous. Without considering whether or not some necessary steps were omitted on this or that detail (in all likelihood there were), we can now, in reviewing the completed phase of French party life, say with complete assurance that the tactics of the ECCI have been fundamentally correct. Correct not only with regard to methods but also with regard to tempo which has corresponded to the *inner rhythm of development of the proletarian vanguard in France*. It is thanks to just this complete harmony, that our French party, after a severe and profound internal crisis, and after the ejection of alien elements, has been able to retain in its ranks the crushing majority of its members, the entire party apparatus and its central publication (*l'Humanité*)—which is of far greater importance in France than in any other country. In this connection, it must be remarked that the French party and the International have to thank Comrade Marcel Cachin for a great deal. There have been misunderstandings between him and the International, but in the decisive moment, he took his post unfalteringly in the camp of the revolution.

The surgical operation undertaken by the Fourth Congress was doubtless a very grave one, and it appeared to some comrades as altogether too risky. It was a question of a final and irrevocable simultaneous break between the party and bourgeois public opinion and its most equivocal institutions in the guise of Freemasonry, the League of the Rights of Man, the radical press and so forth. When this surgical operation was approaching its successful conclusion, the still vacillating Frossard surveyed the scene and saw that he had nothing in common with *this* party. And the very same door which served as a means of exit for Frossard in company with the Masons, the Human Righters and the rest, has also been the door through which two others have entered the party : Monatte and Barbusse.

The entry of Monatte is as far from being a mere personal episode as is Frossard's exit. During and after the war, Monatte represented more clearly and intransigently than anyone else the traditions of revolutionary syndicalism in its heyday. Mistrust of "politics" and "party" formed the most important ingredient of these traditions. This mistrust had an adequate historical justification. During all these years Monatte has been the loyal friend of the Russian Revolution. He never wavered, not even at the most critical moments. But toward the French Communist Party he maintained an attitude of extreme distrust, remaining on the sidelines, outside of it. It was only when the party proved by deeds that it does not shrink from the harshest measures, if need arises, to secure its proletarian composition and its revolutionary character, that Monatte applied for a membership card. This was more than a personal "gesture." It means that the party has broken down the wall of distrust which had separated it from a whole layer of the revolutionary French workers. It is quite likely that internal friction will continue inside the party, which contains elements from different political schools, but the party's genuine proletarian character is henceforward assured, and with it, its revolutionary future.

The entry of Barbusse bears a more individual character. Barbusse does not stand for any revolutionary traditions of prewar times. But by way of compensation, Barbusse is the best embodiment of the indignant conscience of the war generation. As president of the Revolutionary Union of War Veterans, Barbusse has until recently kept up his formal independence from the Communist Party, and thus mirrored the profoundly revolutionary, but uncrystallized, indignation among the workers and peasant masses of the postwar period. As soon as political relations had cleared up, and declaimers of pacifism and the dilettantes of revolution had returned to their old bourgeois feeding troughs, Barbusse entered the door of the party and said, "Here I am! " By this he proved that there is no spiritual avenue other than the Communist Party for all that is left of thought, of honesty and indignation in the war generation. Beneath the restrained lyricism of Barbusse's letter to *l'Humanité* one can sense genuine revolutionary passion. We congratulate the French party upon this conquest !

Scarcely had Frossard and his entourage crossed the threshold, when the events connected with the Ruhr[104] put the party to severe political tests. And the party proved that now, freed from alien elements, it has grown stronger and taller by a head. The repressions that descended upon it have only served to increase its moral cohesion.

Naturally the greatest difficulties still lie ahead. But there is one thing we can say positively : in France a real Communist Party is living and breathing, fighting and growing.

March 25, 1923.

30

Is the Slogan of 'The United States of Europe' a Timely One?

(A Discussion Article[105])

In connection with the slogan of "A Workers' and Peasants' Government," the time is appropriate, in my opinion, for issuing the slogan of "The United States of Europe." Only by coupling these two slogans shall we get a definite systematic and progressive response to the most burning problems of European development.

The last imperialist war was at bottom a European war. The episodic participation of America and Japan did not alter its European character. Having secured what she required, America withdrew her hands from the European bonfire and returned home.

The motor force driving to war was this, that the capitalist forces of production had outgrown the framework of European national states. Germany had set herself the task of "organizing" Europe, i.e., of uniting economically the European continent under her own control, in order then seriously to set about contending with Britain for world power. France's aim was to dismember Germany. The small population of France, her predominantly agricultural character and her economic conservatism, make it impossible for the French bourgeoisie even to consider the problem of organizing Europe, which indeed proved to be beyond the powers of German capitalism, backed though it was by the military machine of the Hohenzollerns. Victorious France is now maintaining her mastery only by Balkanizing Europe. Great Britain is inciting and backing the French policy of dismembering and exhausting Europe, all the time concealing her work behind Britain's traditional mask of hypocrisy. As a result, our unfortunate continent is cut up, divided, exhausted, disorganized and Balkanized —transformed into a madhouse. The invasion of the Ruhr is a piece

341

of violent insanity accompanied by far-sighted calculation (the final ruination of Germany)—a combination not unfamiliar to psychiatrists.

At bottom of the war lay the need of the productive forces for a broader arena of development, unhampered by tariff walls. Similarly, in the occupation of the Ruhr so fatal to Europe and to mankind, we find a distorted expression of the need for uniting the coal of the Ruhr with the iron of Lorraine. Europe cannot develop economically within the state and customs frontiers imposed at Versailles. Europe is compelled either to remove these frontiers, or to face the threat of complete economic decay. But the methods adopted by the ruling bourgeoisie to overcome the frontiers it itself had created are only increasing the existing chaos and accelerating the disintegration.

To the toiling masses of Europe it is becoming ever clearer that the bourgeoisie is incapable of solving the basic problems of restoring Europe's economic life. The slogan : "A Workers' and Peasants' Government" is designed to meet the growing attempts of the workers to find a way out by their own efforts. It has now become necessary to point out this avenue of salvation more concretely, namely, to assert that only in the closest economic cooperation of the peoples of Europe lies the avenue of salvation for our continent from economic decay and from enslavement to mighty American capitalism.

America is standing aloof from Europe, tranquilly biding her time until Europe's economic agony has reached such a pitch as will make it easy to step in and buy up Europe—as Austria was bought up— for a mere pittance. But France cannot stand aloof from Germany, nor can Germany stand aloof from France. Therein lies the crux, and therein lies the solution, of the European problem. Everything else is incidental. Long before the imperialist war we recognized that the Balkan states are incapable of existing and of developing except within a federation. The same is true of the various fragments of the Austro-Hungarian Empire, and of the western portions of Czarist Russia now living outside the Soviet Union. The Apennines, the Pyrenees and Scandinavia are limbs of the European body stretching out toward the seas. They are incapable of an independent existence. The European continent in the present state of development of its productive forces is an economic unit—not a shut-in unit, of course, but one possessing profound internal ties—as was proved in the terrible catastrophe of the world war, and again revealed by the mad paroxysm of the Ruhr occupation. Europe is not a geographical term; Europe is an economic term, something incomparably more concrete—especially in the present postwar conditions—than the world market. Just as federation was long ago recognized as essential for the Balkan peninsula, so now the time has arrived for stating definitely and clearly that federation is essential for Balkanized Europe.

There remain to be considered the question of the Soviet Union, on the one hand, and that of Great Britain, on the other. It goes without saying that the Soviet Union will not be opposed either to the federative union of Europe, or to its own adhesion to such a federation. Thereby, too, a reliable bridge will be secured between Europe and Asia.

The question of Great Britain is far more conditional; it depends on the tempo at which her revolutionary development proceeds. Should the "Government of Workers and Peasants" triumph on the European mainland before British imperialism is overthrown—which is quite probable—then the European Federation of Workers and Peasants will of necessity be directed against British capitalism. And, naturally, the moment British capitalism is overthrown the British Isles will enter as a welcome member into the European Federation.

It might be asked : Why a European Federation and not a World Federation ? But this manner of posing the question is much too abstract. Of course, the world economic and political development tends to gravitate toward a unified world economy, with its degree of centralization dependent upon the existing technological level. But we are now concerned not with the future socialist economy of the world, but with finding a way out of the present European impasse. We have to offer a solution to the workers and peasants of torn and ruined Europe, quite independently of how the revolution develops in America, Australia, Asia or Africa. Looked at from this point of view, the slogan of "The United States of Europe" has its place on the same historical plane with the slogan "A Workers' and Peasants' Government" ; it is a transitional slogan, indicating a way out, a prospect of salvation, and furnishing at the same time a revolutionary impulse for the toiling masses.

It would be a mistake to measure the entire process of the world revolution with the same foot-rule. America came out of the war not enfeebled, but strengthened. The internal stability of the American bourgeoisie is still quite considerable. The American bourgeoisie is reducing its dependence upon the European market to a minimum. The revolution in America—considered apart from Europe—may thus be a matter of decades. Does that mean that the European revolution must align itself with the American revolution? Certainly not. If backward Russia did not (and could not) await the revolution in Europe, all the less can and will Europe await the revolution in America. Workers' and Peasants' Europe, blockaded by capitalist America (and at first, perhaps even by Great Britain), will be able to maintain itself and develop as a closely consolidated military and economic union.

It must not be overlooked that the very danger arising from the United States of America (which is spurring the destruction of Europe, and is ready to step in subsequently as Europe's master) furnishes a very substantial bond for uniting the peoples of Europe who are ruining one another, into a "European United States of Workers and Peasants." This opposition between Europe and the United States stems organically from the differences in the objective situations of the European countries and of the mighty trans-Atlantic republic, and is not in any way directed against the international solidarity of the proletariat, or against the interests of the revolution in America. One of the reasons for the retarded development of the revolution throughout the world is the degrading European dependence on the rich American uncle (Wilsonism, the charitable feeding of the worst famine districts of Europe, American "loans," etc., etc.). The sooner the popular masses of Europe regain the confidence in their own strength which was sapped by the war, and the more closely they rally around the slogan of "United Workers' and Peasants' Republics of Europe," the more rapidly will the revolution develop on both sides of the Atlantic. For just as the triumph of the proletariat in Russia gave a mighty impetus to the development of the Communist parties of Europe, so, and even to an incomparably greater degree, will the triumph of the revolution in Europe give an impetus to the revolution in America and in all parts of the world. Although, when we abstract ourselves from Europe, we are obliged to peer into the mists of decades to perceive the American revolution, yet we may safely assert that by the natural sequence of historical events the triumphant revolution in Europe will serve in a very few years to shatter the power of the American bourgeoisie.

Not merely the question of the Ruhr, i.e., of European fuel and iron, but also the question of reparations fits into the pattern of "The United States of Europe." The question of reparations is a purely European question, and it can and will be solved in the period immediately ahead only by European means. The Europe of Workers and Peasants will have its own reparations budget—as it will have its own war budget—so long as it is menaced by dangers from without. This budget will be based upon a graduated income tax, upon levies on capital, upon the confiscation of wealth plundered during wartime, etc. Its allotments will be regulated by the appropriate bodies of the European Federation of Workers and Peasants.

We shall not here indulge in speculations as to the speed at which the unification of the European republics will proceed, in what economic and constitutional forms it will express itself, and what degree of centralization will be obtained in the first period of the workers' and peasants' regime. All these considerations we may safely leave to the future, remembering the experience already gained by the Soviet Union, constructed on the soil of former Czarist Russia. What is perfectly obvious is that the customs barriers must be thrown down. The peoples of Europe must regard Europe as a field for a unified and increasingly planned economic life.

It might be argued that we are in reality speaking of a European Socialist Federation as an integral part of the future World Federation, and that such a regime can be brought about only by the dictatorship of the proletariat. We shall not, however, pause to answer this argument, since it has been refuted by the international analysis made during the consideration of the question of a "Workers' Government." "The United States of Europe" is a slogan in every respect corresponding with the slogan "A Workers' (or Workers' and Peasants') Government." Is the realization of a "Workers' Government" possible without the dictatorship of the proletariat ? Only a conditional reply can be given to this question. In any case, we regard the "Workers' Government" as a *stage* toward the dictatorship of the proletariat. Therein lies the great value of this slogan for us. But the slogan "The United States of Europe" has an exactly similar and parallel significance. Without this supplementary slogan the fundamental problems of Europe must remain suspended in mid-air.

But will not this slogan play into the hands of the pacifists ? I do not believe that there exists such "lefts" nowadays as would consider this danger sufficient grounds for rejecting the slogan. After all, we are living in 1923, and have learned a little from the past. There are the same reasons, or absence of reasons, for fearing a pacifist interpretation of "The United States of Europe" as there are for fearing a democratic-S.R.'ist interpretation of the slogan "A Workers' and Peasants' Government." Of course, if we advance "The United

States of Europe" as an independent program, as a panacea for achieving pacification and reconstruction, and if we isolate this slogan from slogans of "A Workers' Government," of the united front, and from the class struggle, we shall certainly end in democratized Wilsonism, i.e., in Kautskyism, and even in something more degrading (assuming there is anything more degrading than Kautskyism). But I repeat, we live in the year 1923 and have learned a little from the past. The Communist International is now a reality, and it will not be Kautsky who will initiate and control the struggle associated with our slogans. Our method of posing the problem is diametrically opposed to Kautsky's method. Pacifism is an academic program, whose object is to avoid the necessity of revolutionary action. Our formulation, on the contrary, is an incentive to struggle. To the workers of Germany, not the Communists (it is not necessary to convince them), but to the workers in general, and in the first place to the Social-Democratic workers, who fear the economic consequences of a fight for a workers' government; to the workers of France, whose minds are still obsessed by the questions of reparations and of the national debt; to the workers of Germany, France and of all Europe, who fear lest the establishment of the workers' regime lead to the isolation and economic ruin of their countries, we say : Even if temporarily isolated (and with such a great bridge to the East as the Soviet Union, Europe will not be easily isolated), Europe will be able not only to maintain herself, but to consolidate and build herself up, once she has broken down the customs barriers and has united herself economically to the inexhaustible natural riches of Russia. "The United States of Europe"—a purely revolutionary perspective— is the next stage in our general revolutionary perspective. It arises from the profound difference in the situations of Europe and America. Whoever ignores this difference, will, willy-nilly, drown the true revolutionary perspective in mere historical abstractions. Naturally, the Workers' and Peasants' Federation will not stop in its European phase. As we have said, our Soviet Union affords Europe an outlet into Asia, and from Asia into Europe. We are, therefore, here envisaging only a stage, but a stage of great historical importance, through which we must first pass.

First Published
in *Pravda*, June 30, 1923.

31

Can a Counter-Revolution or a
Revolution be made on Schedule?

"Of course it is not possible. Only trains travel on schedule, and even they don't always arrive on time."

Precision of thought is necessary in everything, and in questions of revolutionary strategy more than anywhere else. But since revolutions do not occur so very often, revolutionary concepts and ideas become encrusted with fat, become vague in outline, the questions are raised in a slip-shod way, and are solved in the same manner.

Mussolini made his "revolution" (that is, his counter-revolution) according to a schedule, made publicly known beforehand. He was able to do this successfully because the Socialists failed to make the revolution when the time for it came. The Bulgarian fascists accomplished their "revolution" through a military conspiracy[106]. All the dates were fixed and the roles assigned. The Spanish officer caste did exactly the same thing[107]. Counter-revolutionary overturns are almost always carried out along this pattern. They are usually synchronized with the moment when the disillusion of the masses in revolution or in democracy has taken the form of apathy and a favorable political situation has thus been created for an organized and technically prepared military coup, whose date is definitely fixed beforehand. Obviously, it is not possible to create artificially a political situation favorable for a reactionary coup, much less to bring it off at a fixed date. But when the basic elements of such a situation are at hand, then the leading party does, as we have seen, choose beforehand a favorable moment, and synchronizes accordingly its political, organizational, and technical forces, and—if it has not miscalculated—deals the victorious blow.

The bourgeoisie has not always made counter-revolutions. In the past it has also had occasion to make revolutions. Did it fix any definite dates for them ? It would be quite interesting and in many respects instructive to investigate from this standpoint the development of the classic as well as of the epigone bourgeois revolutions (here is a topic for our young Marxist scholars !). But even without such a detailed investigation it is possible to establish the following fundamentals involved in this question.

The propertied and educated bourgeoisie, that is, precisely that section of the "people" which took power, did not make the revolution but waited until it was made. When the movement of the lower layers overflowed and when the old social order or political regime was overthrown, then power dropped almost automatically into the hands of the liberal bourgeoisie. The liberal scholars proclaimed such a revolution as "natural" and ineluctable and they compiled vast platitudes which were passed off as historical laws : revolution and counter-revolution (action and reaction—according to Kareyev[108] of blessed memory) were declared to be the natural products of historical evolution, and consequently beyond the power of men to produce arbitrarily, or arrange according to the calendar, and so forth. These "laws" have never yet prevented well prepared counter-revolutionary coups from being carried out. But way of compensation, the nebulousness of bourgeois-liberal thought finds its way, not infrequently, into the heads of revolutionists, causing great havoc and leading to injurious practices.

But even bourgeois revolutions have by no means invariably developed at every stage in accordance with the "natural" laws of liberal professors. Whenever petty-bourgeois, plebeian democracy overthrew liberalism, it did so by means of conspiracy and organized uprisings, fixed beforehand for definite dates. This was done by the Jacobins, the extreme left wing in the Great French Revolution. This is perfectly comprehensible. The liberal bourgeoisie (the French in 1789, the Russian in February 1917) can content itself with waiting for the mighty elemental mass movement and then at the last moment throw into the scales its wealth, its education, its connection with the state apparatus, and in this way seize the helm. Petty-bourgeois democracy, under similar circumstances, has to act differently : it possesses neither wealth, nor social influence, nor connections. It finds itself compelled to replace these by a carefully thought-out and minutely prepared plan for a revolutionary overturn. But a plan presupposes a definite orientation in point of time and therefore also the fixing of dates.

This applies all the more to the proletarian revolution. The Communist Party cannot adopt a waiting attitude in the face of the growing revolutionary movement of the proletariat. To do so is to adopt essentially the point of view of Menshevism. Mensheviks try to clamp a brake on the revolution so long as it is in process of development, they exploit its successes as soon as it is in any degree victorious, and they strive with might and main to keep it from being completed. The Communist Party cannot seize power by utilizing the revolutionary movement from the sidelines but only by means of a direct and immediate political, organizational and military-technical leadership of the revolutionary masses, both in the period of slow preparation as well as at the decisive moment of the overturn. Precisely for this reason the Communist Party has absolutely no use for the great liberal law according to which revolutions happen but are never made and therefore cannot be fixed for a specific date. From a spectator's standpoint this law is correct, but from the standpoint of the leader this is a platitude and a vulgarity.

Let us imagine a country where the political conditions for the proletarian revolution are either completely mature or are obviously and distinctly maturing day by day. In such circumstances what should be the attitude of the Communist Party to the question of an uprising and of setting of date for it ?

If the country is passing through a profound social crisis, when the contradictions become aggravated in the extreme, when the toiling masses are in constant ferment, when the party is obviously supported by an unquestionable majority of the toilers and, in consequence, by all the most active, class-conscious and self-sacrificing elements of the proletariat, then the task confronting the party—its only possible task under the circumstances—is to fix a definite time in the immediate future, a time in the course of which the favorable revolutionary situation cannot abruptly react against us, and then to concentrate every effort on the preparation of the blow, to subordinate the entire policy and organization to the military object in view, so that this blow is dealt with maximum power.

To consider not merely an imaginary country, let us take our own October Revolution as an example. The country was in the throes of a great crisis, internal and international. The state apparatus was paralyzed. The toilers streamed in ever greater numbers to the

banners of our party. From the moment when the Bolsheviks were
in the majority in the Petrograd Soviet, and afterward in the Moscow
Soviet, our party was faced with the question—not of the struggle for
power in general but of preparing for the seizure of power according
to a definite plan, and at a fixed date. The chosen day, as is well
known, was the day upon which the All-Russian Congress of the
Soviets was to convene. Some members of our Central Committee,
from the first, were of the opinion that the moment of the actual blow
should be synchronized with the political moment of the Soviet Congress. Other members of the Central Committee feared that the bourgeoisie would have time to make its preparations by then and would
be able to disperse the Congress, they wanted the blow delivered at
an earlier date. The Central Committee fixed the date of the armed
uprising for October 15, at the latest. This decision was carried out
with a deliberate postponement of ten days because the course of
agitational and organizational preparations showed that an uprising
independent of the Soviet Congress would have sown confusion among
considerable layers of the working class who connected the idea of
the seizure of power with the Soviets, and not with the party and its
secret organizations. On the other hand, it was perfectly clear that
the bourgeoisie was already too much demoralized to be able to
organize any serious resistance in the space of two or three weeks.

Thus, after our party had won the majority in the leading Soviets,
and had in this way secured the basic political premise for the seizure
of power, we were faced with the stark necessity of fixing a calendar
date for the decision of the military question. Before we had the
majority, the organizational technical plan was of course bound to
be more or less provisional and elastic. For us the gauge of our
revolutionary influence was the Soviets which had been created by the
Mensheviks and the Social Revolutionists at the beginning of the
revolution. And the Soviets, on the other hand, furnished us with
a political cover for our conspiratorial work; and afterward, the Soviet
served as the organs of power after it had been actually seized.

What would our strategy have been if there had been no Soviets?
In that case, we obviously should have had to turn to other gauges
of our revolutionary influence : the trade unions, the strikes, the
street demonstrations, democratic elections of all kinds, and so forth.
Although the Soviets are the most accurate gauge of the actual activity
of the masses during the revolutionary epoch, still without the existence of the Soviets we would have been fully able to ascertain the

precise moment at which the actual majority of the working class and of the toilers as a whole was on our side. Naturally at this moment we should have had to issue to the masses the slogan of the formation of Soviets. But by doing so, we would have already transferred the whole question to the plane of military clashes, and consequently before we issued the slogan of forming Soviets we should have had a thoroughly worked out plan for an armed uprising on a fixed date.

Once the majority of the toilers is on our side, or at least the majority in the decisive centers and provinces, the formation of Soviets would be sure to follow our summons. The more backward cities and provinces would emulate the leading centers with more or less delays. We should then be faced with the political task of convening the Soviet Congress and with the military task of ensuring the transfer of power to this Congress. Quite obviously these are only two aspects of one and the same problem.

Let us now imagine that our Central Committee, in the above-described situation, that is, in the absence of Soviets, had met in a decisive session in the period when the masses had already begun to move spontaneously to our side but had not yet ensured us a clear and overwhelming majority. How should we then have laid out our plan of action ? Would we schedule an uprising ?

The answer to this may be adduced from the above. We should have said to ourselves : At the present moment we still do not possess a clear and undisputed majority; but the swing among the masses is so great that the decisive and militant majority necessary for us is merely a matter of the next few weeks. Let us assume it will take approximately a month to win over the majority of the workers in Petrograd, in Moscow and in the Donetz basin; let us set ourselves this task and concentrate the necessary forces in these centers. As soon as the majority has been gained—and we shall ascertain in action if this be the case after a month has elapsed—we shall summon the toilers to form Soviets. For this, Petrograd, Moscow and the Donetz basin would not require more than a week or two; it may be calculated with certainty that the remaining cities and provinces will follow the example of the main centers within the next two or three weeks. Thus the creation of a network of the Soviets would require about a month. After Soviets have been formed in the important provinces, in which we have of course the majority, we shall convene an All-Russian Soviet Congress. We shall require an additional two weeks to assemble this Congress. We have, therefore, two and a half months at our disposal before the Congress. In the course of this time the seizure of power must not only be prepared, but actually accomplished. We should accordingly place before our military organization a program allowing it two months, at most two and a half, for the preparation of the uprising in Petrograd, in Moscow, on the railways, and so on. I use here the conditional tense (we *should have* decided, we *should have* done this and that) because in reality, although our operations were by no means unskillful, still they were by no means so systematic, not because we were in any way disturbed by "historic laws" but because we were carrying out the proletarian uprising for the first time.

But are not miscalculations likely to occur by this method? Seizure of power means war, and in war there can be defeats as well as victories. But the systematic course here described is the best and most direct road to the goal, that is, it enhances the chances of victory to the maximum. Thus, for instance, should it have turned out, a month after the decisive Central Committee session in our foregoing example, that we had not yet the majority of the toilers on our side, then we would not, of course, have issued the slogan calling for the formation of Soviets, for in this case the slogan would have miscarried (in our example we assume that the Social-Revolutionists and the Mensheviks are against the Soviets). And had the reverse been the case, and we had found a decisive and militant majority on our side, say, within two weeks, then this would have abridged our plan and moved up the decisive moment of the uprising. The very same thing applies to the second and third stages of our plan : the formation of Soviets and the convocation of the Soviet Congress. We should not have issued the slogan of the Soviet Congress until we had secured, as I have said, the actual formation of Soviets in the most important centers. In this way the realization of each successive stage in our plan is prepared and secured by the fulfillment of antecedent stages. The work of military preparation proceeds parallel with all the other work according to a rigid schedule. Therewith the party retains throughout absolute control of its military apparatus. To be sure, there is always a great deal that is entirely unforeseen, unexpected and spontaneous in the revolution; and we must of course make allowances for the occurrence of all such "accidents" and adjust ourselves to them; but we can do this with greater success and certainty if our conspiratorial plan is thoroughly worked out beforehand.

Revolution possesses a mighty power of improvisation, but it never improvises anything good for fatalists, bystanders, and fools. Victory comes from the correct political evaluation, from correct organization and from the will to deal the decisive blow.

First published
in *Pravda*, September 23, 1923.

* * *

To Comrade McKay*

Dear Comrade McKay,

1. What practical steps are to be taken to prevent France from employing Negro troops on the European continent?—this is your first question.

The Negroes themselves must offer resistance against being so employed. Their eyes must be opened, so that they realize that when they help French imperialism to subjugate Europe, they are helping to subjugate themselves, in that they are supporting the domination of French capitalism in the African and other colonies.

The working class of Europe, and particularly of France and Germany, must realize that their own most vital interests are involved in this work of enlightening the colored peoples. The day of general resolutions on the right of self-determination of the colonial peoples, on the equality of all human beings regardless of color, is over. The time has come for direct and practical action. Every 10 Negroes who gather around the flag of revolution,—and unite to form a group for practical work among the Negroes, are worth a hundred times more than dozens of the resolutions establishing principles, so generously passed by the Second International. A Communist Party confining itself to mere platonic resolutions in this matter, without exerting its utmost energies towards winning the largest possible number of enlightened Negroes for its ideas, within the shortest possible time, would not be worthy of the name of Communist Party.

2. There is no doubt whatever that the use of colored troops for

---

* The poet McKay, who represented the revolutionary Negroes at the IV World Congress of the Communist International, requested Comrade Trotsky to answer some questions regarding the struggle for emancipation among the Negroes. Trotsky replied to some of these questions in this letter.—**Ed.**

imperialist war, and at the present time for the occupation of German territory, is a well thought out and carefully executed attempt of European capitalism, especially of French and English capitalism, to raise armed forces outside of Europe, so that capitalism may have mobilized, armed and disciplined African or Asian troops at its disposal, against the revolutionary masses of Europe. In this way the question of the use of colonial reserves for imperialist armies is closely related to the question of European revolution, that is, to the fate of the European working class.

3.   There is no doubt whatever that the employment of the economically and culturally backward colonial masses for the world conflicts of imperialism, and still more in the class conflicts of Europe, is an exceedingly risky experiment, from the standpoint of the bourgeoisie itself. The Negroes, and indeed the natives of all the colonies, retain their conservatism and mental rigidity only insofar as they continue to live under their accustomed economic conditions. But when the hand of capital, or even sooner—the hand of militarism, tears them mechanically from their customary environment, and forces them to stake their lives for the sake of new and complicated questions and conflicts (conflicts between the bourgeoisie of different nations, conflicts between the classes of one and the same nation), then their spiritual conservatism gives way abruptly, and revolutionary ideas find rapid access to a consciousness thrown off its balance.

4.   Therefore it is of the utmost importance, today, immediately, to have a number of enlightened, young, self-sacrificing Negroes, however small their number, filled with enthusiasm for the raising of the material and moral level of the great mass of Negroes, and at the same time mentally capable of grasping the identity of interests and destiny of the Negro masses, with those of the masses of the whole world, and in the first place with the destiny of the European working class.

The education of Negro propagandists is an exceedingly urgent and important revolutionary task at the present juncture.

5.   In North America the matter is further complicated by the abominable obtuseness and caste presumption of the privileged upper strata of the working class itself, who refuse to recognize fellow workers and fighting comrades in the Negroes. Gompers' policy is founded on the exploitation of such despicable prejudices, and is at the present time the most effective guarantee for the successful subjugation of white and colored workers alike. The fight against this

policy must be taken up from different sides, and conducted on various lines. One of the most important branches of this conflict consists in enlightening the proletarian consciousness by awakening the feeling of human dignity, and of revolutionary protest, among the Negro slaves of American capitalism. As stated above, this work can only be carried out by self-sacrificing and politically educated revolutionary Negroes.

Needless to say, the work is not to be carried on in a spirit of Negro chauvinism, which would then merely form a counterpart of white chauvinism,—but in a spirit of solidarity of all exploited without consideration of color.

What forms of organization are most suitable for the movement among the American Negroes, it is difficult for me to say, as I am insufficiently informed regarding the concrete conditions and possibilities. But the forms of organization will be found, as soon as there is sufficient will to action.

With Communist greetings,

L. TROTSKY.

First published in English
March 13, 1923
International Press Correspondence, Vol. III, No. 25, p.197.

Explanatory Notes

Index

EXPLANATORY NOTES

(These notes are based on material collected by the Marx-Engels Institute under Ryazanov for the first edition of Lenin's *Collected Works* s. The notes in this volume are supplementary to the notes appended to the first volume of the *First Five Years of the Communist International*.)

[1]Robert Lansing was an American lawyer and diplomat. He was appointed Secretary of State when W. J. Bryan resigned on June 8, 1915. Lansing was a member of the American commission to negotiate the peace at Paris, 1918-19.—Page 6.

[2]The Zimmerwald Conference was called early in 1915 on the initiative of the Italian and Swiss Socialist parties for the purpose of uniting the oppositional elements of the world Socialist movement. Later in the year the conference was held in a little Swiss mountain village of Zimmerwald. The majority of the participants were Left-Centrist in tendency and these "moderates" laid down the line of the conference. The Zimmerwald decisions were for this reason not at all consistently Marxist in character, but, on the contrary, nebulous and semi-pacifist. In his autobiography, Leon Trotsky gives the following account and estimate of Zimmerwald: "The days of the conference, September 5 to 8, were stormy ones. The revolutionary wing, led by Lenin, and the pacifist wing, which comprised the majority of the delegates, agreed with difficulty on a common manifesto of which I had prepared the draft. The manifesto was far from saying all that it should have said, but, even so, it was a long step forward. Lenin was on the extreme left at the conference. In many questions he was a minority of one, even within the Zimmerwald left wing, to which I did not formally belong, although I was close to it on all important questions. In Zimmerwald Lenin was tightening up the spring of the future international action. In a Swiss mountain village, he was laying the corner-stone of the revolutionary International."—Page 11.

[3]L. B. Krassin (1870-1926) became active in the Russian revolutionary movement in the early Nineties. He played an important role in the early days of the Bolshevik party (1903 to 1906), serving several times as member of the Bolshevik Central Committee. The defeat of the 1905 revolution first found him with the "extreme left" (Bogdanov's sectarian *Vpered* group), and then drawing away altogether from the revolutionary movement. He devoted him-

self to his profession, becoming one of the most prominent Russian engineers. With the October 1917 Revolution, Krassin started moving back to the revolutionary ranks. He held various government posts, serving as Soviet Ambassador to Britain and later to France. At the time referred to by Trotsky in the text Krassin held the post of Commissar of Foreign Trade. —Page 18.

4Hoersing was one of the infamous galaxy of German Social Democrats, Noske and Severing in particular, who in positions of government power, succeeded in provoking sections of the German working class into precipitate actions which were then crushed in blood by use of police and troops. At the time of the movement of the miners in Central Germany, Hoersing held the post of *Regierungspraesident*.—Page 20.

5Mirbach was the German Ambassador to Soviet Russia after the conclusion of the Brest-Litovsk Treaty. The Left Social Revolutionaries assassinated him in the summer of 1918 in order, in this way, to provoke war with Germany. —Page 25.

6The Nechayevites were the followers of S. G. Nechayev (1847-82), an anarchist and terrorist at one time associated with Bakunin. He was a "fanatic of conspiracy." He rejected class consciousness and mass movements as unnecessary, holding that a handful of bold and determined leaders could accomplish the revolution.—Page 25.

7Maslow was one of the leaders of the German Communist Party at the time. Together with Ruth Fischer and Hugo Urbahns he headed the opposition to the Brandler leadership and gained the majority at the Frankfurt Convention of 1924. When the struggle broke out in the Russian party after Lenin's death, Maslow lined up against the Russian Left Opposition led by Trotsky. Later, upon Maslow's expulsion from the Comintern, he flirted for a while with the Trotskyist movement only to slide into the ranks of its opponents.—Page 27.

8Monmousseau was a syndicalist who was educated on the ideas of the *La Vie Ouvrière* group. One of the leaders of the French trade union opposition during World War I. Later, together with Rosmer and Monatte, Monmousseau belonged to the "Committee for the Third International." In 1918 to 1921 was one of the leaders of the revolutionary wing in the General Confederation of Labor (CGT). When the split occurred, he became secretary of the CGTU. Subsequently he was a pillar of Stalinism in the French labor movement.—Page 35.

9L. Martov (J. O. Tsederbaum) (1873-1923), the ideological leader of Menshevism, began his career by working with Lenin in 1895 in the Petersburg "League of Struggle for the Emancipation of the Working Class." Collaborated with Lenin in founding *Iskra* and the theoretical magazine *Zarya*. Life-long break with Lenin dates back to 1903. During the period of the October Revolution, Martov occupied a "left" position in Menshevik ranks, remaining in the Second Congress of the Soviets after the departure of the Right S.R.'s and the Mensheviks. But shortly thereafter, he became irreconcilably opposed to the Soviet regime. Permitted to emigrate, he left for Berlin where he founded the central publication of the Mensheviks in emigration (*Sotsialisti-chesky Vestnik*).—Page 37.

10Monatte, one of the leaders of the French Communist Party, which he joined toward the end of 1922. Prior to World War I Monatte stood in the ranks of the French revolutionary syndicalists, who constituted during those war years the core of the opposition in the labor movement to the social-patriots. After the war ended, Monatte continued his revolutionary work but did not immediately join the French CP. When the Frossard group split in the winter of 1922, Monatte finally joined the Communist movement only to leave it subsequently.—Page 46.

11 *La Vague* —one of the typical newspapers published in France at the time, using the cover of the French CP in order to attack Marxism and the revolutionary World Congresses of the Third International. (See note 14). —Page 50.

12The Marseilles Convention of the French CP, sometimes referred to as the first convention of this party, took place in December 1921. The main points on the agenda were: The agrarian question; national defense; attitude toward the trade unions; election tactics; organization of women Communists; press and cooperatives. Sharp differences arose which were shortly to lead to the formation of a left wing. At the time of this convention, the CP had 130,000 members and a parliamentary fraction of 13 deputies. The leading role at Marseilles was played by the Frossard group.—Page 52.

13 An Alsatian by birth, Grumbach participated in the German Socialist movement prior to the first World War. When war broke out, he became a rabid "Alsatian patriot," backing French imperialism and virulently attacking the German Social Democracy. After the split of the French SP (at the Tours Convention) he remained in the ranks of the reformists, then known as the Dissidents.—Page 52.

14Brizon, a teacher by profession, was a Socialist deputy in the French Parliament during World War 1. In 1915-16, he tended toward an internationalist position, participating in the Kienthal Conference. Essentially a pacifist, his internationalism faded quickly. Shifting more and more to the right, he broke with the French CP, turned to journalism, publishing a small newspaper *La Vague* which was devoted to attacking Communism.—Page 56.
15 Henri Fabre, merchant and publisher, was one of the bourgeois fellow-travellers of the revolutionary movement in France. With the formation of the French CP Fabre became one of the cleverest and most articulate opponents of the Comintern and enemy of the left wing inside the party, utilizing his newspaper *Journal du Peuple* for this purpose. His name became widely known in 1921-22 because the then incumbent leadership, headed by Frossard, obstructed the attempts of the ECCI to expel him from Communist ranks.—Page 56.

16The reference here is to the various international, reformist trade union and political bodies which had their headquarters at Amsterdam, London, Vienna and Geneva.—Page 58.

[17]At this Conference in December 1921 Zinoviev delivered the report elaborating the United Front Theses which had just been adopted by the ECCI. The theses and the report were approved unanimously by the 1921 Conference.—Page 59.

[18]Pavlovsky's article appeared in issue No. 10 of the magazine *Communist International*.—Page 62.

[19]The reference here is to the 6 articles written in 1921 by Prof. Faulkner, under the pseudonym of Smith, in the magazine *Ekonomicheskaya Zhizn* (*Economic Life*), issues 284, 285 and 286.—Page 62.

[20]The Washington Conference, sponsored by the U.S. government, convened on November 12, 1921. The main point on the agenda was "disarmament." It led to an intensification of arms expenditures.—Page 65.

[21]G. V. Chicherin, born in 1872, was a diplomat by profession who worked prior to the 1905 revolution in the Czarist Ministry of Foreign Affairs. During the 1905 revolution, Chicherin adhered to the Russian Socialist movement and was compelled to migrate abroad. On returning to Russia in January 1918, he joined the Bolsheviks, serving, from March 1918 until 1930 as Commissar of Foreign Affairs. Died, under Stalin, in isolation and disgrace.—Page 66.

[22]This speech, listed as a "summary" in the original Russian text, was actually a second speech, not previously scheduled but delivered by Trotsky at the December 1921 Conference.—Page 68.

[23]Many of the speakers at this conference produced elaborate charts, tables, graphs, etc., in this way shifting the debate to an abstract consideration of economic theory. It is this that Trotsky had in mind by his reference to "the academic character" of the discussion.—Page 68.

[24]D. B. Ryazanov, born in 1870, was the outstanding Marxist scholar and historian in the Russian revolutionary movement. Joining the Marxist movement as a young man, he early underwent imprisonment and exile. He collaborated in many of the famous Russian and German party publications. Ryazanov joined the Bolsheviks after the February revolution. Up to February 1931, when he was expelled from the party, he remained director of the Marx and Engels Institute. Stalin persecuted him ruthlessly for his outspoken support of the Trotskyist opposition, driving him to death in Siberian exile.—Page 68.

[25]The Moscow Soviet was at the time under the chairmanship of Kamenev. —Page 70.

[26]The reference here is to the KAPD which split away from the Comintern and sought together with other groups to set up a rival organization at the time.—Page 82.

[27]Lenin's letter to the Jena Conference of the German CP, which convened

toward the end of August 1921, was written on August 14, 1921 and made public several months later in the magazine *Communist International*, No. 19, December 17, 1921. Lenin affirmed that in the beginning he defended "and had to defend Levi to the extent that I saw before me those of his opponents who merely shouted about 'Menshevism' and 'Centrism', refusing to see the mistakes of the March action and the necessity of explaining and correcting these mistakes." Levi, explained Lenin, was expelled not for his views but for violating party discipline, and Lenin added: "The more cautiously I approached the evaluation of Levi's mistakes at the (Third) Congress, all the greater is the assurance with which I can now state that Levi has hastened to confirm the worst charges brought against him."—Page 87.

[28]The two reports mentioned by Trotsky are : "On the International Situation and the Tasks of the Comintern"; and "The School of Revolutionary Strategy." The text of the second report appears in this volume on pages 1-43; for the text of the first report see the previous volume, pages 238-261.—Page 88.

[29]This pamphlet was written by Rosa Luxemburg in September 1918 when she was in prison, completely isolated and able to follow the events in Russia only through the dispatches in the bourgeois press. In this pamphlet she sharply criticized Bolshevik policies, particularly the Soviet electoral system, the agrarian policy, etc. That Rosa Luxemburg was in process of revising the views she expressed in this pamphlet is clearly shown by her speech on the question of program at the founding conference of the German CP and by her articles in *Rote Fahne*. She never published this pamphlet in her lifetime. It was issued by Paul Levi, her literary executor, for purely factional reasons.—Page 89.

[30]These Theses on the United Front, unquestionably one of the most important programmatic documents of revolutionary Marxism, were drafted by Trotsky for the enlarged Plenum of the ECCI which convened toward the end of February 1922.—Page 91.

[31] *Le Populaire*, founded by Leon Blum, was, as it remained, the central publication of the French Socialist Party.—Page 92.

[32]The CGT (*Confederation Generale du Travail*—General Confederation of Labor) was the central trade union organization of France. Formed in 1903 it embraced all the existing trade unions. Prior to World War I the CGT was the most revolutionary organization in France. But with the outbreak of war in 1914, the majority of the leaders, headed by Jouhaux, became rabid jingoes. The official CGT leadership savagely opposed the growing left wing movement, which grew rapidly after the war and came under Communist influence. They engineered a split which led early in 1922 to the formation of the Unitarian General Confederation of Labor (*Confederation Generale du Travail Unitaire* or CGTU). This split was marked by a sharp decline in total union membership. In 1920 there were about 2,500,000 workers in the CGT. By 1923 the combined memberships of the CGT and CGTU fell under 100,000.—Page 100.

[33] *La Ligue Civique* was a bourgeois anti-labor, strikebreaking organization

in France. The closest counterpart to it in the U.S. would be the National Association of Manufacturers.—Page 100.

³⁴Renaud Jean was at that time one of the prominent French CP leaders. He was in charge of the work among the peasantry. At the Marseilles Congress he was elected to the Central Committee. He was a delegate to the Fourth World Congress and a co-reporter on the agrarian question. His views on the peasant question tended to approximate those of the Russian Social Revolutionaries. Although he remained in disagreement with the policies of the Comintern, Jean submitted to the decisions of the Fourth Congress.— Page 113.

³⁵William Jennings Bryan typified pacifism in the U.S. in the days before the first World War. His lamentations against war and praises of the advantages of peace invariably ended in a pledge to support war if it became "necessary." The same spirit imbued most of the American Socialist leaders at the time. —Page 115.

³⁶Hillquit, a case-hardened opportunist and one of the founders of the American Socialist Party, was characterized by Trotsky as "a Babbitt of Babbitts, the ideal Socialist leader for successful dentists." In 1918-20 Hillquit simulated sympathy and friendship for the Soviet Union. When the revolutionary tide following World War I subsided, he came forth as one of the most rabid opponents of the pioneer Communist movement in the U.S.— Page 115.

³⁷The reference here is to the enlarged Plenum of the ECCI which convened from February 22 to March 4, 1922.—Page 115.

³⁸Victor Hugo, the famous French novelist of the Nineteenth Century, was a political opponent of Napoleon III (Louis Napoleon) and was exiled by the latter. Hugo's funeral in 1885 was the occasion for one of the greatest mass demonstrations witnessed in Europe.—Page 119.

³⁹The all-European economic conference at Genoa (April 10-19, 1922) was called by the Supreme Allied Council for the purpose of reviving the economic life of Europe. It represented the first attempt by the Allied imperialists to extort "peacefully" a number of economic concessions from the Soviet Union, among them the recognition of the Czarist debts.—Page 119.

⁴⁰Miliukov, an outstanding historian, was the leader of the Russian liberal bourgeoisie and its party, the Cadets (Constitutional Democrats). After the February 1917 revolution, he held the post of Foreign Minister in the Provisional Government and tried to continue the foreign policy of Czarism. After the October revolution, he migrated to Paris, where he edited a Russian daily paper.—Page 120.

⁴¹C. Rappoport was an old Russian revolutionist who went to France toward the close of the last century. He worked for several decades in the French labor movement gaining prominence as a talented publicist. In 1921-23 Rappoport supported the position of the Center (the Frossard group) in the French Party, but broke with Frossard when the split came. Rappoport remained

in the Comintern until the late Thirties. He broke with Stalinism only to break with revolutionary Marxism.—Page 134.

[42]Verfeuil—one of the many French opportunists who sought for a while to remain in the Communist ranks. A journalist by profession, he was with Longuet during World War I. At the Tours Convention Verfeuil first left with the Dissidents, but afterwards returned to the French CP. At the Marseilles Convention he was elected to the Central Committee and used his post to collaborate with Fabre, writing for Fabre's paper *Journal du Peuple*. He was expelled from the French CP in the autumn of 1922.—Page 136.

[43]Ker, elected member of the Central Committee at the Marseilles Convention, was one of the secretaries of the French CP. During the factional struggle he belonged to the Frossard group, but continued loyally to carry out the decisions of the Fourth World Congress which he attended as a delegate. He died suddenly in 1923.—Page 138.

[44]Modigliani, a prominent Italian Socialist, who like many other Italian Centrists regarded membership in the Third International as a mere formality, and who quickly returned to the ranks of the reformists.—Page 139.

[45]Quinton was one of a group of adventurists who flirted with the French Communist movement in order to make a career in the trade union movement.—Page 139.

[46]Daniel Renoult, a journalist, headed one of the many factions in the French CP at the time. He was elected to the Central Committee at the Tours Convention and re-elected at the Marseilles Convention. Attended the 1922 enlarged Plenum of the ECCI as a delegate, and later went to the Fourth World Congress. As editor of the party periodical *l'Internationale*, Renoult collaborated with the Right Wing, but he did not go with Frossard when the split came.—Page 141.

[47]The reference here is to the conference of the representatives of the Second, Two-and-a-half and Third Internationals which took place in Berlin, April 2-6, 1922. At this conference of the Three Internationals, Frossard participated as a member of the Comintern delegation.—Page 141.

[48]The enlarged Plenum of the ECCI convened in June 1922. The resolution in reference was adopted at the June 11 session.—Page 143.

[49]Gustave Hervé, erstwhile anarchist, headed, prior to World War I, the extreme left inside the French SP. Editor and publisher of a periodical *Guerre Sociale* (Class War), he signed his articles in those days with the pen-name *Sans-Patrie* (The Man Without a Fatherland). When World War I broke out Hervé renamed his periodical *Victoire* and converted his "revolutionary anarchism" into "republican" monarchism, hailing the Czar on the day hostilities started. After the war he came forward as a rabid monarchist and reactionary.—Page 150.

[50]Treint, a teacher by profession, was one of the leaders of the pioneer French Communist movement. In 1919-20 he was one of the organizers of

the Left Wing that supported the line of the Comintern. In 1923 he served as one of the political secretaries of the French Party. Expelled from the Comintern in the late Twenties, he flirted for a time with the Trotskyist Left Opposition only to become one of its opponents.—Page 152.

[51]The Saint Etienne Convention of the CGTU took place at the beginning of 1922. The bloc of Communists and syndicalists who favoured adherence to the Red Trade Union International (RILU) won the majority. The Saint Etienne Convention marked the first time in France that a Communist trade union fraction was gathered together and functioned throughout the sessions of the convention.—Page 153.

[52]This ECCI letter, drafted by Trotsky, was sent to the Paris Convention of the French CP which was held in October 1922. The ECCI representative to this Convention was the notorious Manuilsky.—Page 162.

[53]Klara Zetkin (1857-1933)—a veteran of the German labor movement, who joined the Socialist ranks in the days of Bismarck's "emergency laws" against the Socialists. From 1822, she was editor of *Gleichheit* (Equality), a periodical specially aimed at women. Outstanding in her work as the founder, theoretician and activist in the women's movement. She participated in the Spartacus League with Rosa Luxemburg and Karl Liebknecht. In March 1915 organized the International Socialist Women's Conference in Berne. She served as member of the ECCI and as General Secretary of the International Women's Secretariat attached to the Comintern. After Lenin's death, she was used as a pawn by the Stalinist machine.—Page 170.

[54]The unification of the Independent Socialist Party of Germany (ISPG) and of the German Socialist Party (SPG) took place on September 24, 1922.—Page 178.

[55]Rathenau was one of the prominent leaders of the German liberal bourgeoisie. In 1922 he held the post of Minister of Foreign Affairs, advocating a close alliance between Germany and Russia. He was murdered in the summer of 1922.—Page 179.

[56]The reference here is to the passages in *Capital* dealing with crises, in particular pp. 87 and 211 in Volume II, and Chapters XXX to XXXV in Volume III.—Page 198.

[57]Ernest Lafont, lawyer, journalist, deputy, was a typical parliamentarian Socialist and at the same time, a typical representative of a French centrist current. During the first World War Lafont was a chauvinist. In 1920 he started getting radical. At the Tours Convention he remained with the majority, joining the CP. After the Fourth World Congress, he refused to accept the decisions adopted, particularly on the question of the trade union movement, and was shortly expelled.—Page 209.

[58]Herriot was the leader of the French Radical Socialist Party. At that time he was a fervent promoter of the "Left Bloc" and advocated the recognition of the Soviet Union. After the victory of the "Left Bloc," Herriot served as

Premier (from July 1924 to April 1925) and extended recognition to the Soviet Union in October 1924.—Page 212.

[59]Capet was the family name of the French dynasty that ruled in the Eighteenth Century.—Page 213.

[60]Purishkevich was a notorious Russian reactionary, anti-Semite, leader of the Black-Hundred gangs and organizer of pogroms. In the Czarist Duma, he was one of the Black-Hundred monarchist leaders.—Page 213.

[61]After a White Guard coup in May 1921, Vladivostok fell into the hands of the counter-revolution. After a number of fierce battles, the Far East territories were cleared in 1922 of the remaining White Guard bands.—Page 223.

[62]Mernulov was a wealthy landlord in the city of Vladivostok who served as Premier of the White Guard regime. He was a puppet of the Japanese.—Page 223.

[63]N. F. Danielson (Nikolai--on) was a theoretician of the Narodnik (Populist) movement and one of the best educated Russian economists of the Seventies and Eighties. He translated Volume I of Marx's *Capital* into Russian and regularly corresponded with Marx and Engels.—Page 230.

[64]Leslie Urquhart, English industrialist and financier, was the owner, under Czarism, of many mills and factories in the Urals and in Siberia; and director of the Russo-Asia Bank. During the Civil War years, Urquhart was one of the inspirers of imperialist intervention against the USSR. In 1922 he engaged in negotiations for concessions.—Page 244.

[65]The Stroganov family was an ancient Russian trading firm which operated on a large scale as far back as the days of Ivan the Terrible in the Sixteenth Century. Toward the end of the Eighteenth Century this family became converted into operators of large-scale capitalist industry.

The Demidov family provide still another Russian example of the conversion of big mercantile capital into industrial capital. The Demidovs, like the Stroganovs, owned enterprises chiefly in the Urals.—Page 246.

[66]Colrat, friend of the arch-reactionary Poincaré, held the post of Minister of Justice in the 1923 French Cabinet.—Page 246.

[67]Auguste Taine was a prominent French historian and literary critic of the Nineteenth Century. A popularizer and vulgarizer of Hegel's historical outlook, Taine gained fame by his writings on English literature and on the epoch of the French revolution.—Page 247.

[68]The reference here is to Jaures' writings on the Great French Revolution in the *History of Socialism* of which Jaures was the editor.—Page 247.

[69]The Ninth of Thermidor, 1794, was the day on which the Revolutionary Jacobin Convention was overthrown and the counter-revolution set in.—Page 247.

[70] Spengler was a popular reactionary writer in Germany who wrote in 1920-21 a number of books on the decline of Europe that created a sensation at the time. In these writings Spengler advanced the view that European culture was doomed. His writings express, on the one hand, the pessimism of the outlived ruling class ; on the other hand, his philosophy is heavily spiced with the ruthlessness and arrogance of a Prussian feudalist. Spengler's "philosophy" was widely used by the Nazi propaganda machine.—Page 254.

[71] The reference here is the Kronstadt mutiny.—Page 267.

[72] The Fourth Congress resolution on the French question was adopted unanimously at the 29th session of this World Congress, December 2, 1922.—Page 275.

[73] —Delplanque and Lavergne were members of the extreme left wing inside the French CP in 1922. They, along with Heine, were among the leaders of these ultra-leftists, whose main base of support was in the Seine Federation.—Page 277.

[74] This program of action was adopted unanimously at the 32nd session of the Fourth World Congress, December 5, 1922.—Page 285.

[75] The series of treaties listed here were imposed by the victorious powers in World War I on the various members of the defeated coalition led by Germany.

The treaty of St. Germain was concluded on September 10, 1919, between the Entente and Austria. According to the terms of this treaty Austria was dismembered, yielding parts of her territory to Italy, Czechoslovakia, Poland, Rumania, etc. Austria's industry and finances were placed under the control of an "international" reparations' committee.

The treaty of Neuilly was concluded between the Entente and Bulgaria on November 27, 1919. By the terms of this pact Bulgaria lost sections of her territory to Greece and Yugoslavia, particularly along the Aegean shore line. Bulgaria was obliged to pay reparations, expenses for the occupation troops and the like.

The treaty of Trianon was concluded between the Entente and Hungary on July 4, 1920. Hungary ceded slices of her territory to Czechoslovakia and Yugoslavia. This treaty set down no fixed reparations, Hungary's economy being placed under the control of a special commission.

The treaty of Sevres was concluded between the Entente and Turkey on August 10, 1920. Turkey was deprived of two-thirds of her territory. All the rights of German and Austrian investors were annulled. Great Britain's influence in the Middle East was recognized as supreme. The struggle by the Ankara government which then followed and which was supported by the USSR brought this rapacious treaty to nothing.—Page 288.

[76] This resolution was adopted at the 29th session of the Fourth Congress, on December 2, 1922.—Page 276.

[77] Louis Sellier, member of the Central Committee of the French CP, was in

1921-22 one of the leaders of the left-centrist formation inside that party. In 1922 he represented the French CP on the ECCI.—Page 291.

[78]Vaillant-Couturier, orator and deputy, was a member of the Central Committee of the French CP. In the 1921-22 factional struggles he was one of the leaders of the Left Wing. After Lenin's death, he became a staunch pillar of Stalinism.—Page 292.

[79]Souvarine was one of the founders of the French CP. In 1919 he was one of the leaders of the "Committee for the Third International." In 1921-22 he headed the struggle of the Left Wing against Frossard. After Lenin's death he broke with Stalinism only to break also with Marxism. In the days before World War II his name became synonymous with the cynicism, pessimism and defeatism that permeated the ranks of all renegades from the revolutionary socialist movement.—Page 292.

[80]Tommasi, a veteran trade unionist, was one of the outstanding worker-Communists in France. Together with Monatte, Monmousseau and others, Tommasi was one of the leaders of the CGTU at the time.—Page 292.

[81]Dunois, member of the Central Committee of the French CP was prominent at the time. Together with Loriot, Souvarine and others, Dunois had worked for the creation of the French CP. During the 1921-22 factional struggles he belonged to the Left Wing and was one of the four editors who resigned at the Marseilles Convention.—Page 292.

[82]The article by Friedlander, a prominent Austrian Communist, was published in *Bolshevik* which was then issued as the organ of the Fourth World Congress.—Page 297.

[83]Ravenstein, a Dutch CP leader, was the foremost spokesman of the ultra-lefts at the Fourth World Congress.—Page 297.

[84]Mussolini, the founder of Fascism in Italy, started his political career as a left-wing Socialist, who during the First World War became a chauvinist and an agent of the Entente. With the blessing, aid and assistance of the Italian bankers and industrialists and the House of Savoy, he rose to power on October 30, 1922, when the first Fascist ministry was organized. Leon Trotsky, in his biography of Stalin, characterized Mussolini, along with Hitler, as typical representatives of the petty-bourgeoisie which in the imperialist epoch "is incapable of contributing either original ideas or creative leadership of its own." "Both Hitler and Mussolini," wrote Trotsky, "have plagiarized and imitated practically everything and everyone. Mussolini stole from the Bolsheviks and from Gabriele D'Annunzio, and found inspiration in the camp of Big Business. Thus the leaders of the petty-bourgeoisie, dependent on capitalism, are typical second-raters—even as the petty-bourgeoisie itself, whether you view it from the top down or from the bottom up, invariably assumes a subsidiary role in the class struggle."—Page 297.

[85]Nitti—an outstanding leader of the Italian liberal bourgeoisie and one-time Italian Premier of the World War I epoch. In the years following World War I, Nitti sharply criticized the Versailles Treaty and was one of the sponsors

of the still-born "Left Bloc," the pre-Stalinist version of "People's Front," in Italy.—Page 298.

[86]Barabant was one of the French Right Wingers who, while a member of the CP Central Committee, propagated together with Verfeuil and others, the "Left Bloc" orientation. Barabant was expelled for this from the French CP in 1922.—Page 299.

[87]Bonar-Law, a Tory chieftain, who served as member and leader of many British Cabinets, became Premier after the Tory victory in the 1922 elections. In 1923 he resigned from the Cabinet because of ill health and presently died. —Page 300.

[88]Clynes was one of the case-hardened reformist leaders of British Labor Party. He became a member of the MacDonald government.—Page 300.

[89]Buchanan was the British Ambassador to Czarist Russia who continued in this post under Kerensky. He was one of the bitterest foes of the young Soviet Republic.—Page 303.

[90]The offensive on Warsaw was opposed by Leon Trotsky, for the reasons he explained in his autobiography. The scope of the defeat below Warsaw was due primarily to the conduct of the "Western group of the Southern armies," which was then under the political control of Stalin. "He (Stalin)," wrote Trotsky in his biography of Stalin, "wanted at any cost to enter Lwow at the same time that Smilga and Tukhachevsky were to enter Warsaw . . . . At this decisive moment, the line of operations on the Southwestern Front diverged at right angles from the line of operations on the main Western Front: Stalin was waging his own war."—Page 310.

[91]Tardieu, one of the arch-reactionary leaders of the victorious French bourgeoisie, advocated the domestic policy of ruthlessly suppressing French labor and the French revolutionary movement. The pivot of his foreign policy was the merciless pillage of defeated Germany.—Page 311.

[92]Kuno, a big German capitalist, headed the German Cabinet in 1922-23. His government discredited itself during the days of the Ruhr occupation by granting huge subsidies to the leading German monopolies. Kuno was forced to resign in August 1923 under the pressure of the great strike wave of this period.—Page 311.

[93]Rasputinism was a term denoting the complete corruption and denegeration of the Czarist court. Rasputin, an ordinary monk, wormed his way through various intrigues into the top ruling circles and in 1912-16 acquired unbounded influence over the Czar and his family, and actually dictated the Czar's policy on various questions.—Page 313.

[94]This prognosis of the possible "order of revolutions" was retained by Leon Trotsky until 1930, when he wrote: "It is not at all permanently established that the United States will be last in the order of revolutionary primacy, condemned to reach its proletarian revolution only after the countries of Europe and Asia. A situation, a combination of forces is possible in which

the order is changed and the tempo of development in the United States enormously accelerated. But that means that it is necessary to prepare." (See *The Militant* , May 10 1930.)—Page 316.

[95]Soutif was closely associated with Andre Morizet, the author of a book entitled *A Visit to Lenin and Trotsky* . Morizet served as mayor of one of the Parisian suburbs. He and Soutif were among the group of French opportunists who temporarily belonged to the French CP and occupied prominent positions in it.—Page 320.

[96]Burtsev, an old Social Revolutionist, was famous in, pre-revolutionary Russia as a specialist in exposing Czarist provocateurs and agents in the ranks of the revolutionary movement. During the war of 1914-18 he became a chauvinist and after the October Revolution, a supporter of the White Guards.—Page 323.

[97]In October 1923, at the height of the revolutionary ferment in Germany, the Brandler Leadership of the German CP formed in coalition with the Socialists a "Workers' Government" in Saxony. While the German leadership vacillated on the question of assuming the power and while Stalin, behind the scenes, sabotaged the 1923 revolution, the Saxon Communists became absorbed in "constructive measures" instead of turning their position into one of the revolutionary strongholds, as Trotsky advised. The Berlin government sent troops which drove out this coalition government.—Page 326.

[98]Lozovsky, later a pillar of Stalinism, was at the time the General Secretary of the Red Trade Union International, In December 1922, as the representative of the Russian Trade Unions, Lozovsky went to the Hague Congress called by the Amsterdam Trade Union International to discuss the struggle against war.—Page 327.

[99]In Lenin's lifetime, the Lux Hotel in Moscow was used to house workers and delegates to the Third International.—Page 327.

[100]Stolypin, Plehve, Sipyagin were the inspirers of Czarist reaction toward the end of the last century. Their names became synonymous with the hated autocracy, which sought to stamp out the revolutionary movement by savage repressive measures. Plehve was assassinated in 1904. Sipyagin, who served as Czarist Minister of Internal Affairs in the Nineties, was assassinated in 1902.—Page 333.

[101]This article was written on March 25, 1923, as an introduction, or more accurately "in place of an introduction" to a special volume of Trotsky's writings devoted exclusively to France and entitled *The Communist Movement in France*, published in 1923 simultaneously in French and Russian editions. The most important documents dealing with France have been included in volumes I and II of the present work.—Page 334.

[102]Henri Barbusse, celebrated French novelist, depicted the horrors of World War I in his novels, *Light Fire* etc. He became one of the initiators of the anti-militarist organization of French war veterans, but remained outside the

French CP until 1923. After Lenin's death, Barbusse became one of the court writers attached to the Kremlin.—Page 334.

[103]Friesland—a one-time prominent German Communist leader. Friesland left the CP in 1921 together with Paul Levi, first joining the Independent Socialists and then moving over to the official Socialist Party.—Page 336.

[104]The reference here is to the occupation of the Ruhr by the French troops in January 1923. This action precipitated the revolutionary crisis in Germany in 1923, an exceptionally favourable revolutionary situation which was let slip by the German leadership and the already Stalinized International.—Page 340.

[105]This highly important article was written by Trotsky during the Ruhr crisis. Its political line was officially adopted by the Executive Committee of the CI shortly after its publication, against considerable opposition. "It was no mere accident," wrote Trotsky in 1928, "that despite all prejudices the slogan of a Soviet United States of Europe was adopted precisely in 1923, at a time when a revolutionary explosion was expected in Germany, and when the question of state interrelations in Europe assumed an extremely burning character. Every new aggravation of the European and indeed of the world crisis is sufficiently sharp to bring to the fore the main political problems and to invest the slogan of the United States of Europe with attractive power." The slogan appeared in Comintern literature as late as 1926.—Page 341.

[106]The Bulgarian coup was carried out by the Bulgar reactionaries in the summer of 1923. The coup had been a long time in preparation and its success was assured by the vacillation and indecision by Stambulisky's Peasant Party.—Page 347.

[107]The coup in Spain, which placed Primo de Rivera in power, was carried out on September 13, 1923.—Page 347.

[108]Kareyev was a Czarist academician and historian who belonged to the subjective sociological school of Lavrov. Karayev contributed to populist and liberal periodicals, devoting many of his articles to a polemic against the Russian Marxists, who heaped deserved ridicule upon him.—Page 348.

INDEX